The Ultimate
HERB
——— Book ———

The Ultimate
HERB
—— *Book* ——

ANTONY ATHA

COMMISSIONED PHOTOGRAPHY
DAVID MARKSON

C&B
COLLINS & BROWN

635.7
ATH

Contents

First published in Great Britain in
2001 by
Collins & Brown Limited
London House
Great Eastern Wharf
Parkgate Road
London SW11 4NQ

Distributed in the United States and Canada by
Sterling Publishing Co.
387 Park Avenue South,
New York, NY 10016, USA

1 2 3 4 5 6 7 8 9

British Library Cataloguing-in-Publication Data:
A catalog record for this book is available
from the British Library

ISBN: 1-85585-880-0 (hardback)
ISBN: 1-85585-903-3 (paperback)

Project editor: Jane Ellis
Edited and designed by Axis Design Editions Limited
Indexer: Lisa Foottit

Color reproduction by Global Colour, Malaysia
Printed by: Tat Wei Printing & Packaging Co Pty

Some herbs are dangerous and should not be used unless
recommended by a qualified herbal practitioner. Neither the
author nor the publisher accepts responsibility for unauthorized
or irresponsible use of herbal remedies.

Introduction

A study of herbs is both a fascinating and a humbling experience. At the simplest level it is an exploration of a group of plants that have some use, other than their existence as a plant growing in a garden or in a field. An herb might be an ingredient in an old country remedy, a flavoring in the kitchen, or make a fragrantly scented sachet to sweeten the linen closet.

At another, quite different, level such a study establishes a link between the 21st century, with its cell phones and instant global communication, and prehistoric man—a link stretching back hundreds of thousands of years. Herbs are the oldest medicines in the world. Ancient man used various plants to treat various ills. Initially this would have been by instinct, in the same way as animals instinctively avoid poisonous plants and seek out plants that will do them good. Later such knowledge would have been passed down the generations by word of mouth. Finally, a mere 5,000–6,000 years ago, the Sumerians inscribed this knowledge on tablets, followed by the Greeks and Chinese, who wrote the first herbals. At the end of the 10th century the monks of the Benedictine monastery at St. Gall in Switzerland created the first known herb garden. By the 19th and 20th centuries, synthetic medicines became available, an achievement based upon humankind's ancient relationship with plants.

The paths of this formal herb garden are sown with lawn chamomile. Lavender and borage provide contrasting blue colors.

In the Middle Ages herbalism was often linked with magic and sorcery. The herbal astrologers, such as 17th-century Englishman Nicholas Culpeper, set great store by the signs that governed each plant. The *Doctrine of Signatures*, developed by the Swiss Paracelsus and the Italian Giambattista della Porta in the 16th century, decreed that if a plant looked like a particular disease or illness, then that plant could cure it. Such ideas had their fantastical elements and have been decried and derided, bringing herbalism and the science of treatment by herbs into general disrepute.

And yet, strange as it may seem, many of these theories have a basis in fact. Like does sometimes cure like: Culpeper's treatments are not to be dismissed without examination. Herbs do contain many properties that today are being used more and more to treat a variety of ailments, both physical and mental. The major drug companies of the world are investing millions of dollars in research into the properties of various plants, and are discovering within them a potential to heal modern killers such as AIDS and cancer. Headlines in a recent newspaper broadcast the results of a controlled drug test that had concluded that treatment by the herbal remedy St John's-wort was the best treatment available for cases of depression.

It must not be forgotten that apirin, one of today's most familiar painkillers, was developed from the herb meadowsweet, *Filipendula ulmaria*, in 1838. It is therefore increasingly important that the gene bank of herbs available to doctors and scientists is preserved and protected.

The more herbs are studied, the more fascinating they become. But to undertake such a study is not necessary for anyone to enjoy them and use them profitably. Many herbs are attractive, fragrant, flowering plants in their own right that can be included in any herbaceous border. A keen cook can grow a good number of the culinary herbs for the kitchen in a small windowbox. Most herbs are straightforward to cultivate, and many varieties are tolerant of even harsh growing conditions.

Warning

Many herbs are dangerous and have poisonous properties in their raw state, even those that have contributed greatly to the treatment of major diseases. The common foxglove *Digitalis purpurea*, used to treat cardiac malfunction, is a good example. Even apparently harmless herbs used to make herbal teas, such as mint, should not be taken constantly over a period of time.

Anyone suffering from any ailment is strongly advised to seek professional medical help from a doctor or qualified herbal practitioner, and neither the author nor the publisher accepts any responsibility for unauthorized and irresponsible use of herbal remedies. A number of herbs are also subject to legal restrictions in various countries either because they, or parts of them, are poisonous in their raw state, or because they are hazardous in the garden, such as lupin and laburnum seeds, or because they become pernicious weeds outside their country of origin. Such restrictions vary from country to country.

Gardens can look spectacular in winter with the leaves rimmed with frost. The lion reflects the colors of the plants.

What is an herb?

The simplest definition of an herb is a plant that has a use for people separate from its existence as a plant growing in the garden or found in the wild. Many common plants, trees, and ordinary garden perennials, such as the birch, *Betula alba*, and the monkshood, *Aconitum napellus*, are used in the kitchen or medicinally, and so are considered herbs.

Botanists have a very different definition of what an herb is. They describe herbs as small, seed-bearing plants with fleshy, rather than woody, stems, hence the term herbaceous, as in herbaceous border. But this definition ignores many of those plants that have a long tradition of use, both in the apothecary's chamber and in the kitchen. The ginkgo tree, *Ginkgo biloba*, for example, is one of the oldest organisms in the world. Fossils have been discovered containing samples of this tree, dating from before the evolution of mammals. It is immensely important medically, for it contains unique substances that are extremely important in controlling allergic reactions.

The uses of herbs

The main use for herbs is in medicine. Herbal medicine stretches back to the dawn of humankind, for knowledge of healing plants would be instinctive to primitive man, in the same way as animals instinctively avoid eating poisonous plants. This knowledge of the healing properties of various plants—much of it unwritten— was handed down from generation to generation. One of the most fascinating aspects about the study of herbs and herbalism is how modern science and scientific analysis has confirmed so much of this ancient wisdom.

Herbs in the kitchen

People automatically associate herbs with the kitchen, for their smell and taste add flavor to food. It is a minor blessing that many of the requirements of the medieval kitchen and household have disappeared. We no longer

Purple loosestrife is an astringent herb with anti-bacterial qualities. It is used to treat severe fevers and skin infections. It may become invasive in borders.

BEE BALM, OSWEGO TEA

Many herbs are attractive flowering plants that can be grown in the herbaceous border and used in flower arrangements. The flowers of the bergamot are particularly attractive to butterflies. Rosemary is used in the kitchen and has the reputation for warding off anxiety, while elderberries, are the ingredient of elderberry rob, a cordial used to treat colds and flu in winter.

ROSEMARY

ELDERBERRY

need to add pennyroyal, *Mentha pulegium*, to stews to disguise the taste of rotten meat, nor strew lavender or meadowsweet on the floor to sweeten noxious household odors, nor use rue to repel the fleas from the black rats that carried the bubonic plague. But we still add basil and oregano to sauces, and use rosemary to flavor roast lamb. Herbs have become increasingly important in cooking as the world has become more cosmopolitan, and more and more flavors and spices are used everywhere.

The commercial uses of herbs

Herbs have important commercial uses, not only as culinary flavorings, but in the perfume and food industries. The essential oil of many plants is distilled from the leaves and flowers, and used in the manufacture of scents, soaps, and skin tonics. Herbs are also the main ingredient in a number of insect repellents. They are added to liqueurs, used to flavor vermouth, and yellow gentian, *Gentiana luteum*, is one of the main ingredients in Angostura bitters.

Scutellaria laterifolia received the common name mad-dog skullcap because it was considered a cure for rabies. Today it is used as a tonic for the nervous system in humans.

WHITE WATER LILY

herbs used for flavoring drinks and cordials

A number of herbs are taken medicinally in infusions or drunk as soothing tisanes. A number are also used to flavor beers and liqueurs.

- *Angelica archangelica* Benedictine
- *Carum carvi* (caraway) kümmel
- *Chamaemelum nobile* (chamomile) tea
- *Gentiana lutea* (yellow gentian) Angostura bitters
- *Filipendula ulmaria* (meadowsweet) beer, soft drinks
- *Geum rivale* (water avens) chocolate drinks
- *Humulus lupulus* (hops) beer
- *Hyssopus officinalis* (hyssop) Chartreuse and Benedictine
- *Inula helenium* (elecampane) liqueurs
- *Levisticum officinale* (lovage) soft drink
- *Marrubium vulgare* (horehound) beer
- *Mentha x piperata* (mint) Crème de Menthe
- *Rosa canina* (dog rose) rose-hip syrup
- *Salvia elegans* (pineapple sage) soft drinks
- *Taraxacum officinale* (dandelion) tea, beer
- *Verbena officinalis* (vervain) tea

The importance of herbs

For a great variety of reasons, herbs have been essential to humankind for many thousands of years. Although today we may no longer worship herbs for their magical properties, modern science is discovering more and more important medicines derived from many common herbs.

A recent study conducted in Germany showed conclusively that St. John's-wort, *Hypericum perforatum*, was the most effective drug available to treat cases of mild or moderate depression, something that herbalists have known for centuries. Plants and fungi are now the fastest growing source of new medicines in the pharmaceutical industry.

Herbs in religion and legend

In the age of the ancient Druids of Europe a number of herbs were thought to be sacred and to possess magical properties—among them ivy, holly, birch, and vervain—and were worshipped. Mistletoe was a sacred herb, and the Norse god Balder was killed by a dart of mistletoe. As a result of his murder the gods of Valhalla ordained that the plant could grow only at the very tops of trees where it was impossible to reach, and those meeting under it must kiss, as a sign of love and peace. In German legend the elder tree was another magical tree with religious associations. It was the tree from which Judas Iscariot hanged himself. There remains a superstition that if elder wood is burned, there will be a death in the family.

twelve important herbs in conventional and alternative medicine

There has been a recent upsurge of interest in herbs and herbal medicines as more and more people come to realize the properties inherent in many of the traditional herbal medicines. This increased scientific interest and knowledge is extremely important for the future of humankind and may well hold the key to defeating major diseases such as cancer.

Catharanthus roseus
MADAGASCAN PERIWINKLE
The alkaloids contained in the Madagascan periwinkle have proved effective in the treatment of a number of serious cancers, such as Hodgkin's disease and leukemia.

Cephaelis ipecacuanha
IPECAC
An evergreen shrub from Brazil that has been used in the treatment of dysentery for centuries. It is the commonest ingredient in all proprietary cough medicines.

Cinchona pubescens
QUININE
Discovered in 1630, probably by the Jesuits, as a treatment for malaria. It was the first drug that Samuel Hahnemann, founder of homeopathy, tested on himself.

Colchicum autumnale
AUTUMN CROCUS
A very poisonous plant that is, nevertheless, extremely important in the treatment of gout. Its cells are also used for the genetic modification of plants.

Digitalis purpurea
FOXGLOVE
A poisonous herb that is important in controlling cardiac function. It is used to regulate the heartbeat in patients suffering from heart disease.

Erythroxylum coca
COCA
An evergreen shrub from South America, source of the illegal drug cocaine. Extremely important in medicine as a painkiller and in the treatment of terminal illness.

Filipendula ulmaria
MEADOWSWEET
The painkilling substance salycin was discovered in the leaves of meadowsweet early in the 19th century. This is the basis for acetysalicylic acid, from which aspirin was first produced in 1899.

Hamamelis virginiana
WITCH HAZEL
Used for centuries in Europe and North America to treat bruises and sore eyes. Today it is also used internally for dysentery and colitis and other gastrointestinal disorders.

Hypericum perforatum
ST JOHN'S WORT
A recent study has shown that this herb is the best treatment for mild forms of depression. In 1652 Culpeper recommended the herb as a remedy "against melancholy and madness."

Papaver somniferum
OPIUM POPPY
Opium, extracted from this poppy, is probably the oldest painkiller in the world. It is the source of morphine, codeine, and methadone.

Rauvolfia serpentina
SERPENTINE WEED
An evergreen shrub, native of Burma, that is the source of reserpine, the first tranquilizer. Use of this drug has greatly helped the treatment of patients suffering from hypertension and mental illness.

Stachys officinalis
BETONY
One of the most popular herbs from Roman times, with the power to cure almost all known ailments. It is still important in the treatment of headaches and nervous tension.

The hawthorn, the symbol of May, is another tree of legend, associated with pre-Christian fertility rites. The white flowers are never to be brought inside a house, for they are an omen of death or disaster. The May Queen used to be a human sacrifice as part of the May Day ritual.

Herbs in magic and witchcraft

A number of herbs have poisonous or hallucinogenic properties. This is especially true of the poppy family, from which come the drugs opium and heroin. Often these substances are addictive. In medieval times these properties were exploited by witches, magicians, sorcerers, and poisoners, and legends grew up around various plants. Chief among these was the mandrake root, from whose strange shape many superstitions arose. Henbane was a well-known poison, and werewolves were born in the imagination when ointments made from the poisonous nightshades and aconites were applied to the skin.

Herbs in myths

Some herbs are associated with ancient myths dating from the times of the Greeks and Romans. Myrtle was dedicated to Venus, the Roman equivalent of the Greek goddess Aphrodite. They are linked to the Babylonian goddess Ishtar, the great whore of Babylon and goddess of fertility. Myrtle was a symbol of fertility and was often carried by brides on their wedding day. Bay leaves were used to crown returning warriors and also to ward off evil. Doctors were garlanded with bay leaves when they qualified, from which comes the French term *baccalaureate*. Mugwort was hung over doors to prevent damage to the home. The herbal of the Roman Apuleius declares that "if any root of this wort be hung over the door of any house then may not any man damage the house."

Houseleeks and stonecrops growing on roofs were supposed to prevent lightning strikes. The Saxons of northern Europe believed that illness could be transferred to an herb, and then the plants, and thus the ailment, could be disposed of. The 10th-century British *Book of Bald* gave a recipe for a salve to cure "one suffering from nocturnal goblin visitors" that instructed that the herbs then be thrown into running water.

An allegorical portrayal of witches preparing medicines, taken from an old manuscript. The raindrops descending from the clouds symbolize the fertility of the earth. Early medicine was often linked to astrology and the occult.

Herbs in history

The earliest recorded use of herbs dates from ancient Sumerian tablets, between 4500–3500 BC. Around 250 herbs were listed, and the uses of the poppy as a tranquilizer and narcotic were mentioned. Widespread excavations of Bronze Age burial sites have revealed a number of herbs buried with the dead, particularly yarrow, *Achillea millefolia*, which indicates their importance in prehistoric times.

The early instances of herbs used as medicines, or worshipped as sacred plants, show their importance to primeval humans. Knowledge of herbs was passed down from one generation to another by word of mouth. This oral tradition is still important among the indigenous groups of South America, particularly as so much of the rain forest is being destroyed and their natural habitat is disappearing.

Each part of the body was governed by a sign of the zodiac. Astrologists believed that plants which fell under the dominion of a particular sign were the ones best able to cure diseases in that part of the body.

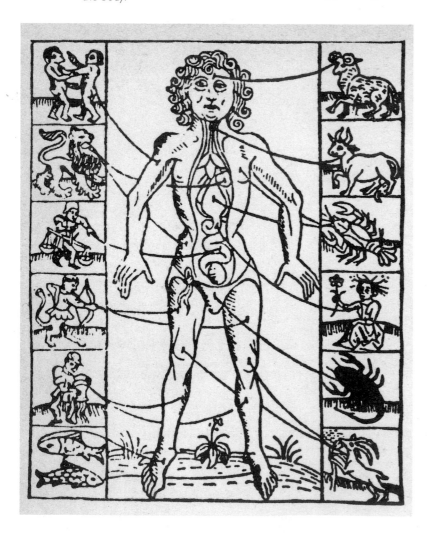

The first books on herbs

The oldest recorded tradition of herbal medicine is found in China. Chinese medicine dates back over 4,000 years, and several of the ancient herbals are used today. The Egyptians, too, have a long tradition of using herbs, and herbs are illustrated on the walls of tombs and carvings. Little of this knowledge has been written down.

It was not until the time of the Greeks that the first Western herbals were written, and the first two herbals that have survived are *Plant Researches* and *Plant-Aetiology* by Theophrastus, written around 300 BC. These were based on the writings of the philosopher Aristotle.

Herbalism and astrology

The practice of astrology was believed to have originated in ancient Babylon. The early astronomers noted the visible planets and ascribed to them certain properties. Venus, the equivalent of the Babylonian goddess, Ishtar, became the goddess of love and harmony, and, opposite her in the planetary system, Mars became the god of war and discord. Astronomers then discovered the celestial zodiac, a circular path along which the Sun, Moon, and planets were thought to travel. This was divided into twelve equal sections, each corresponding to a constellation along this path, and these were endowed with a set of characteristics.

In the 15th century an Italian called Marsilio Ficino wrote a book called *Liber de Vita,* in which he set down the zodiacal signs that rule the different parts of the body, and he also noted the effect that the planets have on each part.

Astrologers believed that everything in the universe is part of a cosmic pattern that has a relationship to every other part. In an attempt to codify this giant web of relationships and establish a connection, known as astrological correspondences, between the planets and assorted scents, colors, precious stones, and herbs, each herb was placed under the domin-ion of a planet. It was also therefore related to the part of the body that the planet governed. As an example burnet saxifrage, *Pimpinella saxifraga*, St. John's-wort, *Hypericum perforatum*, and the viola Johnny-jump-up, *Viola tricolor*, are all herbs that come under the governance of the sun in the astrological system and are therefore supposed to be good for the heart and cardiac diseases. The strange thing is that scientific research has since proven that they are indeed good for the heart.

The first herbals

Herbs were the medicines of the Middle Ages. The first herbals reflect this.

Plant researches and Plant-Aetiology
by Theophrastus, c. 300 BC
Theophrastus was a pupil of Aristotle. These two books are a counterpart of Aristotle's biological works and are influenced by them.

Historia Naturalis (Natural History)
by Pliny the Elder
Thirty-seven books of which Books 12 to 19 are on botany, and 20 to 27 on botany in medicine.

Materia medica
by Dioscorides Pedanius, 1st century AD
Dioscorides was an army physician from Anazarbus. The five books contain descriptions of 600 plants and nearly 1,000 drugs. It was the first conscious attempt to provide a medical system, not an alphabetical list of drugs. It remained the standard work on medical practice for many centuries.

Leech Book of Bald, c. 900
The oldest existing medical book written in the vernacular. The book was written by a scribe named Cild by order of a man named Bald, who was possibly a courtier at the time of King Alfred.

Herbarium Apuleii Platonici, c. 1000
The oldest illustrated herbal. This is a Saxon translation of a 5th-century herbal from the school of Aelfric of Canterbury.

De proprietatibus rerum
by Bartholomeus Anglicus, c. 1250
The major work of the Middle Ages on natural history. The 17th book covers herbs.

Myddfai manuscript, c. 1250
A collection of 900 herbal recipes handed down from generation to generation of Welsh herbalists and doctors.

Banckes's Herbal
by Richarde Banckes, 1525
The first printed English herbal. A translation of a medieval manuscript now lost.

A New Herball
by William Turner, 1551–68
This was published in three parts. Turner was a native of Northumberland. He is known as the father of English botany. He also published *Libellus de re herbaria novus*, 1538, the first book to give the locality of many native English plants, and *Names of Herbs* in 1548.

Herbal by Paracelsus, 1570
Paracelsus's real name was Theophrastus Bombastus von Hohenheim. His herbal set out the Doctrine of Signatures.

The Herball or General History of Plants
by John Gerard, 1597
The most famous herbal in the English language, which was in part a translation by Dr Priest of *Pemptades*, an herbal by the Flemish herbalist Rembert Dodoens. Gerard was much criticized for using this without acknowledgement.

Theatrum Botanicum
by John Parkinson, 1640
A major work that describes about 3,800 plants. It is dedicated to King Charles I.

The English Physician Enlarged
by Nicholas Culpeper, 1652
Culpeper's herbal is widely read and contains descriptions of 577 herbs. He was an herbalist/astronomer and his book is heavily biased towards the effects of the planets on plants and their relationship to each disease. He also propounded the Doctrine of Signatures.

American herbals
Joyfull Newes out of the Newe Founde Worlde by
Nicolas Monardes, 1569
Monardes was a Spanish doctor and his work was translated throughout Europe. It was translated into English by John Frampton.

New England's Rarities Discovered
by John Josselyn, 1672
A description of America's plants and their uses. It includes notes on the medicinal plants used by the Native Americans, a list of weeds introduced by the settlers, and a list of herbs that they attempted to grow.

The American Physitian
by William Hughes, 1672
An account of the remedies used in North America and famous for its description of chocolate.

American Gardener's Calendar
by Bernard McMahon, 1866
The first gardening book published in America, with descriptions of 3,000 species and varieties of plants.

Chinese herbals
Yellow Emperor's Classic of Internal Medicine,
c. 1000 BC
The first book on the principles of Chinese medicine as expounded by Huang Di around 2650 BC.

Tang Materia Medica **by Su Ying,** c. 659
Fifty-four volumes on Chinese plants, commissioned by the rulers of China in the Tang dynasty.

The Atlas of Commonly Used Chinese Traditional Drugs, 1970
Produced by the Chinese Academy of Sciences, this charted the revival of traditional Chinese medicine after the Kuomintang era.

Herbs in history

The Doctrine of Signatures

Side by side with astrology marches an extra-ordinary theory, expounded in the Doctrine of Signatures. This theory was based on the connection between humans and the universe that arose from their essential "oneness." All plants had some connection with people and this was obvious for everyone to see who could interpret the signs correctly. This doctrine is most closely associated with Paracelsus, 1493–1541, a Swiss army physician who became Professor of Medicine at the University of Basle in 1526. His theories proved so heretical to the Christian church that two years later he was expelled from the city and spent the remainder of his life wandering around Europe, teaching, healing the sick, and learning.

At its simplest, the Doctrine held that if a plant looked like a disease, then within that plant lay the properties needed to cure it. The roots of the lesser celandine, commonly called pilewort, look like hemorrhoids, proof positive that it could heal piles. The wild pansy has heart-shaped leaves, and was therefore considered certain to be a cure for heart troubles. Kidney-shaped leaves belonged to plants that could benefit the renal system, while spotted leaves showed that a plant was a cure for acne. Similarly, lungwort, *Pulmonaria officinalis*, was considered a curative for lung disease.

The most complete exposition of this theory was written by an Italian called Giambattista della Porta, 1543–1615. He carried the Doctrine to the extremes of dissecting plants, and, taking it even farther, he asserted that plants common to a region could cure most of the afflictions of the local inhabitants. The theory was that the local climate was responsible not only for the disease, but also for their cure.

As knowledge expanded, and the Age of Reason ushered in a more scientific approach, the reliance of herbalists on astrology and the Doctrine of Signatures waned. Practitioners became more pragmatic and preferred to judge medicines on their results, rather than on how the plants looked. But, again, it is a curious fact that many of the herbs promoted by the Doctrine of Signatures do in fact work.

The lesser celandine does cure piles, the wild pansy does indeed cure valvular disorders of the heart. Even della Porta's theory cannot be too lightly dismissed. Willows, for example, trees that grow in damp places, were considered by him to be a cure for rheumatism. The bark of the willow tree has been shown to contain salicin, a substance once much used in the treatment of rheumatic fever.

The symbolism of herbs and the language of flowers

In his famous herbal written in the 16th century, the Englishman John Gerard declared that "through their beauty and variety of colour and exquisite form they [flowers] do bring to a liberal and gentle mind the remembrance of honesty, comeliness and all kinds of virtues." Florography attributes an individual symbolic meaning to many flowers. Many people are familiar with the heart-rending scene in Shakeseare's *Hamlet* when Ophelia distributes flowers taken from her father's coffin: "There's rosemary, that's for remembrance. I pray you, love, remember. And there is pansies, that's for thoughts."

By exchanging the right flowers lovers can carry on a complicated conversation without words. A white carnation signifies devotion, offering true and chaste love. If a red chrysanthemum is received, this says "I love you also."

A botanical illustration taken from a 19th-century French herbal showing the charming spring-flowering lungwort, *Pulmonaria saccharata*. The spotted leaves indicated to old herbalists that this plant could cure lung diseases.

Herbs and herbalists

The influence of the monks and nuns in the Dark and Middle Ages cannot be overestimated. It was only in monasteries that learning survived in Europe after the fall of the Roman Empire. All gardeners of today owe a huge debt to the monastic scribes and gardeners of that time for the accumulated knowledge they passed down.

Right: Nicholas Culpeper was one of the most famous of the English herbalists. He fought on the Parliamentary side in the English Civil War.

The earliest monastic garden of which there is definite knowledge is that of the monastery of St. Gall near Lake Constance in Switzerland. This became a Benedictine monastery. The Benedictine order attached great importance to manual labor and developed the art of gardening.

The first gardening book was written by the monk Walafred Strabo at St. Gall, who dedicated his book *Hortulus* to the abbot, Grimwald. Monastic gardens were divided into several parts. There was frequently an orchard, a vineyard, and an herbarium. The herbarium was divided between the pot herbs, or vegetables, that went to the kitchen for cooking, and the medicinal herbs that were used by the apothecaries to make decoctions to heal the monks and the poor. In addition, there were often various flower gardens and fishponds, where carp were bred to feed the monks on Fridays.

The ancient uses of herbs

In the Middle Ages herbs were not just used in the kitchen or for medicinal purposes. They were thought to possess magic powers, and were used by many as charms to ward off evil spirits and to keep diseases at bay.

Herbal baths were extremely important in Saxon times, especially vapor baths. The fumes of the herbs dulled the senses of the patient and alleviated pain, and at the same time drove away evil spirits. Cattle were also fumigated.

Herbs were worn as amulets, and this was another practice that had a dual purpose. Wearing the correct herb in a band around the arm or wrist helped the healing process, but more importantly it drove away evil spirits. Reminders of this old superstition can be seen today when people buy sprigs of shamrock or bunches of mistletoe to bring them good luck. Red wool was often worn at the same time, for the color red was believed to be abhorred by evil spirits. Wearing red flannel next to the skin was a country practice designed to prevent colds and influenza in winter.

This power of herbs as magical protectors extended to houses. Herbs were hung above doors to protect both the inhabitants and the cattle from all ills. Saxon books on the use of herbs describe the custom of transferring the disease to the plant and then throwing the plant away into running water.

Strict instructions were also given about when—and often where—to gather herbs. Herbs should be picked at dawn, or in the evening, when night and day divide, and the gatherer must face toward the east. The origins of these ancient superstitions are believed to lie in the worship of Eostre, the Saxon goddess both of fertility and the dawn.

Strewing herbs

In Saxon and Norman times life had moved on from the Dark Ages, when, in the memorable words of the English political thinker Thomas Hobbes (1588–1679), life was "solitary, poor, nasty, brutish, and short." Much of the population lived within the walls of the castles, while others lived in huts and houses outside. Yet life was still primitive. Fresh herbs were laid on the floor to sweeten the air. Lavender, woodruff, and meadowsweet were all herbs favored for the smell that rose up when they were trodden on; these were called strewing herbs.

Latin names

Latin names are a good deal easier to understand than might be thought.

The species name, the one that comes after the plant name, very often says something about the plant.

Primula vulgaris, means the common primrose; *vulgaris* means common.

Paeonia officinale, means the *officinal* (medical) peony. The *officina* was the storeroom of a monastery in which drugs were kept.

Other common species names cover
color: *caeruleus*, blue, *virens*, green;
place: *alpestris*, of mountains, *alpina*, alpine, *pratensis*, of meadows;
habit: *biflorus*, two-flowered, *horizontalis*, horizontal.

Gathering the grapes in the fall to make the wine: In this illustration taken from an old herbal the figures and flowers symbolize the Garden of Eden, from where Adam and Eve were expelled for eating the forbidden fruit.
It is interesting to note the use of containers for growing plants.

Herbs and herbalists

Mentha pulegium, pennyroyal, illustrated in Sowerby's *English Botany*, 1863. This herb had a number of uses in the Middle Ages, in medicine and in the kitchen, where it was employed to disguise the taste of rotten meat.

Herbs as cosmetics

As well as their healing properties herbs were used as charms to beautify. They were particularly important during the 13th and 14th centuries, the Age of Chivalry, when knights on horseback jousted for the favors of their ladies, kings fought crusades to redeem the Holy Land, and England and France were engaged in the Hundred Years War. Many herbs were prepared as lotions and used to clear the skin of freckles and spots; sowbread and watercress were applied to the hair to make it grow, and chamomile to lighten it. Ointments and simples, too, were made by pounding herbs in lard or butter, and rosewater and pastilles were used to sweeten the breath.

Medieval pot herbs

Herbs could be dried and kept over the dreary months of the winter, and were extremely important in the medieval kitchen to add flavor to the monotonous diet of meat and bread. They also helped to keep scurvy at bay, and a number of herbs were recommended as healing agents in cases of scrofula, the old name for scurvy. There is some confusion about the term "pot herbs," for up until the middle of the 19th century the term also included all of the edible vegetables. The list of pot herbs given in *The Countrie Farme*, published in 1600 in England, included a good number of vegetables, but it also contained many herbs that are seldom grown today. These included colewort, sow thistle, succory, arrach, and bugloss. These were all mainly culinary herbs used in the kitchen.

important herbs from around the world

North America

The Native Americans have a long tradition of herbal medicine and a number of the herbs they used, such as echinacea and black cohosh (*Cimicifuga racemosa*), are today used throughout the world.

IMPORTANT HERBS FROM NORTH AMERICA INCLUDE

Ceanothus americanus
NEW JERSEY TEA
Used to treat skin cancer and as a tea substitute.

Chionanthus virginicus
FRINGE TREE
A treatment for liver and gall bladder disorders.

Trillium erectum
BIRTHROOT
For hemorrhages and urinary diseases.

Smilax aristolochiifolia
SARSAPARILLA
Flavoring for soft drinks, tonic.

Hamamelis virginiana
WITCH HAZEL
Used for bruises, eye lotion, and stomach disorders.

Eschscholzia califomica
CALIFORNIAN POPPY
Popular annual used to relieve tension and anxiety.

Hydrastis canadensis
GOLDENSEAL
Tonic herb for digestive disorders.

Echinacea purpurea
PURPLE CONEFLOWER
An important herb popularly used today to enhance the immune system.

Herbs of Central and South America

Central and South America have vast resources of plants, many probably undiscovered even today. This makes the destruction of the valuable rain forest in South America extremely threatening to the future of humankind.

Agave americana
AMERICAN CENTURY PLANT
Source of fiber for rope making. The waste material provides the precursor of steroid drugs.

Capsicum annuum
CHILI PEPPER
Widely used spice. Many uses in herbal medicine especially to aid convalescence.

Cephaelis ipecacuanha
IPECAC
Powerful emetic used in cough mixtures as an expectorant.

Chinchona officinalis
QUININE
A major antimalarial drug, discovered by the Jesuits.

Erythroxylum coca
COCA
The source of cocaine, used for anesthetics. The leaves were chewed by the South American Indians to stave off hunger pangs.

Guaiacum officinale
LIGNUM VITAE, GUAIAC
One of the hardest woods known and also used as an herb tonic. In danger of extinction.

Strychnos-nux vomica
STRYCHNINE
A deadly poison, source of the drug curare. Used in minute amounts to stimulate the nervous system.

Zea mays
CORN
Grown throughout the world as an important food and fodder crop. The flowers were also used as a diuretic in Aztec medicine.

Herbs of India

The Indian subcontinent is the home of many well-known and unusual plants. The Himalayas were the hunting ground for the great plant collectors of the 19th and early 20th centuries.

Cinnamon zeylanicum
CINNAMON
Well-known spice from Sri Lanka used in oriental cooking, drinks, and for colds and stomach complaints.

Dioscoria deltoidea
Yam
Contains steroidal saponins used in the manufacture of steroids.

Elettaria cardamomum
CARDAMOM
The seeds are used as flavoring. A powerful expectorant and detoxifying herb.

Gloriosa superba
FLAME LILY
A poisonous plant used in medicine and genetic engineering.

Nelumbo nucifera
SACRED LOTUS
A commonly used herb in Ayurvedic medicine as a heart tonic and for bleeding disorders.

Piper nigrum
BLACK PEPPER
Used as a spice all over the world.

Rauvolfia serpentina
SERPENTINE WOOD
Compounds in the plant have revolutionized the treatment of psychotic disorders. The first "tranquilizers" came from this plant.

Santalum album
SANDALWOOD
Aromatic oil from the plant is used for perfumes and in aromatherapy.

Herbs of China

A number of herbs are specific to Chinese medicine.

Artemisia annua
Source of a new anti-malarial drug.

Cinnamomum camphora
CAMPHOR
Widely used as an insect repellent, particularly for moths.

Eleutherococcus senticosus
SIBERIAN GINSENG
Widely used as a tonic, and in the background treatment of cancer.

Ginkgo biloba
GINKGO TREE
Particularly effective in the treatment of asthma.

Paeonia officinalis
PEONY
Used to treat eczema in children and as a tonic for the circulation.

Rheum palmatum
CHINESE RHUBARB
A purgative used for chronic constipation and other internal disorders.

the
herb
garden

Herb gardens can be both extremely practical and enormously interesting. Many gardeners devote their herb gardens entirely to kitchen herbs, either confined to small containers, laid out in formal beds, or cultivated as a separate part of the garden. Others plan several borders of special interest, including scented herbs, medicinal herbs, plants for winter dried-flower arrangements, or herbal wildflowers that were used by the apothecaries in monasteries. Often, interesting combinations can be thought up. In general, an herb garden is sure to give pleasure and amusement.

The different types of herbs

There are no hard and fast rules that can be used to distinguish an herb from any other plant. Herbs are often divided into culinary and medicinal plants but even these divisions frequently overlap. Herbs come in many shapes, sizes, and forms; they may be large trees or tiny, low-growing annuals.

The well-known plant rosemary is one example of an herb that belongs to both the kitchen group and the medicinal group of herbs. It is valued as a treatment for nervous disorders and headaches. There is no obvious relationship between the types of plants that are classified as herbs. Many large trees are important herbs. The ginkgo tree, *Ginkgo biloba*, can reach 100ft (30m) in height. Extract from the leaves is used to control allergic reactions. The flowers, bark, and sap of other large trees, such as limes, pines, birch, cinchona (from which quinine is extracted), and guaiac are all used in herbal medicine.

At the other end of the scale a number of annuals are important herbs, such as the marigold, *Calendula officinalis*, or the Californian poppy, *Eschscholzia californica*. Many small, low-growing perennials, such as the woodruff, *Galium odoratum*, and soapwort, *Saponaria officinalis*, are also important herbs.

The only safe definition that can be made is that a plant is an herb at the point in time when it is used for cooking, healing, as a dye plant, for flavoring, for use in cosmetics, or as a perfume. Any of these is a separate and distinct use quite apart from any pleasure it may give as a plant, shrub, or tree growing in a garden.

The importance of medicinal plants

Many gardeners today think of herbs as plants to grow solely for use in the kitchen, for example parsley or mint, which can be cut and used as a garnish, or to add flavor to ordinary dishes. But

Herbs range from annuals, sown and harvested in the same year, to shrubs and trees. Some herbs, such as betony and white water lilies, were sacred.

Stachys officinalis, betony

Origanum vulgare oregano

Achillea millefolium, yarrow

in medieval times herbs were held to be far more important as sources of medicine. Indeed, they were almost the only medicines available.

Plans of old monastic gardens demonstrate how important herbs were. The monastery garden at St. Gall in Switzerland was divided into a kitchen garden, where the vegetables were grown, and a separate physic garden, adjacent to the infirmary. These were both huge areas.

Most monastery gardens were divided into three, with separate orchards, vineyards, and herbariums. The herbarium was the most important of these three and was made up of separate sections for the kitchen plants and those grown for medical purposes. Flowers, such as roses, were also grown for use in medicine as well as to decorate the monastery.

The famous physic gardens of Europe, such as Padua and Bologna in Italy, and Paris in France, date from the 16th century, and were centers for botanical study. The Oxford Physic garden was the most famous in England. The Botanical Garden in Edinburgh, Scotland, was laid out in alphabetical order, but this arrangement broke down with the introduction of so many new plants in the 18th and 19th centuries.

A traditional herb garden laid out in a formal pattern, with each bed surrounded by neatly clipped hedges of box. The gazebo is a striking and unusual addition. The flowers are planted in blocks of contrasting color to enhance the formal effect.

Gillenia trifoliata, Indian physic

some important medicinal herbs

- Achillea millefolium yarrow
- Agastache foeniculum giant hyssop
- Agrimonia eupatoria church steeples
- Angelica archangelica angelica
- Calendula officinalis marigold
- Calluna vulgaris heather
- Cardamine pratensis cuckooflower
- Centaurium erythrea centaury
- Cnicus benedictus St. Benedict thistle
- Echinacea purpurea purple coneflower
- Filipendula ulmaria meadowsweet
- Galium verum yellow bedstraw
- Gaultheria procumbens wintergreen
- Geranium robertianum herb robert
- Geum urbanum bennet
- Gillenia trifoliata Indian physic
- Hypericum perforatum St. John's-wort
- Inula helenium elecampane
- Jasminum officinale jasmine
- Lythrum salicaria purple loosestrife
- Malva moschata muskmallow
- Melissa officinalis lemon balm
- Oenothera biennis evening primrose
- Pulmonaria officinalis lungwort
- Rosa gallica var. officinalis French rose
- Rosmarinus officinalis rosemary
- Salvia officinalis sage
- Sambucus nigra black elder
- Sanguisorba officinalis great burnet
- Saponaria officinalis soapwort
- Solidago virgaurea goldenrod
- Stachys officinalis betony
- Tanacetum parthenium feverfew
- Tanacetum vulgare tansy
- Tussilago farfara coltsfoot
- Valeriana officinalis valerian

Planning an herb garden

Garden design is entirely a matter of personal preference. Choice is limited only by the size, shape, and aspect of the garden itself. Cost, too, can be a major factor. Building permanent features can involve considerable financial outlay, as well as taking up a great deal of time, so projects should be planned carefully.

An herb garden laid out around a fountain surrounded by pleached lime trees. This idea can be copied with fruit trees.

main considerations

● Decide how much room is available in the garden for herbs.

● Check the aspect of the garden. Do you have a sunny, sheltered position that will enable you to grow herbs from hot climates, such as the Mediterranean, or are you confined to herbs that will grow in shade or partial shade?

● What type of herbs do you want to grow? Do you want to grow just a few fresh herbs for the kitchen, or a selection of culinary and medicinal herbs?

● Do you want to research and grow many of the old medicinal herbs, or would you prefer to grow flowering herbs for summer color?

● There are many herbs with strongly scented leaves and flowers that can be used to make potpourris and herbal sachets to perfume the house. A scented border can easily be planned and planted at little cost.

● If you like herbal teas, a number of plants are suitable for infusions and can be grown together to make a handy tea border.

If you want to create a rockery for alpine herbs, a water garden, or even a formal potager, this involves labor and materials, as well as the purchase of plants. You may have the necessary time and skill to do most of the practical work yourself, but if not, you will need to seek professional help. Remember to have a clear plan before you start, and if you are getting quotations from outside contractors, make sure that the specification is as exact as possible. Be generous with estimates; that way you will hopefully avoid any cost overruns.

Planting objectives

The first decision is what type of herbs you want to grow. At one end of the scale the dedicated herb gardener can plan a whole garden of herbs: herbs for the kitchen, Mediterranean herbs, old medicinal herbs, flowering herbs for borders, a garden of herbal wildflowers, beds of bulbs used in herbal medicine, and a water garden full of water lilies with the margins surrounded by meadowsweet. At the other end of the scale, many people are happy with a few culinary herbs growing in a windowbox or in a couple of small containers outside the back door. Grand or small-scale, the choice is yours.

Two ideas for culinary herbs

If you have the room and want to grow herbs for the kitchen, there are two attractive designs that are easy to follow and will enable you to grow plenty of herbs outside in the late spring and summer months.

The first is the traditional wheel. Anybody reasonably competent with tools can build this type of herb bed without professional help. Dig proper foundations and plan everything on paper first before transferring the design to the ground. It is essential to measure everything carefully, and then measure and measure again. If this is not done correctly, the finished design can look very strange. Divide the wheel into six or eight segments, and remember that it is best to have reasonably wide spokes of brick or paving leading to the center, as this makes the plot easier to cultivate.

The next easy design that can be used in any space, whatever its size, is the checkerboard, alternating square slabs with miniature square beds. This can be laid out on any rectangular patch of ground and the extent is limited only by the space available. Again this will enable the gardener to grow plenty of herbs for the kitchen. Grow one type of herb in each square, depending on the size, although you can add edging plants such as marigolds or chives, or grow some spreading herbs, such as thyme, to soften the hard edges of the design.

The orange flowers of the marigolds make a pleasing contrast with the blue and yellow of the lavender and santolina. What could be a color clash is avoided by the bright green foliage of the marigolds.

A small formal pond surrounded by great clouds of the yellow lady's mantle, *Alchemilla mollis*, matched with the purple spikes of the common sage. Old-fashioned roses complete this herbal planting.

Formal or informal design?

Formal herb gardens are always based on a regular geometric shape. The inspiration for the gardens is the knot garden of 16th-century Europe, where herbs were planted in regular patterns. Informal designs of island beds and borders are more suited to the smaller gardens of today.

An unusual wooden planter based on a medieval ecclesiastical design is home to a small bay tree, underplanted with creeping thyme tumbling over the edge.

Formal herb gardens are designed using strict geometrical shapes, squares, circles, diamonds, and triangles, each compartment separated by low growing hedges of box or lavender. Such formal designs are fascinating to plan and construct, and they have an immediate impact, for the shape of the garden creates its own interest, but they do need space and are time consuming to plant and maintain.

The main advantage of formal gardens is that they retain their interest throughout the year and often look at their best when the outlines are revealed by snow and frost in winter.

Informal designs

These are better suited to the ordinary small backyards of many properties today, and herbs can be planted in any part of any garden—beds, borders, raised beds, or containers—to blend in with the overall garden design.

Island beds are one of the simplest and easiest design elements, and these can be planned to reflect a theme or make a color statement. One of the most popular color ideas is the white and silver border, found in so many gardens, and white and silver herbs such as cotton

Opposite: French lavender, *Lavandula stoechas*, growing in a decorated terracotta pot is surrounded by the green leaves and yellow flowers of lady's mantle.

lavender, *Santolina chamaecyparissus*, the curry plant, *Helichrysum angustifolium*, horehound, *Marrubium vulgare*, and alecost, *Tanacetum balsamita*. If you haven't room to devote a single border or bed to a color scheme such as this, remember that white and pale gray link patches of bright color, blending them together.

Other popular color schemes for island beds or borders are blue and white: *Lavandula* 'Hidcote', noted for its deep purple flowers, can be grown with the deep blue monkshood, *Aconitum napellus*, with the white daisy-like flowers of *Tanacetum balsamita* var. *tomentosum* providing a color contrast. This group could be linked by scarlet poppies such as *Papaver orientale* 'Beauty of Livermere', red, or *P. rhoeas* 'Shirley Mixed', mixed red, pink and white.

Scented borders are another excellent idea, and you can include plants that are all suitable for potpourri mixtures. Lavender, pennyroyal, roses, rosemary, lemon beebrush, balm, carnation petals, and heliotrope all have a distinctive scent, while some herbal plants, such as evening primrose, *Oenothera biennis*, or tobacco plants, *Nicotiana sylvestris*, release their perfume on still evenings in summer.

old-fashioned roses

Roses have been used in herbal medicine and cosmetics for thousands of years. An old-fashioned rose garden is certainly worth planning, as the famous 16th-century English herbalist John Gerard said: "The Rose doth deserve the chief and prime place among all floures whatsoever."

The best-known old roses include *Rosa gallica* var. *officinalis*, *R. damascena*, *R. × centifolia*, and *R. × alba*. Important roses that have been used for traditional herbal medicines include *R. canina*, for rose-hip syrup, *R. laevigata* and *R. rugosa*; the latter can also be used for hedging.

Create a sense of mystery

Try to include some element of surprise in any garden design. This may be a wildflower area tucked away in a corner, or a bed concealed by a large shrub, or even a container. Also, keep any planting reasonably simple. All borders and beds are more effective if they are planted in blocks of color. Plant at least three herbs in any group, the only exception is large shrubs, such a rosemary, that will stand on their own.

An herbal potager

The word "potager" is French for a kitchen garden, but over the years the meaning of the word has changed slightly, and it has come to mean a kitchen or herb garden laid out in a formal pattern based on geometrical shapes.

Potagers can incorporate a range of shapes; beds may be circular, square, rectangular, or even triangular. They should have symmetrical divisions with paths or hedges dividing the beds, and a number of separate beds. The beds can be any size, but small beds are easier to manage and enable the gardener to grow a larger variety of plants. The inspiration for formal potagers came from monastic gardens of the Middle Ages in Europe, and the formal knot gardens of 16th-century Europe, so beloved of Le Notre, designer of the famous gardens of Versailles, near Paris, in France.

Herbal potagers need not occupy a great amount of room in a garden. A small potager for the most common culinary herbs might need only six or seven divisions and can be placed near the house so that the herbs can be cut fresh and used immediately. But if there is sufficient room, then the concept of the potager can be extended, and quadrants of a rectangular design might be devoted to a variety of herbal themes; culinary, medicinal, scented plants, dye plants, or plants for potpourris.

Watch out for the varying heights of many of the herbs. Angelica is a tall, stately plant, while rosemary grows into a substantial flowering shrub. Take care how you match the varying heights of the plants—try to achieve an overall balance. Also make sure that the tall plants are supported properly with stakes, otherwise they may flop over and ruin the basic design.

Designing a potager

When designing a potager, draw your plan on paper and measure the space carefully and accurately. It is also essential to list the materials you are going to use for the formal paths and divisions. Hedging with some low-growing plants, such as box or lavender, is excellent, and the paths in between the hedges can be covered

Thyme, oregano, French lavender, and evening primrose are the main features of a mixed bed of herbs. Such a planting shows how attractive herbs can be, grown in a border.

with gravel or wood chippings. The disadvantages of hedging are that it takes time to grow and requires a considerable amount of maintenance to keep it looking orderly and tidy. It is better, if your budget and space allowance permit, to make the paths of brick, which can be laid down in a variety of patterns. Brick paths should be at least five bricks in width, laid side by side. A path three bricks wide might look adequate at the planning stage, and even when the potager is first laid out, but when the plants

grow and flop over the edges of their beds it will soon prove to be too narrow. It is important that you have enough room to reach the various areas of the potager easily.

A potager of culinary herbs

Culinary herbs can be divided into several groups. The first is the important herbs used in cooking that are native to the Mediterranean. These all require hot, dry conditions to flourish and need to be grown in a sunny, sheltered place in the garden. If you cannot offer such a site, then it is best to concentrate on herbs that require less sun and heat. Herbs from the Mediterranean include sage, thyme, rosemary, oregano (although both oregano and its near relative sweet marjoram will tolerate some shade), basil, verbena, and hyssop.

Larger Mediterranean annual and perennial herbs include chicory, globe artichokes, fennel, lovage, and black lovage. If you are planning an herbal potager in a sunny garden then it would be possible to have one section for low-growing scented herbs and another for taller plants. This would make a pleasant fragrant spot that would look attractive throughout the summer.

best culinary herbs for potagers

Allium schoenoprasum chives (flavoring, edging)
Anethum graveolens dill (flavoring)
Artemisia dracunculus tarragon (flavoring)
Borago officinalis borage (drinks, flavoring)
Buxus sempervirens box (hedging)
Calendula officinalis marigold (edging, coloring)
Coriandrum sativum coriander (flavoring)
Foeniculum vulgare fennel (flavoring)
Lavandula angustifolia English lavender (hedging)
Mentha spicata spearmint (flavoring, try growing a number of different varieties)
Myrtus communis myrtle (flavoring)
Ocimum basilicum sweet basil (flavoring)
Origanum majorana marjoram (flavoring)
Origanum vulgare oregano (flavoring)
Petroselinum crispa parsley (flavoring)
Rosmarinus officinalis rosemary (flavoring)
Salvia officinalis sage (flavoring)
Satureja montana winter savory (flavoring)
Thymus vulgaris thyme (flavoring, ground cover)

Herbs for the kitchen

In the Middle Ages the term "pot herbs" meant all green and root vegetables, as well as the culinary and strewing herbs that were used to flavor food and scent the living quarters of castles and monasteries.

Nowadays when we use the term "herb" we think first and foremost of plants that are used in the kitchen to garnish and flavor salads, stews, and sauces. Try to include at least some of the following in your herb garden.

Give rosemary pride of place at the center of a bed. Common rosemary, *Rosmarinus officinalis*, will grow as high and spread as wide as 5ft (1.5m). The variety 'Miss Jessopp's Upright' grows even bigger with an upright habit, while 'Severn Sea' is lower-growing and more spreading. Plant two or three varieties of thyme around the rosemary. Thymes have bright pink

The statue of a satyr copied from ancient Rome has his features largely obscured by sprigs of mint. Mint needs to be confined, otherwise it will threaten to overwhelm the garden.

and purple to white flowers that open when the rosemary flowers are over. Thymes grow only to 12in (30cm) in height with a spread of 16in (40cm). The main thymes used in the kitchen are: common or garden thyme, *Thymus vulgaris* (the variety 'Aureus' has yellow leaves); 'Silver Posy', green leaves with white margins; lemon-scented thyme, *T.* x *citriodora* (the variety 'Aureus' has gold leaves); 'Silver Queen', cream variegated leaves; and caraway thyme, *T. herba-barona*.

If you don't want to surround the rosemary with thyme, plant some oregano on one side. These plants are larger than thyme and are more difficult to accommodate. Sweet marjoram, *Origanum majorana*, is a half-hardy evergreen subshrub often grown as an annual or biennial in colder climates. Oregano, or wild marjoram, *O. vulgare*, is a spreading perennial. Sweet marjoram may grow as high as 30in (75cm). It can be grown in a container and brought inside in the winter when frost threatens. Oregano or wild marjoram may eventually spread to 3ft (90cm) and grow almost as high. There are many attractive varieties that can be grown in herb gardens.

Two more flowering herbs from the Mediterranean are vervain and hyssop. Vervains are grown in many gardens as annuals, but the true medical vervain, *V. officinalis*, is rather an ordinary looking plant and, unless you wish to drink huge quantities of vervain prepared from fresh leaves, it is better ignored. Hyssop, on the other hand, is an attractive flowering plant, a semi-evergreen, small shrub with large spikes of deep blue flowers that bloom from midsummer onward. There is a white form, *Hyssopus* f. *albus*, which is often used in white gardens as an informal hedge.

A bed of salvias

Salvias (sage) deserve a bed of their own, as there is a large number of varieties with different habits and leaf colors. That said, it is an herb where a little goes a long way in the kitchen, and cooks should beware of adding too much of it to any dish, or the flavor may become overpowering. Sage is an attractive plant. Common sage has gray-green leaves, with light lilac-blue flowers. Varieties with colored leaves include 'Aurea', yellow leaves; 'Icterina', yellow and green leaves; 'Purpurascens', red-purple young leaves; and 'Tricolor', gray-green leaves with pink and cream margins.

Mint

Mint is an herb that should be grown on its own, if possible, and even then the varieties should be separated into their own compartments. The species mints are more vigorous than the varieties and will overwhelm them if given sufficient opportunity. The traditional way to confine mints to their allotted place was to plant them in old pails—made from either wood or metal—from which the bottoms had been removed, and this method works just as well today. However, a bed in an herb garden can be divided into sections by digging out the soil and then setting old roofing slates on their edge to

A small octagonal wheel planted with herbs and fringed with chives. This design is easier to cultivate with wider brick paths.

Herbs for the kitchen

A kitchen windowsill devoted to herbs and plants. The addition of fresh herbs from your own backyard brings an added excitement to cooking.

create a number of divisions. Hardboard will achieve the same result, but this material will eventually rot away and will need to be replaced. Refill the bed once the slates are in position so that the soil reaches the top of the slates and they become invisible. The most popular mints to grow for the kitchen are spearmint, *Mentha spicata*—the varieties 'Crispa' and 'Moroccan' are especially recommended; apple mint or round-leaved mint, *M. suaveolens*, is equally popular, 'Variegata' has variegated leaves and is also known as pineapple mint; and *M.* x *villosa alopecuroides* 'Bowles' Mint, the best for mint sauce or flavoring new potatoes.

Parsley

Parsley is another extremely common plant in herb gardens. It is an herb that is best sown at intervals two or three times through the year. Most gardeners prefer to grow parsley in containers. It can be grown as a formal edging with pleasing textures along the sides of a potager bed and then dug up and replaced each year. Hamburg parsley is grown for its roots, which are eaten in the winter as a vegetable.

A choice of herbs for the kitchen

Some gardeners will have to settle for a selection of the following herbs because some of these examples listed can be grown only in hot summers in temperate zones.

Angelica; basil, a tender annual that can be grown in containers and brought indoors in the winter; burnet, also called salad burnet; caraway, a hardy flowering biennial, the seeds can be used in the kitchen in its second year; celery; chervil, a good herb with a delicate flavor; chives, grow as edging in a potager or in containers; coriander, the variety 'Morocco' is best for seed and 'Santo' for the leaves; dill, a useful annual culinary herb grown for its seed and for the feathery foliage that is used to flavor fish; fennel; garlic, plant out individual cloves in the spring and they will be ready to harvest in late summer; lovage, tastes like celery; sweet and chile peppers ; savory; and tarragon.

You can also include some salad vegetables; lettuces, especially the curly leaved 'Lollo rosso' and 'Salad Bowl', can edge a border. Arugula, Good King Henry, garden cress, and corn salad are other good choices.

Even formal gardens can create a sense of mystery and perspective. Here the eye is led down the path and the design is held together by the spires of a white loosestrife.

Herbs for shade

The answer to a question commonly asked by many a would-be herb grower,
"What herbs can I grow in a totally shady garden?" must be the usual one:
"It all depends on the degree of shade and the aspect of the garden."

If your backyard—and this is highly unlikely—really is in total shade, similar, for example, to the interior of a pine forest, nothing will grow. Without light, no plants, nor undergrowth of any sort, will survive for long. On the other hand many herbs will grow quite happily without direct sunlight. To the gardener, there are various different types of shade

The different types of shade

Certain herbs will tolerate one type of shade, some another. Dry shade, as is found under the canopy of large trees, suits a number of bulbs. Moist shade, as in a north-facing garden in the northern hemipshere, is necessary for most ground cover and for woodland herbs, such as trillium and myrrh. If you have a very shady garden or patio, you may well have to experiment to see which herbs will grow. There is no point in trying to grow plants that won't flourish in the conditions you can offer them, even if every gardening book in the world says that they should tolerate deep shade.

Bulbs and perennials grown in shade normally require little or no maintenance. Some, such as snowdrops and primroses, should be split after flowering. You may need to add some leaf mold to dry areas, and dominant plants may require thinning out.

Culinary herbs for shade

Only a few culinary plants will grow in deep shade. As a general gardening rule, vegetables and fruit of all sorts require more sun than flowers. If you live in a town and can

White and purple foxgloves, an important medicinal herb, make imposing plants in the border.

offer only a very shady position but want to grow some culinary herbs, try containers of chives, *Allium schoenoprasum*; spearmint, *Mentha spicata*; parsley, *Petroselinum crispum*; and basil, *Ocimum basilicum*. If you have a larger container, or a raised bed that gets some sun during the day, or, at the very least, plenty of light, you could try to grow *Angelica archangelica*; chervil, *Anthriscus cerefolium*; lovage, *Levisticum officinale*; or black elder, *Sambucus nigra*.

Scented herbs for shade

Even if you have a shady garden you can grow a number of scented plants that prefer a shady position. These include English bluebells; lily-of-the-valley; primroses; sweet cicely, *Myrrhis odorata*, woodruff, and violets. Additionally, both *Artemisia lactiflora* and *Pelargonium tomentosum* should grow satisfactorily in partial shade.

herbal flowers for shade

A number of floral herbs will flourish in shade. However, not all of these will flourish in deep shade. Foxgloves, for example, do best in partial shade. But all are worth trying—you can never predict exactly what will or won't grow. A shady border of flowering herbs could include:

Aconitum napellus monkshood
Ajuga reptans bugle
Aquilegia vulgaris columbine
Camellia spp. camellia
Convallaria majalis lily-of-the-valley
Digitalis purpurea foxglove
Fragaria vesca wild strawberry
Galanthus nivalis snowdrop
Galium odoratum woodruff
Gaultheria procumbens wintergreen
Geranium maculatum spotted cranesbill
Geranium robertianum herb Robert
Hepatica nobilis hepatica
Hyacinthoides nonscripta English bluebells
Lysimachia nummularia creeping Jenny
Primula officinalis primrose
Pulmonaria officinalis lungwort
Scutellaria lateriflora skullcap
Trillium erectum birthroot
Valeriana officinalis valerian
Vinca major great periwinkle
Viola odorata sweet violets

Aquilegia vulgaris, columbine

The striking blue flowers of the monkshood (this variety is 'Bressingham Spire') are welcome in late summer when many other plants are past their best. The plants are poisonous.

Trillium erectum, birthroot

Geranium maculatum, spotted cranesbill

Herbs for partial shade

Almost all the herbs suitable for growing in shade can be grown in partial shade. Few plants need to avoid the sun completely. Conversely, the plants suitable for partial shade can be tried in full shade. Each site has its own micro-conditions, so the only way to know what will grow is to experiment.

Shade-loving plants will tolerate some sun, even if it means that they will need moister soil than normal, and sun-loving plants may well tolerate some shade. The time of day when the sun shines is more important. Shade-loving plants may not welcome the early morning sun. And sun-loving plants will survive early morning or late evening shade, as long as they receive the heat of the sun in the middle of the day.

Most gardens have large areas of partial shade. This may well be under a tree that casts its shadow for part of the day; and in an enclosed town garden in the northern hemisphere, plants growing against north-, west-, or east-facing walls will all be in shade for part of the day. Large shrubs in a smaller garden can also create areas of partial shade.

There are some plants, such as rock roses or lavenders, that really do need an open, south-facing position to be at their best, but most plants will grow perfectly adequately as long as most of their requirements are fulfilled for most of the time.

One of the advantages of a partially shaded environment is that such areas are usually quite sheltered and they are not generally prone to hard frosts in the winter months. You have only to take a look at the frost-free zones created by undergrowth during winter in cold regions to realize this. The other advantage is that in a garden such environments can be controlled quite easily by enriching the soil with compost or leafmold and cutting back the canopy of branches when overhanging trees become too dense and threaten to block out too much light.

Flowering herbs for partial shade

Large numbers of flowering herbs that will grow in shady situations are available to the gardener. A carefully thought out choice will provide flowering plants all through the year. There are also plenty of useful ground-cover plants and climbers that will flourish in partially shaded positions, as well as various perennials, shrubs, and evergreens.

Among the best-known plants for this type of position are *Adonis vernalis*, spring pheasant's eye, a low-growing perennial with yellow flowers in early spring; *Arctostaphylos uva-ursi*, bearberry, an

Passion flowers are still used in herbal medicine as a sedative, as they have a tranquilizing effect. They are good climbers and quickly cover a wall but they are not fully hardy in temperate climates.

evergreen, ground-cover shrub with pinkish-white flowers in early summer, it must be grown in acid soil; *Bellis perennis*, wild daisies that look so unlike their common ancestor found in many lawns—they have balls of varied pink and white flowers, and are usually grown as annuals; *Cardamine pratensis*, cuckooflower or lady's smock, with its clumps of pale lilac to white flowers in late spring and early summer; *Filipendula ulmaria*, meadowsweet, a beautiful wild herb with drifts of white flowers that loves damp places; *Paeonia officinalis*, the common peony, with its crimson, pink, or white flowers in early summer; and *Stachys officinalis*, betony, a magical healing herb with spires of purple flowers in summer.

Other excellent flowering herbs and climbers include: *Aristolochia clematitis*, birthwort; *Chelone glabra*, white turtlehead; *Cimicifuga racemosa*, black cohosh; *Clematis vitalba*, evergreen clematis; *Euonymus patens*, spindle tree; *Hamamelis vir-*

giniana, witch hazel; *Hesperis matronalis*, dame's rocket; *Humulus lupulus*, hops; *Lobelia inflata*, lobelia; *Magnolia officinalis*, magnolia; *Perilla frutescens*, beefsteak plant; *Rosa canina*, dog rose; *Saponaria officinalis*, soapwort; *Symphytum officinale*, comfrey; and *Veronica officinalis*, speedwell.

A flowering herb border in midsummer. The red and pink hollyhocks are matched with the purple *Verbena bonariensis*.

culinary and scented herbs for partial shade

Many of the plants listed above have fragrant leaves or flowers. If you want to grow scented herbs in partial shade then the following are all fragrant:

Aloysia triphylla lemon beebrush
Cardamine pratensis cuckooflower
Filipendula ulmaria meadowsweet
Hamamelis virginianus witch hazel
Hesperis matronalis rocket
Magnolia officinalis magnolia
Melissa officinalis lemon balm
Monarda didyma Oswego tea
Origanum majorana sweet marjoram
Origanum vulgare oregano
Rosa canina dog rose

The culinary herbs listed for growing in shade grow equally well in partial shade. There are others that can be used for flavoring or as tea plants. These include:

Aloysia triphylla lemon beebrush
Geum urbanum bennet
Juniperus communis juniper
Melissa officinalis lemon balm
Meum athamanticum spignel
Monarda didyma Oswego tea
Origanum majorana sweet marjoram
Origanum vulgare oregano
Pycnanthemum pilosum mountain mint
Tanacetum vulgare tansy
Tropaeolum majus nasturtium

Herbs for wet habitats

Wet areas of the garden include ponds, the banks of streams or rivers, as well as marshy fields and meadows. Most of these habitats are wild, often uncultivated areas where wildflowers and wetland herbs flourish.

Monarda didyma, Oswego tea

Many important herbs are found in wetland habitats. These include meadowsweet, the original source of the drug aspirin, which was used for centuries to treat fevers, and *Lobelia cardinalis*.

Wetlands support a large amount of wild-life and contain a great diversity of plants. Some of the plant species that flourish in damp conditions will grow in shade or partial shade, but the majority, perhaps rather surprisingly, require full sun. This is important to remember if you are planning to make a pond or a water feature in a garden. Position the feature where it will be in sun, and be sure not to position it under any trees or large shrubs, for apart from the shade that they cast, the drifting leaves of fall will need removing or the water quality will begin to deteriorate.

Herbal plants for a pond

It is essential to plant some oxygenating plants in a pool before planting anything else. These keep the water clear and ensure that fish and insects can survive. Two of the best are curly water thyme, *Lagarosiphon major* syn. *Elodea crispa*, and water milfoil, *Myriophyllum aquaticum*

(neither of these are herbs). The most significant deep-water plants used as herbs are the water lilies, *Nymphaea lotus* and *N. odorata*. Both these species have a long history of use in herbal medicine, and the white lotus, *N. lotus*, was an important herb in ancient Egypt.

All water lilies need a good depth of water, usually 12–18in (30–45cm), and sun. They will not grow in moving water. Two other aquatic herbs are *Nasturtium officinale*, watercress, and *Nelumbo nucifera*, sacred lotus.

Marginal herbs for wet habitats

A number of plants that flourish in the margins of a pond are important herbs. These grow either in the shallow water at the edge of the pool, or in the damp soil that surrounds a pond. They include *Iris versicolor*, the blue flag, used to treat skin complaints as well as various liver disorders. It can be invasive and needs to be controlled.

Lobelia cardinalis, cardinal flower

Althaea officinalis, marshmallow

Filipendula ulmaria, meadowsweet

Angelica archangelica

An attractive marginal planting of *Polygonum bistortoides*, the pink-flowered bistort, *Caltha palustris*, marsh marigolds, with *Iris pseudacorus*, yellow flag, in the background.

Valeriana officinalis, valerian, was one of the medicinal herbs used in medieval times.

Mentha aquatica, water mint, is a water-loving herb that will grow in up to 6in (15cm) of water. It has attractive light-purple flowers and is used in herbal medicine for diarrhea and stomach disorders. It should not be used in the kitchen.

Filipendula ulmaria, meadowsweet, is another herb that will flourish in damp soil. It has attractive, feathery, creamy plumes of flowers, and a fragrant smell. It is a hugely important medical herb, for the plant contains salycic acid, from which the common painkiller aspirin is obtained. It was also a strewing herb used for the floors of medieval castles and monasteries to provide a pleasing atmosphere.

Lythrum salicaria, loosestrife, flourishes in moist soil. It was widely used in the 19th century to treat cholera in the many epidemics that swept through the new industrial towns.

suitable plants for wet habitats

There are plenty of other herbs and grasses that flourish beside ponds and in moist habitats.

Ajuga reptans bugle
Althaea officinalis marshmallow
Eupatorium cannabinum hemp agrimony
Eupatorium purpureum Joe-pye weed
Lobelia cardinalis cardinal flower
Lobelia dortmanna Dortmann's cardinalflower
Lysimachia nummularia creeping Jenny
Lysimachia vulgaris yellow loosestrife
Menyanthes trifoliata buck bean
Monarda didyma Oswego tea
Succisa pratensis devil's bit scabious
Valerian officinalis valerian

Grasses and other marginals include

Butomus umbellatus flowering rush
Carex elata 'Aurea' golden sedge
Carex pendula hanging sedge
Juncus effusus common rush
Pontederia cordata pickerelweed
Typha angustifolia bulrush
Typha latifolia bulrush
Typha minima lesser bulrush

Herbs for dry habitats

Hot, dry habitats can mean Mediterranean summers with the scent of pines, thyme, and rosemary clinging to the sides of the mountains. Many of the most familiar and best-loved herbs are found in this habitat.

The white daisy-like heads of feverfew are welcome in any color scheme. Here it is grown beneath the feathery heads of fennel. Many of the old traditional names for herbs are related to their uses in herbal medicine: Bruisewort; woundwort; throatwort and the chaste tree are among the most obvious.

The common oregano grows wild in chalky soils.

The sun seems to concentrate and accentuate the essence of the herbs that is distilled into the classic food of the Mediterranean region, with its emphasis on olive oil and deliciously flavored sauces. Plants from this part of the world have adapted to the hot, dry climate over millions of years. Their roots descend below the level of the rocky surface to the cooler, moister soil below, and many have adapted their leaves to store water.

Any gardener in a more temperate clime who wants to imitate these conditions must, as a priority, possess a garden with a sunny, sheltered position. Free-draining soil is the next item of importance, and if you garden on heavy soil, particularly heavy clay, then you will need to construct a raised bed or a small rock garden to make a microclimate where the soil drains freely throughout the year. The one condition that Mediterranean plants will never tolerate is cold damp roots, especially in the winter.

Constructing a raised bed

The first thing to decide is the size and shape of the bed. There is no point in making a raised bed that is out of proportion with the rest of the garden or in the wrong position. As an extreme example, a large raised bed placed in the center of the lawn would look out of place. Choose a site where a raised bed will add to the interest of the garden and check the overall design to see whether you need to construct two beds to add overall symmetry to the scheme.

When you have done that, you will need to choose the materials. This depends entirely on the look and period of the house. A plain brick house would look best with matching brick beds, while stone houses would need beds made from the local material, or something very close to it. Gardeners living in houses with plain plastered or wooden outside walls might consider the cheaper alternative of concrete blocks that can then be rendered and painted.

Whatever the material, when building a raised bed be sure to read a professional manual and follow the instructions carefully. It is very important to calculate the amount of material required correctly and ensure that the foundations are sufficiently deep to support the weight of the walls and the soil. Fill the bottom of the raised bed with rubble, broken bricks, and large

flowering herbs for a dry position

Amaranthus cruentes amaranth
Anthemis nobile Roman chamomile
Armeria maritima seapink
Artemisia absinthium wormwood
Calendula officinalis marigold
Centranthus ruber red valerian
Cheiranthus cheiri wallflower
Consolida ambigua doubtful knight's-spur
Coreopsis tinctoria golden tickseed
Cymbalaria muralis Kenilworth ivy
Dianthus barbatus pink
Drimia maritima squill
Helianthemum nummularium rock rose
Lavandula angustifolia English lavender
Lavandula stoechas French lavender
Linaria vulgaris yellow toadflax
Oenothera biennis evening primrose
Papaver orientale oriental poppy
Pulsatilla vulgaris European pasque flower
Santolina chamaecyparissus lavender cotton
Sedum reflexum Jenny's stonecrop
Sempervivum tectorum houseleek
Silybum marianum milk thistle
Verbascum taxus mullein

stones, then build up the bed in layers of smaller stones, finishing with a layer of gravel before adding the compost and topsoil. By constructing the bed in this way it will be free draining. If you plan to grow acid-loving plants, then fill the bed with ericaceous compost suitable for these. Raised beds are a good way for gardeners with alkaline soil to grow acid-loving plants, such as heather, camellias, and small azaleas.

Culinary herbs

Many of the favorite culinary herbs flourish in hot, dry conditions. They include: *Anethum graveolens*, dill; *Foeniculum vulgare*, fennel; *Hyssopus offic-*

inale, hyssop; *Juniperus communis*, juniper; *Laurus nobilis*, bay tree; *Origanum majoranum*, marjoram; *Origanum vulgare*, oregano; *Rosmarinus officinalis*, rosemary; *Salvia officinalis*, sage; *Satureja montana*, winter savory; and *Thymus vulgaris*, wild thyme.

Grow the larger herbs, such as bay and juniper, in separate containers and plan an herbal potager for the lower-growing culinary plants. These can all be grown in a raised bed if you cannot provide suitable soil conditions.

The vast majority of herbs suitable for hot, dry conditions are scented, and many of them are essential ingredients in potpourri mixtures, scented oils, and culinary preparations.

A handsome old stone lion surrounded by French lavender above and English lavender below. In time, the ivy creeping upwards will soften the hard outlines of the plinth.

Herbs for sun

A number of herbs prefer to grow in sites with full sun and moisture-retaining soil. They can be the most difficult herbs to satisfy, but they flourish best in reasonably heavy soil or in meadows bordering rivers and streams.

Opposite: Orange flowers of *Calendula officinalis*, the common marigold, are contrasted with the deep blue of *Nigella sativum*, black cumin.

Almost all herbs for sun are native of temperate climates that have no extremes of winter and summer weather. A number are perfectly hardy, but they do not enjoy long periods of hot drought in summer. There are plenty of attractive flowering plants that can be grouped in borders, such as the purple coneflower or echinacea, daylilies or hemerocallis, blazing star, liatris, and the oxeye daisy, *Leucanthemum vulgare*. These will flower throughout summer and provide color and interest in the garden.

Establishing a wildflower meadow

This is the ideal environment for a number of herbs that flourish in grassy meadows alongside the native grasses. This scheme can be difficult to establish in an ordinary garden. Very often the soil is too rich and the native grasses swamp the flowering herbs before they have become established and can compete on an equal footing. To make a wildflower meadow you need to apply a selective weedkiller to the chosen area to eliminate all perennial weeds, such as dandelion and dock. Next, strip off the old turf, remove the fertile topsoil, and cultivate the subsoil to a fine consistency. After this, sow a mixture of fine grasses, such as bents and fescues, and flowering plants and herbs. Suitable mixtures can be purchased from specialist suppliers.

Roses for a sunny position

People often forget the importance of roses in herbal medicine, but the keen rose grower can easily plan a bed of old-fashioned roses that can still be used in the kitchen, in herbal medicine, and as one of the essential ingredients in potpourris. There are many roses that will grow happily in partial shade. There are even climbing species that can be grown against an exposed wall. However, the majority appreciate a sunny spot, as long as it is not too dry and the soil is reasonably fertile.

French lavender, *Salvia officinalis* 'Tricolor' and varieties of creeping thyme decorate a path. These herbs love the extra heat provided by the stones.

Viola tricolor, viola

Salvia officinalis 'Icterina', gold variegated sage

herbs suitable for sunny, moist positions

Achillea millefolium yarrow	*Malva sylvestris* common mallow
Alchemilla vulgaris lady's mantle	*Melissa officinalis* lemon balm
Atriplex hortensis **var. rubra** red orache	*Phytolacca americana* pokeweed
Centaurea scabiosa greater knapweed	*Platycodon grandiflorus* balloon flower
Dipsacus fullonum teasel	*Polemonium caeruleum* Greek valerian
Echinacea purpurea purple coneflower	*Primula veris* cowslip primrose
Galega officinalis goat's rue	*Pycnanthemum pilosum* mountain mint
Inula helenium elecampane	*Saponaria officinalis* soapwort
Laurus nobilis bay	*Tanacetum parthenium* feverfew
Leucanthemum vulgare oxeye daisy	*Tropaeolum majus* nasturtium
Liatris spicata blazing star	*Verbena officinalis* vervain

Many of the best culinary herbs flourish in hot, sunny positions, as they are native to the Mediterranean, where they grow on the rocky hillsides and mountains close to the sea. These include all the sages, thyme, and rosemary Try to grow these herbs only if you can offer a warm place in the backyard.

The best old roses for potpourris are some of the gallicas, probably the oldest roses in existence: 'Belle de Crécy', which is deep pink, turning violet; 'Camaïeux', white, splashed with crimson; *Rosa gallica* var. *officinalis*, the French rose, light crimson with gold stamens; and *R. gallica* 'Versicolor', the Rosa Mundi, crimson and white striped flowers.

Other groups of old roses include: Damask roses, supposedly brought to Europe by the Crusaders in the 12th century; the centifolias, the rose of Provence; alba roses, probably the hardiest roses of all; and moss roses.

Salvia officinalis 'Rosea', pink-flowered sage

Pulsatilla vulgaris, European pasque flower

Santolina chamaecyparissus, lavender cotton

Salvia officinalis 'Purpurascens', purple sage

Rosmarinus officinalis, rosemary

Herbs for containers

Probably more herbs are grown in containers than anywhere else, particularly the best-known culinary herbs. A good number are tender and will not survive outdoors during the winter months, so the kitchen windowsill, where there is light and a moist atmosphere, is a most suitable place for them.

Possibly the most common and most popular of all culinary herbs is basil. Sow this herb throughout the summer in individual pots so that the plants can be brought indoors if the weather gets cold in the fall. Grow the standard sweet basil, *Ocimum basilicum*, and also one of the purple-leaved varieties, 'Purple Ruffles' or var. *purpurascens*. If you wish, experiment with some of the scented-leaf varieties, the lemon-scented var. *citriodorum*, 'Cinnamon', or 'Horapha' with a flavor of aniseed and licorice, are all well worth trying.

Chives, *Allium schoenoprasum*, are another good culinary herb that can be kept in a sheltered porch or on the windowsill over the winter. They die down in the winter if left outside but will grow again the following year.

A colorful wooden container planted with Californian poppies contrasted with the dark blue of the veronicas. Californian poppies are very easy to grow and need only sun and warmth to flourish. They are used in herbal medicine as a sedative, as they have mild narcotic properties.

Parsley and mint

Parsley, too, is suitable for growing in individual containers. It is an excellent herb, rich in vitamins A and C. There are two types of parsley; flat-leaf or Italian parsley, and the curled varieties. The best varieties are 'Moss Curled 2' and 'Italian'; the latter is a flat-leaf. Mint, too, is always popular and is a good plant to confine to a container, where it cannot spread and start to rampage through the backyard.

Culinary herbs with colored foliage

The Mediterranean herbs sage, thyme, and oregano are all suitable for containers. Two or three can be included in a small trough. There are a number of good varieties to choose from and the containers can be put out in summer.

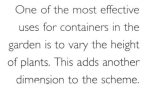

One of the most effective uses for containers in the garden is to vary the height of plants. This adds another dimension to the scheme.

Try to grow herbs with contrasting colors. *Salvia officinalis*, common sage, has varieties with purple, gold, yellow, pink, and variegated leaves. The lemon-scented thyme, *Thymus* x *citriodorus* 'Silver Queen', has cream-variegated leaves. *T. vulgaris* 'Aureus' has yellow-tinged green leaves and 'Silver Posy' has white-margined leaves. The oregano variety *Origanum vulgare* 'Aureum Crispum' has golden leaves and pink flowers, and *O. v.* 'Gold Tip' has leaves with yellow tips.

Scented pelargoniums

Scented geraniums are another group of plants commonly grown in containers either in the house or in an unheated greenhouse. The scented-leaf varieties all have an individual and distinctive aroma. Look out for lemon, rose, apple, pine, cinnamon, and peppermint, among many others. They can be used to make herbal teas, or even as a flavoring for baking.

Grouping herbs in containers

Small containers can be home to a number of plants, for many herbs are not that large, and it is easy to include a small rosemary shrub, thyme, salvia, oregano, and some parsley in an individual container. Such containers can be conveniently placed outside the kitchen door or even on a windowsill, providing there is sufficient room. If you are planning to move containers of any size, make sure that they can be lifted easily, since even fairly small containers filled with compost and plants can be quite heavy.

culinary herbs for containers

Allium schoenoprasum chives

Aloysia triphylla lemon beebrush

Mentha mint

varieties: x *piperata* (peppermint), *spicata* (spearmint), *suavolens* (applemint)

Ocimum basilicum basil

varieties: var. *citriodorum*: 'Dark Opal', 'Genovese', 'Horapha', 'Purple Ruffles', var. *purpurascens*

Origanum majorana sweet marjoram

Origanum vulgare oregano, wild marjoram

varieties: 'Aureum', 'Aureum Crispum', 'Gold Tip', 'Heiderose'

Petroselinum crispum parsley

varieties: 'Italian', 'Greek', var. *neapolitanum*, 'Afro', 'Champion Moss Curled', 'Moss Curled 2'

Salvia elegans **'Scarlet Pineapple'** pineapple sage

Salvia officinalis common sage

varieties: 'Icterina', Purpurascens Group, 'Kew Gold', 'Tricolor'

Thymus x citriodorus lemon-scented thyme

varieties: 'Aureus', 'Bertram Anderson', 'Silver Queen'

Thymus vulgaris common thyme

varieties: 'Aureus', 'Silver Posy'

Patios and window boxes

Patios, especially if they are sunny, are often the best place to grow those herbs that normally flourish in hot climates, while window boxes allow everyone to grow their own fresh herbs for the kitchen wherever they live.

Trailing nasturtiums, *Tropaeolum majus*, look well grown as the center of a display surrounded by African marigolds. Excellent companion plants for the vegetable garden, they deter whitefly and attract the pest-eating blackfly.

In a patio garden, herbs can be planted in containers. The heat of the walls of the house and the hard surface of the patio will greatly increase the temperature, and such places form their own microclimates within larger backyards. They are also extremely useful even if the main garden contains a large space for herbs and vegetables, for they enable the cook to have a number of herbs at hand without having to venture out in the wind and rain when fresh herbs are required for the kitchen. Low-growing herbs can be planted in any cracks in the patio floor, or in prepared spaces. Creeping thymes, carnations, and even lavender and wallflowers can be grown in this way.

The importance of watering

Balance the needs of the cook with the amount of time and effort needed to maintain herbs in containers, and remember that containers need regular watering during the hot months of the summer, for they dry out much more quickly

growing sweet peppers on a patio

Peppers have valuable herbal properties. They are used in the kitchen in a number of dishes, and they are also prepared commercially as hot, spicy sauces. They are also used medically to treat fevers, digestive problems, and to help with convalescence in old age.
Sweet peppers, *Capsicum annuum*, can be grown in a sheltered patio in temperate zones. They are good plants to grow in containers.

Sow the seed in individual pots in spring. Sow two seeds in each pot and discard the weakest if both germinate. The seeds require a temperature of 64–70°F(18–21°C) to germinate. Repot in larger containers until the plants are large enough to plant outside, and keep the compost moist, but not sodden. Train the vines up canes and water with a potassium-rich feed when the fruits start to form. They are ready for harvesting when they are green, swollen, and glossy towards the end of the summer.

than the surrounding soil. Those herbs that are native to the Mediterranean will tolerate dry conditions better than the others, but even they need water because they are used to having their roots deep in the soil where it is cooler and some moisture remains. These conditions cannot be replicated in a container.

Brilliant blue pots planted with lavender and the yellow-flowered santolina. Painted containers give the garden an additional splash of color and have the advantage that they can be moved around throughout the year.

Containers for trees

Containers enable the gardener to make a definite design statement that is not possible in any other way. Formal trees and shrubs can all be grown in containers and some, such as bay and box, can be clipped into geometric shapes to frame the entrance to a town house. As well as bay and box, important for the kitchen and for medicine respectively, the European olive, *Olea europaea*, is becoming increasingly used as a container-grown plant. The fruits can be gathered and pressed at the end of the summer for a small amount of oil. Small citrus trees, such as *C. limon*, lemon, and *C. reticulata*, mandarin orange, can also be grown in containers and given shelter in a cool place indoors over the winter months.

Window boxes

Any of the culinary herbs can be grown in a window box, and a medium-sized box can contain a varied selection that will provide fresh herbs for a good part of the year. Other useful herbs and vegetables that can be grown in window boxes are wild strawberries, *Fragaria vesca*, small tomatoes, the mini-vegetables that have been developed for gardens where there is little room, or any of the wide selection of scented-leaf geraniums.

Herbs for hedges

Many of the major hedging plants, such as yew and privet, are important plants in herbal medicine. A number of other herbs can be planted to make smaller hedges or to line formal borders or beds in a knot garden.

Small hedging plants include box, lavender, cotton lavender, hyssop, some salvias, roses, and germander. The most commonly grown hedging plant is box, formerly used to make a treatment for malaria. The box variety 'Suffruticosa' is the low-growing form found framing so many beds in kitchen gardens, knot gardens, and formal potagers. Box hedging should be planted 8in (20cm) apart any time between early fall and early spring, as long as the soil is warm enough and not too sodden. It needs clipping two or three times during the summer to keep the hedge in shape and to encourage dense, bushy growth.

A variety of herbal hedges

Lavender is a lovely herb when planted as an informal, low-growing hedge along paths or borders. *Lavandule angustifolia* 'Hidcote' is compact with deep-purple flowers. French lavender,

L. stoechas, is another good compact variety, but some people do not like the shape of the flowers. Lavender cotton, *Santolina chamaecyparissus*, makes a spreading, gray hedge. It needs to be clipped in the spring. The sages, *Salvia fruticosa*, and *S. gregii*, are both small, evergreen shrubs that can be planted as unusual hedges. The latter is not fully hardy.

The scented thyme, *Thymus* x *citriodorus*, is another possibility, but it is rather rounded in form. Another herb that makes an attractive and unusual low hedge is rosemary: 'Miss Jessopp's Upright' is the best to grow for this purpose. Beware, however, when trimming it; no rosemary will tolerate savage pruning.

Larger herbal hedging plants

The finest plant for garden hedging is yew, *Taxus baccata*, used in the treatment of some forms of cancer. Yew forms an impenetrable

planting a natural hedge

The sweetbrier rose, *Rosa eglanteria*, is another rose often used as a hedging plant. It has single pink flowers in summer, followed by oval red hips in fall. The foliage is strongly fragrant of apples.

1 When planting any hedge the most important stage in the work is to clear the ground properly. Apply a systemic weedkiller to kill off all perennial weeds. Dig over the whole area.

2 Break up the soil at the bottom of the hole to encourage root penetration and aid drainage. If the soil is very dry, fill the hole with water and then allow it to drain away before planting the rose.

3 Prepare a planting mix, following the instructions on pages 76–9. Firm the mix around the roots of the plant, then fill in around the plant. Water well and keep watering if the weather is dry.

hedge that needs little attention. Yew hedges should be planted 2ft (60cm) apart. They are not as slow-growing as might be imagined. The cedar, *Thuja plicata*, is another excellent hedging plant. Cedars are used to treat cancer, heart disorders, and many other internal complaints.

Holly, *Ilex aquifolium*, also makes an excellent slow-growing hedge. It is used to treat malaria and bronchial complaints, while Chinese privet, *Ligustrum lucidum*, is a toxic plant, used in the treatment of liver complaints.

One of the best formal hedging plants of all is the common beech, *Fagus sylvatica*, used in herbal medicine to treat chronic bronchitis and respiratory infections.

Informal herbal hedges are good decorative features in gardens, especially if they flower in summer. They can be trimmed early in the year or clipped into shape once the flowers have faded. The most popular of these hedging plants is the rose 'Roseraie de l'Haÿ'. Other rugosa roses are also popular choices.

This sweetbrier rose makes a fine decorative hedge and also repels intruders.

herbs for hedging

EVERGREEN

Berberis darwinii Darwin's barberry
Buxus sempervirens 'Suffruticosa' box
Ilex aquifolium holly
Lavandula angustifolia 'Hidcote' lavender
Lavandula stoechas French lavender
Ligustrum lucidum glossy privet
Rosmarinus 'Miss Jessopp's Upright' rosemary
Salvia fruticosa sage
Salvia gregii autumn sage
Santolina chamaecyparissus lavender cotton
Taxus baccata yew

Teucrium fruticans shrubby germander
Thuja plicata cedar
Thymus x citriodorus lemon-scented thyme

DECIDUOUS

Berberis thunbergii barberry
Crataegus monogyna hawthorn
Fagus sylvatica common beech
Hyssopus officinalis hyssop
Hyssopus officinalis f. *albus* white hyssop
Rosa eglanteria vars. sweetbrier rose
Rosa rugosa vars. rugosa rose

Flowering herb borders

Many herbs are attractive flowering plants in their own right. Planning successful flowering borders demands care and attention. For maximum impact several of the plants should flower around the same time, and the foliage and height of the different plants should complement each other.

A wild corner in an old herb garden. The silvery green leaves of the cotton lavender, lavender, and rosemary make a pleasing evergreen corner.

When planning a border, remember the important principles of design—color and contrast. Group plants so that they match each other, and link opposing colors with patches of white flowers or gray foliage plants.

Early flowering herbs

Many of the herbs that flower early in the year are bulbs or early flowering shrubs, a number of which prefer to grow in acid soil. Beds of early flowering herbs are best planned in gardens that can provide acid conditions.

Plant a selection of bulbs—snowdrops to flower early in the year, followed by the blue hepaticas, and the yellow stars of the spring pheasant's eye. Keep these plants in groups, alternating the colors. The common primrose, *Primula vulgaris*, with its pale yellow flowers, can be planted among the bulbs. It flowers slightly later, as do the delicate fritillaries, *Fritillaria meleagris* and *F. thunbergii*, with their purple-spotted, white, red and pink hanging flowers.

Other early flowering herbs include *Arctostaphylos uva-ursi*, bearberry; *Bellis perennis*, ornamental daisy; camellias; *Chaenomeles* spp., ornamental quince; *Cornus mas*, the Cornelian cherry, and *C. officinalis*; magnolias; rosemary; *Vinca major*, the great periwinkle; and varieties of the winter-flowering pansy, *Viola* x *wittrockiana*. The evergreen *Artemisia absinthium* 'Lambrook Silver' is an excellent gray foliage plant that helps to link the colors together.

Shrub borders for late spring

One of the best spring shrubs is *Berberis darwinii*, evergreen with orange-red flowers. Plant it alongside *B.* x *stenophylla*, with yellow flowers, or varieties of *Forsythia suspensa*.

If you want to have a white and pink shrub border, try growing the calico bush, *Kalmia latifolia*, in company with another pink flowering herbal shrub, *Daphne genkwa*, and the white-flowering myrtle, *Myrtus communis*. A pink and

The pink flowers of the chives can be used as decoration in summer salads. Here they show up well against the darker foliage of the sages.

white border based on these shrubs can be complemented by the peonies, *Paeonia officinalis*, pink to red, the white tree peony, *P. suffruticosa*, underplanted with lungwort, *Pulmonaria saccharata*, with its blue and pink flowers, and lily-of-the-valley, *Convallaria majalis*.

Other flowering herbs for late spring include: *Cardamine pratensis*; *Corydalis solida, Polemonium caeruleum*, Jacob's ladder; *Pulsatilla vulgaris*, European pasque flower; *Trillium erectum*, wake robin; and *Vaccinium myrtillus*, bilberry.

Herbs for midsummer borders

Most herbs flower in the summer. The trick of designing a successful herb border is to blend the colors of the flowers and foliage with the varying heights of each plant so that the border makes a harmonious picture.

A blue, pink, and white summer herb border could include the taller herbs at the back, such as *Sambucus nigra* 'Guincho Purple', with its dark foliage and pinkish-white flowers; *Alcea rosea*

summer flowering herbs

EARLY SPRING	LATE SPRING
Adonis vernalis spring pheasant's eye	*Berberis darwinii* Darwin's barberry
Arctostaphylos uva-ursi bearberry	*Cardamine pratensis* meadowsweet
Artemisia absinthium 'Lambrook Silver' wormwood	*Convallaria majalis* lily-of-the-valley
Bellis perennis daisy	*Daphne genkwa* daphne
Cornus officinalis dogwood	*Forsythia suspensa* weeping forsythia
Camellia spp. camellia	*Kalmia latifolia* calico bush
Fritillaria thunbergii fritillary	*Myrtus communis* myrtle
Magnolia spp. magnolia	*Paeonia officinalis* peony
Vinca major great periwinkle	*Polemonium caeruleum* Jacob's ladder
	Pulmonaria saccharata lungwort

Flowering herb borders

'Chater's Double'; hollyhocks, whose flowers come in a range of colors; and *Cynara cardunculus*, cardoon, with pink to purple flowers and silver-gray foliage. In the center of the border, place *Achillea millefolium* 'Cerise Queen' and 'Lilac Beauty', deep and pale pink flowers respectively *A. ptarmica* 'Boule de Neige', the white sneezeweed; *Tanacetum parthenium*, feverfew, with its white daisy-like flowers, or other varieties of white-flowering daisies. Include some lavenders—*Lavandula* x *intermedia* 'Seal'

A majestic flowering herbal border dominated by the striking purple and pink plumes of the buddleias. These all need hard pruning early in spring each year otherwise they become straggly.

has pale purple flowers—and plant lower-growing herbs, such as *Dianthus barbatus*, sweet William, *Salvia officinalis* 'Tricolor', *Linum perenne*, the blue flax, and the pink-flowering *Thymus herba-barona* at the front to spill over the edges.

Borders of annual herbs

Many series of flowering herbs that will provide instant and glorious color in the summer garden have been developed. Grow annuals in a border on their own or plant them at random in herbaceous borders. You can sow hardy annuals in position the previous fall so that they will flower the following summer, or plant out half-hardy annuals in late spring when all danger of frost is over. The Californian poppy, *Eschscholzia californica* 'Ballerina' series, is a very popular annual herb and has attractive white, pink, red, and orange flowers.

Other common herbs that have been developed as annuals include achilleas; hyssop (agastache); amaranthus; clary (*Salvia horminum*); cornflower (*Centaurea cyanus*); poppies; pelargoniums; lobelias; tobacco plants (*Nicotiana*) and vervains. All these annuals have attractive flowers in a color spectrum ranging from deep red through pink, blue, purple, and white.

If you want yellow and orange borders, then choose some of the marigolds (tagetes) that are available in a bewildering range of yellow and orange colors. These plants also make excellent edging plants along paths.

Fall borders of herbs

There is inevitably a somewhat dull period in all gardens as summer draws to a close. The main flowers of the year are over, the leaves start to fall from the trees, but the gorgeous fall colors have yet to arrive.

The dedicated herb gardener can plan a border of late-flowering herbs that will provide a bright spot in the garden as summer ends. Some herbs start flowering in midsummer and continue in bloom into the fall.

There are many suitable flowering herbs for a late summer border, which will help to liven up this dull time of year. These include yarrow (*Achillea* spp.), which has pink, red, and white flowers; coneflower (*Echinacea* spp.), with purple and red flowers; boneset (*Eupatorium perfoliatum*), white flowers; hyssop (*Hyssopus officinalis* f. *roseus*), pink flowers; blazing star (*Liatris spicata*), mauve-pink flowers; Oswego tea (*Monarda didyma*), red flowers; soapwort (*Saponaria officinalis*), pink flowers; costmary (*Tanacetum balsamita*), white flowers; and tansy (*T. vulgare* var. *crispum*), which has yellow flowers and feathery foliage.

summer flowering herbs

EARLY SUMMER

Achillea millefolium 'Cerise Queen' yarrow
A. ptarmica 'Boule de Neige' sneezeweed
Alcea rosea 'Chater's Double' hollyhock
Cynara cardunculus cardoon
Dianthus barbatus carnation
Lavandula × *intermedia* 'Seal' lavender
Salvia officinalis 'Tricolor' sage
Sambucus nigra 'Guincho Purple' black elder
Tanacetum parthenium feverfew

LATE SUMMER

Achillea spp. yarrow
Echinacea spp. coneflower
Eupatorium perfoliatum boneset
Hyssopus officinalis hyssop
Liatris spicata blazing star
Monarda didyma Oswego tea
Saponaria officinalis soapwort
Tanacetum balsamita costmary
Tanacetum vulgare var. *crispum* tansy

Two matching formal borders of flowering herbs. Gardens with plenty of space available can use this type of border to great effect, and here the picture is complemented by the wall opening smothered with climbing roses at the height of summer.

A medicinal herb border

There are few herbs that are not connected with medicine. Many are used to treat various illnesses and ailments. There has recently been a great expansion in the research by drug companies into the properties of herbs, and their potential to treat fatal diseases such as AIDS and cancer.

An herbal border dominated by lemon balm, which has the reputation for treating melancholy. It is a popular herbal tea.

It is interesting to plan and plant specific borders of medicinal herbs because there are so many possibilities. One option is to concentrate on herbs that would have been grown by the monks in the Middle Ages. These include the species herbs called *officinalis* or *officinale*, for example *Salvia officinalis*. The official was the place in the monastery where the medicines were prepared and administered.

Another idea might be to group together herbs that were used to treat a specific ailment, such as bronchial disorders. This would include herbs such as agrimony, coltsfoot, hound's tongue, hyssop, lavender, and marshmallow. Another would be to grow all the plants that are used to make herbal teas and drunk as infusions for indigestion or nervous disorders. Such a border would include various mints, vervain, lemon balm, and chamomile. There is considerable overlap, for nearly all the best-known medicinal herbs were used to treat ailments. Another welcome planting could include scented herbs used in potpourri mixtures, for many medicinal herbs have strongly scented leaves.

Medicinal herbs of legend

If you wanted to research the herbs that were used in ancient worship and legend, then a border could be planned using these on their own. Meadowsweet and mistletoe were sacred to the Druids, an ancient religious group of northern Europe. A mixture containing laurel leaves, picked from the bay tree, *Laurus nobilis*, was smoked by the ancient Greeks at the Temple of Apollo at Delphi, Greece. Combined with other herbs, laurel was reputed to have narcotic qualities. Yarrow, revered in the Bronze Age, is found in the burial mounds of that period, while balm, *Melissa officinalis*, was considered the "elixir of life," capable of rejuvenating the elderly, by the 16th-century Swiss herbalist Paracelsus. Horehound, *Marrubium vulgare*, was one of many sacred herbs of the Egyptians, known by them as the seed of Horus. Horus was the divine son of the goddess Isis, who used a magic penis to conceive him, fashioned from the remains of her murdered lover Osiris.

Plan your planting carefully

It is important to try to create a harmonious planting. Many of the old physic gardens where the herbs were planted in blocks, often in alphabetical order, are dull and of interest only to the dedicated collector. A good medicinal border in an ordinary garden should be attractive to look at as well as of historic interest. Consider the colors of the flowers, as well as the time of year in which they bloom, and take the position of the border into account. Some herbs prefer full sun, others need some shade: Is the border

A number of medicinal herbs grow well in damp conditions. The planting around the antique fountain includes Indian physic, lavender, yellow flag iris, and dame's rocket.

Medicinal herbs are often colorful. This well-planned border, lined with low-growing clipped box hedges, includes yellow evening primrose, achillea, borage and feverfew.

A medicinal herb border

This flowering border is dominated by hollyhocks and the globe thistle, *Echinops bannaticus*. These are excellent plants for a late summer flowering border with contrasting foliage. Hollyhocks were formerly used to treat sore gums and made an excellent mouthwash. The roots were dried and used to treat intestinal worms.

against a wall or fence, or are you planning an island bed? All these factors influence the design and planting of a successful border.

Flowering borders

A flowering border that will provide color for most of the year and that will look particularly attractive in late summer could include the following medicinal herbs. Borage, *Borago officinalis*, has bright blue flowers lasting from midsummer onward; borage is used to flavor drinks, as a tonic to drive away melancholy, and as an herbal treatment for coughs and colds. Pot marigolds, *Calendula officinalis*, can be planted in clumps at the front of the border, the bright orange flowers will make a vivid contrast with the borage. Pot marigolds are used in a number of herbal healing ointments; the young leaves can be added to salads, and the flowers are used in hair tonic preparations.

If the border is backed by a wall or trellis the common or summer jasmine, *Jasminum officinale*, can be grown as a climber. It is often used in aromatherapy to treat depression, nervous tension, and impotence. Alternatively you could grow the Japanese honeysuckle, *Lonicera japonica*, which has a number of medicinal uses. Lavender is a charming herb in summer with its gray-blue leaves and fragrant purple, lilac, blue, or white flowers. It can be planted at the front of the border and then interspersed with clumps of contrasting marigolds.

Both height and color can be provided by including the French rose, *Rosa gallica* var. *officinalis*, with its light crimson, semi-double flowers, or its close relative the Rosa Mundi, *R. g.* 'Versicolor', with its white flowers splashed with red. In moist, slightly acid soil you can plant the storax, *Styrax officinalis*, which grows into a substantial shrub with cinnamon-scented white flowers in early summer. It is used to treat a number of common complaints including coughs, colds, bronchitis, and mouth ulcers.

Any flowering border can be embellished by bee balm, *Melissa officinalis*—the variety 'Aurea' has green leaves marked with gold; rosemary, *Rosmarinus officinalis*, which complements the lavenders and flowers earlier in the year; and sage, *Salvia officinalis*—also evergreen, the variety 'Tricolor' has green, cream and pink leaves. Don't forget to plant white flowers in your border to join the other colors together. Feverfew, *Tanacetum parthenium*, and pyrethrum, *T. cinerariifolium*, have white daisy-like flowers, and many of the varieties have yellow centers.

Medicinal plants for a potpourri

Many gardeners who wish to develop herb plots like to cultivate one area of the garden where the plants can be used to make a scented potpourri mixture. A border of scented medicinal herbs could include any or all of the following herbs, the French rose, *Rosa gallica* var. *officinalis*; southernwood, *Artemisia abrotanum*; lavender, *Lavandula angustifolia* 'Hidcote'; clove-scented carnations, *Dianthus caryophyllus*; sage, *Salvia officinalis* Purpurascens group; wild thyme, *Thymus vulgaris* 'Silver Posy'; jasmine, *Jasminum officinale*; tansy, *Tanacetum vulgare*, 'Tom Thumb'; black cumin, *Nigella sativa*; Oswego tea, *Monarda didyma*; applemint, *Mentha suaveolens* 'Variegata'; rosemary, *Rosmarinus officinale*; as well as the scented pelargoniums. Choose varieties with foliage that will blend in with the other plants, or ones that will provide an additional perfume, since scented pelargoniums have leaves of many different fragrances.

A border of plants for herbal teas

Herbal teas or tisanes can be prepared from a number of herbs. Plants for tisanes include lemon beebrush, *Aloysia triphylla*; chamomile, *Chamaemelum nobile*; bee balm, *Melissa officinalis*; peppermint, *Mentha* x *piperata*; pineapple sage, *Salvia elegans* 'Scarlet Pineapple'; and vervain, *Verbena officinalis*.

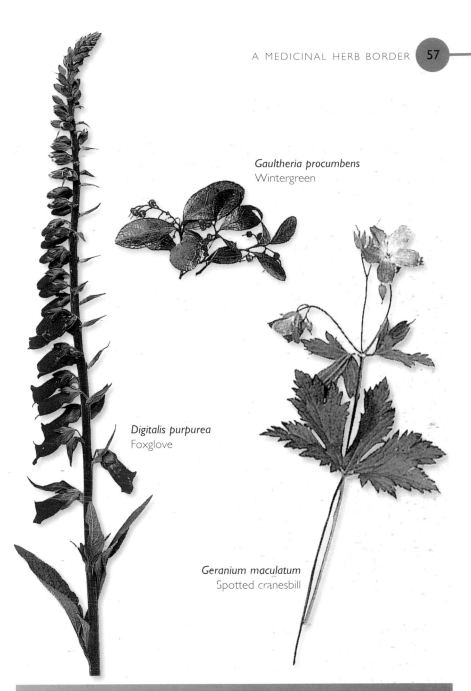

Gaultheria procumbens
Wintergreen

Digitalis purpurea
Foxglove

Geranium maculatum
Spotted cranesbill

some poisonous medicinal herbs

- *Aconitum napellus* monkshood
- *Adonis vernalis* spring Pheasant's eye
- *Aloe vera* aloe
- *Aquilegia vulgaris* columbine
- *Arnica montana* mountain arnica
- *Artemisia vulgaris* common wormwood
- *Asclepias tuberosa* butterfly milkweed
- *Atropa belladonna* deadly nightshade
- *Buxus sempervirens* box
- *Caltha palustris* marsh marigold
- *Chamaemelum nobile* lawn chamomile
- *Cimicifuga racemosa* black cohosh
- *Colchicum autumnale* autumn crocus
- *Digitalis purpurea* foxglove
- *Eupatorium cannabinum* hemp agrimony
- *Glycyrrhiza glabra* licorice
- *Heliotropium arborescens* heliotrope
- *Helleborus niger* black hellebore
- *Hyoscyamus niger* black henbane
- *Iris pseudacorus* yellow flag
- *Ligustrum vulgare* European privet
- *Lobelia siphilitica* great blue lobelia
- *Mandragora officinarum* mandrake
- *Paeonia officinalis* peony
- *Papaver* spp. poppy
- *Phytolacca americana* pokeweed
- *Pulmonaria officinalis* lungwort
- *Sanguinaria canadensis* bloodroot
- *Sempervivum tectorum* houseleek
- *Solanum dulcamara* woody nightshade
- *Symphytum officinalis* comfrey
- *Verbena officinalis* vervain

Wildflowers and herbs

Many herbs are wildflowers, and a number of useful herbs are generally regarded as mere weeds: Dandelions, nettles, and yarrow are the bane of many a gardener. Keen herbalists set aside part of their garden to grow common herbs and wildflowers, or seek out the wild herbs on wasteground.

A number of important herbs are usually found as wildflowers throughout the world. They include comfrey, creeping buttercup, nettles, and elder trees.

The basic steps for cultivating a wildflower garden are described on pages 42–3. A number of other factors should also be considered when planning a wildflower area. First of all you need to sow seed that will suit your soil. There is no point in sowing a wildflower mixture suitable for chalky soil in acid, upland areas. Obtain mixtures of wildflowers that are native to the area where you live. Make sure that the flowers have plenty of room. They should be given the advantage of some space when you sow them, otherwise the more rampant grasses may overwhelm the flowers before

they can become established. Make sure that the soil has a low fertility and try to eradicate all perennial weeds before you start. Scatter the seed in early fall or spring and protect it from the birds by covering the area with netting if possible, as the seed needs to be left open on the ground to germinate.

Wildflower meadows should be cut in late summer when the flowers are over and have had a chance to set seed. If the growth in the fall is vigorous, then the meadows should be cut again before winter sets in. Rake up all the cuttings and remove them from the site.

Herbs from the wild

Generally speaking, all herbs are, or were, wild-flowers: It is usually the species plant that is used in herbal medicine. Some common wild-flowers are not grown in gardens but can be sought out and prepared as decoctions for herbal treatment. Check with a good wildflower guide where plants are likely to be found and use the illustrations to aid identification. Among them are: agrimony or church steeples, *Agrimonia eupatoria*, used for coughs; betony, *Stachys officinalis*; birch, *Betula alba*, the leaves are used; sweet gale, *Myrica gale*, the leaves are infused as a tonic; burdock, *Arctium lappa*, used as a tonic and diuretic; celandine, *Chelidonium majus*, the juice is supposedly a cure for warts; centaury, *Centaurium vulgare*, a good antiseptic; cleavers or goosegrass, *Galium aparine*, a cure-all herb once used for leprosy; cowslip primrose, *Primula veris*, the leaves make a sedative tea; fig-wort, *Scrophularia nodosa*, a cure for sore throats and circulatory disorders; horehound, *Marrubium vulgare*, a syrup makes a good cough medicine; marshmallow, *Althaea officinalis*, another herbal cough medicine; meadowsweet, *Filipendula ulmaria*, a scented herb used for stomach upsets, and red clover, *Trifolium pratense*, for treating headaches and skin complaints.

A wild-looking herb border dominated by the feathery, textural leaves of the fennel and brightened by the bright red cardinal flower, *Lobelia cardinalis*.

herbs found in the wild

- *Agrimonia eupatoria* church steeples
- *Althaea officinalis* marshmallow
- *Anagallis arvensis* scarlet pimpernel
- *Arctium lappa* burdock
- *Centaurea cyanus* cornflower
- *Centaurea scabiosa* greater knapweed
- *Clematis vitalba* evergreen clematis
- *Cymbalaria muralis* Kenilworth ivy
- *Cynoglossum officinale* hound's tongue
- *Dipsacus fullonum* teasel
- *Echium vulgare* viper's bugloss
- *Filipendula ulmaria* meadowsweet
- *Fumaria officinalis* drug fumitory
- *Galega officinalis* goat's rue
- *Galium verum* yellow bedstraw
- *Geranium robertianum* herb robert
- *Hesperis matronalis* dame's rocket
- *Lysimachia vulgaris* yellow loosestrife
- *Marrubium vulgare* horehound
- *Myrica gale* sweet gale
- *Onopordum acanthium* Scotch cotton thistle
- *Ophioglossum vulgatum* adder's tongue
- *Phytolacca americana* pokeweed
- *Plantago major* common plantain
- *Primula veris* cowslip primrose
- *Prunella vulgaris* selfheal
- *Scabiosa succisa* devil's bit
- *Scrophularis nodosa* figwort
- *Sedum acre* goldmoss stonecrop
- *Taraxacum officinale* dandelion
- *Tussilago farfara* coltsfoot
- *Veronica officinalis* speedwell

Herbs in winter

All gardens look bare in winter. Leaves fall, perennial plants die back, annuals, like the year, fade away. That is not to say that winter gardens cannot be of interest. Every garden should have some plants in flower in each month of the year. Plants that flower in the winter are doubly important—because of their rarity.

There are times in winter when any garden looks wonderful. Early in the morning after a crisp frost, the grass and plants sparkle as if they have received a dusting of powdered sugar. Or after a slight fall of snow when you can appreciate the outlines of hedges and evergreen shrubs. But without snow, gardens need some plant interest.

Successful winter gardens require careful planning. If the design of the garden permits, the first, most important thing is to grow permanent hedges of evergreen trees or of deciduous trees that retain the leaves of the old year until the new buds arrive the following spring, such as beech or hornbeam. Good evergreen herbal hedges include box, *Buxus sempervirens* 'Suffruticosa'; French lavender, *Lavandula stoechas*, yew, *Taxus baccata*; and rosemary, *Rosmarinus officinalis*—this last herb should be clipped only lightly after flowering.

A fine winter scene when the garden is covered with frost and the shapes of the seedheads are thrown into sharp silhouette.

Evergreen herbal shrubs

Rosemary and lavender can also be grown as shrubs. Indeed, this is probably more common, and they can be planted in beds with lavender cotton *Santolina chamaecyparissus*, or some bushes of common sage. Any bed that includes these shrubs will provide a color point in the early winter. Rue, *Ruta graveolens*, the herb of grace, is another evergreen herb, with striking blue-gray foliage during the winter months. The variety 'Jackman's Blue' is the most commonly grown. This can be grown in company with the yellow-leaved feverfew, *Tanacetum parthenium* 'Aureum' or 'Golden Moss'.

Herbs with seed heads

Many gardeners leave their borders over winter and tidy them early in spring in the following year. The garden benefits from the shape of the stems and seed heads that give form and interest over the winter months. Whether you follow this practice or not is a matter of personal taste. The disadvantage is that with plants that self-seed freely, too many will germinate the following spring and they will need to be controlled. Herbs with striking seed heads include hollyhocks, wild carrot, teasels, yellow gentian, opium poppies, red orache, evergreen clematis, dill, and fennel.

Flowering herbs for winter gardens

Early in the new year, the first flowers start to appear. The first is the snowdrop, and although this is seldom used as an herb, it has been proposed as cure for frostbite. The earliest snowdrops emerge very early in the year although the main flowering is a month later.

They are preceded by the black hellebore, *Helleborus niger*, with its lovely, drooping, cup-shaped flowers. The small comfrey, *Symphytum ibericum*, also flowers at this time and makes an excellent ground-cover plant. The early flowering shrubs should also have a place in the winter garden, especially as so many of them are wonderfully fragrant. The Japanese Cornelian cherry, *Cornus officinalis*, is one, the mezereon, *Daphne mezereum* , with its pink or reddish purple flowers, another, and the flowering witch hazel, *Hamamelis mollis*, a third.

Finally, the most colorful and rewarding winter herbs are the flowering heathers. You can prepare a special bed, providing you have soil that is acid enough and a reasonably damp position. The pink, red, and white sprigs of flowers will provide color for several months.

Often seedheads look their best when they are rimmed with frost. Here fennel stands out against the background of the formal yew hedge.

When planning the planting of the garden it is important to ensure that there are a number of evergreen and silver plants that provide color and contrast in the dark months of the year.

how to
grow
herbs

Growing herbs is not much different from growing any other garden plants. Many are tolerant of a variety of soils and conditions, but there are significant exceptions, and you should check the requirements of each one before including it in an herb garden or a special herb border. If you wish to grow Mediterranean herbs in a temperate climate, you must offer them a hot, sunny position. Similarly, forget about growing the wild herbs from peaty uplands unless you can provide acid soil and a damp position. Grow only those herbs that will appreciate what your garden can offer.

Soil types

Soil is alkaline, neutral, or acid. The first thing that any gardener should do in any new garden is to measure the pH (the scale of alkalinity and acidity) of the soil, because its acidity or otherwise will dictate the type of plants you can grow and the success you will have with your garden.

Some plants will grow only in acid soil, while others prefer alkaline. Attempts to match acid-loving plants with alkaline soil may cause the death of the plant; likewise alkaline-loving plants fare badly in acid conditions. The reason is that the lime present in alkaline soils locks in the nutrients that plants such as rhododendrons, heathers, and camellias need to flourish. These plants are described scientifically as calcifuges—lime-haters. Plants that grow best in extremely alkaline soil are called calcicoles.

Experienced gardeners may be able to tell what type of soil any garden has just by looking at its plants, but it is extremely easy to measure the pH of the soil using a simple test kit. Neutral soil has a pH of 7, acid soils are below 7, and alkaline soils above. The ideal soil has a pH of between 6.5 and 7 and most plants will grow well in this type of soil.

Sandy soil is light and free-draining, and therefore often dries out quickly in hot summers. It can be improved by digging in layers of organic matter, such as garden compost.

Hollyhocks are spectacular plants and should be grown at the back of the border. The most popular forms are *Alcea rosea* 'Chater's Double', with double flowers in a variety of colors. A. r. 'Indian Spring' has single flowers, white, pink, or yellow.

Peaty soil is easy to work, moisture-retentive. It is essential for camellias and rhododendrons.

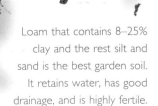

Loam that contains 8–25% clay and the rest silt and sand is the best garden soil. It retains water, has good drainage, and is highly fertile.

Clay soil is dense, difficult to work, and needs drainage. However, it is fertile and the texture can be improved quite easily.

Soil and soil improvement

In addition to the pH, soils can be light and free-draining, sandy or stony, heavy clay or heavy silt, or various stages in between. Chalky soil is alkaline, it may be heavy or light and very often is covered by only a thin layer of topsoil. Peaty soil is light and acid, but may not be very fertile. It is tempting to say "blessed is the gardener who is possessed of fertile soil" but in practice the solution for every gardener who wants to improve the quality of the soil is the same whether the soil is heavy clay or light sand—add plenty of bulky organic matter each year. On clay soils this helps break up the very fine particles that make clay so dense and makes the soil lighter and easier to cultivate. On sandy soils it makes the soil less free-draining, more able to retain moisture, so plants grow better. Clay soils will also benefit from the incorporation of coarse gravel and grit, since this will improve their drainage.

Cultivating the soil for herbs

To dig or not to dig. In prior times there was no question over how an herbal potager or kitchen garden should be treated. Gardeners dug. Not only did they dig, but they double dug, taking out a trenchload of soil and digging the garden to two spade depths. Nowadays this is very seldom done and many gardeners hardly dig the vegetable plot at all.

This is by no means a hard-and-fast rule. If you are preparing a new bed or laying down an herbal potager, the soil must be properly dug, all perennial weeds removed, and most importantly any "pan" should be broken up to allow the roots of the plants to penetrate deep into the soil. Pans are layers of dense soil, and either occur naturally where a solid layer forms below the topsoil, or are caused by repeatedly rotavating the garden to a fixed depth. A hard pan usually has to be dug with a good garden fork, as a spade will seldom penetrate the crust. Similarly, if you have a beautiful kitchen garden with thick fertile soil, then digging the soil properly is an excellent idea. But on certain soils, especially really heavy clay, it does more harm than good, for it exposes the heavy subsoil, which is almost impossible to cultivate. On this type of soil it is better to spread a good layer of compost on the top of the soil and plant directly into that. The roots of the plants and the worms will pull the compost in and improve the soil far better than any gardener ever will by digging.

Acidic soil

Neutral soil

Alkaline soil

testing your soil

Simple soil test kits to measure the pH of the soil in your garden are available at garden centers and are simple to use. It is essential to test the soil, as it shows the types of plants that will grow best in your garden.

1 Take a sample of soil from the garden and then add the chemicals as instructed in the kit. Shake the test tube and leave it to stand.

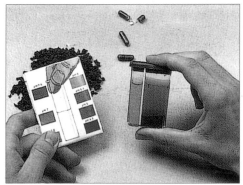

2 The color shows the acidity or alkalinity of the soil. Yellow means the soil is acid; dark green alkaline. Try to take samples from various parts of the garden.

3 Soil meters do the same as the chemical soil-testing kit but are more expensive. The advantage is that you can easily test a range of soils across the garden at one time.

Using fertilizers and manures

All plants need certain chemical nutrients in the soil to grow and flourish. The vast majority of the time these nutrients are present naturally, but it is a good idea to give most plants a helping hand—be it organic or inorganic—at certain stages of their development. Then they can grow to their best.

A checkerboard planting of creeping thyme and other fragrant herbs surrounds a garden bench. Make sure that the soil in each square is fertile; feed if necessary.

Nutritional help for plants can come in a variety of guises. At one extreme it comes in the form of composted stable manure, at the other, chemical fertilizer. Both have much the same effect on the plant. The choice depends on cost, availability, and personal inclination. It is difficult, for example, to obtain well-composted stable manure in a large city.

The main nutrients

The three nutrients that all plants need to flourish are: Nitrogen (N), which promotes leafy growth; potassium (potash) (K), which helps plants form flowers and fruit; and phosphorus (phosphate) (P), which promotes healthy root growth. In addition, plants need a variety of secondary nutrients, such as magnesium, calcium, and sulfur, and trace elements, such as iron, zinc, copper, and molybdenum.

For practical purposes, all of these can be ignored in the ordinary garden by the ordinary gardener. If the soil is lacking in any of them, then the plants will develop symptoms of deficiencies or disease. If this becomes significant and serious, it is worth having the soil tested professionally, for if any of the trace elements or secondary nutrients are missing, they can be added artificially quite easily, as can the three main nutrients. Nitrogen is the nutrient that most often drains from the soil, especially in periods of heavy rain, but it is the one most readily replaced by manure and compost.

Organic fertilizers

It is a good idea to add as much bulky organic matter to your soil as possible each year. As already discussed, this helps to improve the structure, and it also contributes nutrients that are broken down in the soil by various micro-organisms. These are then taken up by the roots of each plant. Using bulky organic fertilizers may be costly if you have to buy stable manure, but all gardeners can make their own compost heap of fall leaves, grass clippings, soft pruning, and kitchen waste—such as vegetable peelings, eggshells, coffee grounds, and tea leaves—that can be added to the garden each year. In many gardens, particularly those with large lawns and a good quantity of grass, this may have all the nutrients that are required.

Organic fertilizers, such as garden compost or stable manure, have one disadvantage. The amount of fertilizer that they contribute to the soil is far less than would be contributed by applying chemicals. For example, the total per-centage of the three main nutrients in animal manure and garden compost is only 1.9% and 1.6% respectively. A popular chemical fertilizer contains around 21% in a balanced NPK for-mula of 7:7:7. You would have to put a great

Fennel, *Foeniculum vulgare*, is a popular herb in the kitchen and is much used to flavor fish dishes and soups. In Roman times it was taken as an antidote in cases of mushroom poisoning. This is one of the many plants that does best in fertile loam, for it prefers full sun, but it does require moisture-retaining soil that does not dry out.

common fertilizers

nitrogen

INORGANIC

SULFATE OF AMMONIA 21% nitrogen. A good top dressing. Makes the soil more acid.

NITROCHALK 26% nitrogen. Use as top dressing on acid soils.

NITRATE OF SODA 16% nitrogen. Fast-acting. Good for some vegetables.

ORGANIC

DRIED BLOOD 13% nitrogen. HOOF AND HORN 13% nitrogen. Use as a base dressing.

phosphorus (phosphate)

INORGANIC

SUPERPHOSPHATE 17% phosphate. Apply early in the year.

ORGANIC

BONEMEAL 20% phosphate. Slow-releasing, so ideal to add to soil when planting trees and shrubs. Can also be used as top dressing.

potassium (potash)

INORGANIC

SULFATE OF POTASH 50% potassium. Apply in early spring.

ORGANIC

ROCK POTASH 11% potash. Apply in fall or winter.

WOOD ASH

This is best applied in the fall. It contains 1% potash, 0.1% nitrogen and 0.3% phosphorus.

general fertilizers

INORGANIC

CHEMICAL FERTILIZERS Use balanced 7.7.7 NPK formulas.

ORGANIC

FISH, BLOOD, AND BONE This is not made to a specific formula, so check the label for the proportions of each nutrient.

LIQUID FEEDS These are usually balanced formulas. Apply weekly to garden during growing season.

Using fertilizers and manures

deal of garden compost on the garden to provide the equivalent nutrient boost. On the other hand, the benefits of bulky organic fertilizers go well beyond their primary role. They usually contain a high level of micronutrients, which help to maintain the nitrogen content of the soil over a long period, and provide an environment in which worms thrive. This benefits the structure of the soil and makes for healthier root growth and better plants.

Garden compost and farmyard manure are the two obvious sources of organic manure and soil improver, but there are other forms available. Leafmold is one. This can be made separately in the fall and added when the leaves have rotted down. Beware—this can take a long time, up to two years. The process can be accelerated by putting the fallen leaves through a leaf shredder, which increases their surface area.

Spent mushroom compost is another soil improver usually available at garden centers and nurseries. It is alkaline and should never be used where you want to grow acid-loving plants. Seaweed is good if you live on the coast and can gather it yourself, but it must be washed first in order to remove the salt.

Straw can be used if you live in the country and can purchase old bales at small cost from farmers. Compost it by mixing it with manure or a compost activator before putting it on the garden—uncomposted it may rob the soil of nitrogen. It may also contain weedkillers.

Mulches repress weed growth. Organic mulches rot down and add to the soil's fertility. The most economical mulch is garden compost made from grass cuttings and leaves. Commercially mulches can be expensive, depending on the area to be covered.

Coarse bark is expensive and best confined to ornamental beds.

Cacao fiber is slow to break down. It is also expensive.

Farmyard manure should be dug into the soil.

Leaf mold makes an excellent mulch for shrubs and flowerbeds.

Wood chippings make a good mulch. Hire a chipper to make your own.

The business end of a garden, with a greenhouse surrounded by herb beds. Grow some herbs near the kitchen, ready for the cook.

Liming the soil

Lime is the other traditional soil improver, used to dilute acid soil. It can also be a great help in improving the texture of clay soil. Making acid soil more alkaline can enable you to grow better brassicas, cabbages, and brussels sprouts. Test the pH of the soil before applying lime. If it is above 6.5–7, the soil does not need it. Do not add manure in the year when you lime. Some professional gardeners lime their gardens in rotation every three years.

Mulches

Another way to improve the quality of both your soil and the plants you grow is to apply mulches to shrubs and over beds. These will rot down during the course of the year. The purpose of a mulch is twofold—it prevents weed growth, and it helps to retain moisture in the soil. Ideally mulches should be applied early in the year when the soil is wet and before weeds have started into full growth.

Mulches need to be at least 2in (5cm) thick to prevent weeds, and this can be quite expensive if you have to buy bags of chipped bark, wood chippings, or cocoa shells. One traditional gardening tip is to cover the soil with two or three sheets of newspaper first and then spread the mulch more thinly over the top. At the end of the summer it will all have disappeared, absorbed by the combined action of weather, worms, and other organisms.

Sowing seeds

Raising healthy plants from seed can be a rewarding process. It is also extremely simple, and much the cheapest way of propagating large numbers of new plants. Seeds can be sown either inside in trays of prepared compost, or outside, where they are to grow—"in situ" in gardening terminology.

The majority of the herbs that gardeners grow from seed are annuals, biennials, and some herbaceous perennials. These include parsley, basil, borage, coriander, and marigolds. Seeds can be sown in seed trays inside or outside—depending on the plant and its specific requirements. Most plants germinate when the soil reaches a certain temperature. If the seeds require a high temperature, such as coneflowers (*Echinacea* spp.) or hops, they should be started off indoors in spring and planted out in position at the beginning of summer. If you sow seeds in degradable pots, then individual plants do not suffer when they are planted out.

Basic rules

Different herb seeds have different requirements, so read the instructions on the package carefully. Most small seeds just need to be scattered on the surface or covered lightly with soil, while larger seeds need to be buried deeper in the ground. Some larger seeds should be soaked overnight before sowing.

Herb seeds germinate at different temperatures. If you are planting outside, then make sure that the soil is warm enough. Check with a garden thermometer—the optimum temperature is 68°F (20°C). Sow thinly. If you want to raise just a few plants indoors, sow two or three seeds in pot and discard the weakest if they all germinate. This applies particularly to any large seeds, such as parsley.

Make sure that the seed bed or soil is properly prepared, moist, and can drain freely. Check the germination time of the seeds you are planting. Some seeds, such as parsley and parsnips, take up to 90 days to germinate, so don't give up too early.

direct seeding

Some seeds are best sown where they are to grow. These include seedlings that are difficult to prick out and transplant, such as dill, and seedlings with long roots. Hardy annuals, too, are often best sown outside in the fall, and thinned the following spring.

1 Prepare the bed by digging over the soil and raking it to a fine consistency. Break up large lumps and remove stones.

2 Sow the seed in drills as directed on the package, or sprinkle them over the soil where you want them to grow.

3 Sieve a covering of soil over the seeds if necessary. Large seeds need to be pressed into the soil individually.

4 Water the seeds with a fine rose to make sure that the soil is damp, and keep it damp until the seedlings have emerged.

care of seedlings

If seedlings are kept in compost that is too cold and too wet, or are too crowded in the soil, they can be subject to fungal diseases. Spray the seedlings from time to time with a suitable fungicide as an avoidance measure and take care to keep all containers as clean as possible. If you are keeping trays on a windowsill, be sure to turn the tray every day, as otherwise the plants will grow lopsided toward the light. Put them outside as soon as possible: Shade them from direct sunlight to start with and water them with a diluted liquid fertilizer.

Scarifying and stratifying herb seeds

Some herbs have specific requirements before their seed will germinate properly. This involves two processes: scarification and stratification. Scarification applies to certain large seeds with a hard outer coating, such as rock roses (*Helianthemum* spp.). In the wild they would remain in the ground over winter and the outer coating of the seed would rot, allowing the seed to absorb water and start into growth. Without this process, some large seeds need to have their outer coating weakened to allow growth to take place. This is usually carried out using sandpaper, or by chipping the coating with a knife.

Stratification is when the seeds germinate better after a period of either hot or cold. You can achieve either of these effects artificially by keeping seeds in a plastic bag mixed with peat substitute and sand, either near a heat source if the seeds need a period of warmth, or the refrigerator if they need cold. The majority of seeds do not require this treatment, but read the instructions on each seed package carefully.

Tomato plants and French marigolds are both good companion plants and help to deter a number of harmful insects.

indoor sowing

Sow seeds indoors in early spring to start plants into growth. Sow the seeds in a seed tray or individual pots using seed compost that has the right texture and contains the correct amount of nutrients for seedlings to flourish. Water the compost from below if it dries out.

1 Fill the seed tray with seed compost and level off ¼in (0.6cm) below the rim. Water the compost and press it flat.

2 Sprinkle the seeds thinly on the surface of the compost. Sow only the number that you plan to use at any one time.

3 Some seeds need to be covered with a fine layer of compost (use a plastic pot or sieve). See package directions.

4 Cover the seed tray with glass or plastic and keep it in a good light but out of direct sunlight.

Propagating

This means taking one piece of a plant and using it to grow a new plant. It is one of the most satisfying aspects of gardening, a process that dates backs thousands of years. It is an essential skill that all true gardeners should master.

The commonest form of propagation is by taking cuttings. The principle behind all the various methods is the same: You take a portion of a plant and stick it in the ground or, more frequently, in cutting or rooting compost. If it is kept moist, roots will eventually emerge and the cutting will grow into a new plant having the same characteristics as the parent. The various methods of taking cuttings differentiate only between different plants that root best from different parts of the parent plant taken at different times of the year. Herbs can all be propagated by taking cuttings of one sort or another, and you can check in the plant directory to see what method applies. A good cuttings compost can be prepared by mixing equal parts of peat or peat substitute with perlite or sharp sand. If cuttings are left in the original compost for any length of time, they will need to be fed with a liquid feed every two weeks throughout the growing season.

Greenwood cuttings are taken from the same group of herbs as softwood cuttings, just slightly later in the year when the shoots are more developed. The process is exactly the same. Water both softwood and greenwood cuttings with a weak fungicide solution once a week.

Semi-ripe cuttings

Where possible, choose non-flowering shoots or remove the flowerheads. New roots develop from the cambium, a layer of cells in the plant that cause the stems to thicken. The root-producing hormones present in each plant are inhibited by the flower-producing hormones. The practical steps for taking semiripe cuttings

semi-ripe cuttings

Large numbers of evergreen and deciduous shrubs can be propagated by semiripe cuttings, including herbs such as bay, daphne, witch hazel, and sage. These should be taken toward the end of summer when the new wood has started to ripen.

1 Remove the lower leaves. Cuttings cannot support many leaves and develop new roots at the same time.

2 On large-leaved plants cut the remaining leaves in half to lessen the surface area. Dip the stems in rooting hormone powder.

3 Insert the cuttings in a pot. Keep it moist in a propagating frame in the same way as softwood cuttings.

are shown below. They will take longer to strike (for the roots to form) than softwood cuttings. Some shrubs that are commonly propagated by semiripe cuttings root better if the cutting is taken with a section of the old wood attached. Pull the sideshoot away from the plant and this will remove a strip of the main stem. Trim this with a sharp knife so that it is neat and tidy, and then follow the steps for softwood cuttings.

Leaf-bud cuttings

This is an economical way of propagating a number of plants from one stem. It is used for shrubs such as camellias. Select a non-flowering

shoot in late summer and make a cut just above each leaf. Trim the shoots just under 1in (2.5cm) below each leaf and remove a sliver of bark from the stem. Pot these so that the leaf axils (the point where the leaf joins the stem) are just above the surface of the compost. No hormone rooting powder is needed for these cuttings.

Root cuttings

It is essential to take root cuttings when the plant is dormant in the winter. Either dig up a young plant or, if that is not possible, remove enough soil so that some portions of the root are exposed. Trim off a young root close to the

softwood and tip cuttings

These are usually taken in late spring and early summer from plants that develop very rapidly. Examples would be, bearberry, broom, lavender, rosemary, and turtlehead.

1 Take the cuttings when the new shoots are 2–4in (6–12cm) long. Trim them just below a node (a leaf joint).

2 Remove the lower leaves, since leaves that touch the compost will rot. Dip the stem in rooting hormone.

3 Mist the cuttings to keep them moist, and water the compost well with a fine rose when you have potted them.

4 Push the cuttings into the rooting medium around the sides of the pot. Include four or five cuttings in each pot.

5 Put them in a mist unit or a propagating frame, or put a plastic bag over the pot—use wire to keep it off the leaves.

6 Secure the bag with a rubber band. Keep softwood cuttings in a moist atmosphere, otherwise they will die off.

7 Cuttings need good light but no direct sunlight. and a temperature of 70°F (21°C). They should root in 1–5 weeks.

8 Once the cuttings have rooted, they can be potted in individual pots and hardened off before being placed outside.

Propagating

Many cuttings can be grown in pots. A gravel bed prevents the pots becoming waterlogged. Serious gardeners often take cuttings each year as replacement plants for their own gardens and also as gifts for fellow enthusiasts.

main stem. Remove any fibrous roots and cut the root into pieces about 2–3in (5–7.5cm) in length. Make a diagonal cut on the end furthest from the main stem so that you will remember to insert the cuttings in the compost the correct way up. Insert the root cuttings in compost with the top of each cutting flush with the surface; water, then cover with a thin layer of coarse grit. Dust with fungicide powder if necessary.

Hardwood cuttings

This is the best method for propagating a number of valuable shrubs and herbal plants. Select healthy shoots from this season's growth in fall

or early winter. They can be rooted in a cold frame or in a prepared trench. Cut off the shoots where the new growth of this season has started and trim the shoots above and below a leaf joint so that they are 6–9in (15–23cm) long. Remove a sliver of bark from the rooting end and treat the base with hormone rooting powder. Insert the cuttings in a prepared trench that has a good layer of coarse grit in the bottom. Fill in the trench. Evergreens treated in this way need the leaves removed from the bottom two-thirds of the stem and any large leaves cut in half to reduce transpiration.

Internodal cuttings

These are taken from plants, such as clematis, that root best from softwood cuttings taken early in the spring. Cut the stem just above a leaf joint and again about 2in (5cm) below the joint. Remove one of the pair of leaves. Insert the cuttings in the compost so that the leaf joint is just above the level of the surface.

Layering

This is done by pegging down long branches into the ground. Roots will spring from the leaf joints. As with strawberries, the runners will have already established their own roots and it is

root cuttings in water

Some plants, especially mints and other moisture-loving plants will root perfectly well in a jar of water. Varieties of yarrow can also be treated in this way. Fill the jar only half way because the roots tend to form near the surface.

1 Choose a number of non-flowering shoots in late summer or early fall and strip away the lower leaves.

2 Put the cuttings in a jar of water. Keep it in good light but avoid direct sunlight.

3 Leave the cuttings in the jar until strong roots have formed. Remove any leaves that turn brown.

4 Pot the cuttings individually, using a standard potting compost. Let them harden off and develop before planting.

merely a question of moving them around the garden. This has two benefits. It rejuvenates the clumps, and it makes two plants out of one. Division does not simply apply to woody perennial plants but also to bulbs, such as snowdrops, rhizomatous plants such as irises, and suckering shrubs such as phygelius. Dividing larger plants can be done in two ways. Either dig up the plant and insert two garden forks, back to back, in the center and prise the plant apart by pushing both, or take a spade and slice through the rootball.

Dividing rhizomes

When rhizomes form congested clumps, they should be dug up and divided. To divide a clump of irises, dig up the clump and split it up by hand. Trim the old rhizomes, leaving young healthy root sections, each with at least one bud. Dust all cut surfaces with fungicide powder, trim leaves back to a maximum of 6in (15cm), and replant the rhizomes about 5in (12cm) apart. Place firmly in the soil; the rhizome should be at soil level and the leaves upright.

plant division—herbs with a fleshy crown

One of the easiest ways to increase the number of plants is to divide up established clumps of perennial herbs and replant them. Slightly different techniques apply to different plants.

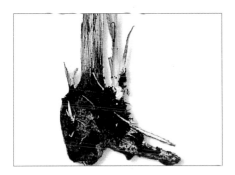

1 Dig up a plant in the spring when the soil is warming up and it has just started into growth.

2 Cut the roots into sections and replant as many as you require. This is the root of a comfrey.

plant division—herbs with fibrous roots

Many small plants or herbs are best divided by hand. The clumps should be split when flowering is over.

1 Dig up the plant and then pull apart the rooted sections. Replant them separately. Discard any old and woody sections from the center.

2 Split congested clumps of spring-flowering bulbs in the same way. It is a good idea to give all bulbs a foliar feed after flowering.

plant division-herbs with a rhizome

Herbs that spread by runners or rhizomes are easy to increase by division. Mint and the attractive ground-covering herb bugle are good examples.

1 Dig up rhizomes and cut into pieces, each with some healthy roots. Each piece of the old plant will quickly make strong new plants.

2 Either plant the divided cuttings directly outside or pot them individually until they have grown on and are large enough to transplant.

Planting

At its very simplest, planting any new herb, whether it is a tree, shrub, perennial, or biennial, simply means digging a hole, placing the plant in it, and refirming the soil around the roots. However, preparing the soil well and following a few simple planting and aftercare techniques will give your plants the best possible chance to become established quickly, and flourish in your garden.

When planting an herbaceous or flowering border, make sure the colors blend well, like this attractive pink, yellow, and blue scheme. Plot your design on paper before planting it in the border.

Commercial foresters with thousands of small trees to plant in a short space of time, make a slit with a spade, wedge the young sapling into the slit in the soil and stamp it closed. The process takes less than a minute. Gardeners do not have to work under such constraints and since young plants are expensive it is worth taking time to plant them properly.

Preparing, siting, and garden design

Once you have decided on the main garden design, carefully mark out all the beds and areas with pegs and string. Look at the aspect of the garden and of the different beds—this is most important when you are growing herbs. If you are planning a permanent herbal bed or border,

choose a south-facing, sunny position for it. If you do not have a sunny area in your garden, then you will have to select herbs that flourish in either shade or partial shade and avoid planting species, such as thyme and rosemary, that will flourish only in sun and heat.

If you are preparing a border in a new garden or carving one out of a lawn, prepare the ground properly to ensure that the plants will grow well. First of all, remove any turf piece by piece and make a stack of it in an out-of-the-way corner of the garden. Place the pieces of turf one on top of another, face downward. Eventually they will rot down and can be used as topsoil. Then dig over the whole area with a good garden fork. This is much easier than trying to use a spade, which will be blocked by stones and pebbles. Remove all the weeds you can find, including the roots.

When you have done this, spread a good layer of well-rotted garden compost over the whole area and fork it in lightly. If this is not available, sprinkle the bed with a general fertilizer, applying it at the recommended rate. Rake the soil level and leave it to settle for at least a week before planting.

New beds can be prepared at any time providing that the soil conditions are suitable, but planting is best done in the spring or fall. If you are planting large trees or shrubs, plant in the fall if you can. This also applies if you are planting container-grown plants, which, in theory, can be planted at any time. If you plant while the soil is still relatively warm, the roots will have the best chance of establishing themselves before the growing season.

planting

It is not generally advisable to plant out in midsummer, but if you have to, make sure that the plant, container or hole, and the surrounding soil are really moist. Check on the plant every day, watering it until its roots have become established.

1 Dig a good-sized hole—check that it is deep enough to hold the contents of the container—and fork in some garden compost or a peat-substitute. Fill the hole with water.

2 Remove the plant from the container and place it in the hole. Firm the soil around the roots with your fingers. Gently tread the soil down, and water well.

Herbal potager

If you want to create an herbal potager, a formal ornamental herb bed, prepare the beds and plan your planting carefully. Plant large herbs, such as rosemary, on their own, surrounded by lower-growing shrubs, but plant smaller herbs in groups of three or five All gardens look better if the flowers appear in blocks, and it is more effective to group plants in odd numbers rather than even ones.

Planting in a wall

Planting small spreading plants in walls or among paving stones can be done more easily than might be imagined. When planting in a wall, use heavy soil or garden compost that will not readily dry out and crumble away, exposing the roots of the plant. Put some soil in the cracks in the wall and then gently insert the small plants, so that the roots are not damaged. Firm them in, adding more soil, and wedge the soil into position with a small stone if necessary.

Make sure that you plant in walls on a cool, wet day or, if the weather is dry, soak the wall thoroughly so that the moisture from the soil is not absorbed by the stones or brick. Keep the wall and plants moist until the roots have become established.

Planting a tree

Trees are expensive and it is worth taking trouble to ensure that they are planted properly. If you are planting a container-grown tree in the middle of a lawn, remove a good square of turf, not a circle—squares are much easier to mow around and keep tidy. Dig out all the soil, putting it into a wheelbarrow or on a garden sheet for easy removal. Dig down until you have reached the subsoil or the pan and break this up

planting in a rock garden

This is best done in the spring or early fall. Allow more room between the plants than you think is necessary, as they will grow and spread quickly.

1 Rake back the gravel mulch, dig a planting hole in the soil below, and firm in the plant. Make sure that the plants are watered in well.

2 Replace the gravel mulch around the plant. This helps to retain the moisture in the soil—the roots need moisture to become established.

planting a small tree or shrub

This sequence of pictures demonstrates the basic techniques of planting a tree or shrub, which is best done in the fall. The shrub being planted here is a narrow-leaved bay and the planting area is in shady woodland with dry soil.

1 Dig a good-sized hole and bank up the soil, as here, or place it in a wheelbarrow for removal. Break up any pan with a garden fork or crowbar.

2 Water the hole and let it drain. Add a handful of bonemeal and some compost to bring the base of the stem to level of the surrounding soil.

3 Remove the shrub from the container and firm the soil and some compost around its roots with your hands. This ensures there are no airpockets.

4 Fill the hole and firm down the soil gently as shown. Water well, check the plant daily, and keep watering until the shrub is established.

Planting

with a garden fork or a crowbar so that the roots can reach right down into the earth. Check the diameter of the container and then hammer in a stake to which the tree can be secured when it is planted, placing the stake as close to the edge of the container as possible. High stakes should be placed on the side of the prevailing wind. Diagonal stakes should be inserted facing the prevailing wind. Make sure that all stakes are firmly in the ground and that the tree is properly secured with professional tree ties, which avoid damaging the bark.

Replace the soil in the hole until the container will rest 2–3in (5–7.5cm) below the surface of the soil. Mix the topsoil with garden compost or peat and add a sprinkling of bonemeal at the bottom of the hole. Fill the hole with the topsoil and compost mix until the container is at the correct level. Knock the tree out of the container, tease out the roots, and trim away any that are damaged. Put the plant in the hole and then firm it in place using the topsoil and compost. Water well and allow the soil to settle for three or four days before topping up the level.

A fine lavender hedge stretching down a path. Lavender should be cut back hard every spring or it becomes "leggy."

planting in a wetland area

Planting marginal plants in a boggy area of the garden is exactly the same as any other form of planting. Dig a large enough hole, put the plant in the hole, check that the roots are properly spread out, and then fill in around the plant, making sure that the roots are firmly in the soil.

1 Dig a hole that is slightly bigger than the container. Here the gardener is planting out rhizomes of yellow flag in a boggy area.

2 Water the container well and tip the plant out. It is particularly important that all marginals are planted in properly moist conditions.

3 Place the rhizome in the hole and firm the soil gently around the roots. Make sure that the rhizome is not planted too deeply.

4 All marginal plants must be watered in well, and kept moist if there is any chance at all of the soil drying out in a dry spell in spring or early summer.

Planting a shrub

There is little difference between planting a tree and planting a shrub, but if you are planting a bare-root shrub or tree, such as a rose, take special care to ensure that the roots are properly spread out and in direct contact with the compost. Make sure that the shrub is standing upright, then fill in around the roots, pressing the compost in with your fingers. Tread the plant in gently when the planting has been completed. Water it well.

Planting large aquatics

In a small pond, all aquatics are best planted in special planting baskets. To plant the sacred herb (water lily) choose a basket that will accommodate the roots of the plant and then line it with burlap or porous close-weave plastic. Add heavy soil to the basket and then put the plant in the basket. Fill the basket with soil and then add a good layer of heavy gravel on top. This will keep the soil in place and prevent any fish from disturbing the plant. Lower the basket into the pond, having checked the correct depth for the lily you have chosen. If the pond is too deep, put the basket on top of a submerged pier of bricks.

planting in a wall

Gently insert the small plants, so that the roots are not damaged. Firm them by adding more soil and wedge the soil into position if necessary.

practical tips for planting

● Make sure the stake is inserted before you plant the tree. Hammering a stake in after planting can damage the roots.

● Do not plant any tree deeper than the soil mark on the container.

● Dig a good big hole, about twice as large as you think is necessary

● Don't cram a container-grown plant into a small space, for the roots will have difficulty establishing themselves if you do.

● All trees once established grow amazingly quickly and are easier to keep tidy if the space around them is clear.

● For the same reason prepare the soil and compost mix properly. Imagine the difficulty roots would have penetrating a solid clay wall without some help.

● **Water well**
All plants need water to become established when first planted.

● If you are planting a tree or shrub in the middle of a lawn, dig a square hole not a round one. This is easier to mow around and keep tidy.

● When digging a planting hole, use a wheel barrow or a garden sheet so that you can pile up the soil as it is removed.

● **Planting a tree**
Stake all trees before planting. Upright stakes should be driven in on the side of the prevailing wind.

● Diagonal stakes should be driven in on the side opposite the prevailing wind.

● **Planting a shrubbery or a rock garden**
Make sure that all plants have room to expand, and allow much more space between them that you think is necessary. All shrubs and plants grow very quickly once they become established.

● **Moving an established tree**
If you have to move an established tree or shrub, dig out a really large hole around the roots and take as much of the rootball and soil as possible.

● If the tree or shrub has a taproot, try to get as much of this out of the ground as possible. Prepare the new position well and water the shrub in.

● Cut back the top growth quite severely so that the plant has less foliage to support initially. You may have to sacrifice one year's flowers when you do this.

Protecting your herbs

The first thing that the herb gardener has to do in the fall is to assess how many of the herbs that are growing in the garden will need protection over the cold months. This depends on the hardiness of the individual herb, the general climate, and whether or not there are any microclimates that create particularly hot or cold spots within the garden.

An old-fashioned cold frame open for ventilation. Ventilate them on sunny days—even in winter.

In ordinary temperate zones, protection may simply mean avoiding planting sun-loving herbs in a part of the garden that becomes a frost pocket in the winter. However, some herbs will need indoor protection. These include plants such as scented-leaf pelargoniums, basil, vervain, and Oswego tea. Grow them in individual containers—some small trees, such as lemon and orange trees, also make excellent container-grown plants—then move them inside to the protection of a cool, frost-free place as fall advances.

The real trouble with keeping plants indoors during the winter is that they need a cool, light room where the central heating does not pene-

cloches

Cloches come in many forms and can be homemade or bought in kit form from garden centers. This is a simple tunnel cloche with plastic ribs and a clear plastic cover, which can easily be removed when you need to give the plants some air or reduce the temperature inside.

1 When the cloche is closed, it offers good protection to young plants from bad weather, such as heavy rain, wind, and frost, and also from birds and rabbits.

2 On fine days the cover should be removed to allow air to circulate and to stop excessive heat building up in the tunnel. Cloches can quickly become very humid and this spreads disease.

trate—such a space can be difficult to find in most houses. A cool porch is the best place for many plants, but some are adversely affected by drafts. You may need to use trial and error to see how happily certain frost-tender plants survive. The other place where tender herbs can be overwintered is in an unheated greenhouse or cool conservatory that can be kept above freezing. Here almost all plants will survive the winter perfectly happily.

In winter, make sure that watering is kept to a minimum; plants should not be kept permanently damp. Remove all dead leaves to avoid the spread of disease and ventilate the greenhouse or conservatory on sunny days to stop it becoming too hot. This also improves the health of the plants.

Overwintering out of doors

Evergreen or tender shrubs can be protected in frosty areas in a number of ways. Covering them with straw or bracken and then wrapping the plant in burlap was a traditional method, but it is very labor-intensive and the materials may be difficult to get hold of. Nowadays many gardeners wrap tender plants in garden fleece or netting. Netting may not seem much of a protection, but it breaks up the wind and it is surprising how effective it can be. Garden fleece should be removed on warm days if possible to allow the plant more air. It is not very robust but it will keep the frost at bay and allow the moisture and light to penetrate.

Tender perennial herbs growing in a border may need additional protection for their roots. This is easily provided by covering them with 2–3in (5–7.5cm) of garden compost when the foliage has died down.

Cloches and cold frames

These are usually used to give protection to young seedlings or cuttings of hardy plants in their first year. As a general gardening point, young plants are much more susceptible to cold than mature specimens and a shrub that may need protection in its first two years will

survive quite cold winters unprotected after that. Cold frames are extremely useful and enable the gardener to sow seeds earlier in the year, before the soil has warmed up enough for them to germinate in outside conditions. Similarly, you can use cloches to protect young tender plants when they start to grow, or they can be used to force early crops of vegetables and herbs. You can make your own or buy kits at a garden center.

A great advantage of cloches is that they are portable and can be moved around. They not only protect young plants, such as coriander, in the spring, but also extend the season of hardy perennial herbs into the fall. They also give protection to plants against the birds, rabbits, and rodents that menace many gardens.

Cold frames are excellent for starting seedlings earlier in the year than is normally possible. They also allow the gardener to overwinter a number of plants.

herbs that may need protection

Aloysia triphylla vervain	*Lavandula* lavender
Cedronella canariensis false balm of Gilead	*Lippia citriodora* lemon beebrush
Coriandrum sativum coriander	*Monarda didyma* Oswego tea
Cynara scolymus globe artichoke	*Olea europea* olive
Foeniculum vulgare fennel	*Origanum vulgare* oregano
Galega officinalis goat's rue	*Pelargonium graveolens* rose geranium
Gentiana lutea yellow gentian	*Rosmarinus officinalis* rosemary
Hesperis matronalis dame's rocket	*Satureja montana* winter savory
Laurus nobilis bay	*Thymus vulgaris* common thyme

Companion planting

A few useful herbs can be used to protect nearby plants from pests and diseases, or they may attract the beneficial insects that consume predators. Some plants also grow better when they are planted in company with others.

The vast majority of companion planting belongs in the kitchen garden, where pests and diseases can cause havoc in a short time. One of the major pests in the kitchen garden is the cabbage-white butterfly, with its black-tipped, black-veined wings. The caterpillars of these butterflies hatch from the eggs laid on brassicas and in large infestations the winter greens can disappear almost overnight. Companion planting is the classic way to prevent this and other similar pest problems. The butterflies dislike the smell of certain plants and if these are planted alongside the brassicas, then the damage is minimized. French marigolds are well-known companion plants for protecting brassicas from cabbage-white butterfly; when rows of these are included in the vegetable patch, the effect can be remarkable. Some gardeners hold that it is the scent of the marigolds themselves that deters the butterflies, others that secretions from their roots enter the system of other plants and makes them unpalatable to butterflies and aphids. Tomatoes planted alongside brassicas have a similar effect. Tomatoes generally are good companion plants, for they also deter flea beetles and a chemical in their roots is toxic to some weevils.

The other major kitchen garden pest is the carrot root fly. This can be prevented by erecting physical barriers of plastic sheets around the plants, but you can also deter them by the scent of chives, *Allium schoenoprasum*, or other commonly grown alliums, such as onions and garlic. Strong-smelling herbs, such as mint, catnip and hyssop, are also a help in confusing butterflies and moths, and generally attract bees, which help to pollinate all flowers and fruit.

Some herbs are beneficial to vegetables, fruit, and other plants. Chives help to prevent blackspot on roses and scab on apples; sage repels cabbage-white butterflies and is beneficial to all vegetables when grown alongside them. A number of herbs attract hoverflies, which feed on aphids such as blackfly and whitefly, and therefore benefit the garden. These include chamomile and wild marigolds,

A formal vegetable garden with the beds confined by hedges of low-growing box. Use onions planted in early spring and that produce seed heads first, as they will not keep long.

Tagetes minuta. Nasturtiums repel whitefly but attract blackfly and they are therefore often grown as a trap for these pests.

Complementary plants

The habit of some plants makes them very suitable to grow with others. Tall-growing plants with large leaves, such as comfrey and angelica, provide shade and shelter. Ground-cover plants, such as ajuga, help to keep the roots of climbers, such as clematis, cool and prevent the topsoil drying out. Most flowering herbs attract bees and other insects that help to pollinate the fruit into the garden, and a number attract beneficial insects, such as hoverflies.

Caring for plants

The best cure for garden ills is constant care and a quick response to any problems that occur. Very often the onset of pests, such as caterpillars, for example, can be nipped in the bud if they are spotted early. Pick them off and squash them before they have time to do any lasting damage. As a general rule, remove all dead leaves and plants. This will keep the garden healthier. Similarly, if you spray at the first sign

Chives are an excellent herb with a delicate onion-like flavor often used for summer soups. They help to deter carrot root fly in the kitchen garden and also black spot on roses.

of disease, this prevents it spreading. Whether you use organic sprays or not is up to the individual gardener. However, effective organic sprays are available that will safely combat most of the garden problems that arise.

good companion plants

All the herbs that are listed below have a beneficial effect on the vegetable garden. Some attract pollinating or other beneficial insects, and others repel certain common garden pests.

Chives *Allium schoenoprasum*
Chives deter carrot root fly and also, strangely enough, help to prevent the spread of black spot on roses and scab on apples. They can be planted as an edging around a rose bed.

Chamomile *Chamaemelum nobile*
Chamomile helps to improve the yield of a number of vegetables and also attracts the beneficial hoverfly.

Hyssop *Hyssopus officinalis*
The blue flowers of the hyssop attract bees and other pollinating insects. Hyssop improves the yield of grapevines and deters cabbage-white butterflies.

Marjoram *Origanum majoranum*
As well as attracting bees, marjoram acts as a protective companion plant when it is grown with brassicas.

Sage *Salvia officinalis*
This herb repels cabbage-white butterflies, so makes a useful addition to the kitchen garden.

Wild marigolds *Tagetes minuta*
All marigolds deter cabbage-white butterflies and whiteflies and are the most commonly used companion plant. The wild marigold, or muster John Henry, deters a number of other insects, including wire worms, millipedes, and eelworms, and it also attracts hoverflies.

Nasturtium *Tropaeolum speciosum*
Nasturtiums deter a number of aphids, but they also act as a diversion for blackfly, which they attract away from other, more valuable plants.

Pests and diseases

All plants are susceptible to pests and diseases. Prevention is much better than cure, and all gardeners should try to create a healthy environment for their plants by practicing good garden hygiene. Acting quickly at the first signs of disease will significantly reduce any problems that do occur.

Scabious is attractive to a number of insects, notably bees and butterflies. It is important for any garden to contain a number of attractive plants like this.

The first rule of healthy plants is to ensure adequate ventilation. A large number of plants in an enclosed space or a crowded greenhouse is a recipe for disaster, so open the doors and windows on fine days in winter. Pay attention to pruning, particularly of trees and shrubs, and ensure that the center of each plant is open so that as much air as possible can circulate.

Spraying, organic or non-organic

The approach that you take to spraying and pest control depends entirely on how strictly you adhere to organic principles. There are organic alternatives to most normal garden pesticides; you have to decide whether these are sufficiently effective for it to be worth using them since they may involve more work. It is important to read the instructions on the labels and to follow them carefully.

Major pests

ANTS Ants cause more damage than is commonly realized. They feed on the honeydew excreted by aphids and will farm the aphids, carrying them from plant to plant, and thus spreading these pests around the garden. They also cause damage to the roots of plants by tunnelling underground and they will eat newly sown seeds. If you find a small nest, destroy it by pouring boiling water over it. Large nests may have to be dealt with by an exterminator. Dust affected areas with an insecticide.

APHIDS There are many aphids but the best-known are green peach aphid and blackfly. They all suck the sap from plants and so weaken them. Fava beans, philadelphus, some mints,

and salad herbs may be affected. Pinch out the growing tip of fava beans, and spray affected plants with a contact or systemic insecticide, or use a solution of liquid detergent. However, this may not be as effective.

BIRDS These are particularly troublesome when it comes to young seedlings, which they find with unerring instinct. The only solution that really works is to net everything at risk and to keep the plants netted throughout the growing season. You may well find, however, that city birds are less well-educated than their country counterparts and that plants that disappear overnight in the country survive perfectly well on a city roof garden.

CATERPILLARS Companion planting will go a long way to preventing these pests. If your vegetables and herbs do become infected with caterpillars, pick them off by hand and spray with a suitable pesticide—the only trouble is that this may be too late. Biological control by the bacteria *Bacillus thuringiensis* is effective on a large scale, but expensive.

EELWORMS This is a soil-born pest that causes serious damage. There is no control readily available. However they are not enormously common. They may be deterred by a companion planting of Mexican marigolds.

SLUGS AND SNAILS These can be a major problem, especially in moist or damp conditions. Certain plants, such as young herbs and lettuces, are particularly prone to slug damage. There are two methods of control: trapping

natural pest control

EARWIGS Trap them under upturned flower pots on canes filled with straw. Burn the straw every other day.

CATERPILLARS. Pick them off by hand.

GREENFLY. Spray with washing up liquid solution.

SLUGS Trap them under upturned grapefruit halves or sink a pot filled with sweet liquid into the soil into which they will fall and drown.

ANTS. Destroy their nests by pouring boiling water over them when you find them. Encourage predators, such as hoverflies by planting herbs that attract them to the garden.

USE companion planting to deter butterflies. Surround young plants by a layer of grit. Slugs and snails do not like crawling over rough, hard surfaces.

and deterrents. Place hollowed-out, upturned grapefruit halves near the plants to trap them. Alternatively, sink a shallow pot half-filled with sweetened liquid in the soil near the plants; they will fall into this and drown. Deter them by putting collars of plastic around young plants—plastic bottles cut into halves or thirds with the top and bottom removed are ideal. Alternatively, surround the plants with a circle of grit, since slugs do not like sliding over sharp surfaces. As a last resort, scatter slug pellets around the plants.

WHITEFLY The scale-like nymphs of these small insects attack brassicas grown out of doors and they are also pests that are found in greenhouses. Spray with a suitable insecticide.

Common diseases

BLACK SPOT This commonly affects roses. Spray regularly with a suitable fungicide.

DAMPING OFF A disease of seedlings, which makes them collapse and die, damping off is usually caused by damp compost that is too

cold or by overcrowding. To control it, water seedlings regularly with a suitable fungicide, throw away any seedlings that have been affected, and disinfect the seed trays or containers of affected plants before using them again.

GRAY MOLD (botrytis) This is caused by cold, damp conditions and affects fruit such as strawberries. Keep plants as dry and well-ventilated as possible to prevent it. Little can be done to arrest the disease, but removing and burning infected leaves will stop it spreading.

FUNGAL DISEASES These cause mold, mildew, and wilts, and thrive on humid conditions. Fungal diseases are difficult to control; improved ventilation is the best way of preventing them. The same applies to leaf spots, but here a fungicidal spray may prove effective.

Good garden hygiene and regular checks are the best antidote to pests and diseases. This border is full of shrubs in full bloom and looks spectacular in midsummer.

Harvesting and storing

One of the beauties of growing herbs is that so many can be dried and stored for use during the winter months. Also, a number of culinary herbs, such as poppies and coriander, are grown for their seeds. These can be collected in the fall when the seedheads have ripened.

Cut ripe seedheads of a number of herbs, such as larkspur shown here, just before the seed pods start to split. Store them carefully in a dry place until the seed is ripe.

The herbs that you choose to dry and store depend very much on the use to which they will be put in the home. Dry culinary herbs, such as mint, basil, and thyme, by hanging them upside down in a warm, airy room—keep them out of direct sunlight. You can also dry them in a cool oven or in a microwave. Another way is to lay them on paper on a table in an airy room and turn them over once a day. When the herbs are dry, the leaves can be stripped away from the stems and stored in a screwtop jar or a paper bag. Dried herbs will last for several months before they lose their flavor. You can use many dried herbs in pot-pourri mixtures, and certain herbs, such as lavender, can be used in herbal sachets for scented pillows or as moth repellents.

Collecting seeds

The seeds of many herbs are collected for use as flavoring, while the ripe seeds of annual and perennial herbs are used for sowing the following year. How you collect the seed depends on the family of plants to which the herb belongs. The commonest families have a variety of seedheads and each one has to be collected in a different way.

BORAGE FAMILY (Boraginaceae) The seeds are relatively large, like small black nuts, and ripen one by one over a period. Put a cloth under the plant and gather the ripe seed when it falls.

CARROT FAMILY (Umbelliferae) The seeds are held in the flat flowerhead. Cut off the head when it is brown and ripe and shake the seed out onto a piece of paper.

releasing seeds

The easiest way to release ripe seeds is to shake them gently out onto a sheet of white paper and then place them in a marked envelope for safe keeping. Seeds vary enormously from plant to plant in size, number, and how they are stored on the plant.

1 Hollyhock seed is held in a brown circular capsule that opens when the seed is ripe. The seeds are profuse. Shake them out onto a piece of white paper.

2 Ripe poppyheads develop holes in the top when the seed is ripe, and the seeds can be easily shaken out. The difficulty is to limit the number you retain.

3 Larkspur holds its seeds in elongated seed pods that split when the seeds inside are ripe. The seed pods are shown in the picture above.

Daisy family (Compositae) The seeds are often held on an open flowerhead with feathery hairs attached. Collect the flowerhead and shake out the seed onto a piece of paper.

Pea family (Leguminosae) Most members of this family hold their seeds in pea-like pods. Collect the pods when they are ripe and starting to split open.

Poppy family (Papaveraceae) Poppies form large, hard heads. When the seed is ripe, the head develops small holes in the top. Collect the capsule head and shake out the seed.

Primrose family ((Primulaceae) The seed is contained within a case that turns brown when it is ripe. Cut off the case and shake the fine seed out onto a piece of white paper.

Preserving herbs

Drying does not apply just to the flowers and leaves. The roots of a number of herbs, particularly medicinal ones, are often dug up and dried before being used in medicinal preparations.

Some culinary herbs do not dry well and these can often be frozen successfully. These include basil, tarragon, fennel, chervil, parsley, and chives. Store them in plastic bags.

Dried seedheads are very decorative and come in a variety of shapes and form. The herbs illustrated are, from the left, opium poppies; evening primrose; marshmallow; teasel; and blue vervain.

Dry herbs by hanging them upside-down in a light, airy room, out of direct sunlight. When dry, they can be used for winter flower arrangements, or the leaves can be used as flavoring in the kitchen.

cleaning and storing seeds

Make sure seed is dry before storing. A lot of seed contains dust, which should also be removed before storing. Anyone sensitive to dust should not clean seed.

1 Remove the dry heads from the stems by rubbing them between your hands. Pick out the large stems and leaves by hand.

2 Shake the seed through a coarse sieve to remove debris. Sieve very fine seed again through a finer sieve, which will clean it better.

3 Blow on the seed very gently to remove any remaining dust. The seed can now be placed in a bag or envelope for storing.

LAVENDER HIDCOTE

4 Label the envelope with the correct name of the plant. Store in a cool, dry place, such as an old metal box in the greenhouse.

the herb directory

This directory lists common herbs alphabetically by Latin name, each plant illustrated with a color photograph. Herbs may be used in the kitchen, as medicines, for scents, or as dye plants. Each description tells some of the history of each herb, particularly those herbs that have been used in herbal medicine for thousands of years. There is a concise guide to the cultivation requirements of the plants at the end of each entry.

The study of herbs is a fascinating pursuit and is surrounded by myths and strange magical theories. At the start of the 21st century it is extraordinary that so many of the ancient myths are now being confirmed by present-day scientific investigation and that so much medical research is being devoted to the properties of each plant.

key to directory symbols

 MEDICINAL herbs used in herbal or modern medicine.

 FEATURE FLOWER herbs with notably decorative flowers.

 POISONOUS herbs that must be handled with caution.

 COSMETIC herbs used to make cosmetic products.

 CULINARY herbs used to flavor or garnish food.

 FEATURE FOLIAGE herbs with notably decorative foliage.

 SCENTED herbs with pleasant scents when fresh or dried.

 FULL SHADE herbs that prefer a site in full shade.

 FULL SUN herbs that prefer a site in full sun.

 PARTIAL SHADE herbs that prefer shade with some sun.

Acanthus mollis

Acanthus

bear's breech

Acanthus is a tall, upright plant. It was used as a medicine by the Greeks for the treatment of fevers but is no longer used today. It is best known for its leaves, which have become a commonly used architectural symbol. They can be found carved at the head of Corinthian columns in grand buildings and medieval churches. Their form was also used by the famous 19th-century English craftsman and designer William Morris as the inspiration for some of his famous wallpaper patterns. The acanthus plant reaches 4ft (1.2m) in height and looks good in a formal herbaceous border, where its long spires of white flowers and purple bracts stand out in late summer.

Acanthus is indigenous to the Mediterranean and likes hot, dry conditions, so it will flourish in a dry, sunny bed. The name comes from the Greek *acanthus*, meaning a spine, and refers to the spiny leaves. As a garden plant it is quite slow to become established and does not like being moved. *Acanthus mollis* is fully hardy and *Acanthus spinosus* is the hardiest species. Other members of the genus are more tender and you'll need to protect them in hard winters.

The flowering spikes of the acanthus look dramatic when grown at the back of a bed. The colors will blend with any scheme.

vital statistics

FAMILY Acanthaceae	**PERENNIAL** **ZONE 6**	**FOLIAGE** Long, deeply lobed dark green leaves that are shiny above.	**SOIL** Well-drained soil.	**FLOWERING** Late summer.
OTHER VARIETIES AND SPECIES A. mollis Latifolius Group, A. hirsutus, A. hungaricus, A. spinosus	**HEIGHT** 5ft (1.5m) **SPREAD** 18in (45cm)	**NATURAL HABITAT** Native of the Mediterranean and northwestern Africa, grows on dry rocky hillsides.	**PROPAGATION** Sow seed in spring at 50°F (10°C). The seed takes some time to become established. Divide established plants in spring or take root cuttings in early winter.	**USES** Formerly medicinal.
	FLOWERS White, with purple bracts on long stalks, 3ft (1m) high.	**SITE** Prefers full sun, but will tolerate partial shade.		

Achillea millefolium
Yarrow

bloodwort, milfoil, hierba de las cortaduras, nosebleed, soldier's woundwort, thousand leaf

Achilleas form a large genus of about 85 species, of which 35 are commonly found in cultivation. *A. millefolium* was traditionally most often used as a poultice. Many of its common names, such as soldier's woundwort, refer to its ability to staunch the flow of blood from a wound. It was also once used as a remedy for fever. Sprinkle the young leaves lightly over salads. They are also dried and used as a substitute for hops to flavor beer—another common name for the plant is field hop.

This plant is a wild herb that grows uninvited and unwanted on lawns and is difficult to get rid of. It can resist even the best selective weedkillers. The modern cultivars bred from the original plant are very attractive in borders and rockeries, with their wide range of colors. The pink, red, yellow, and white flowers on flat daisy-like heads appear through most of the summer and may continue into the fall.

Achilleas also grow well in containers: Use them to add color and form to an herbal bed. Plant the taller species in flower displays, where their blooms make a striking contribution. Smaller species look good in rock gardens. A number of the larger species, such as the varieties of *A. ptarmica* (sneezeweed) reach over 2ft (60cm) and make good focal plants in an herbaceous border. However, all yarrows are invasive and will need controlling.

Garden varieties of *A. millefolium* have been developed in a number of colors and they are popular plants for herbaceous borders and alpine beds.

vital statistics

FAMILY
Asteraceae/Compositae

OTHER VARIETIES AND SPECIES
A. filipendulina 'Cloth of Gold', *A. f.* 'Gold Plate', *A. millefolium* 'Burgundy', *A. m.* 'Cerise Queen', *A. m.* 'Lilac Beauty', *A. m.* 'Sammetriese', *A. ptarmica*, *A. p.* 'Perry's White', *A. p.* The Pearl Group

PERENNIAL ZONE 3

HEIGHT
6–24in (15–60cm)

FLOWERS
White, pink or red, depending on the cultivar, produced in flat clusters at the end of the flower stalk.

FOLIAGE
Lance-shaped, with many divided leaves that look lacy, hence the name millefolium.

NATURAL HABITAT
Grassland in the northern hemisphere, especially lawns.

SITE
Prefers full sun but will tolerate partial shade.

SOIL
Flourishes on poor soils that must be well-drained. Good for chalky and coastal gardens although some, such as *A. ageratum* 'W. B. Childs' and *A. ptarmica* cultivars prefer rather moister conditions.

PROPAGATION
By seed sown in the spring or divide in spring or fall.

FLOWERING
Midsummer to fall.

USES
Formerly used in folk medicine to staunch wounds and quell fevers. It is also used as a digestive tonic and dye plant. Use the young leaves (sparingly) for variety in salads.

Aconitum napellus
Aconite
friar's cap, monkshood, mousebane, Venus' chariot, wolfsbane

The common monkshood has indigo flowers in late summer and is a striking plant in an herbaceous border reaching 5ft (1.5m) in height. It was considered a remedy against poisons and a cure for snakebite but it was seldom used, even in medieval times, because the pollen caused irritation of the eyes. Today the roots of *A. napellus* are dried and used in herbal medicine as a sedative as well as in the treatment of influenza.

However, do not grow this plant in the kitchen garden, as all parts of it are extremely poisonous and the roots can easily be mistaken for those of horseradish. The leaves and sap of the plant are an irritant and care must be taken when handling them. The active principle, aconitine, is one of the most deadly poisons known—it was even used to coat the tips of poisoned arrows. In India, where monkshood grows in the wild, the shepherds in the foothills of the Himalayas used to muzzle their sheep to prevent them from eating the plants. The plant prefers moist soil and some shade and should be cut down in fall.

Caution: All parts of this plant are poisonous and must not be taken in any form.

The tall "hoods" of the typically blue or purple flowers can be seen in late summer and early fall. Other species have yellow, and occasionally white blooms.

vital statistics

FAMILY
Ranunculaceae

OTHER VARIETIES AND SPECIES
A. anthora, A. 'Bressingham Spire', A. x cammarum 'Bicolor', A. lycoctonum, A 'Spark's Variety'

PERENNIAL ZONE 4

HEIGHT
5ft (1.5m)

SPREAD
12in (30cm)

FLOWERS
Indigo, hooded. Some species are pale yellow or light blue,

FOLIAGE
Dark green deeply divided leaves.

NATURAL HABITAT
Mountainous regions in Europe, northern India and China.

SITE
Full shade or partial shade.

SOIL
Broadly tolerant of most soils and conditions but prefers moist well-drained soil.

PROPAGATION
By seed sown in the spring or divide in late fall.

FLOWERING
Mid- to late summer.

USES
All parts of the pant are extremely poisonous and must be handled with care. The roots are dried and used in herbal medicine.

Adonis vernalis
Spring pheasant's eye

This is a charming, small herb and is used today as a heart tonic in herbal medicine. The name *Adonis* commemorates the mythological Greek hunter, lover of the goddess Venus, who was killed by a wild boar. The tears that Venus wept changed into these flowers while Adonis's blood turned into roses.

Adonis was allowed to return to the land of the living from Hades for six months each spring and when he returned *A. vernalis* started to bloom. The flowers are brilliant yellow in color, with separated petals, and always turn to face the sun. They appear just before the bright green leaves that die down later in the summer. Plant them in groups in rock gardens, where they will thrive. They are rhizomatous and are easily divided once the plants have become established.

Caution: All parts of this plant are poisonous and must not be taken in any form.

The spring pheasant's eye is an attractive flower for the early months of the year, with clear yellow star-shaped flowers and feathery foliage.

vital statistics

FAMILY
Ranunculaceae

OTHER VARIETIES AND SPECIES
A. amurensis (prefers shade and acid soil), *A. annua* (annual), *A. brevistyla* (from China, prefers shade and acid soil).

PERENNIAL ZONE 5

HEIGHT
8–10in (20–25cm)

SPREAD
18in (45cm)

FLOWERS
Bright golden yellow with a distinct sheen.

FOLIAGE
Pale green, finely divided and rather feathery

NATURAL HABITAT
Native to Asia and Europe, the genus contains both annuals and perennials. Often found on mountains and on grassland.

SITE
Full sun or partial shade.

SOIL
Prefers well-drained, dry alkaline soil, this plant will not flourish in acid soil.

PROPAGATION
Sow seeds in the fall or divide after flowering is over.

FLOWERING
Early spring.

USES
In herbal medicine as a heart tonic.

Agastache foeniculum
Blue giant hyssop

Blue giant hyssop is a popular herb, favored by beekeepers for the long spires of blue-purple flowers that are most attractive to bees.

This herb is native to the prairies of North America and is not totally hardy in temperate zones. A tea made from the leaves was used by the Native Americans in herbal medicine to alleviate the symptoms of fevers, coughs, and colds. You can also use the leaves in as a flavoring in soups and sauces.

Its most notable feature is the long, dense spikes of violet-blue flowers, which last from midsummer until early fall. These dense blooms are most attractive to bees and are a favorite plant of beekeepers. The brightly colored flowers make a striking addition to a formal bed of herbs or an herbaceous border. It likes a sunny position and grows well in hilly areas.

The long serrated leaves of the plant look a little like mint. They are green on top, with a pronounced tip and whiteish-green underneath. They are pleasantly anise-scented when crushed and this gives the plant its common name.

vital statistics

FAMILY
Labiatae

OTHER VARIETIES AND SPECIES
A. barberi, A. f. 'Alabaster' (white flowers), *A. mexicana*

PERENNIAL ZONE 5

HEIGHT
3–5ft (90cm–1.5m)

SPREAD
12in (30cm)

FLOWERS
Purple-blue flowers held in long spikes.

FOLIAGE
Triangular, sharply toothed leaves on short stalks. The leaves are aromatic.

NATURAL HABITAT
Prairies of North America. Plants of the genus are found in hilly areas around the world.

SITE
Full sun.

SOIL
Well-drained soil.

PROPAGATION
Sow seed in spring at 55–64°F (13–18°C). The plant is relatively short lived so it is advisable to divide in spring or take semiripe cuttings in late summer. Keep the cuttings in a frost-free environment over the winter.

FLOWERING
Late summer to fall.

USES
Medicinal, culinary, bee plant.

Agrimonia eupatoria
Church steeples
agrimony, cockleburr, sticklewort

A common perennial, in medieval times this plant had very many uses in herbal medicine. It was believed to have a binding effect on the bowels and heal internal wounds. A decoction (an extract usually obtained by boiling the dried roots of the plant) made with wine was used to treat snakebites. The plant was used to clear urinary disorders and was thought to cure both colic and coughs. It was also prescribed in the treatment of agues and the "bloody flux" (dysentery). When mixed with pig's fat, it was believed to cure old sores and to help to draw splinters from the flesh. Finally, it was also used to ease cases of earache.

The plant is particularly common in chalky soils. It is distinguished by its gray-green leaves, greenish above and grayish underneath, with scalloped edges. The leaves appear in pairs on a stalk, larger pairs alternating with smaller ones. The flowers are pale yellow and star-shaped, carried on tapering spikes. They have a scent of apricots and are popular with bees. The seed heads form burrs that stick to clothing in the late summer and fall.

The tall, slender spikes of flowers of *Agrimonia eupatoria* give the plant its common name of church steeples.

vital statistics

FAMILY	PERENNIAL ZONE 5	FOLIAGE	SOIL	FLOWERING
Rosaceae		Gray-green above, gray beneath, with scalloped margins; small and large pairs appear alternately on the stalk.	Well-drained soil but will grow in short grass.	Summer.
OTHER VARIETIES AND SPECIES	HEIGHT			USES
A. repens	6in–2ft (15–60cm)		PROPAGATION	Formerly medicinal, bee plant.
	SPREAD	NATURAL HABITAT	Sow seed in spring, divide established plants in the fall.	
	18in (45cm)	Chalky soil in northern Europe.		
	FLOWERS	SITE		
	Long spikes of pale yellow. Apricot-scented, star-shaped.	Full sun.		

Ajuga reptans

Bugle

Bugle is one of the most attractive and useful ground-covering plants for the garden. In herbal medicine it was used to stop the flow of blood from wounds, hence the common name of carpenter's herb, and it was also used to treat ulcers, sores, and internal and external bruises. A decoction made from the leaves was also thought to be good for healing broken bones. It was also sometimes given to people who suffered delirium tremens, a condition brought on by excessive alcohol consumption.

A number of varieties have been developed, some with attractive variegated and bronze foliage. Among the most popular are 'Atropurpure', with green and red leaves, the bronze-leafed 'Braunherz', 'Burgundy Glow', with cream-edged red leaves, and 'Catlin's Giant', which has bronze-purple leaves.

Attractive spires of bright blue flowers appear in late spring and early summer. Grow the plants around the edge of an herbaceous border or in an alpine garden. Although they prefer to grow in some shade, those with variegated leaves need a good deal of sun to develop their full leaf color.

The creeping common bugle is usually grown as a ground-covering plant, but it was traditionally used as a treatment for a wide range of ailments.

vital statistics

FAMILY
Lamiaceae/Labiatae

OTHER VARIETIES AND SPECIES
A. genevensis, A. pyramidalis, A. reptans 'Alba', A. r. 'Jungle Beauty', A. r. 'Variegata'

PERENNIAL ZONE 4

HEIGHT
6in (15cm)

SPREAD
24–36in (60–90cm)

FLOWERS
Bright to dark blue flowers carried on upright spires.

FOLIAGE
Dark green, oval and spreading. Cultivated varieties often have variegated foliage.

NATURAL HABITAT
Europe and western Asia.

SITE
Can grow in full shade. Variegated forms need partial sun.

SOIL
Prefers moist soil and will not flourish in dry conditions. Will grow in poor soils.

PROPAGATION
Spreads freely and may need to be controlled. Propagate by division in spring.

FLOWERING
Late spring and early summer.

USES
Formerly medicinal.

Alchemilla vulgaris
Lady's mantle

This plant, formerly classified as *Alchemilla arvensis*, parsley piert, or parsley breakstone, is a common herb found throughout the northern hemisphere. It was used in the treatment of bladder complaints, kidney and bladder stones, and in cases of jaundice. You can use it as an herb in salads.

A. vulgaris is another herb that had many uses in medieval medicine. It was held to be efficient in treating wounds and inflamed sores. It was used for eye infections, to aid conception, and to prevent miscarriage. It is now used in herbal medicine for digestive and menstrual disorders.

The alchemilla most commonly grown in gardens is *A. mollis*. This enchanting hardy perennial with soft green leaves and small yellow flowers is native to Turkey and the Caucasus. It was a favorite plant of the celebrated English garden designer Gertrude Jekyll. It is found edging many herbaceous borders and you'll find it particularly useful for growing among paving stones (where it will self-seed). Many people let it hang down over the edges of lawns. It grows in most soils and is extremely rampant: You may need to take action to keep it where you want it. There are many other species, such as *A. alpina*, alpine lady's mantle, some of which are smaller and can be grown in rock gardens.

The tiny flowers of *A. mollis*, the most commonly grown species, are held in clumps, and are often used for cutting.

---

vital statistics

FAMILY Rosaceae	**PERENNIAL ZONE 5**	**FOLIAGE** Soft, yellow-green pleated leaves.	**SOIL** Prefers moist rich soil, but will flourish in poor sparse conditions.	**FLOWERING** Summer.
OTHER VARIETIES AND SPECIES *A. alpina, A. erythropoda, A. mollis, A. xanthoclora*	**HEIGHT** 24in (60cm)	**NATURAL HABITAT** Grassland and light woodland in Europe and western Asia, and mountainous regions throughout the world.	**PROPAGATION** Sow seed in spring, divide established plants in the spring or fall.	**USES** Herbal medicine, dried flower arrangements.
	SPREAD 30in (75 cm)			
	FLOWERS Very small, greenish-yellow held in clumps.	**SITE** Sun or partial shade.		

Allium fistulosum
Welsh onion

S ometimes called the ciboule, the Welsh onion is an evergreen plant that retains its leaves even in the hardest frosts. These onions make a useful winter vegetable for salads or seasoning, but since they do not form a true bulb they do not keep for any length of time after they have been pulled. If they are left from year to year they will grow into a large clump that requires dividing and replanting.

Onions were valued as herbs in the 16th and 17th centuries. According to Gerard the "juice stuffed up the nose, purgeth the head, and draweth forth raw flegmaticke humors." And they were also used to draw the poison from boils and sores and the juice, if mixed with pennyroyal, "anointed upon a bald head in the Sun, bringeth the haire againe very speedily." They were also thought to be good for colds and coughs.

Sow Welsh onions in the spring or late summer in rows 9in (23cm) apart, thinning the plants to 8in (20cm). Spring-sown onions will be ready for harvesting in early fall, onions sown in late summer will be ready the following spring.

The tall stems of Welsh onions can be used like chives, but have a stronger flavor.

vital statistics

FAMILY
Liliaceae

OTHER VARIETIES AND SPECIES
A. fistulosum 'White Evergreen',
A. f. 'Ishikura', *A. schoenoprasum* (chives), *A. tuberosum* (Chinese chives)

PERENNIAL
ZONE 4

HEIGHT
18in (45cm)

SPREAD
9in (23cm)

FLOWERS
Very small balls of white flowers in spring.

FOLIAGE
Long, green, hollow leaves that last all year. Small bulbs form just below the ground.

NATURAL HABITAT
Northern hemisphere. Usually found growing in wild mountainous regions.

SITE
Sun.

SOIL
Fertile, well-drained soil.

PROPAGATION
Sow seed in spring or late summer or divide established plants in spring.

FLOWERING
Late spring.

USES
Culinary, medicinal.

Allium sativum
Garlic

Common garlic is easy to grow in the kitchen garden. Cloves can be planted out in the fall and harvested at the end of summer.

Common garlic, a relation of the onion, can be classed either as an herb or a vegetable. It has been one of the plants most commonly used in medicine for many hundreds of years. In the 17th century the herbalists regarded it with great suspicion and believed that it should not be used internally in any great quantity because it "sent humours to the brain." Today, some people still avoid the pungent-flavored herb—a matter of taste rather than scientific belief. Garlic is now a popular herbal medicine taken in capsule form to ward off the common cold and to aid digestion. Medical research suggests that it helps to lower both cholesterol and blood pressure. As it is a close relation of the onion, the growth habit and appearance are very similar, and you'll find it easy to grow.

Garlic is commonly used in the kitchen to flavor stews and sauces, probably more so than any other herb. *Poulet a l'ail* is one classic dish that depends on garlic for its flavor, aïoli, the "golden butter" of Provence in France, is another.

vital statistics

FAMILY
Liliaceae

OTHER VARIETIES AND SPECIES
A. oleraceum (field garlic), A. ursinum (wild garlic), A. vineale (crow garlic)

ANNUAL BULB ZONE 3

HEIGHT
6–12in (30–60cm)

SPREAD
10in (25cm)

FLOWERS
Single head of pale pink or greenish-white flowers.

FOLIAGE
Short, flat upright gray-green leaves.

NATURAL HABITAT
Southern Europe, central Asia.

SITE
Open and sunny.

SOIL
Does best on well-drained, light, alkaline soil.

PROPAGATION
Plant individual cloves in the fall, about 4in (10cm) deep and 7in (18cm) apart. Most varieties need at least two months at temperatures between 32–50°F (0–10°C). Do not plant on recently manured ground.

FLOWERING
Summer.

USES
Probably the most commonly used herb in the kitchen, particularly in stews and salads. Herbal medicine.

Allium schoenoprasum
Chives

You can use both the flowers and leaves of this onion-related herb as flavoring, particularly for summer soups and in salads. Freeze surplus leaves for use in the winter, when the foliage dies down completely. It is very high in vitamin C, and is used in herbal medicine to aid the digestion and as a mild stimulant. The onion family in general, particularly the ordinary garden onion, *Allium cepa*, was much revered in herbal medicine. Among other uses, a roasted onion eaten with sugar and oil was used in cases of persistent coughs. Eating onions was thought to increase male virility, and leeks, another member of the family, could be boiled and then applied warm to ease bad cases of hemorrhoids.

If you are not growing *A. schoenoprasum* for their attractive purple flowerheads, then cut the plant to the ground two or three times during the growing season to promote fresh growth from the base. Chinese chives, *A. tuberosum*, have star-like white flowers and are eaten as a vegetable in China. You can easily grow the plant in containers kept in the kitchen. They are sometimes made into an herbal spray to prevent mildew in the garden.

Its late spring flowers make chives one of the most attractive herbs. These pink-purple globe-like heads of *A. schoenoprasum* are edible as well as highly decorative.

vital statistics

FAMILY
Liliaceae

OTHER VARIETIES AND SPECIES
A. s. var. *sibiricum* (Siberian chives), *A. s* 'Forescate' (pink flowers), *A. tuberosum* (garlic chives)

PERENNIAL
ZONE 3

HEIGHT
8–12in (20–30cm)

SPREAD
12in (30cm)

FLOWERS
Pink or purple many-petaled balls held on long stalks.

FOLIAGE
Long thin green leaves.

NATURAL HABITAT
Found throughout North America, Europe, and Asia, generally in damp places.

SITE
Open and sunny.

SOIL
Prefers moist, rich soil.

PROPAGATION
Sow in seed trays indoors in spring and then plant out in groups of three or four seedlings. Divide established groups every three or four years in spring or fall.

FLOWERING
Summer.

USES
Commonly used in the kitchen for flavoring and as a garnish. Use the flowers in salads and as an edible garnish. Cut and freeze the chives for use over the winter when the foliage dies down.

Aloe vera ✛✿⊗◗❧○

Aloe

Barbados aloe

Aloes are evergreen, tropical plants with short-stemmed rosettes and clumps of fleshy, succulent leaves. The plant is commonly used in herbal medicine. The sap of *Aloe vera* is made into an ointment and used as an antiseptic to heal wounds and burns (hence the common name "burn plant"). It is also used in face creams and other cosmetics. Aloe was used as a purgative (to clear the bowels) but this is discouraged—it can cause internal bleeding.

The plant grows best in fertile, well-drained soil with plenty of grit. In temperate zones aloes are popular houseplants. They need a minimum winter temperature of 41°F (5°C). As well as those grown in the United States, there are species from South Africa, Madagascar, and the Cape Verde islands.

The distinctive, spiked leaves of the plant are quite long. They sometimes reach 2ft (60cm) in length and in some species they are variegated. In the summer the plant carries large spikes of yellow or red flowers on stalks, and a mature plant may carry as many as four stalks at any one time. Sow seed in the spring under glass and then repot annually at this time.

Caution: Can cause internal bleeding.

Aloes are popular tropical plants with succulent leaves that are often grown as houseplants. *Aloe vera* has spikes of yellow flowers in summer.

vital statistics

FAMILY Aloeaceae/Liliaceae	**TENDER TROPICAL EVERGREEN SUCCULENT ZONE 11**	**FOLIAGE** Large pale green spotted to 2ft (60cm) often with pink margins. Teeth-like spikes.	**SOIL** Well-drained, fertile, although they will survive very dry conditions.	**FLOWERING** Spring.
OTHER VARIETIES AND SPECIES A. aristata, A. bakeri, A. rauhii, A. variegata (partridge-breasted aloe), A. v. 'Walmsley's Blue', A. zebrina	**HEIGHT** 2ft (60cm) **SPREAD** Indefinite. **FLOWERS** Large yellow tubular spikes..	**NATURAL HABITAT** Tropical and subtropical areas. **SITE** Indoors needs good light out of direct sun. Grows in full sun out of doors.	**PROPAGATION** Sow seed when it is ripe, at a minimum temperature 70°F (21°C) or separate offsets in early summer.	**USES** Herbal medicine.

Aloysia triphylla
Lemon beebrush
lemon verbena

This herb is a perennial, deciduous shrub that is a native of Chile and Argentina. The essential oil (Spanish verbena) distilled from these plants is used as a flavoring in cakes and drinks, and for fragrance in potpourris. Tea made from the lemon-scented leaves is sold in France as *vervaine* and used for easing cases of indigestion. You can also use the dried leaves in potpourris and for flavoring food. Pick the leaves when young. You can grow the plant outdoors in mild areas at the foot of a sunny, warm wall or along a sheltered border. However, you may find it altogether easier to grow the plant in a container which can then be moved indoors in winter and during cold snaps.

It flowers on the new growth of the current year, so cut it back hard early in spring to a basic framework of branches, in the same manner as *Buddleia davidii*. Train it against a sunny, warm, and sheltered wall. The highly aromatic leaves are followed by small, pale lilac-colored flowers in late summer. It can be prone to red spider mite infestation.

Caution: Large doses or prolonged use can cause internal irritation.

The lemon-scented leaves and late summer flowers make lemon verbena a decorative container plant. It is half-hardy and needs to be given shelter in cold weather.

vital statistics

FAMILY Verbenaceae.	**HALF-HARDY SHRUB ZONES 7–10**	**FLOWERS** Pale lilac to white held in slender tufts.	**SITE** Full sun.	**FLOWERING** Late summer.
OTHER VARIETIES AND SPECIES None	**HEIGHT** 6ft (1.8m) or more in its natural habitat.	**FOLIAGE** Narrow, lance-shaped bright green leaves that have oil-bearing glands on the underside.	**SOIL** Rich, well-drained. **PROPAGATION** Take semiripe cuttings in summer.	**USES** Flavoring and tea in the kitchen. Herbal medicine.
	SPREAD 4ft (1.2m)	**NATURAL HABITAT** Fields and along highways in Chile and Argentina.		

Althaea officinalis
Marshmallow
mortification plant, sweet weed, wymote

Marshmallows, as the name suggests, grow best in damp places. The main use of the plant in medieval times was as a medicine to treat many ailments, particularly sore mouths, and as a gargle to ease chest complaints, coughs, and bronchitis. Lozenges made from the powdered roots were used to cure throat infections and coughs. It was also used as a poultice to treat wounds and to aid women who were having difficulty in childbirth.

The roots were used to make the squashy candy marshmallows. Try using both the leaves and shoots in salads.

It is a tall plant, reaching 4ft (1.2m) in height with a large number of soft, gray green leaves and clumps of very pale pink, five-petaled flowers that grow up the stem in rather the same way as a hollyhock.

Marshmallows are one of the oldest medicinal herbs. The roots were used to make the candy marshmallows.

vital statistics

FAMILY
Malvaceae

OTHER VARIETIES AND SPECIES
A. armeniaca, A. cannabina, A. o. alba, A. o. 'Romney Marsh'

PERENNIAL ZONE 3

HEIGHT
4ft (1.2m)

SPREAD
2ft (60cm)

FLOWERS
Pale pink-lilac growing up the stem of the plant.

FOLIAGE
Gray green soft hairy leaves with five lobes.

NATURAL HABITAT
Damp places by streams and in marshes by the sea. Native of Europe but found throughout the world.

SITE
Full sun.

SOIL
Prefers rich, moist soil.

PROPAGATION
Sow seed in spring, take cuttings in early summer or divide the roots in early spring.

FLOWERING
Late summer.

USES
Culinary, herbal medicine.

Althaea (Alcea) rosea
Hollyhock

For hundreds of years the Latin name for hollyhocks was *Althaea*, but this name has recently been changed, and correctly they are now known as *Alcea*. As they are members of the mallow family, they have been included here with marshmallow. Hollyhocks were used in herbal medicine as a mouthwash and to treat disorders of the gums. They had other medicinal uses—as a cure for incontinence, to prevent miscarriage, to treat chest complaints, and as a remedy for the "bloody flux" (dysentery). The root was also dried, ground to a powder, and then boiled in wine to treat worms in children. It has many of the same properties as *Althaea officinalis* but is generally less effective.

Hollyhocks are biennials and are a favorite garden plant, found in many herbaceous borders in summer. They are tall and stately, and carry large tubular flowers on spikes. The flowers self-seed freely in well-drained soil. There is a variety of colors available, from pink to lilac, deep red and blue.

Hollyhocks are common garden flowers that bloom in late summer and are favorite plants for a cottage garden effect.

vital statistics

FAMILY Malvaceae	**BIENNIAL** **ZONE 5**	**FOLIAGE** Pale green, heart-shaped, hairy leaves usually with five lobes.	**SOIL** Fertile, well drained.	**FLOWERING** Summer.
OTHER VARIETIES AND SPECIES A. ficifolia, A. r. Chater's Double Group, A. r. 'Indian Spring', A. r. 'Nigra'	**HEIGHT** 8ft (2.5m)	**NATURAL HABITAT** Native of western Asia.	**PROPAGATION** To grow as a biennial sow seed in situ in late summer. Transplant in early fall when two or three leaves have developed.	**USES** Herbal medicine.
	SPREAD 2ft (60cm)	**SITE** Full sun.		
	FLOWERS Range of colors from yellow to pink, purple, and deep red.			

Amaranthus hypochondriacus
Amaranth
lady bleeding, lovely bleeding, pilewort, Prince-of-Wales feather, red cockscomb

As its Latin name implies, *A. hypochondriacus* has been used in herbal medicine for thousands of years. The ancient Greeks held that it contained special healing properties. It was used to staunch the flow of blood from a wound or in cases of severe nosebleeds, and was used to treat venereal disease. It was also used as a cure for diarrhea and excessive menstruation.

Amaranth is a spectacular annual that is found in many planting schemes in public parks, where it is valued for its lance-shaped, purple-green leaves and crimson plumes of flowers. The variety 'Green Thumb' has brilliant yellow-green flowers. The two most commonly grown species are *A. caudatus*, love-lies-bleeding or tassel flower, and *A. cruentes*, red amaranth. *A. caudatus* has long pendant tassels of flowers, usually crimson or purple, that trail down (some varieties have different colored flowers). The flower plumes of *A. cruentes* stand stiffly upright, followed in the fall by red, purple, or yellow seed heads. *A. caudatus* is sometimes grown as a grain crop in poorer countries.

Many varieties have been developed; among the most popular is *A. cruentes* 'Golden Giant', with striking golden seed heads. The varieties of *A. tricolor* are also popular: 'Flaming Fountain' has red leaves, 'Illumination' has rose-red upper leaves tipped with gold, and 'Joseph's Coat' has attractive many-colored leaves of gold, crimson, green, yellow, and brown.

Amaranths are spectacular colorful annuals with long plumes of flowers. They were used in medicine by the ancient Greeks.

vital statistics

FAMILY
Amaranthaceae

OTHER VARIETIES AND SPECIES
A. caudatus, *A. cruentes*, *A. retroflexus* (green amaranth), *A. polygamus*, *A. tricolor*. There are many varieties that have been developed as annuals.

HALF-HARDY ANNUAL

HEIGHT
3–4ft (90–1.2m)

SPREAD
12–18in (30–45cm)

FLOWERS
Tiny maroon flowers held upright, making an erect feathery plume.

FOLIAGE
Lance-shaped, purple-green leaves.

NATURAL HABITAT
Wasteland and fields in temperate and tropical regions throughout the world.

SITE
Full sun and shelter.

SOIL
Moderately fertile, well-drained soil, although *A. caudatus* will tolerate poor soil.

PROPAGATION
In temperate climates sow seed under glass in spring at 68°F (20°C). Plant out in position in early summer when all danger of frost has passed.

FLOWERING
Summer.

USES
Bedding plant, dried flowers, formerly medicinal.

Anagallis arvensis ✚ ❁ ⊗ ◯ 🌿 ○
Scarlet pimpernel
poor man's weather glass, red chickweed

A. arvensis, or the common pimpernel, has scarlet (or, more rarely, pink) flowers that bloom in late spring or summer. It seeds freely, so is suitable for a wild garden.

The scarlet pimpernel is a common weed or wildflower found in many gardens in temperate regions in the northern hemisphere. The juice of the plant applied to a wasp or bee sting is said to bring instant relief.

The plant's name was the alias adopted by the dashing hero of Baroness Orczy's novel about the French Revolution, *The Scarlet Pimpernel*. It gets its common name of "poor man's weather glass" because the flowers will open only in sunny weather. This plant does not tolerate very cold conditions.

The bog pimpernel, *A. tenella*, was used in medieval times as a medicine for various ailments. It was used to treat diarrhea, piles, cataracts, and scurvy.

The two species commonly grown in gardens are the blue pimpernel, *A. monellii*, which comes from the Mediterranean and has deep blue flowers in summer, and *A. tenella* 'Studland', which forms a mound covered with pink flowers. *A. tenella* will flourish in a moist position in the backyard. Propagate both of these species by division in spring.

vital statistics

FAMILY
Primulaceae

OTHER VARIETIES AND SPECIES
A. a. var. *caerulea, A. monellii* (both blue flowers), *A. tenella* 'Studland' (deep pink flowers)

PERENNIAL ZONE 5

HEIGHT
4–8in (10–20cm)

SPREAD
4in (10cm)

FLOWERS
Scarlet five-petaled flowers that only open on sunny days.

FOLIAGE
Heart-shaped, mid-green, ribbed leaves, held in pairs on a long stalk.

NATURAL HABITAT
A weed of cultivated ground. Common in fields, gardens, and wasteland.

SITE
Full sun.

SOIL
Cultivated varieties and species prefer fertile, moist, well-drained soil.

PROPAGATION
Sow seed in a cold frame in spring or take soft tip cuttings of garden varieties in spring and early summer.

FLOWERING
Summer.

USES
Rock or bog garden plant, formerly medicinal.

Anemone nemorosa

Wood anemone

European thimbleweed, windflower

A flower of the woods, the wood anemone is a creeping perennial widely grown in shaded areas in temperate climates. Bathing in a decoction made from the leaves was formerly recommended as a cure for leprosy and for malignant ulcers. The juice of the leaves was stuffed up the nose to cure headaches, and an ointment made from them was applied to the eyelids in cases of cataracts.

The species plant has single white- or pink-tinged flowers with, usually, six petals and a yellow center. A number of varieties have been developed and one can be found to suit most backyards and color schemes. 'Allenii' has deep lavender-blue flowers; 'Bracteata Pleniflora' has semi-double white flowers with a ruff of leaves, 'Robinsoniana' has pale blue flowers and 'Vestal' has double white flowers.

Wood anemones grow best in light soil in shade or semi-shade and flourish in deciduous open woodland. These plants flower in the spring and then die down. They are called windflowers because the flowers are supposed to open only when the wind is blowing.

Anemones form an attractive genus of flowers that bloom in the spring and fall. Spring-flowering anemones include varieties of the popular *A. blanda*, with many different colors. The wood anemone is a creeping woodland plant.

---

vital statistics

FAMILY
Ranunculaceae

OTHER VARIETIES AND SPECIES
A. altaica, A. apennina, A. obtusilosa, A. ranunculoides, A sylvestris (snowdrop anemone)

RHIZOMATOUS PERENNIAL ZONE 4

HEIGHT
3–6in (8–15cm)

SPREAD
12in (30cm)

FLOWERS
White or pink-tinged.

FOLIAGE
Rounded tripalmate leaves with narrow leaflets that are divided and toothed.

NATURAL HABITAT
Woods and mountain pastures of Europe.

SITE
Shade or partial shade.

SOIL
Moist, well-drained, humus-rich.

PROPAGATION
Separate the rhizomes in spring or sow seed in early summer when the seed is ripe.

FLOWERING
Spring to early summer.

USES
Formerly medicinal.

Anethum graveolens
Dill
dilly

Dill is a popular herb that can be grown in most soils. It needs to be kept moist, otherwise it will quickly run to seed.

Dill is an attractive plant with fine feathery leaves and flat yellow flowerheads made up of a multitude of small bright yellow flowers. It is a popular herb in the kitchen, especially in Scandinavian countries, where it is used in pickling and fish dishes—particularly gravadlax, salmon pickled with dill. The main parts of the plant used in the kitchen are the leaves, which should be picked when young and fresh, and the seeds, which contain an essential oil. These are more strongly flavored than the leaves and are used in cakes and bread. Freeze the leaves for use later. You can also cut and dry the flowers for flower arranging.

Dill was a popular plant in herbal medicine. It was traditionally used to prevent nausea, to cure excessive gas and to treat hiccups. Dill water was formerly given to babies who were suffering from gas and digestive disorders, and in the words of 17th-century English herbalist Nicholas Culpeper, it was "a gallant expeller of wind and provoker of terms."

There is only one species in the genus, which can be seen on wasteland and in cornfields. It grows best in soil that is fertile and well drained, prefers full sun and does not like the cold.

vital statistics

FAMILY
Umbelliferae

OTHER VARIETIES AND SPECIES
A. g. 'Dukat', A. g. 'Sowa'

ANNUAL

HEIGHT
2–3ft (60–90cm)

SPREAD
12in (30cm)

FLOWERS
Tiny, bright yellow, held on large, flat heads.

FOLIAGE
Blue-green, fine, feathery leaves.

NATURAL HABITAT
Found on wasteland in the northern hemisphere. Native of southwestern Asia and India.

SITE
Full sun.

SOIL
Most, likes dry conditions.

PROPAGATION
Sow seed in spring where the plants are to grow. Thin to 12in (30cm) apart.

FLOWERING
Summer.

USES
Culinary, dried flowers.

Angelica archangelica
Angelica

Angelica is a tall, stately plant that is usually found growing at the back of an herbaceous border or tucked away in the kitchen or herb garden. All parts of the plant were used in herbal medicine. The juice of the leaves was used as an eye tonic. A decoction of the stems was used in cases of the ague or fever, as it promoted perspiration and helped to lower body temperature. It was also used as an expectorant (clearing the lungs of fluid) to cure cases of bronchitis, pleurisy, coughs, and other chest infections. A syrup made from the stalks was used to cure colic, indigestion, and heartburn.

As well as its former uses in medicine, angelica is one of the ingredients in a number of liqueurs, such as Benedictine (originally made by Benedictine monks in France). You can try candying the stalks, and use angelica peel to decorate cakes. You can also prepare the stalks in the same way as rhubarb.

Angelica has tiny yellow flowers that are carried in large clumps held out on long stalks. It is native to wet areas in the northern hemisphere and so it will flourish in moist conditions in the backyard. This self-seeding plant is usually grown as a biennial.

The name comes from the Latin *herba angelica* (angelic herb). It was believed that the herb would cure all ills, and protect against evil in general.

vital statistics

FAMILY	PERENNIAL	FOLIAGE	SOIL	FLOWERING
Apiaceae/Umbelliferae	ZONE 3	Large, sparse, bright green	Deep moist soil is preferred.	Summer.
	Sometimes grown as a biennial.	leaves on long stalks		
OTHER VARIETIES AND			PROPAGATION	USES
SPECIES	HEIGHT	NATURAL HABITAT	Sow seed in a cold frame and	Culinary, formerly medicinal,
A. atropurpurea, *A. gigas*,	6–7ft (2m)	Damp sites in	transplant the seedlings when	flavoring.
A. sylvestris		northern Europe.	they are young. They generally	
	SPREAD		flower within two to three	
	3ft (90cm)	SITE	years.	
		Shade or partial shade,		
	FLOWERS	although *A. sylvestris* prefers full		
	Tiny, greenish-yellow flowers.	sun.		

Anthriscus cerefolium
Chervil

C hervil is a fine and delicate herb both in appearance and flavor. It is one of the *fines herbes* of French cuisine and is used as a flavoring in salads, particularly potato salad. Try adding it to soups and stews—at the last minute, otherwise the flavor will be lost. It was also an important medicinal herb in medieval times. Chervil was used to thin blood clots, to treat severe bruising, in cases of kidney stones, to provoke urine, as a treatment for pleurisy, and as a tonic for general health and well-being.

The plant grows wild in southern Europe and the Near East, and has become naturalized in North America. Its fern-like leaves have a flavor reminiscent of parsley and fennel.

Grow this plant in the shade. Sow seeds in late summer for an early spring crop, and then again in the spring for a summer crop.

Caution: Use only cultivated chervil, wild chervil can be easily confused with similar looking plants that are poisonous.

Chervil is not as widely used in the kitchen as it should be, for it has a fine and delicate flavor. It was an important medicinal herb in medieval times to thin blood clots and treat kidney stones.

vital statistics

FAMILY
Umbelliferae

OTHER VARIETIES AND SPECIES
A. sylvestris, Chaerophyllum aureum (golden chervil)
C. bulbosum (bulbous chervil)

HARDY ANNUAL

HEIGHT
2ft (60cm).

SPREAD
1ft (30cm).

FLOWERS
Tiny white flowers held in umbels (flowerheads on stalks that grow from a single stalk).

FOLIAGE
Finely cut leaves have a subtle aniseed flavor.

NATURAL HABITAT
Banks and waste ground. Native of Europe and western Asia.

SITE
Needs partial shade in summer months but likes sun in winter.

SOIL
Light, fertile soil that does not dry out.

PROPAGATION
Sow seed in spring (for summer plants) and late summer (for winter leaves). Thin plants to 6in (15cm) apart and water regularly during the summer.

FLOWERING
Spring to summer.

USES
Culinary, formerly medicinal.

Anthyllis vulneraria
Kidney vetch

Kidney vetch was formerly a popular medicinal herb but is seldom found in herbal medicine today. It was applied to wounds and also used to treat coughs, bronchial complaints, and as a laxative. It is an attractive garden plant and is frequently found in rock or alpine gardens or growing in wildflower meadows. It has a spreading habit and the plant makes good ground cover. In the summer the flowers emerge on upright stalks, usually yellow tinged with red, although there are many naturally occurring color variations, including orange, red, purple, and white. The flowers are attractive to bees and butterflies. Cut the flowers down when flowering is over and another flush will emerge later in the year. If the flowers are left on the plant the seed heads make attractive shapes for winter floral decorations. The kidney vetch is a tolerant plant and will survive in poor, dry conditions although the flowering period will be shorter and the growth less vigorous. The variety *coccinea* has bright-red flowers.

Anthyllis vulneraria is at home in a wildflower garden and will tolerate most soil types, as long as they are well drained.

vital statistics

FAMILY
Leguminosae/Papilionaceae

OTHER VARIETIES AND SPECIES
A. vulneraria var. *coccinea*, *A. hermanniae*, *A. montana*

PERENNIAL ZONE 4
Annual or short-lived perennial

HEIGHT
12 in (30 cm)

SPREAD
18 in (45 cm)

FLOWERS
Many color varieties occur.

FOLIAGE
Light-green, silky, hairy leaves, whitish underneath. There is a large terminal leaflet.

NATURAL HABITAT
Native of Europe and northern Africa. Found on chalky soil, dunes, and on the coast.

SITE
Sun.

SOIL
Well-drained, light, or sandy.

PROPAGATION
Sow seed in the fall, divide established plants in spring, self-seeds.

FLOWERING
Summer

USES
Formerly medicinal, bee plant, dried-flower arrangements.

Apium graveolens
Celery
wild celery

Grow this common garden vegetable in the summer for pulling and eating in the winter. It is often eaten raw, and is also used as an ingredient in salads. The classic French method of cooking celery is to blanch the hearts, stew them in butter, and coat them with a meat glaze. Also try braising celery in the oven.

As well as its uses as a kitchen vegetable the seeds are often used in herbal medicine. They dissolve many of the harmful accretions of uric acid, and a decoction made from the seeds is thought to help in rheumatic illnesses and to be a diuretic (increasing the flow of urine). It is also used as a general tonic, and has been prescribed for arthritis and high blood pressure.

There are two sorts of celery, self-blanching, or American green celery, which is easier to grow and is ready to eat toward the end of summer, and trench celery. This is generally planted in a trench and the stems blanched by earthing them up as the plants grow. They can also be blanched with collars made of strips of heavy-weight lightproof paper. This celery is ready to eat from early winter.

These tiny yellow flowers are produced in the second year. They are followed by seeds used in herbal medicine and in the kitchen.

vital statistics

FAMILY
Apiaceae/Umbelliferae

OTHER VARIETIES AND SPECIES
A. graveolens var. dulce,
A. nodiflorum

HARDY BIENNIAL ZONE 4
Grown as an annual vegetable.

HEIGHT
12–18 in (30–45cm)

SPREAD
4in (10cm)

FLOWERS
Small, yellowish flowers.

FOLIAGE
Flat leaves with serrated edges, used as a seasoning and garnish in the kitchen.

NATURAL HABITAT
Wasteland and pasture in Europe.

SITE
Sun or partial shade.

SOIL
Very fertile, moist, well-drained soil with lots of organic matter.

PROPAGATION
Sow seed in spring under cover at a soil temperature of 50–59°F (10–15°C). Prick out seedlings when they are as young as possible. Grow at an even temperature. Plant in early summer.

FLOWERING
Summer.

USES
Culinary, herbal medicine.

Aquilegia vulgaris
Columbine

Aquilegias are among the most charming flowers of early summer and many varieties have been developed. The traditional *A. vulgaris* is one of the most popular.

Aquilegias are one of the most charming flowers in the garden, with nodding, graceful blooms that are held aloft on long stalks above neat green clumps of leaves. They were formerly much valued in herbal medicine. A decoction of the leaves was used to cure sore throats and mouth ulcers, and also to treat jaundice. It was also taken to clear obstructions of the liver.

The traditional *Aquilegia vulgaris* blooms in early summer. It is a dark blue or violet color, although other colors are available. Modern varieties come in all shades of deep violet through blue and yellow, to pink and white. Many are bicolored, which adds to their attraction.

Their delicate appearance belies their toughness. They self-seed and can become invasive, so you may need to control them if you have them in an herbaceous border. They thrive in neutral to alkaline soil and prefer sun or partial shade.

Caution: All parts of all species of the plant are poisonous, especially the seeds, and they should not be consumed in any way.

vital statistics

FAMILY
Ranunculaceae

OTHER VARIETIES AND SPECIES
McKana Hybrids, Mrs Scott-Elliot Hybrids, Music Series are all commonly grown.
A. v. 'Nivea' (white flowers), *A. v.* 'Nora Barlow' (green, red), *A. canadensis* (scarlet, yellow), *A. caerulea*, (blue, white)

SHORT-LIVED HARDY PERENNIAL ZONE 5

HEIGHT
36in (90cm)

SPREAD
18in (45cm)

FLOWERS
Usually deep violet. Other varieties have a range of colors.

FOLIAGE
Attractive mid-green leaves divided into three leaflets with indented edges.

NATURAL HABITAT
Grows wild in open woodland in eastern North America, and in Europe.

SITE
Sun or partial shade.

SOIL
Rich, moisture-retaining.

PROPAGATION
Sow seed in spring, although alpine species may take two years to germinate. Self-seeds freely. Divide named varieties in spring. *Aquilegias* hybridize freely and often do not come true from seed.

FLOWERING
Early summer.

USES
Formerly medicinal, border perennial.

Arctium lappa

Greater burdock

bardana, burrseed, clotburr, cockleburr, hareburr

The greater burdock is a common wild plant of uncultivated land. It has long roots up to 3ft (90cm) in length, which may be dug up and cooked. They are cultivated as a vegetable in Japan, and were eaten by Native Americans as a vegetable. Try candying the stalks in the same way as angelica.

The plant has widespread medicinal uses. It has a reputation as a cure for skin complaints, notably eczema, and it was formerly considered a treatment in cases of sciatica and gallstones. The seeds are used today in Chinese medicine as a cure for throat and bronchial infections. To use the roots for cooking, gather one-year-old plants before flowering in the spring or early summer. Herbalists split and dry the roots before preparing them.

The plant's most notable feature is the thick, hairy stems, which carry purple flowers in the summer. These then later form the large burr-like seed heads that stick to clothing and the coats of animals during the fall and are so difficult to remove. The leaves are large and coarse with white undersides.

The greater burdock has many uses in herbal and Chinese medicine. It gets its common name of "clotburr" from the large burr-like seed heads that form when flowering is over.

vital statistics

FAMILY Compositae	**BIENNIAL** **ZONE 3**	**FOLIAGE** Large, coarse, broadly triangular, white on the underside.	**SOIL** Rich, moisture retaining.	**FLOWERING** Summer.
OTHER VARIETIES AND SPECIES A. pubens (common burdock), A. minus (lesser burdock)	**HEIGHT** 6ft (1.8m)	**NATURAL HABITAT** Meadows throughout North America, Europe, and Asia.	**PROPAGATION** Sow seed in spring. Generally the plant can be found growing in the wild.	**USES** Formerly medicinal, culinary.
	SPREAD 3ft (90cm)			
	FLOWERS Reddish-purple tubular flowers followed by large seed heads.	**SITE** Sun or partial shade.		

Arctostaphylos uva-ursi
Bearberry
kinnikinnick, manzanita

The bearberry is an attractive ground-cover shrub that will grow only if you can provide acid soil. It also prefers some shade. The bearberry is valued by the practitioners of herbal medicine in the treatment of urinary, bladder, and kidney infections. As with all herbs and herbal preparations, it should not be used for unsupervised treatment in the home.

It has small, dark green, glossy, evergreen leaves and sprays of pink-tinted white flowers in summer. These are followed by bright red berries in the fall. They grow wild in North America and northern Europe.

The name comes from the Greek word *arktos*, meaning "bear." *A. alpina*, the alpine bearberry, is a similar creeping shrub. Other species are larger; *A. manzanita*, Parry manzanita, native to California, reaches 10ft (3m). A number of good varieties are available, among them 'Vancouver Jade', with pink flowers, and 'Wood's Red', with pink flowers followed by large red berries. The berries make a gray or blue dye.

Bearberries can be grown as ground-cover plants in acid soil. Their pink flowers are followed by red berries in the fall.

FAMILY
Ericaceae

OTHER VARIETIES AND SPECIES
A. u-u. 'Vancouver Jade', A. u-u. 'Wood's Red', A. manzanita, A. alpina, A. patula, A. pumila

EVERGREEN SHRUB ZONE 3

HEIGHT
6ft (1.8m)

SPREAD
3ft (90cm)

FLOWERS
Small sprays of pink-tinted white flowers. Red fruit in fall.

FOLIAGE
Small, glossy, evergreen, smooth, dark green leaves.

NATURAL HABITAT
North America and northern Europe. Favors conifer woods.

SITE
Sun or partial shade.

SOIL
Prefers light, acid soil with some moisture.

PROPAGATION
Sow seed in fall. Take semi-ripe cuttings in summer or layer in the fall.

FLOWERING
Summer.

USES
Herbal medicine, dye plant.

Armeria maritima
Thrift seapink

Thrift is a common plant that often grows near the coast. The plant was once considered a treatment for obesity, nervous disorders, and urinary infections, but it is now thought to cause allergic reactions and is no longer used.

The flowers are attractive, generally pink, and held aloft on stalks with the grass-like foliage forming a dense clump. A number of varieties have been developed for growing in alpine and rock gardens. These include 'Alba', with white flowers; 'Bee's Ruby', which is taller with deep pink flowers; and 'Bloodstone', with dark red flowers.

Thrift is found in clumps along cliff edges and along salt marshes, as well as in mountainous regions in North America and Europe. *A. arenaria*, now reclassified as *A. alliacea*, has white to deep purple flowerheads and is native to the mountains of Europe. The flowers look good in rock gardens and along garden paths.

The ordinary form of thrift, *Armeria maritima*, grows in clumps by the sea and has attractive pink flowers. Garden varieties have been developed with deeper pink and red flowers.

vital statistics

FAMILY
Plumbaginaceae

OTHER VARIETIES AND SPECIES
A. alliacea (Jersey thrift), *A. alpina, A. juniperifolia, A. pseudoarmeria*

PERENNIAL ZONE 4

HEIGHT
8in (20cm)

SPREAD
12in (30cm)

FLOWERS
Profuse clumps of pink, white and purple rounded heads.

FOLIAGE
Short, dark green, narrow leaves, like stiff grass.

NATURAL HABITAT
Coastal and mountainous regions and salt marshes of Europe, North America, and also Asia.

SITE
Sun or partial shade.

SOIL
Prefers light, slightly acid, well-drained soil.

PROPAGATION
Sow seed in fall. Take semi-ripe cuttings or divide in summer. Self-seeds.

FLOWERING
Summer.

USES
Formerly medicinal, dried flower arrangements.

Arnica montana
Arnica
leopard's bane, mountain arnica, mountain tobacco

Arnica carries brilliant, single, yellow flowers held aloft on a long stalk above a rosette of green downy leaves, hence the common name of mountain daisy. Some species are native to North America, and it is found in mountainous regions of Europe. It has long been valued as the herb to heal bruises above all others. There are a number of other species that have similar medicinal properties.

Arnica is a bitter herb that is thought to stimulate the heart and immune system. As well as being commonly used in ointment form in many countries to heal bruises, it is also used in homeopathic medicine to treat epilepsy, shock, paralysis, trauma, and throat infections. A salve of arnica was used by the Shakers.

Arnica is a creeping rhizomatous perennial and is frequently grown in rock or alpine gardens for its striking flowers.

Caution: In its natural state arnica is poisonous and can cause toxic reactions and skin irritations. In common with most medicinal herbs, it is not for self-medication.

Arnica is probably the best-known herb for treating bruises. It should be propagated by division or by seed sown in the fall. It is a plant of mountainous regions and hillsides.

vital statistics

FAMILY Compositae	**PERENNIAL ZONE 3**	**FOLIAGE** Green downy leaves forming a rosette at the base of the plant.	**SOIL** Prefers rich, light, slightly acid, well-drained soil.	**FLOWERING** Summer.
OTHER VARIETIES AND SPECIES *A. angustifolia, A. chamissonis, A. nevadensis, A. sachalinensis*	**HEIGHT** 20in (50cm)	**NATURAL HABITAT** Mountainous regions of Europe and western Asia.	**PROPAGATION** Sow seed in fall or spring. Divide in spring.	**USES** Herbal medicine.
	SPREAD 12in (30cm)			
	FLOWERS Large, single deep yellow or orange-yellow flowerheads.	**SITE** Sun.		

Artemisia abrotanum
Southernwood
lad's love, crusader herb, sagebrush

Southernwood was formerly a very popular medicinal herb, and was used to cure numerous ailments ranging from dropsy and jaundice to intestinal worms. The medieval Crusaders used it to ward off the plague, hence one of its many common names.

A. absinthium, wormwood, is one of the main ingredients of the potent French liqueur absinthe, and was also used to expel intestinal worms. Roman wormwood, *A. pontica*, was considered effective in treating stomach complaints. In the 16th century this species had such a reputation for promoting appetite that the Germans, who specialized in its production, were thought to be able to eat for hours on end without sickness or indigestion.

Artemisias are widely grown in many gardens for their lovely silver, white, and gray foliage, and a number of varieties have been developed. Among those most commonly grown are: 'Powys Castle', with deeply divided foliage; *A. absinthium*, 'Lambrook Mist', 'Lambrook Silver'; and *A. ludoviciana* var. *latiloba*.

A. abrotanum is popular with gardeners because its leaves are highly aromatic and the shrub is generally hardy. It is also often used in flower arrangements.

vital statistics

FAMILY
Asteraceae/Compositae

OTHER VARIETIES AND SPECIES
A. caucasica, A. frigida, A. lactiflora, A. ludoviciana, A. schmidtiana

DECIDUOUS OR SEMI-EVERGREEN SHRUB OR PERENNIAL
ZONE 4

HEIGHT
16–36in (40–90cm)

SPREAD
24–36in (60–90cm)

FLOWERS
Small grayish or greenish-yellow daisy-like flowers held in dense clumps.

FOLIAGE
Gray, silver or white with deeply cut or divided leaves.

NATURAL HABITAT
Dry rocky hillsides throughout North America, Europe and Asia.

SITE
Sun.

SOIL
Prefers fertile soil that must be well drained.

PROPAGATION
Sow seed in fall or spring. Divide in spring or fall. Take greenwood cuttings or heel cutting from non-flowering side shoot in summer.

FLOWERING
Summer.

USES
Medicinal, insect repellent, foliage border plant, dried flower arrangements.

Artemisia dracunculus
Tarragon
estragon

Tarragon is an herbaceous perennial that is a common and popular herb in the kitchen. Historically, it was used to cure toothache, as a treatment for snakebite, and also to help stimulate the appetite.

It is an essential flavoring in *sauce béarnaise* and *sauce verte*, and is one of the traditional herbs in *omelette aux fines herbes*. The herb also adds piquancy to all kinds of soups and fish dishes. Nowadays it is often confined to tarragon vinegar, but the best Dijon mustard is made with tarragon and *Poulet a l'estragon* is one of the classic French methods of cooking chicken. A little of the herb goes a long way. You can also use the needle-shaped leaves in salads and as a seasoning.

If you grow tarragon as a kitchen herb, cut the leaves and use them when young. Cut off the flower heads when they form. You can also dry the leaves for a supply during the fall and winter. Strip the leaves from the plant when drying is complete and store them in airtight bottles. French tarragon is not totally hardy and protection may be needed in hard winters in cold areas. Do not confuse *A. dracunculus*, French tarragon, with *A. dracunculoides*, Russian tarragon. This has relatively little flavor, is rather bitter, and is also difficult to dry successfully.

Tarragon is a popular herb for the kitchen and can easily be dried and kept over winter. Use sparingly, the flavor goes a long way.

vital statistics

FAMILY
Compositae

OTHER VARIETIES AND SPECIES
A. absinthium (wormwood),
A. abrotanum (southernwood)

PERENNIAL ZONE 4–5

HEIGHT
2–3ft (60–90cm)

SPREAD
2ft (60cm)

FLOWERS
Insignificant, white or gray.

FOLIAGE
Lance-shaped, light to mid-green leaves.

NATURAL HABITAT
Dry hillsides in North America, Europe, and central Asia.

SITE
Sunny.

SOIL
Light, well drained.

PROPAGATION
Divide roots in spring (the most successful method) or take softwood cuttings in summer.

FLOWERING
Summer.

USES
Culinary.

Artemisia vulgaris

Mugwort

felon herb, sailor's tobacco

One of the oldest herbs used in medicine, mugwort was usually infused as a tea to cure stomach ailments and to treat menstrual disorders. It was also prescribed to hasten delivery during childbirth. It was considered to be a cure for sciatica and an antidote for overindulgence in opium. Today mugwort is an ingredient in insect repellents, and it has been used in Chinese medicine as a treatment for rheumatism for thousands of years.

The plant's fine, feathery foliage is attractive in rock gardens. Occasionally, mugwort used to find its way into the kitchen as a flavoring in meat dishes. It is seldom used nowadays and is definitely not recommended. The Latin name comes from the Greek hunter goddess Artemis.

Caution: Artemisia is potentially toxic. Use only *A. dracunculus* or *A. dracunculoides* (Russian tarragon) in the kitchen.

All artemisias are potentially toxic except *A. dracunculus* and *A. dracunculoides*, Russian tarragon. It should only be used in medicine by qualified practitioners.

vital statistics

FAMILY
Compositae (daisy).

OTHER VARIETIES AND SPECIES
A. dracunculus (tarragon),
A. absinthium (wormwood),
A. abrotanum (southernwood).

PERENNIAL ZONE 4

HEIGHT
6ft (1.8m).

SPREAD
18in (45cm).

FLOWERS
Small, reddish-brown.

FOLIAGE
Fine, silvery foliage, often aromatic.

NATURAL HABITAT
Native of central Europe.

SITE
Open and sunny.

SOIL
Light, well-drained.

PROPAGATION
Sow seed in situ in spring or take cuttings in summer.

FLOWERING
Late summer.

USES
Herbal medicine, culinary.

Asclepias tuberosa
Pleurisy root
butterfly milkweed, Canada root, fluxroot, swallow-wort, tuber root

The asclepias are a large group of plants that come mostly from North and South America and southern Africa. They are both evergreen and deciduous, and the genus contains both subshrubs and perennials. A number of the species have medicinal properties and were formerly used by Native Americans to treat a wide variety of illness-es. The name of the plant comes from the Greek God Aesculapius, the god of healing. The long, tuberous root is used in herbal medicine in the treatment of chest complaints and pleurisy.

The plants have brightly colored flowers that are attractive to bees, and they are good plants for herbaceous borders or a wildflower garden. Some species are hardy but others require pro-tection during hard winters if they are grown in areas prone to severe frosts.

A. tuberosa has bright orange-red flowers held in flat clumps at the end of long, unbranched stems. The flowers are followed by fruit in the fall. The leaves are arranged in a spiral around the stalk and are bright green, thin, and lance-shaped. Like all milkweeds, the sap of the pleurisy root is acrid and may cause some skin irritation. Use gloves when handling the plant.

Caution: The plant is potentially poisonous and must not be taken at home in any form.

Although toxic to handle, the plant is a treatment for pleurisy and chest complaints.

---

vital statistics

FAMILY Asclepiadaceae	**PERENNIAL ZONE 4**	**FOLIAGE** Mid- to light green, long and lance-shaped, held in spirals.	**SOIL** Well-drained, sandy soil mixed with gravel.	**FLOWERING** Summer to early fall.
OTHER VARIETIES AND SPECIES *A. curassavica, A. hallii, A. incarnata, A. speciosa, A. syriaca*	**HEIGHT** 36in (90cm) **SPREAD** 12in (30cm)	**NATURAL HABITAT** Dry areas on the prairies of North America. **SITE** Full sun.	**PROPAGATION** Sow seed in fall or spring. Divide in spring. Take root cuttings in spring.	**USES** Formerly medicinal, cut flowers.
	FLOWERS Brilliant red-orange flowers held in flat clumps.			

Atriplex hortensis
Orache
red orache

This plant is an extremely useful herb from a fairly large genus. Many of the species can be found growing in the wild in North America and Europe. Various species have had a number of uses in herbal medicine through the ages. Leaves of the plant were used to treat sore throats and jaundice. It was also taken as a tonic and as a cure for menstrual problems.

The species most commonly cultivated is *A. hortensis*, a half-hardy annual that has green, yellow, or reddish-purple leaves. Grow this plant together with other plants that have ornamental leaves in summer flower beds. You could also use a clump of plants to make an impact in an herbaceous border. The most striking variety is *A. h.* var. *rubra*, which has blood-red or purple-red foliage and flowering spikes. The flowers of this plant are upright and feathery, and are usually green or brown.

You can grow orache as a vegetable. Harvest the leaves for use in salads or for cooking and eating like spinach. If you are growing them for the kitchen, make sure the plants have plenty of water. Pick the leaves when they are young, as the older ones become tough and stringy. If the plant is allowed to mature, the stems can be cut and used in dried flower arrangements.

Orache is both a culinary and medicinal plant. It is also grown in herbaceous borders for its decorative qualities.

vital statistics

FAMILY
Chenopodiaceae.

OTHER VARIETIES AND SPECIES
A. hortensis var. rubra, A.h. green-leaved, *A.h.* gold-leaved, *A. patula* (common orache), *A. littoralis* (grass-leaved orache)

HALF-HARDY ANNUAL

HEIGHT
4ft (1.2m)

SPREAD
12in (30cm)

FLOWERS
Small red or green spikes of flowers, depending on the species grown.

FOLIAGE
Spinach-like, succulent, red to green, triangular leaves growing from the stem. The leaves may be 17in (18cm) long.

NATURAL HABITAT
Wasteland and coastal regions throughout Europe.

SITE
Open, sunny.

SOIL
Moist, well drained.

PROPAGATION
Sow seed in spring when the soil temperature has reached 50°F (10°C). Thin plants to 18in (45cm). Water in dry periods to prevent bolting.

FLOWERING
Summer to early fall.

USES
Culinary, formerly medicinal, dried flowers.

Atropa belladonna ⊕❀⊗🌿○
Deadly nightshade
belladonna, dwale, poison black cherry

One of the most popular plants of the medieval poisoner, deadly nightshade must be treated with extreme caution. In the Middle Ages it was applied as a poultice and today it is used for muscle spasms.

This is one of the most poisonous plants that exists and no part of the plant should be consumed in any way under any circumstances. On no account should this plant be cultivated anywhere that children or cattle frequent.

Although it is such a poisonous plant, a drug produced from the leaves and roots is extremely important to medicine. The plant contains a number of alkaloids that have narcotic, diuretic, and sedative properties. These are used to make treatments for a number of complaints, including muscle spasms.

It is the largest of the nightshades and reaches 3ft (90cm) in height. It has a long stem, with big, oval green leaves in unequal pairs, the lower being smaller than the upper one. The flowers are trumpet-like and purple, and are followed by the large, shiny black berries. It can be found growing wild on wasteland and woods in northern Europe.

This plant is a member of the potato family and is easily confused with common or black nightshade, *Solanum nigrum*.

Caution: Extremely poisonous.

---

vital statistics

FAMILY	PERENNIAL	FOLIAGE	SOIL	FLOWERING
Solanaceae	ZONE 5	Round, oval, green leaves in unequal pairs growing from the main stem.	Moist, well-drained.	Summer.
OTHER VARIETIES AND SPECIES	**HEIGHT**		**PROPAGATION**	**USES**
Solanum nigrum (black nightshade), *S. dulcamara* (woody nightshade), *S. crispum* (potato vine)	3ft (90cm)		Not advised under any circumstances.	Medicinal.
	SPREAD	**NATURAL HABITAT**		
	18in (45cm)	Wasteland in Europe.		
	FLOWERS	**SITE**		
	Long, tubular purple flowers followed by large, black fruit.	Open, sunny.		

Baptisia australis
Blue wild indigo

Although the original name of this plant comes from the Greek, *bapto*, meaning "to dye," true indigo color comes from several species of the subtropical shrubs *Indigofera*, a number of which can be found in gardens in temperate regions. Roots of baptisia, or blue wild indigo, were used by the Native Americans as a tea, and the leaves were made into a poultice to cure sores.

Baptisia comes from eastern North America, where it can mainly be found in dry woodland and grassland. It is a spreading perennial with attractive green leaves, rather like large clover leaves. Its erect blue spikes of pea-like flowers, sometimes marked white or cream, emerge in the early summer. These are followed by large pods that contain the seeds. Use it as a decorative plant in an herbaceous border or a wild flower garden, where it contributes good color early in the gardening year.

One of the most attractive and colorful of all herbs, the blue wild indigo plant has prominent spikes of purple-blue flowers in early summer. It is seldom used as a dye plant, but the roots were made into a popular herbal tea by Native Americans and the leaves used as a poultice to treat wounds.

vital statistics

FAMILY
Leguminosae/Papilionaceae

OTHER VARIETIES AND SPECIES
B. alba, B. bracteata, B. lactea, B. tinctoria

PERENNIAL ZONE 4

HEIGHT
3–5ft (90–1.5m)

SPREAD
30in (60cm)

FLOWERS
Deep blue, pea-like flowers held upright on a long stalk.

FOLIAGE
Deep green, clover-like leaves divided in three.

NATURAL HABITAT
Open woodland and dry grassland in North America.

SITE
Sun.

SOIL
Rich, dry and open.

PROPAGATION
Sow seeds in early spring or in the fall when ripe. Soak the seeds overnight in warm water before sowing. Divide the plants in spring or fall.

FLOWERING
Early summer.

USES
Formerly medicinal, dye plant.

Bellis perennis
Lawn daisy
English daisy, wild daisy

The common lawn daisy has a number of uses in herbal medicine and was formerly employed as an antiseptic.

Nowadays most of the daisies found in gardens are the lovely ornamental daisies grown as annuals and found in many bedding schemes and containers. The common daisy of lawns and pastures, *Bellis perennis*, ancestor of the beautiful bedding plants of today, was a popular herb with many uses in medieval times.

Today the leaves are sometimes prescribed by homeopathic practitioners as a soothing tea. In homeopathic medicine the herb is also recommended for the relief of internal inflammation and wounds, and as an antiseptic lotion to bathe cuts, sores, ulcers, wounds, and bruises. In medieval times a decoction of the leaves taken internally and a poultice of the leaves applied externally were used to treat tuberculosis of the lymphatic glands. Another of its properties was to dissolve congealed or coagulated blood. It was also used in the treatment of pleurisy and pneumonia, and an infusion boiled in asses' milk was believed to be effective in treating consumption of the lungs.

vital statistics

FAMILY Asteraceae/Compositae	**PERENNIAL ZONE 3**	**FOLIAGE** Deep green, oval-shaped, ground-hugging rosette	**SOIL** Fertile, well-drained	**FLOWERING** Spring to summer.
OTHER VARIETIES AND SPECIES *B. p.* Pomponette, Roggli and Tasso Series.	**HEIGHT** 3in (7.5cm)	**NATURAL HABITAT** Lawns and pasture in northern Europe and Asia.	**PROPAGATION** Sow seeds in early spring or summer.	**USES** Herbal medicine, culinary.
	SPREAD 4in (10cm)	**SITE** Sun or partial shade.		
	FLOWERS White-fringed, many-petaled, with yellow centers.			

Borago officinalis
Borage
bugloss, burrage

Borage's bright blue, star-shaped flowers turn pink with age. The plants provide a good splash of color in an herb garden, although the tall stems may need staking.

Borage is an attractive herb to grow in the backyard. The whole plant appears to be covered with a myriad of hairs, and the flowers—the main glory of the plant—emerge from narrow hanging hairy bells into bright blue stars with a pale center.

It is a fine herb for the kitchen. Try using it to flavor summer drinks, especially fruit and wine cups—the blue flowers add a cucumber flavor. You can also use the leaves in salads and add the flowers for decoration. The flowers are sometimes candied or fried in batter.

Borage was formerly an important medicinal herb and a number of properties were attributed to it. The roots were used to cure coughs, catarrh, and other chest infections; distilled water made from the leaves helped to relieve sore eyes and throats; and the seed and leaves were a folk remedy for increasing the supply of milk in nursing mothers. It was also helpful in cases of ringworm and other sores. Traditionally, borage was thought to have beneficial effects on both the heart and the mind. It was considered a cure for heart disease, and was used to treat people suffering from depression.

It is a substantial plant, most attractive to bees and therefore a favorite of beekeepers. Borage grows well in most soils and most conditions, but it does prefer sunny spots. It is fast growing, and will reach 2–3ft (60–90cm) in favorable conditions.

vital statistics

FAMILY
Boraginaceae.

OTHER VARIETIES AND SPECIES
B. Alba (white flowers), B. pygmaea

HARDY ANNUAL

HEIGHT
2–3ft (60–90cm)

SPREAD
18in (45cm)

FLOWERS
Blue, star-shaped flowers that turn pink with age.

FOLIAGE
Dull green leaves that give off a cucumber scent. They are exceptionally hairy.

NATURAL HABITAT
Native of Mediterranean.

SITE
Open, sunny.

SOIL
Most reasonable fertile well-drained soils.

PROPAGATION
Sow seeds in late spring. The plants will need staking. Place the seedlings 1ft (30cm) apart. They have a long taproot.

FLOWERING
Summer.

USES
Culinary, formerly medicinal.

Buxus sempervirens
Common box
boxwood, bush tree

Box is sometimes used in homeopathic medicine to treat fevers and rheumatism, and the leaves produce a red dye. It is an extremely useful garden plant and is grown everywhere, either as low, formal, evergreen hedges in a kitchen or herb garden, or trimmed into topiary shapes and planted in containers as focal points in town and country gardens. Prune this evergreen, oval-leafed plant frequently.

There are a number of excellent varieties, notably 'Elegantissima', which is dense with white margined leaves; 'Latifolia Maculata', dark green foliage marked with yellow; and 'Suffruticosa', compact and slow-growing. In the 18th and 19th centuries boxwood was much used in furniture making, as well as in the manufacture of mathematical and other scientific instruments. This was because it is particularly hard and dense, and does not shrink and expand as much as other woods when subjected to changes in atmospheric pressure. It was also the wood that was often used for wood engraving.

Caution: The plant is toxic and should never be used at home for medical purposes: The sap of the leaves may cause skin irritations.

The flowers of common box are inconspicuous. The plant is grown for its dense foliage, ideal for topiary and hedging.

---

vital statistics

FAMILY Buxaceae	**EVERGREEN ZONE 4**	**FOLIAGE** Small, leathery, rounded, evergreen leaves that may be variegated, according to the variety grown. The plant withstands frequent clipping.	**SITE** Partial shade.	**FLOWERING** Spring.
OTHER VARIETIES AND SPECIES *B. balearica, B. microphylla, B. s. 'Elegantissima', B. s. 'Handsworthiensis', B. s 'Marginata', B. s. 'Suffruticosa'*	**HEIGHT** 16ft (5m) maximum. **SPREAD** 16ft (5m) maximum. **FLOWERS** Small, star-shaped, yellow-green flowers.	**NATURAL HABITAT** Hills and woodland throughout Europe and northern Africa.	**SOIL** Most reasonable fertile well-drained soils. **PROPAGATION** Semi-ripe cuttings in late summer, layering.	**USES** Herbal medicine.

Calamintha sylvatica
Woodland calamint

Calamint was a well-known herb in medieval times, but nowadays is seldom used in herbal medicine. It is an attractive garden plant and the name comes from the Greek, *kalaminthe*, meaning "beautiful mint."

The plant is frequently grown in an herbaceous border or in a rock garden where the scented leaves can be appreciated. Its small clusters of flowers attract bees and butterflies.

The woodland calamint has pale pink to lilac, tubular flowers on upright stalks with broad, pointed leaves that smell of mint when they are crushed. *C. grandiflora* is the species most commonly grown today in herb gardens, where it makes a bushy plant and the pink flowers remain on the plant for some considerable time—from early summer to mid-fall.

You can use calamint in the kitchen to flavor roast meat or to make a pleasant herbal tea. In medieval times the herb was used to cure stomach ailments, as an antidote to sickness, and as a cure for leprosy. It was also used to hinder conception and to induce abortions. In addition, it was used as a cure for depression.

Caution: It should not be taken in any form by pregnant women.

Common calamint had a number of uses in herbal medicine but is now seldom used. The leaves can be used to make an herbal tea.

vital statistics

FAMILY Labiatae	**PERENNIAL** **ZONE 4**	**FOLIAGE** Bushy rhizomatous perennial with green pointed, round (ovate) leaves, lighter green below.	**SOIL** Most reasonably fertile well-drained soils.	**FLOWERING** Summer.
OTHER VARIETIES AND SPECIES *C. cretica, C. grandiflora, C. nepeta, C. n. ssp. nepeta*	**HEIGHT** 18in (45cm)		**PROPAGATION** Sow seed in a cold frame in spring, or divide established plants in spring.	**USES** Formerly medicinal, culinary.
	SPREAD 18in (45 cm)	**NATURAL HABITAT** Light woodland throughout Europe and the Middle East.		
	FLOWERS Clusters of tubular pink flowers.	**SITE** Partial shade.		

Calendula officinalis
Pot marigold
garden marigold, holigold, marigold, Mary bud

Pot marigolds are one of the most colorful of all herbs and among the easiest annuals to grow. Try the young leaves in salads (they are slightly bitter), and sprinkle the flowers on salads and soups as garnish. You can also dry the flowers and use them as food coloring. The Latin name comes from *Calendae*, meaning "first day of the month," because they can be found in flower for most months of the year.

Medicinally, the pot marigold had many uses. A tea was made from the flowers and taken to soothe all manner of gastric complaints, including colitis and ulcers. However, its main use was as an ointment to treat burns, scalds, bruises, and other wounds. The Shakers regarded calendula ointment as a treatment for gangrene.

These plants are members of the daisy family, and have attractive orange and yellow flower heads. Many varieties are available. They used to be grown as a vegetable but this is not so common nowadays. The pot marigold should not be confused with other marigolds, which are classified under *Tagetes*.

Pot marigolds were widely used in the kitchen and in the herbarium to flavor dishes and treat a number of ailments.

vital statistics

FAMILY
Asteraceae/Compositae

OTHER VARIETIES AND SPECIES
Many cultivars including *C. o. Bon Bon Series, C. o. Pacific Beauty Series* and *C. o. Prince Series*

PERENNIAL ZONE 3
Usually grown as an annual.

HEIGHT
1–2ft (30–60cm)

SPREAD
8in (20cm)

FLOWERS
Pale to deep orange.

FOLIAGE
Pale green, pointed or spoon-shaped hairy leaves

NATURAL HABITAT
Arable and wasteland. Native of southern Europe and North Africa.

SITE
Sunny.

SOIL
Most garden soils.

PROPAGATION
Sow seeds in situ in spring. Thin seedlings to 6in (15cm) apart.

FLOWERING
Summer.

USES
Culinary, herbal medicine, dye plant.

Calluna vulgaris
Heather
ling, Scotch heather

A genus consisting of just one species, the common purple heather of Scotland is naturalized in North America, and can be found in mountain regions throughout Europe. It is widely used in herbal medicine.

It has been developed as a garden plant and there are now over 500 varieties available, with varied foliage ranging from green to gold, and flowers ranging in color from deep pink to white. It will flourish only in acid, peaty soil, and does not tolerate lime. Heather flowers at the end of summer and the flowers remain on the shrub for four to six weeks.

In the highland regions of Scotland the stems were used as brooms or as roofing thatch. Heather still has a considerable reputation as a medicinal plant in primitive regions. It has both sedative and antiseptic properties. An infusion made from the stems of the dried flowers was used to treat coughs and colds, and for kidney and urinary infections. It was also held to be effective in the treatment of rheumatism and arthritis, when sprigs of heather added to the bathwater helped to relieve the pain. Bees love the flowers, and heather honey is much sought after for its healing properties.

Common heather, *Calluna vulgaris*, is purple. Many garden varieties have been developed with red to white flowers. It is still used as a medicinal plant in many primitive areas.

vital statistics

FAMILY Ericaceae	**EVERGREEN** **ZONE 3**	**FOLIAGE** Green, becoming deep purple-brown in winter.	**SOIL** Acid and peaty..	**FLOWERING** Late summer.
OTHER VARIETIES AND SPECIES Many garden varieties are available.	**HEIGHT** 4–24in (10–60cm)	**NATURAL HABITAT** Europe and western Asia.	**PROPAGATION** Take semi-ripe cuttings in summer. Layer in spring.	**USES** Herbal medicine, bee plant.
	SPREAD 12–60in (30–75cm)	**SITE** Sun.		
	FLOWERS Generally purple with pink, red, and white varieties.			

Caltha palustris
Marsh marigold
American cowslip, meadowbright, palsywort, water dragon

The marsh marigold is a popular plant for the margins of water gardens or other moist sites. The yellow flowers that emerge in late spring are a sure sign that summer is on the way. The plant was formerly used in herbal medicine to treat warts. The name *Caltha* is derived from the Greek *kalathos*, meaning "goblet." This refers to its saucer-like flowers, which grow to up to 2in (5cm) wide.

The plant is rhizomatous and spreads quickly, forming a dense clump. It is invasive and you may need to control it. The leaves are kidney-shaped and dark green. There are a number of varieties, but the most commonly grown is 'Flore Pleno', which has large double flowers.

You can plant marsh marigolds in the water itself—they will grow in depths of up to 8in (20cm), but they prefer moist margins. They like a sunny or partially shaded position. Plant seeds in a cold frame in winter or fall. Once established, the plants can be divided after they have flowered or in the fall.

Caution: All parts are an irritant and gloves should be worn when handling them.

The giant buttercup-shaped flowers and large lily-like leaves of the marsh marigold form full, golden borders along water gardens, marshes, and river banks.

---

vital statistics

FAMILY
Ranunculaceae

OTHER VARIETIES AND SPECIES
C. natans, C. palustris var. *alba, C. p.* var. *palustris, C. p.* var. *radicans* 'Flore Pleno'

PERENNIAL ZONE 3

HEIGHT
4–16in (10–40cm)

SPREAD
18in (45cm)

FLOWERS
Bright yellow, goblet shaped, like a large buttercup.

FOLIAGE
Dark green, kidney-shaped leaves with notched edges.

NATURAL HABITAT
Ponds and marshland in the northern hemisphere.

SITE
Sun.

SOIL
Moist, rich and boggy.

PROPAGATION
Sow seed as soon as it is ripe in damp compost. Divide in spring or late summer.

FLOWERING
Spring.

USES
Formerly medicinal.

Campanula rapunculoides
Rampion bellflower

This culinary herb was cultivated as a root vegetable in the 16th and 17th centuries. It is closely related to spiked or horned rampion, *Phyteuma spicatum*, a medicinal herb whose leaves were boiled with milk, the resulting drink acting as a diuretic (increasing the flow of urine). Horned rampion was also used to treat jaundice and for infections of the liver and gall bladder.

Rampion bellflower has thin, lance-shaped leaves growing from a strong purple stalk. This has a milky sap. The plants die down in the winter to a rosette of leaves at the base.

The plant may reach 3ft (90cm) in height. It is a biennial and in the summer of the second year it carries purple or blue star-shaped flowers that are smaller than the majority of the bellflowers.

If you are growing the plant as a vegetable, sow the seed in the spring. Then thin the young plants to 6in (15cm). In cold areas, lift and store them in the fall before the first frost of winter. Once established, the plant can become invasive. Try the roots in salads in the summer, cooked or eaten raw.

Rampion bellflower is found on wasteland and prefers sandy places. Try the roots in salads as an unusual addition.

vital statistics

FAMILY Campanulaceae	**BIENNIAL** ZONE 4	**FOLIAGE** Thin, lance-shaped green leaves that are broader and oval at the base of the plant.	**SOIL** Fertile, well-drained.	**FLOWERING** Summer.
OTHER VARIETIES AND SPECIES *C. glomerata, C. lactiflora, C. latifolia, C. persicifolia, C. rapunculoides, Phyteuma orbiculare, P. spicatum*	**HEIGHT** 3ft (90cm) **SPREAD** 18in (45cm)	**NATURAL HABITAT** Meadows in the northern hemisphere.	**PROPAGATION** Sow seed in spring.	**USES** Culinary, formerly medicinal.
	FLOWERS Light blue to purple, star-shaped.	**SITE** Grown as a vegetable, it does best in partial shade.		

Cardamine pratensis

Cuckoo flower
lady's smock

This delicate, charming perennial owes its common name to the arrival of the cuckoo in spring, which supposedly coincides with the opening of the first flowers. The Latin name of the plant comes from the Greek *cardia*, meaning "heart," and *damao*, "strengthen," and refers to its herbal properties as a heart tonic and a cure for heart troubles. It is also used to treat skin complaints and asthma.

It is one of the most common wildflowers and occurs naturally in moist sites and meadowland in North America and Europe. The blooms are pink, lilac, or white, and are held upright in sprays on thin stalks.

It is chiefly used as a culinary rather than a medicinal herb. You can add the leaves to salads, as they have a pleasant hot flavor with a hint of mustard, and the plant can be grown for this purpose in gardens. Nowadays it is chiefly grown as a flowering perennial in shaded, moist herbaceous borders. A number of varieties have been developed, such as 'Edith', with double flowers that fade from pink to white, and 'Flore Pleno', with double lilac-pink flowers.

Pale-shaded, pretty flowers with rosettes of leaves characterize the cuckoo flower, which can be seen growing in moist woodland, meadows, and streamsides.

vital statistics

FAMILY
Brassicaceae/Cruciferae

OTHER VARIETIES AND SPECIES
C. p. 'Flore Pleno', *C. trifolia*

PERENNIAL ZONE 3

HEIGHT
12in (30cm)

SPREAD
9in (23cm)

FLOWERS
Purple, lilac, or white flowers.

FOLIAGE
Lower leaves are rounded or kidney shaped.

NATURAL HABITAT
Moist meadows and woods with open spaces. Native of North America, Europe, and northern Asia.

SITE
Partial shade.

SOIL
Moist soil.

PROPAGATION
Sow seed in a cold frame in summer or fall, and plant out in spring. Plants can be divided after flowering. Take semiripe cuttings in late summer and grow under cover in winter.

FLOWERING
Spring to early summer.

USES
Culinary, formerly medicinal.

Carthamus tinctorius
Safflower
American saffron, dyers' saffron, false saffron

An attractive addition to the herb garden, the flowers of safflower have been used for centuries as a dye. The plant is grown commercially for its seeds, which produce oil used for cooking and for cholesterol-reducing diets. The herb is also used to treat coronary artery disease and to help with menstrual or menopausal problems. It is widely sold as a health-food product. In medieval Europe the herb was used to clear the phlegm from the lungs of people suffering from pulmonary consumption.

Safflowers are decorative annuals: Plant them in a group as a colorful feature in an herb garden from summer into fall. The bright yellow-orange flowers, shaped like thistles and surrounded by green bracts, are held upright above bright green spiny leaves. The flowers produce both yellow and pinkish-red dyes, traditionally used to dye the robes of Buddhist monks. Use them as a dye at home or dry the flowers and save them for winter flower arrangements.

This popular herb has many uses in herbal medicine and is valued as a treatment for heart disease. It produces the saffron dye used to color the robes of Buddhist monks.

vital statistics

FAMILY Compositae/Asteraceae	**HALF-HARDY ANNUAL** **ZONE 6–7**	**FOLIAGE** Lance-shaped, spiny green leaves growing from the main stalk.	**SOIL** Light, well drained.	**FLOWERING** Summer.
OTHER VARIETIES AND SPECIES *C. t.* 'Lasting White', *C. t.* 'Orange Ball', *C. t.* 'Summer Sun'	**HEIGHT** 2–3ft (60–90cm) **SPREAD** 9in (23cm)	**NATURAL HABITAT** Dry land around the Mediterranean and western Asia.	**PROPAGATION** Sow seed at 50–59°F (10–15°C) from early to late spring. Plant out when all danger of frosts has passed.	**USES** Culinary, dye, dried flowers, herbal medicine.
	FLOWERS Red, yellow, and orange thistle-like flowers.	**SITE** Sun.		

Carum carvi
Caraway

Caraway is a small plant that belongs to the carrot family and is very similar to dill and fennel. It has been used in herbal medicine for centuries for cases of colic in babies and small children, as a cure for indigestion, and to promote gas. Nicholas Culpeper, the famous 17th-century English herbalist, also considered that it improved eyesight.

The plant has small white flower heads and fine feathery, fern-like foliage. It has long white roots that you can lift and cook as a vegetable. These have much the same flavor as parsnips, only somewhat stronger. The commonest use for caraway in the kitchen is the dried seeds that have a distinctive, pungent taste. Use these to flavor cakes and bread, particularly rye bread, and a number of cooked meats, such as goulash and sausages. They are also used to flavor the liqueurs kümmel and schnapps, and are sprinkled over cooked cabbage.

Caraway grows well in most soils, and likes full sun. It makes attractive ground cover. Sow young plants in spring or late summer so that they can establish themselves over winter. The flowers and then the seeds will follow the next summer. Gather the seed when it is ripe. You can also cut the leaves when they are young and use them in salads.

Caraway was mentioned in the Bible and has been cultivated for over 5,000 years.

FAMILY	BIENNIAL ZONE 3–4	FOLIAGE	SOIL	FLOWERING
Apiaceae/Umbelliferae		Fern-like, fine green.	Light, well-drained soil.	Summer.
	HEIGHT			
OTHER VARIETIES AND SPECIES	12–30in (30–75cm)	NATURAL HABITAT	PROPAGATION	USES
None		Dry grassland and meadows. Native of Europe and Asia.	Sow seeds in late summer in situ. Thin to 6in (15cm) apart. It will carry flower heads and seeds in its second year.	Culinary, formerly medicinal.
	SPREAD			
	12in (30cm)	SITE		
		Full sun.		
	FLOWERS			
	Small and white.			

Cedronella canariensis
Herb of Gilead

This herb is grown for the cedar-like scent, which gives it its Latin name. The leaves of the plant can be dried and used to make a scented tea. It has no connection with the fragrant poplars referred to as Balm of Gilead, nor the original Balm of Gilead, *Balsamodendron opobalsamum*, a rare tree that grows in countries bordering the Red Sea.

It is a half-hardy or greenhouse evergreen perennial or subshrub that comes from the Canary Islands, off the northwestern coast of Africa. The plant has square stems that rise to a height of 18–36in (45–90cm). Its small and fragrant leaves are topped by spikes of large, tubular, white, pink, or lilac flowers, which appear in spring and summer.

The leaves give off their cedarwood scent when they are crushed, and the plant is used as an insect repellent in hot countries. In temperate climates you can grow the plant outside as an annual. Give it a warm, sheltered place in an herb garden or patio, and bring it into a cool conservatory or greenhouse during the cold weather. It needs a minimum winter temperature of 41°F (5°C). You can use both the leaves and the flowers of the plant for potpourri.

This fragrant plant is best grown as a container plant in temperate climates, for it will not survive a frost. It has fragrant leaves and pretty pink flowers.

vital statistics

FAMILY
Labiatae

OTHER VARIETIES AND SPECIES
None

PERENNIAL ZONE 7–8

HEIGHT
3ft (90cm)

SPREAD
2ft (60cm)

FLOWERS
Two-lipped white, pink, or lilac held in long clusters.

FOLIAGE
Light green, aromatic leaves with three lobes, toothed.

NATURAL HABITAT
Sunny rocky slopes on the Canary Islands.

SITE
Full sun.

SOIL
Light, well-drained soil.

PROPAGATION
Sow seeds in the spring.

FLOWERING
Summer.

USES
Insect repellent, tea, potpourri.

Centaurea cyanus
Cornflower

bachelor's button, bluebonnet, bluebottle, blue centaury, cyani, hurtsickle

Cornflowers are hardy annuals available in blue, claret, red, or pink. The juice of the cornflower, or a distillation of the leaves, was formerly used to heal ulcers, sores, and wounds. It was also used as an eyewash to treat inflammation of the eyes.

The traditional color of the cornflower is deep blue, and many gardeners prefer to grow this color and no other. Before modern farming practices eliminated unwanted weeds, it was an herb commonly found in cornfields, hence its common name "hurtsickle," for the tough stems blunted the sickles of the reapers.

The leaves are gray-green, hairy underneath, long and thin. The flowers are thistle-like and carried on long stalks, with numerous small blue petals surrounding a darker center. Cornflowers are popular annuals for the summer border. Sow them in situ in the spring (or fall the previous year), and then thin them if necessary. A number of series have been developed, including the Standard Tall Group and Baby Series, but individual varieties are available, such as 'Blue Diadem', 'Blue Ball', and 'Florence Blue', and these are often preferred.

You can dry the flower heads for use in potpourris. Also, add the petals to salads as a garnish. A blue ink is produced from the juice of the petals, and extracts from the cornflower are used in hair preparations.

Swathes of the tall-stemmed cornflower grow, predictably, in cornfields but also in gardens. Its petals can be used to make a watercolor paint.

vital statistics

FAMILY
Compositae

OTHER VARIETIES AND SPECIES
C. cyanus Baby Series,
C. c. Florence Series

HARDY ANNUAL

HEIGHT
9–36in (25–90cm)

SPREAD
6–10in (15–25cm)

FLOWERS
Usually bright blue, daisy-like with a darker center.

FOLIAGE
Gray-green, lance-shaped, hairy, alternate.

NATURAL HABITAT
Native of parts of North America, Europe, and the Mediterranean. Found in cornfields and on wasteland.

SITE
Full sun.

SOIL
Fertile, alkaline loam.

PROPAGATION
Sow seeds in the spring or fall in situ.

FLOWERING
Summer.

USES
Herbal medicine, dried flowers, potpourri, bee plant.

Centaurea scabiosa

Greater knapweed

greater knapweed

This is a larger plant than its relative, the cornflower (*Centaurea cyanus*), and bears a large thistle-like, scaly green head crowned with deep purple to red flowers. In medieval times greater knapweed was used by herbalists, and a distillation was made from the roots and applied to sores and ulcers. It was also considered an excellent bruise herb, and a decoction was both drunk and applied outwardly to the affected part. It was also used as a cure for sore throats.

After flowering, the seed head opens to reveal its shiny black seeds lying in a bed of thistle-like down, which carries them away on the wind. You can grow knapweed in the garden as a specimen plant, but it is most often found growing wild in limestone soil, in moist places on banks, and along the verges of highways. They thrive even in poor soils, but like chalky spots in full sun. The plant reaches 4ft (1.2m) in height and spreads widely, each branch topped by a single flower. Their upright stems look good in borders and beds, but the plant likes plenty of space.

The large, colorful flowers attract bees and butterflies. You can cut and dry the flowers and stems to make winter flower arrangements.

The greater knapweed is a common wild plant. Centaureas are named after the mythological centaur, Chiron, renowned for his knowledge of herbs.

vital statistics

FAMILY
Compositae

OTHER VARIETIES AND SPECIES
C. nigra, C. nemoralis, C. cyanus

PERENNIAL ZONE 3

HEIGHT
12–36in (30–90cm)

SPREAD
24in (60cm)

FLOWERS
Large, deep crimson, thistle-like.

FOLIAGE
Mid-green, deeply lobed. The lower leaves form a large rosette, the upper leaves are stalkless.

NATURAL HABITAT
Native of northern Europe. Found on grass and scrubland.

SITE
Full sun.

SOIL
Moist, well-drained.

PROPAGATION
Sow seeds in the spring or fall.

FLOWERING
Summer.

USES
Formerly medicinal, specimen garden plant.

Centaurium erythraea

European centaury
bitterherb, centaury, lesser centaury

Centaury is a delicate plant with clusters of small star-shaped, carnation-pink flowers held aloft on stalks. It is used in homeopathic medicine for the treatment of liver and gall bladder complaints.

The plant is found on wasteland or dunes, and flourishes on poor, dry, alkaline soils. The flowers are sensitive to the light and open best on bright sunny days and close at night, or as Nicholas Culpeper, the 17th-century English herbalist, put it more poetically, "their flowers open and shut as the sun either showeth or hideth his face." The leaves are gray-green, rounded with prominent veins, and form a rosette at the base of the plant.

A tonic made from this herb was much used in former times, in spite of its extremely bitter taste. It was taken as a tea to tone up the liver, ease difficult or painful menstruation, help in cases of jaundice and hepatitis, and increase the appetite. It was also thought to be effective in lowering the temperature in cases of fever, and the juice of the herb mixed with honey was applied to the eyes to clear the sight. It is also one of the ingredients of vermouth.

One of the common names of this plant indicates its properties. The herb is extremely bitter to the taste and was described by Culpeper as "wholesome but not toothsome."

FAMILY
Gentianaceae

OTHER VARIETIES AND SPECIES
C. Scilloides

BIENNIAL OR SHORT-LIVED PERENNIAL ZONE 4

HEIGHT
12in (30cm)

SPREAD
4in (10cm)

FLOWERS
Small, star-shaped, deep pink.

FOLIAGE
Gray-green, basal, forming a rosette at the base of the plant.

NATURAL HABITAT
Dry grassland of Europe and western Asia.

SITE
Full sun.

SOIL
Dry, poor, alkaline.

PROPAGATION
Sow seeds in the spring or fall. Self-seeds. Divide in spring.

FLOWERING
Late summer.

USES
Herbal medicine, culinary.

Centranthus ruber
Red valerian

This is a common garden plant and flourishes in dry alkaline soils. It is a useful culinary herb and should not be confused with true valerian (*Valeriana officinalis*), which has many useful herbal properties. The name comes from the Greek, *kentron*, meaning "a spur," and *anthos*, "a flower," and refers to the shape of the flowers.

The leaves are long, pointed, and fleshy, and the flowers are held in clumps at the end of the leaf stalks, several of which rise from the base of the plant. The flowers are usually pink or red, although there is a white form, *C. r. albus*. This is less vigorous than the species plant.

Grow valerian either in an herbaceous border or near dry walls, where it will seed itself freely. Its persistent roots allow it to survive in barren spots. The leaves are very succulent: Pick and eat them in salads or lightly boil them in the same way as spinach. In France the roots are used to make soup.

These blood red flowers make a distinctive display against a wall. The colorful clusters attract butterflies and other insects.

vital statistics

FAMILY Valerianaceae	**PERENNIAL ZONE 4**	**FOLIAGE** Green, pointed, and fleshy.	**SOIL** Dry, stony, alkaline.	**FLOWERING** Summer.
OTHER VARIETIES AND SPECIES *C. r. albus, C. r. atrococcineus, C. r. coccineus*	**HEIGHT** 36in (90cm)	**NATURAL HABITAT** Native of Mediterranean and southwestern Asia. Grows on cliffs, old walls, and wasteland.	**PROPAGATION** Sow seeds in the spring. Divide in spring.	**USES** Culinary.
	SPREAD 18in (45cm)	**SITE** Full sun.		
	FLOWERS Pink, crimson, or white, held in clusters at the top of the stem.			

Chamaemelum nobile (Anthemis nobile)
Roman chamomile
chamomile, garden chamomile, ground apple, whig plant

Chamomile is one of the best known of all herbs. It is a member of the daisy family and has the typical daisy-like flower heads and feathery foliage common to many members of that family. If you plant it closely in suitable conditions (well-drained, light, sandy soil and full sun), it will form a dense green "chamomile lawn," which releases an apple-like fragrance when trodden on. The variety 'Treneague' is the best one to choose for this purpose because it is non-flowering and has strongly scented foliage.

Chamomile has had many uses. It was a medieval "strewing herb," scattered on the floor to scent the room. The essential oil was used to relieve swellings and pains in the joints, while the most popular use is in the well-known chamomile tea, which settles the stomach, promotes the appetite, cleanses the liver, and relieves fevers. In Beatrix Potter's story, it was administered by Mrs. Rabbit to Peter after his adventures with Mr. McGregor. It can also be applied externally to cuts and sores, and is used in homeopathic medicine. The oil is also used in shampoos, eye lotions, and various cosmetics.

Caution: Contact with foliage may cause skin rash. Do not use the oil during pregnancy.

Roman chamomile is probably the best-known herbal tea and is also the herb that can be grown as a lawn. These need sandy well-drained soil and a sunny position.

vital statistics

FAMILY Compositae	**PERENNIAL ZONE 3–4**	**FOLIAGE** Green, feathery, small, apple-scented leaves.	**SOIL** Well-drained, light sandy soil. Cultivated forms prefer richer soil.	**FLOWERING** Summer.
OTHER VARIETIES AND SPECIES *C. nobile* 'Flore Pleno', *C. n.* 'Treneague', *Anthemis tinctoria*	**HEIGHT** 12in (30cm)	**NATURAL HABITAT** Found on dry grassland throughout Europe. Naturalized in North America.	**PROPAGATION** Sow seeds in the spring or divide in spring.	**USES** Medicinal, tea, cosmetic, essential oil.
	SPREAD Indefinite.			
	FLOWERS Small, white, daisy-like with a yellow center.	**SITE** Full sun.		

Chelidonium majus
Celandine
great celandine, tetterwort

Celandine is a member of the poppy family. Medicinally, it was an important herb in medieval times. The flowers are bright yellow, four-petaled, and held in small clumps at the end of the stems. The leaves are rather like those of columbine, green on top but grayish underneath, but not as rounded.

Traditionally, the bright orange sap was thought to be a cure for warts, tetters (a form of ringworm), and corns, and was applied directly. It was highly regarded as a cure for cataracts and other eye complaints.

The plant is named for *chelidon*, the Greek for "swallow," and there is an old legend that if the eyes of young swallows were put out with a needle when they were in the nest, then the parent birds would replace them using the sap of the celandine. The flowers and roots of the plant were used to treat liver complaints, and the roots boiled to make a cough medicine, and to treat inflammation of the gall bladder and jaundice. The sap is also used as an orange dye. It was once grown as a cottage garden plant, but is now regarded mainly as a weed.

Caution: The plant is poisonous and the sap can cause skin irritation.

Celandine is no longer used in herbal medicine. The sap is an irritant and the plant must be handled with care.

vital statistics

FAMILY
Papaveraceae

OTHER VARIETIES AND SPECIES
C. majus 'Flore Pleno'

BIENNIAL
ZONE 4

HEIGHT
18–36in (45–90cm)

SPREAD
18in (45cm)

FLOWERS
Bright yellow with four petals.

FOLIAGE
Pale blue-green leaves divided into three leaflets, rounded teeth, grayish underneath.

NATURAL HABITAT
Native of Europe and western Asia. Found mainly in woodland and wasteland.

SITE
Full sun to partial shade.

SOIL
Well-drained, flourishes in most soils.

PROPAGATION
Sow seeds in the spring or fall.

FLOWERING
Spring to summer.

USES
Formerly medicinal.

Chelone glabra
White turtlehead
balmony, salt-rheum weed, shellflower, snakehead

Turtlehead is an attractive flower and deserves to be better known. It needs moisture-retaining soil and grows well in a boggy part of the garden. Other common names include fishmouth, snakemouth, and snakehead.

Turtlehead is an attractive herb. It is a native of North America, and grows in moist woodland and mountainous areas. It is increasingly being used in herbal medicine as the source of a tonic to treat the liver and digestive system. It has laxative effects and is used for colic, constipation, anorexia, and poor digestion.

It is named for the shape of the top lip of the flower, which resembles the head of a tortoise or turtle. The flowers are white, pink, or purple, depending on the species grown, with two lips and beards. *C. glabra* has white or pink-tinged white flowers with a white beard. The flowers are held on erect stalks and appear from mid-summer onwards. The leaves are large, mid-green, veined, and lance-shaped. The plant is very distinctive and is welcome when grown beside a stream or in a bog garden, where the soil remains moist. It makes a spectacular addition to a summer border.

vital statistics

FAMILY
Scrophulariaceae

OTHER VARIETIES AND SPECIES
C. lyonii, C. obliqua, Penstemon barbatus

PERENNIAL ZONE 3

HEIGHT
24–36in (60–90cm)

SPREAD
18in (45cm)

FLOWERS
White, pink, or purple, with two lips and a beard.

FOLIAGE
Dark green, shiny, toothed leaves.

NATURAL HABITAT
Native of North America. Flourishes in moist woodland, mountainous and marshy areas.

SITE
Partial shade.

SOIL
Moist soil.

PROPAGATION
Sow seeds in the spring. Take soft tip cuttings in late spring or early summer.

FLOWERING
Summer.

USES
Herbal medicine.

Chenopodium bonus-henricus
Good King Henry
goosefoot

An excellent herb with a variety of culinary uses that gets its common name of goosefoot from the shape of the leaf. It was a popular herb and used to be more widely cultivated than it is today. It is a perennial plant and the young spears, which you can cook and eat like asparagus, are harvested in their second year.

Grow Good King Henry from seed sown in the spring and then thin it so that the plants are 1ft (30cm) apart. The herb prefers a warm, sunny position in the kitchen or herb garden. Pick the leaves a few at a time, and cook and eat them like spinach. Cut the plant to the ground in the winter and then mulch it with compost or peat. You can then gather the first spears that appear the following year and eat them.

The plant belongs to the same genus as *C. ambrosioides*, wormseed or Mexican tea, an aromatic herb whose oil is used in veterinary preparations to destroy worms and internal parasites in dogs. The leaves of this plant are used to flavor some Central American dishes. However this latter herb must be treated with extreme caution, for taken in excess it can cause severe vomiting, convulsions, and even death.

An excellent culinary herb, which can be grown in most kitchen gardens and eaten as spinach or cut and eaten the following year in the same way as asparagus.

vital statistics

FAMILY Chenopodiaceae	**PERENNIAL ZONE 5**	**FOLIAGE** Triangular, rounded, and wedge-shaped.	**SOIL** Well-drained, light, rich soil.	**FLOWERING** Summer.
OTHER VARIETIES AND SPECIES *C. album, C. ambrosioides, C. botrys, C. quinoa*	**HEIGHT** 24in (60cm)	**NATURAL HABITAT** Native of Great Britain. Other members of family come from South America and China.	**PROPAGATION** Sow seeds in the spring.	**USES** Culinary.
	SPREAD 16in (40cm)			
	FLOWERS Small, greenish-yellow flowers held in clusters.	**SITE** Full sun.		

Cichorium intybus
Chicory
succory, wild chicory

Wild chicory comes from the Mediterranean but it has spread widely throughout the northern hemisphere and is now a common weed in pastureland in North America. Chicory has a bitter taste and is not to everybody's liking, but it is full of vitamins and has many medical properties. In its wild state it is a clump-forming perennial with a rosette of mid-green, spoon-shaped, basal leaves, with narrower leaves above. The plant has many stems and in the summer each stem carries a pale blue, sometimes white or pink, flower head with many narrow petals, similar to a dandelion, with a smaller center. The plant has a long taproot.

Chicory is best known today as a winter vegetable and there are two types grown in the vegetable garden, forcing and non-forcing. Witloof, or Belgian chicory, is the traditional forcing type that produces chicons--tight blanched heads—that you can braise or eat raw in salads. Non-forcing chicory is grown without blanching and you can cut this when it's ready in the fall. 'Sugar Loaf', 'Crystal Head', and 'Snowflake' are all good non-forcing varieties. The most popular chicory today is the non-forcing radicchio types, with their red and white-veined leaves. Commonly used today in salads, these include 'Rosso di Chiogga' and 'Rosso di Treviso'.

An infusion made from the leaves was formerly used to treat stomach complaints, gout, rheumatism, and as a laxative. The bruised leaves were also sometimes applied locally, as they were thought to help remedy cases of pimples and swellings.

The roots of chicory are sometimes roasted for a healthy, caffeine-free alternative to coffee.

FAMILY Asteraceae/Compositae	**PERENNIAL ZONE 3**	**FOLIAGE** Lance-shaped and toothed basal leaves, narrower leaves above.	**SOIL** Most types.	**FLOWERING** Late summer, fall.
OTHER VARIETIES AND SPECIES *C. i.* 'Witloof Belgian', *C. i.* 'Bianco di Milano', *C. i.* 'Pain de Sucre', *C. i.* 'Sugar Loaf', *C. i.* 'Rosso di Chiogga', and 'Rosso di Treviso'	**HEIGHT** 4ft (1.2m) **SPREAD** 24in (60cm) **FLOWERS** Blue, dandelion-like flowers that open in the morning.	**NATURAL HABITAT** Wasteland and dry banks. Native of Europe and the Mediterranean. **SITE** Full sun.	**PROPAGATION** Sow seeds in the spring or fall.	**USES** Herbal medicine, culinary.

Cimicifuga racemosa
Black cohosh
black snakeroot, bugbane, rattleweed, squawroot

Bugbanes are hardy herbaceous perennials, native to North America, China, and Japan. A drug obtained from the plant is used in herbal medicine to treat bronchitis and other chest complaints, and it is used in homeopathy to ease labor pains and treat depression.

The plants can reach a height of 4–6ft (1.2–1.8m) and are chiefly grown for their spires of bottlebrush flowers, which emerge in late summer. The individual flowers are star-shaped, with fine leaves that change color in fall.

The name *Cimicifuga* comes from the Latin, *cimex*, meaning "a bug," and *fugo*, meaning "to flee," a reference to the insecticidal properties of the plant. The rhizomatous roots have also long been used by Native Americans to cure menstrual and menopausal problems, and to treat general pains and fevers, hence the common name of squawroot.

Bugbanes are good plants for a shady border and prefer soil that does not dry out. You'll find the flowers and the leaves are excellent for flower arrangements, although the flowers do have a rather unpleasant smell.

Caution: The plant is poisonous and should not be used for home treatment.

Bugbanes are attractive plants that make a welcome addition to the backyard in late summer when many other flowers are over.

vital statistics

FAMILY
Ranunculaceae

OTHER VARIETIES AND SPECIES
C. americana, C. japonica, C. simplex and cvs., *C. rubifolia*

PERENNIAL ZONE 3

HEIGHT
5ft (1.5m)

SPREAD
24in (60cm)

FLOWERS
Long feathery white spires of small white flowers.

FOLIAGE
Alternate long, green, sharply toothed leaves divided into three.

NATURAL HABITAT
Shady woods and hillsides of eastern North America.

SITE
Shade or partial shade.

SOIL
Rich, moisture retaining.

PROPAGATION
Sow seeds in the fall when they are fresh, or divide them in spring.

FLOWERING
Late summer.

USES
Herbal medicine, insecticide.

Cnicus benedictus

Blessed thistle

Holy thistle, cardin, spotted thistle, St. Benedict's thistle

This thistle was regarded as cure-all in the Middle Ages and was grown in monastery gardens.

The holy thistle is an unusual prickly plant that you can grow in the garden as an ornamental for its distinctive flower heads. It is also a valuable plant in herbal medicine, and is used to treat cases of anorexia, loss of appetite, dyspepsia, and depression. Holy thistle is also used as a digestive tonic.

Like most thistles, it is a branching annual, with hairy red stems that spring from a long taproot. It has long, white-veined, pale green leaves. The thistle heads are bright yellow and are surrounded by spiky brown bracts, followed by single seed pods in the fall. You can cut and dry the plant to make a dramatic element in winter flower arrangements.

In the Middle Ages this herb was grown in monastery gardens and had a reputation as a cure-all, hence its various common names. It was thought to be a good treatment for fevers, and was even believed to cure the bubonic plague. A poultice of the leaves was supposed to relieve chilblains and burns, and to heal wounds.

Caution: Excess can cause vomiting.

vital statistics

FAMILY Compositae	**HARDY ANNUAL**	**FOLIAGE** Pale green, long, spiny, deeply divided leaves.	**SOIL** Well-drained. Tolerates most soils.	**FLOWERING** Summer.
OTHER VARIETIES AND SPECIES None	**HEIGHT** 2ft (60cm) **SPREAD** 12in (30cm)	**NATURAL HABITAT** Native to southern Europe, flourishes on poor ground in cultivated fields.	**PROPAGATION** Sow seeds in the spring where the plants are to grow.	**USES** Herbal medicine, dried flowers and seed heads.
	FLOWERS Yellow flowers that nestle in the middle of prickly thistle-like heads.	**SITE** Sun.		

Colchicum autumnale

Autumn saffron

meadow crocus, naked ladies, upstart

This beautiful flower of the fall emerges before the leaves of the plant. This premature appearance gives the plant one of its common names, naked ladies. It is used in herbal medicine to treat gout, rheumatism, and pains of the joints, as well as diarrhea and nausea.

Colchicum autumnale is a charming sight, with generally pink flowers shaped like large goblets, although there are yellow and white varieties. The lance-shaped leaves emerge in winter and last until the middle of the summer. Although similar in looks and habit, colchicums are not the same as the true fall-flowering crocuses that belong to the genus *Crocus*; these include the species *Crocus niveus*, with white to lilac flowers, and *C. nudiflorus*, which has deep purple flowers. The genus is closely related to lilies.

Colchicum roots are poisonous and were treated with great caution even in medieval times. But the herb has been used for centuries and minute amounts were taken by the Greeks to treat gout, dropsy, and fevers.

Caution: All parts of the plant are poisonous; handling them may cause irritation of the skin.

Although the shape is similar, this plant is quite different from the common crocus of spring and fall. It is extremely poisonous.

vital statistics

FAMILY Liliaceae	**PERENNIAL** **ZONE 3**	**FOLIAGE** Green, glossy, lance-shaped leaves emerge after the flowers and last through the winter.	**SOIL** Rich, moisture retaining.	**FLOWERING** Fall.
OTHER VARIETIES AND SPECIES *C. agrippinum, C. cilicicum, C. variegatum.* There are lots of species with many varieties.	**HEIGHT** 8in (20cm)		**PROPAGATION** Sow seeds in the fall, plant out corms in the summer.	**USES** Herbal medicine.
	SPREAD 4in (10cm)	**NATURAL HABITAT** Mountainous areas or damp pastureland in southeastern Europe.		
	FLOWERS Upright, lavender-pink or white goblet-shaped flowers.	**SITE** Sun or partial shade.		

Consolida ajacis (Consolida ambigua)
Doubtful knight's spur

The doubtful knight's spur is a close relative of the delphinium and was formerly classified in the same genus. It was frequently used in herbal medicine. The flowers are grown for their attractive colors. The dried stems and seed heads are particularly attractive: Use them for dried flower arrangements. The flowers closely resemble those of the delphinium and are generally blue, purple, or lilac, although white and pink forms are available. They bloom throughout the summer. The best known annual varieties are the Giant Imperial Series that will reach 3ft (90cm) in height, or the Dwarf Hyacinth or Dwarf Rocket Series, which grow only half as high.

They do not flourish in cold damp soils and like some sun. They do best when they can be sown in the fall to flower the following summer. All of the cultivated species are hardy. The seed can be scattered throughout a flower bed. The young plants will need protection in areas that are prone to frosts.

The plant had several uses in herbal medicine, particularly as an insecticide, but all parts of the plant are poisonous, particularly the seeds, and it is no longer used. It should not be taken in any form.

Caution: All parts of this plant are poisonous.

Doubtful knight's spur are grown as annuals. The sap of the plant can be used as an ink.

vital statistics

FAMILY Ranunculaceae	**HARDY ANNUAL**	**FOLIAGE** Dark green, feathery, finely divided.	**SOIL** Fertile, well drained. They will not flourish in damp conditions.	**FLOWERING** Summer.
OTHER VARIETIES AND SPECIES *C. ajacis* Dwarf Rocket Series, *C. a.* Dwarf Hyacinth Series	**HEIGHT** 1–3ft (30–90cm) **SPREAD** 12–18in (30–45cm), depending on the variety.	**NATURAL HABITAT** Native to the Mediterranean and western and central Asia. **SITE** Open, sunny.	**PROPAGATION** Sow seeds in situ in fall in mild climates or in spring: seeds sown in fall flower earlier and provide better plants.	**USES** Cut and dried flowers, formerly medicinal.
	FLOWERS Blue, purple, white, and pink held on erect spikes.			

Convallaria majalis
Lily-of-the-valley
May bells, May lily

This well-known flower of the spring has long been used in herbal medicine and as a perfume. It is a rhizomatous perennial, and the creeping rhizomes produce pairs of large, green, pointed leaves, generally shaped like narrow ovals. Some varieties have striped foliage. The flowers are carried on separate leafless stalks in late spring and consist of sprays of small, white, sweet-scented bells. Pink forms can also sometimes be found.

The plant does best in a damp shady border, and although sometimes difficult to establish, they can become invasive given suitable conditions. The volatile oil is used as a popular fragrance in the perfume industry.

Lily-of-the-valley has been used as a medicinal herb for thousands of years, and in the Middle Ages the spirit of the flowers distilled in wine was considered an effective treatment for epilepsy, disorders of the nerves, convulsions, and disordered speech. Distilled water made from the plant was a cure for eye inflammation. Recently it has been discovered to have many of the properties of digitalis and is used in herbal medicine to treat heart disease and angina.

Caution: All parts of this plant are poisonous.

This beautifully scented plant needs suitable conditions to flourish. It is an important herb in the treatment of heart disease.

vital statistics

FAMILY
Convallariaceae/Liliaceae

OTHER VARIETIES AND SPECIES
C. montana, C. transcaucasica, C. m. 'Albostriata' (striped leaves), C. m. 'Flore Pleno' (double flowers), C. m. var. rosea (pink flowers)

PERENNIAL ZONE 4

HEIGHT
12in (30cm)

SPREAD
6in (15cm) depends on variety.

FLOWERS
Small, white, bell-like, sometimes pink. They are extremely fragrant.

FOLIAGE
Green, broad, oval and pointed. Some varieties have prominent veins.

NATURAL HABITAT
Woodlands in Asia, Europe, and North America.

SITE
Sun or partial shade.

SOIL
Fertile, well-drained, leafy, moist soil.

PROPAGATION
Sow seeds in fall. Divide the rhizomes in the fall.

FLOWERING
Late spring, early summer.

USES
Herbal medicine, perfume industry.

Coreopsis tinctoria
Golden tickseed
calliopsis

The *Coreopsis* species form a large genus of annuals and perennials that are native to North America and belong to the daisy family. As the name *tinctoria* implies, it is largely used as a dye plant. The common name "tickseed" is a literal translation from the Greek, *koris*, meaning "a bug," and *opsis*, meaning "like." This refers to the shape of the seed, which is rather like a tick.

The flowers are usually yellow, although bright red, purple, and dark brown varieties occur. They have a typical daisy-like shape, but often with larger and fewer petals than most daisies. Some flowers are yellow with a red center. The leaves are held in pairs and are dark green, thin, and lance-shaped. A number of varieties have been raised as annuals for bedding plants. These include 'Mahogany Midget', dark red-brown with a yellow center, and 'Tiger Flower', crimson and gold. The *Coreopsis* genus is important as a dye plant: The flowers are used to produce yellow, red, orange, and bronze dyes.

Coreopsis makes a good accent plant in a flowerbed, where the bright yellow, red, and orange flowers stand out in high summer. Unselected seed gives a good variety of color.

FAMILY	HARDY ANNUAL	FOLIAGE	SOIL	FLOWERING
Compositae		Dark green, small, and needle-like.	Fertile, well-drained.	Summer.
	HEIGHT			
OTHER VARIETIES AND SPECIES	2–3ft (60–90cm)		PROPAGATION	USES
C. auriculata, C. grandiflora (both perennials), *C. tinctoria* 'Super Dwarf Gold', *C. t.* 'Tiger Flower'		NATURAL HABITAT	Sow seeds in spring where they are to grow.	Dye plant.
	SPREAD	Prairies in North and Central America.		
	12in (30cm)			
		SITE		
	FLOWERS	Sun.		
	Daisy-like, usually golden yellow with a darker center, sometimes deep red.			

Herbal beauty treatments

Over the ages people have yearned for perfect complexions. Herbs have long been used for cosmetic preparations to achieve this goal. Whether they work or not remains a matter of opinion, but it may well be that some of the old treatments are just as effective and cheaper than modern lotions and creams.

Chamomile and bran face mask

YOU WILL NEED:

1 tsp dried chamomile flowers

2 tbsp bran

1 tsp acacia (or clear) honey

¾ cup (5 fl oz/150 ml) boiling water

Put the chamomile flowers in a bowl and pour the water over them. Let it cool for 30 minutes or so. Mix the bran with the honey and then add 3 tbsp of the chamomile liquid. Apply this mixture as a face mask and leave in place for 10 minutes. Rinse off with warm water. It softens and smooths the skin, leaving it fresh and clear.

Anthemis Nobile Chamomile

Tanacetum parthenium
Feverfew

Feverfew complexion moisturizer

YOU WILL NEED:

1 large handful feverfew leaves

1¼ cups (10 fl oz/300 ml) milk

Put the leaves and milk in a saucepan and simmer them together for 20 minutes. Let the milk cool and then strain it into a bottle. Keep the bottle in the refrigerator. This helps with dry skin and discourages skin blemishes.

Fennel cleanser

YOU WILL NEED:

1 tbsp fennel seeds

1 cup (8 fl oz/250 ml) boiling water

1 tsp acacia (or clear) honey

2 tbsp skim milk

Crush the fennel seeds in a bowl and then add the boiling water. Let this infuse for 30 minutes or so. When the water has cooled, strain it into another bowl and add the honey and milk. Stir together. Funnel the liquid into a bottle and keep it in the refrigerator. This acts as a skin cleanser.

Lemon beebrush hair rinse

There are a number of herbal tonics that can be applied to the hair as stimulants. This is one of the best scented.

YOU WILL NEED:

1 handful of lemon beebrush leaves

1 cup (8 fl oz/250 ml) boiling water

Strip the lemon beebrush leaves from the stalks and place them in a bowl. Pour the boiling water over them and let it stand for at least 1 hour. Strain, bottle, and then use as a hair rinse after conditioning.

Aloysia triphylla Lemon beebrush

Pelargonium Scented Pelargonium

Chamomile conditioning rinse

This is especially useful for people with blonde hair, as it lightens and emphasizes the highlights.

YOU WILL NEED:

2 tbsp chamomile flowers

2½ cups (20 fl oz/575 ml) boiling water

1 handful scented geranium leaves

Put the flowers and water in a saucepan and bring the water to a boil. Simmer for 20 minutes. Strain the hot liquid onto the geranium leaves. Leave the mixture to infuse for 40 minutes and then strain it into a bottle. Apply after you have shampooed the hair, leave for a few minutes, and then rinse out.

Scented hand cream

YOU WILL NEED:

1 tsp beeswax

¼ tsp clear honey

¼ cup (2 fl oz/50ml) almond oil

¼ cup (2 fl oz/50ml) orange-flower water or rosewater

Put the beeswax, honey, and almond oil in a bowl and stir over a pan of hot water until they have blended. Add the flavoured water and stir vigorously until it has blended with the oils. Remove from the heat, continue stirring, and then put it in a jar or bowl. This makes an excellent hand cream.

Dame Trot's honey face mask

YOU WILL NEED:

2 lb (900g) clear honey

4 dried bryony roots

⅔ cup (5 fl oz/150 ml) rosemary infusion

Dice the bryony roots and make a standard decoction. Strain off the liquid. Put the roots in the honey with the rosemary infusion and simmer until the rosemary infusion has evaporated. Strain and store for use.

Tagetes patula French marigold

Isis lotion

This is a skin cleanser

YOU WILL NEED:

1¼ cups (4 oz/110g) buttermilk

1 handful each of elderflowers, marigold petals, scented geranium leaves, and 1 chopped garlic clove.

Simmer all the ingredients gently for 40 minutes and then let the mixture stand for 5 hours. Strain. Reheat the lotion adding 1 tablespoon clear honey until the honey has dissolved. Cool, bottle, and use.

Egyptian skin tonic

Take three of the following herbs: chickweed, pansy, bedstraw, meadowsweet, scarlet pimpernel. Make a standard infusion. Wash the face with this every night and allow the conditioner to dry naturally. This preparation is said to improve the complexion and remove pimples.

Angel water for sunburn

Take a handful each of rosemary, sow thistle, *Sonchus oleraceus*, and white water-lily leaves. Prepare a standard infusion with 2½ cups (20 fl oz/575 ml) of boiling water. This makes an effective treatment for sore skin and cases of sunburn.

Herbal hair and scalp lotion

Take equal parts of chamomile leaves, nettles, parsley, and rosemary. Prepare a standard infusion. Apply this daily to the scalp. To combat dry and brittle hair, prepare some essential oil of one of these herbs and massage the scalp with it twice a week. Cleavers substituted for one of the herbs acts as a cure for dandruff, and parents whose children have acquired nits can try adding a pinch of rue to the mixture.

A cure for baldness

It has been claimed, although not proven, that an infusion of betony, maidenhair fern, and scarlet pimpernel massaged into the scalp once a day will alleviate the onset of baldness. Whether it persuades hair to regrow from bald scalps is another matter.

Stachys officinalis
Betony

Taraxacum officinale Dandelion

Hair coloring and restoration

There are a number of treatments available, depending on the result that is required. The following claims have been made for the following treatments.

1. An infusion of mature leaves taken from a privet hedge will add a chestnut coloring to hair.

2. For a lighter effect, add some quince juice, if you can get it, to the privet infusion.

3. Fair hair can be lightened by rinsing it in an infusion of chamomile leaves.

4. The peel of several green oranges steeped in oil for three months and applied to white or gray hair will restore its color.

5. An infusion of rosemary and red sage will return the original color to dark hair that has started to gray.

Beauty bath

Make an essential oil of marigold petals and hyssop. Add a tablespoon of this oil to the bath each night. This will restore bloom to the skin and help to remove wrinkles.

One or two drops of any essential oil mixed with 2 teaspoons of almond oil makes a fragrant bath oil that is relaxing after a hard day's work.

Slimming bath

Prepare a standard infusion of dandelion, horsetail, and rosemary. Add two tablespoons of it to the bath water. Why on earth anyone would think that this should work, no one really knows.

A bath for a magical sleep

Sprinkle a tablespoon of the diced dried roots and leaves of valerian in the bath. Traditionally this was supplemented with a pinch of dried henbane root, but this is not a practice to be recommended as the herb is toxic and you should avoid swallowing the bathwater if henbane has been added.

An old Welsh sleeping draft

Prepare an infusion of red clover heads, hops, and lettuce. Drink a wineglassful before going to bed.

Mulberrry water

For a restful night and pleasant dreams take equal quantities of mulberry leaves, cowslip primrose leaves, and mullein. Make a standard infusion. Drink a wineglassful before going to bed.

Agastache foeniculum Blue giant hyssop

Coriandrum sativum

Coriander
Chinese parsley, cilantro

Coriander is both an attractive plant in the garden and one of the favorite spices in the kitchen. The leaves, berries, and roots are all used in a large number of dishes in many different cuisines. Sow the seeds of this annual in the spring where you want the plant to grow.

You can chose from varieties that produce either a large quantity of leaves or flowers. The leaves, or cilantro, are bright green, a bit like flat-leaf parsley, and you can pick and use them fresh in salads or cook them in spicy dishes. The plant bears attractive, small, white, sometimes purple-tinged flowers in clumps at the end of stalks. These are one of its main attractions. When the flowers are over, the seeds appear, which are then harvested, dried, and ground into a spice. They are one of the main ingredients of curry powder. In Roman times they were used as a preservative for meat.

The herb is also used medicinally and reputedly aids digestion, and contributes to longevity and an improved love life. It was used as an aphrodisiac in ancient Persia (modern Iran). The oil is used to make perfume, and is added to the alcoholic drinks vermouth and Chartreuse as a flavoring.

Coriander is one of the oldest herbs used in cooking and was introduced to Chinese medicine nearly 1,500 years ago. The seeds and leaves have surprisingly different flavors.

vital statistics

FAMILY
Umbelliferae

OTHER VARIETIES AND SPECIES
C. s. 'Cilantro', C. s. 'Morocco', C. s. 'Santo'

ANNUAL

HEIGHT
1–2ft (30–60cm)

SPREAD
9in (23cm)

FLOWERS
Small white and pink flowers held on flat heads.

FOLIAGE
Aromatic. Bright green, shiny, stalked lower leaves, narrower, more divided upper leaves.

NATURAL HABITAT
Wasteland. Native of southwestern Asia and North Africa.

SITE
Full sun.

SOIL
Fertile, well drained.

PROPAGATION
Sow seed in spring and early summer and thin to 6in (15cm) apart.

FLOWERING
Summer.

USES
Culinary, herbal medicine.

Crataegus laevigata, C. monogyna
Smooth hawthorn
oneseed hawthorn, May, quickset, thorn-apple tree

There are many species of hawthorn, with varying uses in cooking and in medicine. It is also called "bread-and-cheese," for the leaves were used in sandwiches.

The hawthorn is an excellent decorative tree for large or small gardens at all seasons of the year. Both *C. laevigata* and *C. monogyna* are important medically and have similar medicinal properties. The flowers emerge in spring, hence the name May, and are white, pink, or red, depending on the variety grown. The traditional May, *C. laevigata*, has white flowers. The leaves are small and attractive, and turn a glorious yellow and red in the fall. The flowers are followed by bright red, sometimes yellow or black berries, which remain on the trees until they are eaten by birds. Hawthorn is grown as a hedge in some countries—its spiky thorns are a good defense against potential intruders.

May is associated with many ancient country customs. "Going a-maying" was a euphemism for courting. The May Queen and the maypole, around which people danced on May 1, were connected with fertility rites. The name comes from Maia, the Roman goddess of the plains and mother of the messenger god Mercury.

Medicinally *C. laevigata* and *C. monogyna* are interchangeable. May has been used for centuries for dropsy, and heart and stomach pains. It has a number of recognized healing properties. The berries are used in herbal medicine to treat heart disease and circulatory disorders, and a decoction of the leaves is used to treat asthma and sore throats, and to lower high cholesterol.

vital statistics

FAMILY
Rosaceae

OTHER VARIETIES AND SPECIES
C. l. 'Coccinea Plena', *C. l.* 'Paul's Scarlet', *C. l.* 'Rosea Pleno Flora', *C. m.* 'Biflora', *C. m.* 'Stricta'

DECIDUOUS TREE ZONE 4

HEIGHT
25ft (8m)

SPREAD
25ft (8m)

FLOWERS
White or pink, held in clumps that can cover the whole tree.

FOLIAGE
Rounded, small leaves with three or five lobes, mid-green, turning yellow or red in the fall.

NATURAL HABITAT
Woodland and scrub in temperate zones in the northern hemisphere.

SITE
Full sun or partial shade.

SOIL
Will grow in most soils except very damp, waterlogged conditions.

PROPAGATION
Sow seed when ripe in the fall. Germination may take 18 months. Bud cultivars in summer or graft in winter.

FLOWERING
Late spring.

USES
Herbal medicine.

Crocus sativus
Saffron crocus

The saffron crocus, with its lilac flowers, sometimes streaked with white in the fall, is a lovely plant. But the saffron that one plant produces is such a tiny amount—around 2,000 bulbs are needed to produce 1oz (28g) of the herb—that the ordinary gardener should grow the plant for decoration rather than the expensive yellow dye and spice used in cooking.

Saffron has been an important herb for thousands of years, used mostly as flavoring in the kitchen and as a dye. It was brought to Europe by the Crusaders in the Middle Ages and many centers that specialized in the cultivation of the bulb sprang up throughout Europe. Saffron Walden in England was one of them. Today the main supply of saffron comes from Kashmir in northern India, and from Spain.

It is still used largely as a flavoring in dishes such as paella and risotto, in the traditional fish stews of France and Italy, and in Middle Eastern cooking. It is also used to make saffron cakes and sweetmeats. In herbal medicine it is sometimes used to treat high blood pressure and to improve the circulation.

The source of the prized spice, saffron, which has the reputation of being the most expensive substance in the world. Luckily, most recipes require the addition of only a few strands.

vital statistics

FAMILY
Iridaceae

OTHER VARIETIES AND SPECIES
Other fall-flowering crocuses include *C. bannaticus*, *C. nudiflorus*, *C. serotinus*. There are also many cultivars.

PERENNIAL BULB ZONE 4

HEIGHT
6in (15cm)

SPREAD
6in (15cm)

FLOWERS
Lilac with bright orange stigma.

FOLIAGE
Fine grass-like leaves that usually emerge shortly after the flowers.

NATURAL HABITAT
Dry regions. Native of Greece and Asia Minor.

SITE
Sun or partial shade.

SOIL
Does best in poor, well-drained soil.

PROPAGATION
Plant bulbs in late summer and divide clumps after flowering.

FLOWERING
Fall.

USES
Culinary, dye plant, herbal medicine.

Cymbalaria muralis
Kenilworth ivy
ivy-leaved toadflax

The name of the plant, *muralis*—of walls—reflects its habit of growing in walls and stony places. It requires a dry position.

This trailing plant is commonly found growing in old walls, where it seems to manage to survive with no moisture whatsoever. The plant was formerly used as a salad herb and the young leaves have a pleasant flavor.

Grow Kenilworth ivy in rock gardens or other areas where there is little moisture, no competition, and some shade (it will not flourish in full sun). It has attractive leaves, light green, with reddish undersides, shaped a bit like ivy leaves, thus the plant's common name. The small flowers, appearing in fall, are lilac or white, rather like those of the antirrhinum (snapdragon), with two lips. Sometimes the lips are tipped with yellow.

If you grow it in good soil in a fertile part of the garden, the plant may well become invasive and it will need to be controlled. It is easy to raise from seed. The flowers are sometimes used to make a yellow dye but this is not permanent.

vital statistics

FAMILY Scrophulariaceae	**PERENNIAL ZONE 5**	**FOLIAGE** Light green with red undersides shaped like rounded ivy.	**SOIL** Well-drained, poor.	**FLOWERING** Spring to summer.
OTHER VARIETIES AND SPECIES None	**HEIGHT** 4in (10cm)	**NATURAL HABITAT** Old walls and crevices in dry regions. Native of the Mediterranean.	**PROPAGATION** Sow seeds in the spring. Divide in spring, self-seeds.	**USES** Culinary, dye plant.
	SPREAD Indefinite, trailing.			
	FLOWERS Pale lilac, sometimes white, like those of a small snapdragon.	**SITE** Partial shade.		

Cymbopogon citratus
Lemon grass

Native to India, *Cymbopogon* is a genus of coarse ornamental grasses. It has scented leaves that are used in oriental cookery and formerly as an ingredient in herbal medicines and cosmetics. *C. citratus* is a clump-forming perennial with hollow stems and erect or arching, blue-green, rough leaves that have a strong scent of lemon. Grass-like flowers are carried in clumps in summer. The Latin name comes from the Greek, *kymbe*, "a boat," and *pogon*, "a beard," a reference to the shape of the flower buds that hang down like beards.

The leaves have many uses. You can use them in the kitchen, fresh or dried and ground into a powder. They are a vital ingredient in a number of Eastern dishes, particularly meat or fish, and are especially popular in Thai cooking. You can also infuse them as a tea that is said to aid digestive problems.

A decoction of the plant is used in herbal medicine to cure minor fevers. It is also used to treat ringworm, lice, and scabies. The essential oil, lemon grass oil, is used in cosmetics, and for flavoring in the food industry.

Several of these grasses have fragrant leaves with geranium, ginger, and rose scents, as well as lemon. They are all used for flavoring and in the perfume industry.

vital statistics

FAMILY Gramineae	**PERENNIAL ZONE 8–10**	**FOLIAGE** Narrow blue-green leaves turning brown when dried.	**SOIL** Fertile, well-drained.	**FLOWERING** Late summer.
OTHER VARIETIES AND SPECIES *C. martinii* (ginger grass), *C. nardus* (citronella grass)	**HEIGHT** 2–3ft (60–90cm)	**NATURAL HABITAT** Tropical and subtropical grassland. Native of India.	**PROPAGATION** Sow seed at 55–64°F (13–18°C) in early spring. Propagate by division in late spring.	**USES** Culinary, herbal medicine.
	SPREAD 2–3ft (60–90cm)			
	FLOWERS Small greenish-white, grass-like flowers.	**SITE** Will not survive frost and is best moved into a greenhouse or conservatory in winter.		

Cynara cardunculus Scolymus Group
Globe artichoke

Artichokes are easy to grow and flourish in fertile, well-drained soil in full sun. They have recently been discovered to contain an important herbal ingredient used in the treatment of liver disease and blood disorders. They are clump-forming perennials and the roots may need protecting in winter when the temperature falls below 5°F (15°C).

They are useful for three purposes. Both globe artichokes and their close relations, cardoons (*Cynara cardunculus*), have been popular vegetables since Roman times. To enjoy an ancient delicacy, simply cut the heads of globe artichokes, boil them, and serve them with melted butter or hollandaise sauce. The stems of cardoons are blanched in the fall in the same way as celery and then cut into pieces and boiled until tender. Some gardeners ignore them as vegetables and grow them in herbaceous or decorative borders for their spectacular, gray-white, thistle-like foliage. Great purple flowerheads emerge in the summer. The plants are large and will reach 6ft (1.8m), given favorable conditions. They prefer well-drained soil and a sunny position. You may need to protect them from slugs, aphids, and other garden pests.

The globe artichoke has recently been discovered to be an important medicinal herb. A compound called cynarin has been found in the leaves. This is extracted and then used in drugs for the treatment of liver and gall bladder com-

plaints, and to lower lipid and blood cholesterol levels. In addition to this, both globe artichoke and cardoon flowers are very popular with bees. You can cut the flowers when they are fresh and then dry them for use as interesting features in winter flower arrangements.

Globe artichokes have recently been discovered to have important medical properties and are valued in the treatment of high cholesterol levels.

FAMILY
Compositae

OTHER VARIETIES AND SPECIES
C. c. Scolymus Group 'Green Globe', *C. c.* Scolymus Group 'Purple Globe', *C. c.* Scolymus Group 'Camus de Bretagne', *C. c.* Scolymus Group 'Violetta di Chioggia'

PERENNIAL ZONE 6

HEIGHT
5–7ft (1.5–2m)

SPREAD
4ft (1.2m)

FLOWERS
Purple, thistle-like, emerge from many-leaved buds.

FOLIAGE
Large, thistle-like, deeply divided leaves, gray-green above and white underneath.

NATURAL HABITAT
Well-drained grassland of the Mediterranean. Probably a native of northwestern Africa.

SITE
Open and sunny.

SOIL
Does best on dry, well-drained soil.

PROPAGATION
Sow seed in spring. Divide in late spring. Take root cuttings in winter.

FLOWERING
Late summer.

USES
Culinary, herbal medicine.

Cynoglossum officinale
Hound's tongue
dog-bur, dog's tongue, gypsy flower, sheeplice, woolmat

Hound's tongue is a wildflower of dry, grassy woodland areas. The plant contains an effective healing substance and for years had many uses in herbal medicine. The leaves were made into a compress to cure burns, bites, wounds, and sores. The juice of the leaves was supposed to prevent hair loss. The roots were cooked and made into pessaries to cure piles, and a distilled water made from the leaves was used to alleviate the sores caused by gonorrhea. It was also taken for coughs and for cases of diarrhea.

It is a biennial, which flowers and sets seed in its second year. The common name of hound's tongue comes from the Greek *kyon*, "a dog" and *glossa*, "a tongue," which refers to the shape and soft surface of the leaves. The leaves and stems of the plant are often hairy.

The flowers are hooded, dull red or maroon, occasionally white, and are favored by bees and butterflies. The plant smells unpleasantly.

Caution: The plant is now thought to contain carcinogenic substances and is a skin irritant. It must be used only under medical supervision.

The plant was formerly used as a painkiller, but is now thought to be carcinogenic and should be used only by qualified practitioners. It is an attractive wildflower.

vital statistics

FAMILY Boraginaceae	**BIENNIAL** ZONE 4	**FOLIAGE** Basal rosette of rounded, oblong gray-green leaves, followed by pointed leaves in the second summer.	**SOIL** Fertile, moist, well-drained soil.	**FLOWERING** Summer.
OTHER VARIETIES AND SPECIES C. amabile, C. nervosum, C. zeylanicum	**HEIGHT** 18–24in (45–60cm)		**PROPAGATION** Sow seed in spring.	**USES** Herbal medicine.
	SPREAD 12–18in (30–45cm)	**NATURAL HABITAT** Dry, grassy areas in western Asia and Mediterranean.		
	FLOWERS Loose clusters of deep purple flowers on branching stalks.	**SITE** Sun or partial shade.		

Cytisus scoparius
Scotch broom
broom, link

This plant gets its name from the long twiggy shoots that were bound together to make brooms. They were also used to thatch the roofs of houses.

The bright yellow flowers of broom are one of the sights of spring. Both broom and its near relative, gorse, grow on wasteland in North America and Europe, and have long been used in herbal medicine.

The twiggy branches of the plant were used to make brooms and baskets, and were also used as thatch in places where reed was not available. It had a reputation as a strong purgative and diuretic, and was used to cure kidney and liver complaints. The leaves are high in tannin (a natural substance that can be used to mature animal hide into leather) and so the branches were sometimes used to tan leather. The flower buds were also pickled and eaten in the same way as caper flowers.

The herb has been discovered to contain alkaloids, particularly sparteine, that have an effect similar to curare, the poison used by the South American Indians to tip their arrows and darts. This causes death by muscular paralysis. An extract of broom is used by qualified practitioners to regulate the action of the heart.

Caution: Parts of this plant contain poison and should not be taken.

vital statistics

FAMILY
Leguminosae

OTHER VARIETIES AND SPECIES
C. adecumbens, C. multiflorus, C. sessilifolius. A number of garden varieties have been developed in colors ranging from deep yellow to white, pink, and red.

PERENNIAL SHRUB ZONE 4

HEIGHT
6ft (1.5m)

SPREAD
6ft (1.5m)

FLOWERS
Clusters of yellow, fragrant, pea-like flowers on long stalks.

FOLIAGE
Small green leaves divided into three held on a short stalk.

NATURAL HABITAT
A native of western Europe.

SITE
Sun or partial shade.

SOIL
Sandy, well-drained, neutral to acid soil.

PROPAGATION
Sow seed in spring or fall. Take semi-ripe cuttings in summer.

FLOWERING
Spring to early summer.

USES
Herbal medicine, culinary, dye plant.

Datura stramonium
Jimson Weed
devil's apple, Jamestown weed, mad-apple, stinkweed, thorn-apple

The shrubby members of this genus have now all been reclassified as members of the genus *Brugmansia*. The annuals remain as *Datura*. The chief kind, which has been used in herbal medicine for centuries, is the poisonous *D. stramonium*, the thorn apple, used by the *thuggi* of India to assassinate people.

It is a bushy plant with unpleasant smelling leaves that look a bit like rather large, limp ivy. It also has white, funnel-shaped flowers that form large egg-shaped spiny fruit, filled with black kidney-shaped seeds. While all parts of the plant are extremely poisonous, with similar properties to deadly nightshade, (*Atropa belladonna*), alkaloids extracted from the thorn apple are now used in drugs to treat Parkinson's disease and to relieve spasms and asthma attacks. The leaves are also made into an herbal smoking mixture to sooth asthma sufferers and an extract is used in some cough medicines. It was formerly used to treat epilepsy, convulsions, and other mental disorders.

Caution: Poisonous. No part of the plant should be taken in any form.

Although the thorn apple contains a deadly poison, the plant is now much valued in herbal medicine. It is used to treat Parkinson's disease and to help in cases of severe asthma.

vital statistics

FAMILY Solonaceae	**HALF-HARDY ANNUAL**	**FOLIAGE** Green, prickly, broadly heart-shaped.	**SOIL** Well-drained, fertile, moist soil.	**FLOWERING** Summer.
	HEIGHT 2–3ft (60–90cm)			
OTHER VARIETIES AND SPECIES *D. ceratocaula, D. inoxia*		**NATURAL HABITAT** A native of South America, it flourishes on wasteland.	**PROPAGATION** Cultivation is not recommended. The plant self-seeds freely.	**USES** Herbal medicine.
	SPREAD 18in (45cm)			
	FLOWERS White, trumpet-shaped flowers followed by egg-shaped spiny fruits.	**SITE** Sun or partial shade.		

Daucus carota
Wild carrot
beesnest plant, Queen Anne's lace

All the carrots that have been grown as a vegetable since Roman times have been bred from this wild carrot. It is the wild carrot that is used in herbal medicine because it still contains properties lacking in its cultivated descendants. It is widely distributed and can be found growing along the coast around the Mediterranean, and in temperate climates in Asia. It has become naturalized in North America. Its habit is similar to the cultivated carrot, but it is taller, the stalks are rougher, and the roots are "small, long and hard and unfit for meat, being somewhat sharp and strong," in the words of an old English herbal. The most noticeable features are the large clumps of small white flowers with purple-flushed central flowers. You can cut and dry these to make a fine addition to a winter flower arrangement.

Traditionally, the herb was used to treat conditions of the bladder and the kidneys, and it is still used in herbal medicine to treat kidney stones, gout, and urinary and menstrual problems. It is also used as an ingredient in face creams. All carrots contain beta carotene; if they are eaten regularly, this helps to improve eyesight, especially night vision.

Wild carrots can often be found growing beside the sea and have prominent flower heads made up of tiny white flowers, often pinkish-purple in the center.

vital statistics

FAMILY
Umbelliferae

OTHER VARIETIES AND SPECIES
All cultivated carrots, *Daucus carota* ssp. *sativus*, have been bred from the wild carrot.

BIENNIAL ZONE 5

HEIGHT
3ft (90cm)

SPREAD
12in (30cm)

FLOWERS
Small, white, held in large tufts with purple-tinged flowers.

FOLIAGE
Green, paler than the cultivated varieties, deeply divided, on long rough stalks.

NATURAL HABITAT
Native of the Mediterranean. Widely distributed throughout the northern hemisphere.

SITE
Sun.

SOIL
Prefers well-drained, light, sandy loam.

PROPAGATION
Sow seed in spring or in late summer, self-seeds freely.

FLOWERING
Summer.

USES
Herbal medicine, dried flower arrangements.

Dianthus caryophyllus
Carnation
gillyflower, pink

Pinks have become obsolete in medicine in the West, but are still used in Chinese medicine. Many pinks are attractively scented and remain favorite garden plants.

Pinks are among the most attractive small flowers in the garden and are deliciously scented, especially the old-fashioned varieties. You can use the flowers of the clove pink, *Dianthus caryophyllus*, to make cordials and to flavor drinks. Also try adding them to soups and salads as a garnish.

Pinks flourish on chalky light soil in a sunny position and do not need too fertile a soil. They do not like being damp and waterlogged during the winter. Cut them back quite hard when flowering is over to keep them neat and tidy. You can raise pinks from seed, but named varieties are best raised from cuttings or pipings taken during the summer and rooted in a sandy compost. Pipings are a method of propagation peculiar to pinks and carnations. Simply pull out the central portion of a shoot and remove the bottom leaves. As well as its uses in the kitchen, you can add the dried flowerheads to potpourris. It was formerly used in herbal medicine but is not used today.

D. chinensis, the Chinese pink, is used in Chinese medicine to stimulate the digestive system and to cure urinary infections, particularly cystitis. It is also used to control fevers.

vital statistics

FAMILY Caryophyllaceae	**PERENNIAL ZONE 6**	**FOLIAGE** Gray-green, thin, spiky leaves on many thin stems.	**SOIL** Prefers light and chalky soil.	**FLOWERING** Summer.
OTHER VARIETIES AND SPECIES *D. barbatus, D. deltoides, D. monspessulanus, D. superbus.* Large numbers of garden varieties have been developed.	**HEIGHT** 2ft (60cm)	**NATURAL HABITAT** Native of the Mediterranean. Grows wild on hillsides and pasture land.	**PROPAGATION** Sow seed or take cuttings or pipings.	**USES** Culinary, formerly medicinal.
	SPREAD 18in (45cm)			
	FLOWERS Rose pink. Other varieties have flowers from red to white.	**SITE** Open, sunny.		

Dictamnus albus
Gas plant
diptam, burning bush, dittany, false dittany, fraxinella

This is a hardy perennial, native to the Mediterranean, and has been used in herbal medicine for over a thousand years. It is not related to the dittany of Crete, *Origanum dictamnus*, a member of the mint family. It is known as the burning bush because the leaves and flowers give off a volatile oil that can ignite in hot, dry conditions. It is a spectacular looking plant, with highly scented leaves, smelling of lemons and balsam, and spikes of white, pink, or purple flowers with long stamens. It makes a good addition to the herbaceous border, reaching 2–3ft (60–90cm) in height, and flowers in midsummer. The plant prefers light, dry soil. The leaves are shaped rather like those of the ash tree and give the plant one of its common names, from *fraxinus*, the Latin word for ash.

The roots of the plant have long been used to treat fevers and were formerly considered a cure for epilepsy. Today they are used in herbal treatments for skin diseases because they are known to control bacterial and fungal infections.

Caution: Contact with the plant may cause skin irritation, especially in sunlight.

This is an attractive garden perennial and an important medicinal herb. It can sometimes ignite in hot weather, causing bush fires.

vital statistics

FAMILY	PERENNIAL	FOLIAGE	SOIL	FLOWERING
Rutaceae	ZONE 5	Green, ash like, growing on many branches, very fragrant.	Prefers light, well-drained, alkaline soil.	Summer.
OTHER VARIETIES AND SPECIES	**HEIGHT**	**NATURAL HABITAT**	**PROPAGATION**	**USES**
D. albus var. *purpureus*	2–3ft (60–90cm)	Native of the southern Europe and western Asia. Found on open woodland and dry grassland.	Sow seed in late summer, divide in spring, or take root cuttings in fall or early winter.	Herbal medicine.
	SPREAD			
	18in (45cm)			
	FLOWERS	**SITE**		
	White or pink. *D. a.* var. *purpureus* is pinkish-purple.	Sun or partial shade.		

Digitalis purpurea
Foxglove
dead men's bells, dog's finger, fairy gloves

Foxgloves are common wildflowers and have been grown in gardens for many years. They have also been used in herbal medicine for a long time, but their use as a heart tonic was not discovered until 1785. The leaves contain digitoxin and digitalin, which are used to strengthen the contractions of the heart and to treat heart failure. However, all parts of the plant are poisonous and great care must be taken that children do not eat the seeds. In earlier times the leaves were used as a poultice to heal wounds, and an ointment made from the leaves was used to treat "scabby heads."

The long spires of white and purple flowers are a glorious sight in late summer. Grow them at the back of an herbaceous border or against a dark background for full effect. A number of species are grown, all of which have similar herbal properties. The one most commonly used in medicine today is *D. lanata*, the woolly foxglove, with off-white or caramel colored flowers. They all produce many seeds and generally self-seed freely given suitable conditions.

Caution: All parts of the plant are poisonous and should not be taken in any form. Contact with the leaves may cause skin irritation.

The medicinal properties of foxgloves were discovered by an English doctor, William Wittering, in the 18th century.

vital statistics

FAMILY
Scrophulariaceae

OTHER VARIETIES AND SPECIES
D. ferruninea, D. grandiflora, D. laevigata, D. lanata, D. lutea. Large numbers of garden varieties have been developed.

BIENNIAL
ZONE 4
Some species are perennial.

HEIGHT
4–5ft (1.2–1.5m)

SPREAD
2ft (60cm)

FLOWERS
Purple, white, and pink flowers.

FOLIAGE
Broad, basal leaves. Smaller leaves between flowers.

NATURAL HABITAT
Native of western and central Europe. Found wild worldwide in temperate climates. Open ground, banks, rocky hillsides.

SITE
Sun or partial shade.

SOIL
Light, moisture-retaining soil, but will grow in most soils.

PROPAGATION
Sow seed in spring. Self-seeds.

FLOWERING
Summer.

USES
Medicinal.

Dipsacus fullonum
Teasel
Fuller's teasel

The teasel grown commercially is Fuller's teasel, *D. fullonum* ssp. *fullonum*. It is used in the cloth industry. Teasels are common plants found on wasteland and have large, rounded, oblong heads covered with hooked spikes. The spikes are irritating to the skin when they are brushed against. The leaves are green and oblong, and the upper leaves form a cup around the stem that collects water. The heads are light green, with the light purple flowers working their way up the head forming a band around it. At no time do they cover it completely. As they ripen, the heads turn from green to gold, and this is a good point to cut them for use in dried flower arrangements. Left any longer and the rains of summer and fall turn them a rather unattractive, dingy brown.

The spiked heads, which are hard and abrasive when dry, soften when wet and are used in the wool industry to raise the fibers on woven cloth. No manufactured product achieves the same effect. In former times the roots were considered to be cleansing and the water found in the cups of the leaves was used to get rid of freckles on the face.

Teasels are one of the rare instances where nature cannot be duplicated by any manufactured product, and they are still used in the weaving industry.

FAMILY Dipsacaceae	**BIENNIAL** **ZONE 5**	**FOLIAGE** Light green pairs forming a cup around the plant stem.	**SOIL** Moisture-retaining soil or clay.	**FLOWERING** Summer.
OTHER VARIETIES AND SPECIES *D. inermis, D. pilosus*	**HEIGHT** 5–6ft (1.5–1.8m)	**NATURAL HABITAT** Native of Europe and Asia. Found wild throughout the world. Usually grows on wasteland or in damp places.	**PROPAGATION** Sow seed in spring or fall where the plants are to grow. Self-seeds.	**USES** Cloth industry, flower arrangements, formerly medicinal.
	SPREAD 2ft (60cm)			
	FLOWERS Pale lilac or purple, forming a ring around the seed head.	**SITE** Sun or partial shade.		

Echinacea purpurea
Purple coneflower

Purple coneflowers are attractive garden plants with widely spread, large daisy-like petals. They are purply-pink in color, surrounding a prominent, central, golden-brown head or cone. It is a native of North America and was used by the Native Americans as a cure-all, particularly in the treatment of septicemia, snakebite, and rabies.

In the garden coneflowers are a welcome addition to an herbaceous border—especially as they flower from midsummer onwards and the flowers remain into the fall, when many others are over. A number of good garden varieties have been developed ranging from red, through orange, to purple and white.

Coneflowers have remained an important medicinal herb over many centuries. The roots are still used in herbal medicine to stimulate the immune system and promote healing. The herb is also used in the treatment of all forms of skin disease, and is also recommended for the treatment of boils, abscesses, herpes, and venereal disease. Its most common use, however, is to ward off the onset of the common cold and to alleviate the effects of a sore throat.

Echinacea is one of the most popular herbal remedies. The name comes from the Greek *echinops,* meaning "hedgehog," referring to the spines in the center of the flowers.

vital statistics

FAMILY
Compositae

OTHER VARIETIES AND SPECIES
E. angustifolia, E. p. 'Bright Star', *E. p.* Lustre Hybrids, *E. p.* 'The King', *E. p.* 'White Lustre'

PERENNIAL ZONE 4

HEIGHT
2–3ft (60–90cm)

SPREAD
18in (45cm)

FLOWERS
Purple-pink with a prominent golden-yellow central cone.

FOLIAGE
Oval, toothed, rough, hairy basal leaves with lance-shaped, toothed stem leaves.

NATURAL HABITAT
Native of North America, found in open woodland and across the prairies.

SITE
Sun or partial shade.

SOIL
Fertile, well-drained, moisture-retentive soil.

PROPAGATION
Sow seeds in late spring; they need a temperature of 55°F (13°C) to germinate. Divide in spring or fall but take care—the plants don't like too much root disturbance.

FLOWERING
Mid- to late summer.

USES
Herbal medicine.

Echium vulgare
Viper's bugloss

Viper's bugloss is an old medicinal herb that also has several uses in the kitchen. It is best known for its lovely violet-blue flowers, which open from purply-pink buds and make a spectacular sight in summer. The old herbalists used the leaves and flowers of the plant as a poultice for snakebite, because the markings on the leaves and flowers resemble the features of a snake, hence its common name. There are many garden varieties. 'Blue Bedder' has light blue flowers, and the dwarf hybrids are smaller, with flowers of varying colors, from pink and purple to blue and white.

Viper's bugloss is seldom used in herbal medicine today, but the flowers and the leaves have mild tonic and antiseptic qualities and are sometimes added to drinks in the same way as borage. An infusion of the leaves is also used in herbal medicine to treat fevers and headaches. They are still sometimes candied or cooked as a vegetable (they taste a bit like spinach). However, this isn't recommended, as they can cause slight stomach upset.

Caution: All parts of the plant may cause mild stomach upset, and contact with the leaves may produce skin irritation.

The viper's bugloss is an attractive wildflower with brilliant blue flowers. A number of garden varieties have been developed. It is used mainly in the kitchen.

vital statistics

FAMILY Boraginaceae	**BIENNIAL ZONE 5**	**FOLIAGE** Bristly, lance-shaped gray-green leaves.	**SOIL** Light, well-drained.	**FLOWERING** Early to midsummer.
OTHER VARIETIES AND SPECIES E. v. 'Blue Bedder', E. candicans, E. pininana, E. wildpretii	**HEIGHT** 2–3ft (60–90cm)	**NATURAL HABITAT** Native of Europe and western Asia, this plant is naturalized in North America. .	**PROPAGATION** Sow seeds in late spring; they need a temperature of 55–61°F (13–16°C) to germinate healthily.	**USES** Culinary, formerly medicinal.
	SPREAD 12in (30cm)			
	FLOWERS Brilliant blue, (pinkish violet in bud) carried on short spikes.	**SITE** Full sun.		

Eryngium campestre
Field holly
field eryngo

Many members of this genus are used in herbal medicine in different countries around the world. The oldest and best known is the common sea holly, *Eryngium maritaimum*, which is found near the coast. This striking plant has very spiny, gray, holly-like leaves, and in the summer powder-blue flowers surrounded by spiny bracts grow like a star from beneath them.

The best known of the garden species is *E. giganteum*, Miss Willmott's ghost. It is a magnificent spectral presence in the herbaceous border in the dusk of a summer evening, with almost pure white bracts.

The plant had a reputation as an aphrodisiac and was thought "to strengthen the spirit procreative." Sweetmeats made from the roots were sold as "eryngoes," aphrodisiac lozenges. The roots have healing properties and were boiled and applied to bad wounds to help the healing process. *E. foetidum*, false coriander, is used both medicinally and in the kitchen in the Caribbean. *E. campestre*, field eryngo, is used in herbal medicine for skin complaints, urinary infections, and whooping cough in Eastern Europe. You can use the flowerheads for dried flower arrangements.

Field eryngo, *Eryngium campestre*, with its narrow, pale green leaves and whiteish flowers, is closely related to sea holly and has the same use in herbal medicine. It is a popular medicinal plant in Eastern Europe.

vital statistics

FAMILY
Apiaceae/Umbelliferae

OTHER VARIETIES AND SPECIES
E. alpinum, *E. amethystinum*, *E. bourgatii*, *E. foetidum*, *E. giganteum*

PERENNIAL
ZONE 5

HEIGHT
12–18in (30–45cm).

SPREAD
12–18in (30–45cm)

FLOWERS
Large, pale blue flowerheads surrounded by spiny bracts.

FOLIAGE
Gray, spiny, holly-like leaves.

NATURAL HABITAT
Mediterranean shores and western Asia, Eastern Europe.

SITE
Full sun.

SOIL
Light, well-drained, poor to moderately fertile soil.

PROPAGATION
Sow seeds in fall when ripe. Divide in spring. Take root cuttings in late winter.

FLOWERING
Summer.

USES
Herbal medicine, flower arranging.

Erysimum cheiri (Cheiranthus cheiri)
Aegean wallflower

The Aegean wallflower may still be found growing wild in walls and rough places around the northern hemisphere. The plant is originally a native of the Mediterranean region, but has long been recognized as a garden plant in more temperate climates, and many modern strains have been developed in varied colors ranging from red, orange, yellow, and purple through to the palest cream. There are also dwarf varieties, which look attractive in rock, or alpine, gardens.

Wallflowers are grown for their scent; the Latin name is said to come from the Arabic *cheire*, a sweet-scented plant. Since then, botanists have reclassified them as *Erysimum*. Each plant produces a number of stalks and the four-petaled flowers appear in dense clumps at the ends. They are perennials, but you can treat them as biennials and plant them in summer to flower in spring the following year. The plant is used to make an aromatic oil used for perfumes.

Wallflowers, with their heavily scented blooms, are one of the sights of old walled gardens in early summer. They prefer a sunny site with well-drained soil.

---

vital statistics

FAMILY
Brassicaceae/Cruciferae

OTHER VARIETIES AND SPECIES
E. c. Bedder Series, *E. c.* Fair Lady Series, *E. c.* 'Harpur Crewe', *E. c.* 'Ivory White'

BIENNIAL ZONE 5

HEIGHT
10–24in (25–60cm)

SPREAD
12–16in (30–40cm)

FLOWERS
Yellow, orange flowers held in long clumps.

FOLIAGE
Green, narrow, tapering leaves formed on many branches.

NATURAL HABITAT
Well-drained alkaline soil in temperate regions in the northern hemisphere.

SITE
Full sun.

SOIL
Well-drained, light soil.

PROPAGATION
Sow seeds in the spring or late summer.

FLOWERING
Late spring, early summer.

USES
Aromatic oil.

Jellies, syrups, & sweets

The dazzling variety of flavors available from herbs lend themselves to a similar variety of uses in the kitchen. These recipes include traditional preparations for accompaniments to meat dishes and desserts, as well as candies.

HERB JELLIES

Herb jellies are traditionally served with meat dishes. Mint jelly is the classic accompaniment for roast lamb, and is sweet enough to be popular with children.

Mint jelly

YOU WILL NEED:

3 lbs (1.35kg) cooking apples

3 cups (25 fl oz/700 ml) water

1 small bunch fresh mint

3 cups (25 fl oz/700 ml) plain vinegar

sugar (see below for quantity)

3 level tbsp chopped fresh mint

green food coloring

Wash the apples, cut in quarters, and then put them in a preserving pan with the water and the bunch of mint. Simmer until the apples are soft and pulpy. Add the vinegar, bring to the boil, and boil for 5 minutes. Tip the mixture into a jelly bag and strain overnight. The next day measure the liquid and allow 1 lb (450g) sugar for every 2½ cups (20 fl oz/575 ml) liquid. Put the juice and sugar in the preserving pan, heat slowly until the sugar has dissolved, and then boil rapidly until setting point is reached. Add the chopped mint and a few drops of food coloring to make the jelly nice and green. Boil until setting point. Pour the jelly into warmed jars.

Mentha spicata Mint

Sambucus nigra Black elder

Elderberry and apple jelly

YOU WILL NEED:

1½ lbs (700g) elderberries

1½ lbs (700g) cooking apples

1 lemon

sugar (see below for quantity)

water

Cut the apples in quarters. Put the elderberries and apples in a preserving pan, cover them with water, and then simmer gently until the fruit is soft and pulpy. Strain over night through a jelly bag. Add the juice of the lemon and the rind and pips tied in a cheesecloth bag. Measure the liquid and allow ¾ lb (350g) sugar to every 2½ cups (20 fl oz/575 ml) juice. Heat gently, stirring until the sugar has dissolved and then boil rapidly until setting point is reached. Remove the bag of lemon rind and pour into warmed jars.

Eryngo conserve

This is an old recipe for sweets that originally came from Colchester, England. They were supposed to be mild aphrodisiacs, as Gerard delicately put it in his *Herbal*, "The roots are exceeding good, … nourishing and restoring the aged, and amending the defects of nature in the younger."

Lift the roots of the eryngo plant, sea holly, *Eryngium maritimum*, in the spring or fall. Wash them carefully and then simmer gently until soft. Put the cooked roots in cold water and peel them when they are cold enough to handle. Add ¾ lb (350g) sugar for every 1 lb (450g) roots and then boil the sugar and roots gently until the sugar has crystallized. Cool and store in a cool, dark place.

Coltsfoot cough taffy

This is another old recipe. The candy was sucked as a cure for coughs.

Gather a bucketful of coltsfoot leaves, *Tussilago farfara*. Stew them in 2½ cups (20 fl oz/575 ml) water until they are soft, and then strain off the liquid and set it aside. Put 1 lb (450g) sugar and 1 lb (450g) molasses with a knob of butter in a pan. Add enough of the hot coltsfoot liquor to melt the sugar and then boil everything rapidly, without stirring, until the taffy reaches setting point. Remove from the heat and stir in ½ tsp baking powder. Be careful, it will foam up. Stir the taffy until it is really thick, roll it out on a tray, cut it into strips and then twist it to make taffy bars.

Flavored syrups

Make a thin syrup with 2½ cups (20 fl oz/575 ml) water and ½ lb (225g) sugar. Simmer for 10 minutes. Add a handful of scented geranium leaves, elderflowers, or young blackcurrant leaves. Let the flavoring infuse in the hot syrup for 30 minutes, then strain and freeze until required.

Rose-hip syrup

YOU WILL NEED:
1½ lbs (700g) rose hips from the dog rose,
R. canina
7½ cups (60 fl oz/1.75 liter)water
1 lb (450g) sugar

You can make double the quantity if you wish depending on the number of rose hips available. The juice is extracted in two stages. Mince the hips coarsely and bring 5 cups water to the boil. Add the hips to the boiling water. Bring back to the boil, skim off the scum, and boil for 5 minutes. Remove from the heat and allow to cool for 15 minutes. Put the pulp through a fine sieve twice, to remove the hairs. Set the liquid aside. Boil the last pint of water and add the sieved pulp. Leave it to cool as before and pass it through the sieve twice. Return both sets of liquid to the pan and simmer until the liquid is reduced by half. Add the sugar and stir well until the sugar is dissolved. Bottle, seal, and store in a cool, dark place until required.

Pelargonium graveolens Rose geranium

Herbal cures & preparations

The study of herbal remedies provides a fascinating insight into the medical practices of our ancestors. Modern science is now confirming that some of these traditional old cures really do show evidence of being effective.

PREPARING HERBS FOR TRADITIONAL MEDICINE

The main ways that herbs were taken in medicine were as infusions, decoctions, and ointments.

Infusions

A standard infusion can easily be prepared by pouring 2½ cups (20 fl oz/575 ml) boiling water over 5 tablespoons dried herbs, (or three handfuls of fresh herbs) and leaving the mixture for three or four hours. It should then be strained and bottled. It will keep fresh for three or four days.

Decoctions

These are generally prepared from the roots of herbs: ½oz (10g) of dried root should be simmered in 2½ cups (20 fl oz/575 ml) water until the liquid has been reduced by half. Strain the liquid and store as an infusion. It will keep for slightly longer.

Eschscholzia californica California poppy

Hypericum perforatum St. John's-wort

Ointments

Herbal ointments can be made by pounding 5 tablespoons crushed herbs in 1½ cups (12 oz/340g) lard and then heating this until the herb is thoroughly incorporated. Strain the fat before it cools and then add some beeswax to harden the mixture. Alternatively, you can pound one part by weight of fresh herbs into two parts of bland cold cream. A mortar and pestle is a help when doing this.

Essential oils

These are prepared by adding 2 tablespoons finely crushed fresh herbs to ¾ cup (5 fl oz/150 ml) pure vegetable oil. Add 1 tablespoon plain vinegar and leave in warm sunlight to mature for three weeks. To make an extra strong oil, strain the mixture at the end of each week and replace the herbs with fresh ones. **Warning:** All essential oils must be used with care. In excess, they are poisonous and need careful measuring even when used externally.

Symphytum officinalis Comfrey

Tinctures

Use ¾ cup (3oz/80g) powdered herb to 5 cups (40 fl oz/1.1 liter) surgical alcohol. Keep the tincture in a warm place and shake vigorously every other day for three weeks. Then store in a cool, dark place.

Poultices

Poultice herbs are applied to sores and inflamed parts and kept in place with a bandage. The easiest way to prepare a poultice is to mix a standard infusion with cornstarch until it has become a thin paste. Spread the paste onto a clean linen bandage and apply to the sore. Useful poultice herbs include, comfrey, poppy, St. John's-wort, and adder's tongue.

SOME ANCIENT HERBAL TONICS

There are a great number of herbal tonics that have been used down the ages to treat a number of complaints, ranging from constipation to infertility. It is very important to treat all these with caution. Occasional use of some of the more innocuous tonics may not do any harm, but they should never be used regularly and all complaints should be taken first of all to a doctor. Nevertheless, they are of interest, for they show the herbal treatments that were used in past centuries.

The tonic of the Druids

An ancient general tonic supposedly prepared by the Druids in pre-Roman Britain.
Take equal parts of the leaves of the following herbs: chervil, heather, Japanese honeysuckle *Lonicera japonica*, (not Dutch honeysuckle, *L. caprifolium* nor woodbine, *L. periclymenum*), red clover, and vervain. Prepare a standard infusion. Take a tablespoon at night and in the morning.

The drink of Paracelsus

Take equal quantities of the dried leaves and flowers of the following herbs: rosemary, marigold, sundew, and the rock rose, *Helianthemum nummularium*. Prepare a standard infusion.
These herbs are governed by the sun, and the tonic is supposed to have a brightening effect on the whole system. The normal intake was a cupful on rising in the morning.

Celestial potion

This ancient tonic was supposed to conserve youth and physical fitness, and cure impotence. It must be treated with great caution, and is not recommended, for the fruit and seeds of the lily-of-the-valley are toxic if eaten.
Take equal quantities of the dried flowers and leaves of lily-of-the-valley, loosestrife, sweet marjoram, and vervain. Prepare a standard infusion. A cupful a day was the recommended intake.

Convallaria majalis Lily-of-the-valley

Eschscholzia californica
Californian poppy

Californian poppies are one of the easiest of all annuals to grow. The juice of the poppies is mildly narcotic and it was used by the Native Americans to relieve toothache. The milky extract of the plant is also a sedative and is used in herbal medicine to relieve tension and anxiety. Spanish settlers in North America used it as a hair tonic.

Californian poppies have very attractive orange, red, and yellow four-petaled, poppy-like flowers that last for a very short time, and attractive gray-green, lance-shaped, deeply divided leaves. They make good cut flowers. Seal the stems after they have been cut by burning them before putting them in water. A number of garden varieties have been developed. Ballerina Series and the popular Thai Silk Series are compact with semi-double, yellow-tinged, orange, or pink flowers. In suitable conditions they self-seed freely and you may need to control them.

Caution: Contains a mild opiate.

Californian poppies are among the easiest annuals to grow. In hot climates they will seed themselves in gravel and in cracks in brick paths. They make good accent flowers.

vital statistics

FAMILY
Papaveraceae

OTHER VARIETIES AND SPECIES
E. caespitosa (perennial),
E. c. Ballerina Series, *E. c.* 'Dali',
E. c. Thai Silk Series

PERENNIAL ZONE 3

HEIGHT
12–24in (30–60cm)

SPREAD
6in (15cm)

FLOWERS
Pale, yellow, orange to cream and white, four-petaled.

FOLIAGE
Gray-green, deeply divided, and fern-like.

NATURAL HABITAT
Native to California and western North America, found in grassy open areas and coastal plains.

SITE
Full sun.

SOIL
Light, well-drained, poor soil.

PROPAGATION
Sow seeds in spring or fall where the plants are to grow.

FLOWERING
Summer.

USES
Herbal medicine, flower arranging.

Eupatorium spp.
Agrimony
agueweed, boneset, feverwort, hemp agrimony, Indian sage, joe-pye weed, thoroughwort

The many common names of these plants is a good indication of the many uses of the *Eupatorium* genus in herbal medicine. The Latin name commemorates Mithridates Eupator, the 1st-century-BC ruler of Pontus, an ancient country in Asia Minor, who is credited with discovering that one of the species could be used as an antidote to poison. Hemp agrimony, *E. cannabinum*, is a tall plant with pink and white flowers held in clusters. The flowers are popular with bees and butterflies, and the plant prefers damp conditions. It was used to treat arthritis, colds, and influenza, and as a tonic to cure constipation. It was a medieval wound herb, used to cure internal and external wounds and bruises. It is used today as a homeopathic cure for influenza. The herb stimulates the immune system, but it is thought that it may cause damage to the liver if taken in excess.

Boneset, *E. perfoliatum*, was formerly a common treatment for colds and influenza. It is used in herbal medicine to ease muscle pain, lower fevers, relieve chest congestion, and bronchitis, and to treat skin diseases.

The plant has small white, sometimes purple-tinged, flowers held in dense flat heads, and large leaves, dark green and shiny above, and white and downy beneath.

Joe-pye weed, *E. purpureus*, is a native of North America and is a larger plant than hemp agrimony. Both plants like moist damp conditions and flourish by ponds and streams and on boggy ground. Joe-pye weed has pinkish-purple flowers held in large clusters, and thin, oval, dark green leaves that smell of vanilla when they are crushed. It was one of the traditional herbs of the Native Americans and was used to treat fevers. Today it is still used in herbal medicine to treat disorders of the kidney, prostate, and urinary system.

Caution: *E. cannabinum* may damage the liver.

The fluffy flowerheads of this herb suit an informal garden. The plant is a staple in herbal, homeopathic, and Native American medicine.

---

vital statistics

FAMILY Asteraceae/Compositae	**PERENNIAL ZONE 3**	**FOLIAGE** Green, rough, and large, lance-shaped and coarsely toothed, emerging on upright stems.	**SOIL** Fertile, moisture-retaining, rich soil.	**FLOWERING** Summer.
OTHER VARIETIES AND SPECIES *E. aromaticum, E. rugosum, E cannabinum* 'Album', *E. c.* 'Flore Pleno', *E. purpureum* ssp. *maculatum* 'Atropurpureum'	**HEIGHT** 5–9ft (1.5–2.7m) **SPREAD** 2ft (60cm) **FLOWERS** White, pink, and purple, depending on the species.	**NATURAL HABITAT** Widespread in North and South America, Europe, and Asia. Prefers damp places. **SITE** Full sun or partial shade.	**PROPAGATION** Sow seeds in spring or divide in the fall.	**USES** Herbal medicine, bee plant.

Euphrasia officinalis

Eyebright
euphrasy, red eyebright

The common name of eyebright relates to the use of the plant as a cure for blindness in the Middle Ages. The flowers resemble diseased eyes.

Eyebright belongs to a group of hardy annual and perennial plants native to Europe. It is used in homeopathic medicine for all manner of bronchial infections, and as a cure for herpes and eczema.

The plant is an annual and grows about 8in (20cm) high. It forms tufts of small, deeply toothed, rounded leaves on narrow stalks. The flowers appear at the end of stems and are small, white and purple, lipped like a snapdragon, to whose family this plant belongs, with a yellow throat. The flowers are extremely short-lived and last only a few hours. The Latin name comes from the Greek *euphraino*, meaning "to delight," which is a reference to the plant's use as a cure for blindness.

The appearance of the flower was considered very similar to eyes suffering from blindness, disease, and conjunctivitis. This led to the practice of using the juice of the plant as a cure for blindness as well as various forms of eye infection. It was either taken internally or dropped into the eyes. It is claimed that it has in fact occasionally restored sight to the blind. It was also considered a treatment for cases of "a weak brain or memory."

vital statistics

FAMILY
Scrophulariaceae

OTHER VARIETIES AND SPECIES
E. alpina, E. montana, E. rostkoviana

ANNUAL

HEIGHT
8in (20cm)

SPREAD
8in (20cm)

FLOWERS
White, purple-tinged, small, three-lobed lower lip with a yellow throat.

FOLIAGE
Small, rounded toothed, green leaves appear on upright stalks.

NATURAL HABITAT
Common in grassland throughout Europe.

SITE
Sun.

SOIL
Fertile, well-drained soil.

PROPAGATION
Sow seeds in spring.

FLOWERING
Summer.

USES
Herbal medicine.

Filipendula ulmaria (Spiraea ulmaria)
Meadowsweet
bridewort, dolloff, meadsweat, pride of the meadow, Queen of the meadows

Meadowsweet is an attractive plant with creamy-white, sweet-smelling flower-heads, and deeply divided, dark green leaves. It has been an important herb for thousands of years, and in medieval times was used as a strewing herb and as a cure for fevers. It grows in water meadows and damp places. The plants appear very similar to the astilbes grown in many gardens, but belong to a different family.

As in so many cases recently, the botanists have reclassified the plant. It is now listed under the name *Filipendula*. The original name *Spiraea* came from the Greek *speiro*, meaning "spiral." This was a reference to the flexible branches that were twisted into garlands; a corruption of this name is found in the name aspirin. Salicylic acid, the basis of aspirin, was discovered in the plant at the beginning of the 19th century. It seems the reputation of the plant as a cure for fevers in the Middle Ages was well founded.

The leaves and root of the plant were also used as a dye, and a tea made from the leaves is still prescribed by herbalists to reduce fever. The dried flowers are sometimes used to flavor beer and other drinks.

Meadowsweet is an important medicinal herb. It contains salicylic acid, the basis of aspirin. It was also called Queen of the Meadow.

vital statistics

FAMILY Rosaceae	**PERENNIAL ZONE 3**	**FOLIAGE** Dark green above, white and downy underneath.	**SOIL** Rich, moisture-retaining soil.	**FLOWERING** Early to late summer.
OTHER VARIETIES AND SPECIES *F. rubra, F. palmata, F. u. 'Aurea', F. u. 'Multiplex', F. vulgaris*	**HEIGHT** 2–3ft (60–90cm)	**NATURAL HABITAT** Found in damp meadows and beside streams in temperate regions throughout the northern hemisphere.	**PROPAGATION** Sow seeds in fall or spring at 50–55°F (10–13°C). Divide plants in spring.	**USES** Medicinal, culinary, dye.
	SPREAD 18in (45cm)			
	FLOWERS Creamy-white, fragrant flowers held in terminal clusters.	**SITE** Sun or partial shade.		

Filipendula vulgaris
Dropwort

Dropwort is a close relative of meadowsweet but flourishes on dry chalky soils and will grow in any well-drained garden. It was formerly much used in herbal medicine but is no longer used today. It was best known as a cure for asthma, shortage of breath, and diseases of the lungs. It was also used in the treatment of urinary infections.

It has fern-like green leaves, and in the summer, large clumps of white, often pink-tinged flowers, held on slender stems. They are sweet smelling. It makes an attractive plant in an herbaceous border and a number of garden varieties have been developed, such as *F. v.* 'Multiplex', which has creamy-white flowers, and *F. v.* 'Rosea', with pink flowers.

The common name of dropwort was given to it because it gave relief to those who had problems urinating freely. The roots were the parts mostly used, ground into a powder, or a decoction was sweetened with sugar and taken with white wine.

Dropwort used to be an important medicinal herb with many uses. It is no longer used in medicine today but it makes an attractive garden plant.

vital statistics

FAMILY Rosaceae	**PERENNIAL ZONE 3**	**FOLIAGE** Dark green and fern-like.	**SOIL** Light, well-drained loam.	**FLOWERING** Early to late summer.
OTHER VARIETIES AND SPECIES *F. rubra, F. palmata, F. u.* 'Aurea', *F. u.* 'Multiplex', *F. v.* 'Multiplex', *F. v.* 'Rosea'	**HEIGHT** 2–3ft (60–90cm) **SPREAD** 18in (45cm)	**NATURAL HABITAT** Native of Europe, found in dry grassland. **SITE** Sun.	**PROPAGATION** Sow seeds in fall or spring.	**USES** Formerly medicinal.
	FLOWERS Creamy-white, fragrant flowers emerge from pink buds.			

Foeniculum vulgare
Fennel
Florence fennel, sweet fennel, wild fennel

Fennel is popular both as a vegetable and flavoring in the kitchen, and has many uses in herbal medicine. It is grown for the large bulb and leaves. The bulb has an aniseed flavor and you can eat it cooked or raw. The sweetness and flavor of the bulb depend on the variety grown. The leaves are often used in the south of France to flavor fish dishes and soups, and the seeds are gathered and used as an ingredient in *finocchiona*, a delicious salami from Florence, Italy. You can also infuse them as a tea. The name comes from the Latin *faenum*, meaning "hay," because of the scent of the leaves.

It was formerly a medicinal herb much used for all ailments of the stomach and as an antidote for anyone who had eaten poisonous mushrooms. It was held to be good for the blood, to help asthmatics or those troubled by shortness of breath, and was regarded as a treatment for obesity. It is used in herbal and homeopathic medicine to treat colic and indigestion as well as to sooth sore gums and throats.

Fennel is one of the most useful herbs, and finds favor with both cooks and herbal practitioners. The tiny yellow flowers are held in clumps on the end of long stalks.

vital statistics

FAMILY Umbelliferae	**PERENNIAL ZONE 6**	**FOLIAGE** Green, very sparse with fine lacy, feathery leaves.	**SOIL** Well-drained fertile soil.	**FLOWERING** Summer.
OTHER VARIETIES AND SPECIES *F. v.* 'Purpureum', *F. v.* 'Giant Bronze', *F. v.* var. dulce	**HEIGHT** 3–6ft (90cm–1.8m) **SPREAD** 2ft (60cm).	**NATURAL HABITAT** Native of southern Europe, found in well-drained soil in coastal areas.	**PROPAGATION** Sow seeds in situ in spring or indoors at 55°–64°F (13°–18°C).	**USES** Culinary, herbal medicine.
	FLOWERS Tiny yellow flowers held in large clusters on long stalks.	**SITE** Sun.		

Fumaria officinalis
Fumitory
drug fumitory, earth smoke, hedge fumitory

Fumitory was an herb of Saturn. Herbal astrologists believed it cured those parts of the body also ruled by this planet, notably the liver and spleen.

Fumitory is a member of the poppy family, Papaveraceae, and is closely related to the genus *Corydalis*. This climbing herb has similar properties to most poppies, but it is less powerful. It also has similar shaped flowers. It is a twining annual and occurs naturally throughout Europe and western Asia. The flowers are small and tubular, usually pink, but there are red and white forms as well. The leaves are small, gray-green like corydalis, and fern-like. The stems need supporting with pea sticks or netting if they are to climb successfully.

The name fumitory means "smoke of the earth" and comes from the smoke-like smell of the roots. Legend had it that the plant grew out of spirals of smoke. In medieval times the herb was used to cure various complaints, including jaundice, leprosy, scabies, sore throats, and sore eyes, and it was also used as a cure for melancholy. The juice mixed with vinegar was thought to heal acne. It is still used in herbal medicine for liver and gall bladder disorders and to cure inflammation. Externally, it is used in the treatment of eczema and dermatitis.

vital statistics

FAMILY
Papaveraceae

OTHER VARIETIES AND SPECIES
F. capreolata (white fumitory), *F. martinii*, *F. muralis* ssp. *muralis* (few-flowered fumitory), *F. parviflora*

HARDY-ANNUAL

HEIGHT
6–12in (15–30cm)

SPREAD
6–12in (15–30cm)

FLOWERS
Small, tubular, pink, red, or white flowers held in sprays.

FOLIAGE
Gray-green, small, deeply divided, triangular leaves with notched ends.

NATURAL HABITAT
Native of Europe found in light, arable soils and grassland.

SITE
Sun.

SOIL
Light, well-drained soil.

PROPAGATION
Sow seeds in spring. Self-seeds freely.

FLOWERING
Summer.

USES
Herbal medicine.

Galega officinalis
Goat's rue
professor weed

A hardy perennial herb that makes an attrac- tive plant for a decorative flowerbed. It is used in herbal medicine for digestive problems and to increase the supply of milk in nursing mothers. It has upright spires of pea-shaped flowers, usually white or mauve, sometimes pink or bicolored. The leaves are alternate and lance- shaped, soft gray-green and pointed. The Latin name comes from the Greek *gala*, meaning "milk." This refers to the plant's ability to increase the milk yield in animals, and it is still sometimes used as animal fodder. The common name of goat's rue comes from the unpleasant smell of the leaves when they are crushed.

The herb was formerly used to treat fevers, smallpox, measles, and all kinds of distempers. It was also a recommended footbath for travel- ers, such as pilgrims, who suffered from sore feet. Cheesemakers sometimes used the plant instead of rennet (a substance for curdling milk made from young cows' stomachs).

Goat's rue can make an attractive garden plant but the leaves give off a noxious odor when crushed. Good garden varieties include *G. o.* 'Alba', with spires of white flowers.

vital statistics

FAMILY
Leguminosae

OTHER VARIETIES AND SPECIES
G. x hartlandii 'Alba', *G. x h.* 'Candida', *G. officinalis* 'Alba', *G. orientalis*.

PERENNIAL ZONE 5

HEIGHT
3–5ft (90cm–1.5m)

SPREAD
3ft (90cm)

FLOWERS
Large spires of blue, lilac, pink, or white pea-like flowers.

FOLIAGE
Lax, spreading, soft green, pinnate leaves.

NATURAL HABITAT
Native of central and southern Europe and western Asia. Found on hillsides or meadows.

SITE
Sun or partial shade.

SOIL
Moist, well-drained soil.

PROPAGATION
Sow seeds in spring; soak the seed overnight. Divide plants in fall or spring. The plants need staking in a border and will self-seed freely.

FLOWERING
Summer.

USES
Herbal medicine.

Galium odoratum
Woodruff
master of the wood, sweetscented bedstraw, woodward

Sweet woodruff is an excellent ground-cover plant in open woodland. Its sweet smell comes from the substance coumarin present in the plant. In the 17th century it was thought to be an aphrodisiac.

This is an attractive herb, best grown in woodland, where it makes a wonderful ground-cover plant. You can infuse the leaves to make an herbal tea—it was also valued as an herbal bath to refresh tired limbs. It has small, bright green, lance-shaped leaves that are rough to the touch and scented. The flowers are small, white and star-like with four petals. It is related to the common weed *G. asperula*, goose grass, stickie willie or cleavers, whose burrs stick to dog's coats and other passing animals, thus spreading its seed. It is another herb that is named for the Greek *gala*, meaning "milk," because several species of the plant were used to curdle milk in cheese-making.

Sweet woodruff is an ancient herb. In the Middle Ages it was used as a strewing herb to give a pleasant scent to houses, since the foliage, when cut, gives off a pleasant smell of freshly mown hay. It was used as a medicine to cure stomachache and to stop nosebleeds.

The roots of the plant can be used as a dye and its flowers are a great help if you want to attract bees to your garden. Both *G. odoratum* and *G. asperula* are still used in herbal and homeopathic medicine. *G. asperula* is used to treat mononucleosis, tonsillitis, benign cysts, and many other skin complaints. *G. odoratum* is used for varicose veins and phlebitis.

vital statistics

FAMILY
Rubiaceae

OTHER VARIETIES AND SPECIES
G. album (hedge bedstraw),
G. aparine, *G. orientalis*,
G. saxatile (heath bedstraw),
G. verum

PERENNIAL ZONE 3

HEIGHT
9in (23cm)

SPREAD
Indefinite.

FLOWERS
Small, bright, fragrant, funnel-shaped with four petals.

FOLIAGE
Bright green, small, lance-shaped, rough, and scented.

NATURAL HABITAT
Native of Europe and Siberia. Found in woodland, meadows, and wasteland.

SITE
Partial shade or shade.

SOIL
Moist, well-drained soil.

PROPAGATION
Sow seeds in late summer. Divide after flowering.

FLOWERING
Late spring to early summer.

USES
Herbal medicine, insect repellent, household, dye plant, bee plant.

Galium verum

Yellow bedstraw
curdwort, cheese rennet, lady's bedstraw, maid's hair, yellow cleavers

Yellow bedstraw is an herb of poor soils. It is found growing near the sea and in dry grassland on several continents. The herb contains properties that relax spasms and act as a diuretic. It is used in herbal medicine for kidney and bladder complaints.

At one time it was used to stuff mattresses, hence its common name. It has upright yellow flowers held in small spires on stalks that smell sweetly of honey. It is a good herb to grow in a wildflower meadow because grown in a mass it clothes a field or bank with its startling yellow flowers. The creeping roots yield a red dye, and the leaves produce a yellow dye that is used to color cheese, butter, and margarine. The herb has the property of curdling milk and is one of the species that is used in cheese-making, hence one of its common names.

Lady's bedstraw has many of the same properties as sweet woodruff. It was used to stuff mattresses, for the dried herb gives off a delicious scent of honey.

vital statistics

FAMILY
Rubiaceae

OTHER VARIETIES AND SPECIES
G. album (hedge bedstraw), G. aparine, G. mollugo, G. odoratum, G. orientalis, G. saxatile (heath bedstraw)

PERENNIAL ZONE 3

HEIGHT
1–3ft (30–90cm)

SPREAD
Indefinite.

FLOWERS
Tiny, yellow, honey-scented flowers.

FOLIAGE
Green, narrow, and threadlike.

NATURAL HABITAT
Native of Europe, western Asia, and northern Africa. Found in dry grassland and near the sea.

SITE
Sun or partial shade.

SOIL
Dry or well-drained, reasonably fertile soil.

PROPAGATION
Sow seeds in late summer. Divide after in spring or fall.

FLOWERING
Summer.

USES
Herbal medicine, dye plant.

Gaultheria procumbens
Wintergreen

Canada tea, checkerberry, eastern teaberry, hillberry, partridge berry, spiceberry

Wintergreen was used in North America to help breathing when carrying heavy burdens.

Teaberry or wintergreen is an evergreen perennial shrub that has creeping stems and makes good ground cover. Tea is made from the leaves and the essential oil is used in the perfume industry. Grow the plant in neutral to acid, lime-free soil, with ample moisture. Conditions that suit rhododendrons and camellias will also suit wintergreen. It is a native of northern America. The best known member of the genus is the shallon or salal, *G. shallon*, a compact shrub for acid soil, whose pink flowers hang down in sprays rather like small, rounded lockets. Both wintergreen and shallon flourish in partial shade and will grow well in a peat bed or alpine garden if you can be find a good shady spot for them. They will perform well in full sun only if the soil is permanently moist.

The leaves of the plant are dark green, oval, and shiny, paler beneath, and the flowers are white or pale pink, followed by scarlet berries. The oil extracted from wintergreen was often used as an ointment to relieve aches and pains, and also as a treatment for catarrh, but it is not so popular nowadays.

vital statistics

FAMILY Ericaceae	**EVERGREEN SHRUB ZONE 4**	**FOLIAGE** Oval and shiny, bright green above, paler underneath.	**SOIL** Moisture-retaining, acid, reasonably fertile soil, with plenty of humus.	**FLOWERING** Summer.
OTHER VARIETIES AND SPECIES *G. andenothrix, G. cuneata, G. miqueliana, G. mucronata, G. shallon*	**HEIGHT** 6in (15cm)	**NATURAL HABITAT** Native of North America. Found on damp acid soils in woods or beside the sea.	**PROPAGATION** Sow seeds in the fall. Separate rooted suckers in spring or take semiripe cuttings in summer.	**USES** Herbal medicine, tea plant.
	SPREAD To 3ft (90cm)			
	FLOWERS Bell-shaped, white, or pale pink, followed by red berries.	**SITE** Partial shade.		

Gentiana lutea

Yellow gentian

bitterroot, bitterwort, pale gentian

Several gentians are used in herbal medicine. The name comes from Gentius, King of Illyria, an ancient country on the northern shore of the Adriatic Sea, who reputedly discovered the medicinal properties of the plant. Sometimes called the great yellow gentian, this is both a striking and important plant. It grows to 5ft (1.5m) and carries spires of pale yellow flowers with soft green centers. The basal rosette leaves grow to 12in (30cm) long.

It is one of the bitterest herbs known. It is used in herbal medicine as a tonic, to stimulate the digestive system, and to treat liver complaints and anorexia. It is also an ingredient in tonic water and certain aperitifs.

Both *G. burseri*, large-leaved gentian, and *G. scabra*, Japanese gentian, are bitter herbs that are generally used in herbal and Chinese medicine to treat stomach and liver problems. Both have the blue flowers that the gentian is best known for. The close relatives of the gentian, *Gentianella*, the felworts, sometimes also called baldmoney, were formerly used in herbal medicine and were said to take away weariness and to heal the udders of cattle. Gentians were traditionally used as a cure for snake and dog bites.

Yellow gentians are called bitterwort and are among the bitterest herbs known. They are used in the manufacture of Angostura bitters, the essential part of the cocktail pink gin.

---

vital statistics

FAMILY
Gentianaceae

OTHER VARIETIES AND SPECIES
G. acaulis (trumpet gentian),
G. asclepiadea (willow gentian),
G. burseri var. *villarsii*, *G. scabra*
(Japanese gentian), *Gentianella campestris* (field felwort)

PERENNIAL ZONE 5

HEIGHT
5ft (1.5m)

SPREAD
2ft (60cm)

FLOWERS
Five-petaled, star-shaped pale yellow flowers, held in clusters.

FOLIAGE
Strongly ribbed, blue-green basal leaves with pointed stiff leaves up the stalk.

NATURAL HABITAT
Native of the mountains of Europe. Found on mountain pastures and in thin woodland.

SITE
Partial shade.

SOIL
Moisture-retaining, fertile soil, with plenty of humus.

PROPAGATION
Sow seeds in the fall. Divide them in spring.

FLOWERING
Summer.

USES
Herbal medicine, flavoring, dried seed heads.

Geranium maculatum

Spotted cranesbill
alum root, crowfoot, spotted geranium, wild geranium

American cranesbill contains medicinal properties that are important in the treatment of injury and stomach ailments, including dysentery, cholera, gastroenteritis, and ulcers.

This cranesbill is a native of North America and has been important in herbal medicine for many years. It is a pretty plant with flowers varying in color from lilac to pink. The distinctive leaves are widely divided into five or seven sections. They are spotted, hence the common name, and turn yellow, gold, and red in the fall. Even though its natural habitat is in shaded woodland or on low ground, it can easily be grown in the herbaceous border in a sunny position. It self-seeds freely, and rapidly forms a good clump. As with most established cranesbills, it makes a good ground-cover plant.

Spotted cranesbills form thick rhizomes that are dried and powdered, and used in the preparation of various herbal remedies to treat diarrhea, dysentery, cholera, and bleeding. They are also used in the treatment of internal and external ulcers, and a gargle is used to heal mouth infections and sore gums and throats.

vital statistics

FAMILY
Geraniaceae

OTHER VARIETIES AND SPECIES
G. phaeum 'Mourning Widow', G. pratense (meadow cranesbill), G. robertianum, G. sylvaticum. There are many species and cultivated varieties.

PERENNIAL ZONE 4

HEIGHT
2ft (60cm)

SPREAD
18in (45cm)

FLOWERS
Lilac-blue to pink, occasionally white, five-petaled, flowers.

FOLIAGE
Broad, mid-green, toothed, with widely spaced lobes,

NATURAL HABITAT
Native of eastern North America and Canada. Found in woodland areas.

SITE
Sun or partial shade

SOIL
Moisture-retaining, fertile soil.

PROPAGATION
Sow seeds or divide in the fall. Self-seeds freely.

FLOWERING
Early summer.

USES
Herbal medicine.

Geranium robertianum
Herb robert
dragon's blood, Robert geranium, storkbill, wild crane's-bill

Herb robert was important in herbal medicine in the 17th century. The herbalist Gerard claimed that it would "cure miraculously ruptures and burstings."

Herb robert is a common wildflower, and an important medicinal herb, found in woodland and walls throughout the northern hemisphere. It has thin red stalks, small, bright rose-pink flowers with white centers and rather sparse, deeply divided green leaves that hang down from the stalks.

The plant can be found in many backyards and on wasteland, and is usually regarded as a weed. Its most marked feature is the unpleasant smell it emits from its leaves, which gives it the common name of stinking cranesbill. In spite of this drawback, some gardeners do grow herb robert in drifts as a backdrop to other plants.

It was highly regarded as a wound herb in the Middle Ages for its ability to staunch the flow of blood. It was also a cure for ulcers and sores, and was taken in cases of kidney stones and other urinary disorders. In herbal medicine today it is used internally in the treatment of ulcers and gastric infections, and externally to cure sore throats, boils, and skin blemishes.

vital statistics

FAMILY
Geraniaceae

OTHER VARIETIES AND SPECIES
G. maculatum, G. phaeum (Mourning Widow), G. pratense (Meadow cranesbill), G. sylvaticum. There are many species and cultivated varieties.

ANNUAL OR BIENNIAL
ZONE 4

HEIGHT
1–2ft (30–60cm)

SPREAD
12in (30cm)

FLOWERS
Small, bright rose-pink, with whiteish centers, in clusters.

FOLIAGE
Drooping, green, and deeply divided. Red veins and stalks.

NATURAL HABITAT
Found throughout the northern hemisphere. Common in walls and wasteland.

SITE
Sun or partial shade.

SOIL
Will grow in any dry well-drained soil, including gravel.

PROPAGATION
Sow seeds in spring. Self-seeds freely.

FLOWERING
Early summer.

USES
Herbal medicine.

Geum rivale

Water avens

avens root, cure-all, Indian chocolate, purple avens, throat root

This herb is less important medically than its near relative, herb bennet, but it contains many of the same medicinal properties and has been used as a cure-all by a number of the Native Americans. As its common name implies, it is a plant that needs a good deal of moisture. Grow water avens in fertile soil that retains moisture.

It has attractive, dusky-pink to dark orange flowers with prominent long sepals (outer petals) that are held up on long stalks. The basal leaves are divided, but the stem leaves are broadly rounded in shape, divided into three parts. They are a bright, shiny green. There are a number of good garden varieties that boast larger flowers than the species plant. They come in a variety of colors that include yellow, pale apricot, and deep orange.

Water avens is an astringent, antiseptic herb that is used in herbal medicine to reduce inflammation, lower fevers, and as a digestive tonic. The whole plant is used to make decoctions or liquid extracts that are given for the treatment of bowel disease, diarrhea, and fever.

A number of varieties of purple avens have been developed, including; 'Coppertone', (apricot-copper flowers), 'Lemon Drops', (lemon-yellow flowers), and 'Tangerine', (bright orange flowers).

vital statistics

FAMILY
Rosaceae

OTHER VARIETIES AND SPECIES
G. coccineum, G. montanum, G. reptans, G. urbanum. There are many colorful garden varieties available.

PERENNIAL ZONE 4

HEIGHT
1–2ft (30–60cm)

SPREAD
18in (45cm)

FLOWERS
Pinkish orange, bell-shaped, hanging down in clusters.

FOLIAGE
Deeply divided basal leaves. Round, bright green, shiny stem leaves divided into three.

NATURAL HABITAT
Native of temperate regions worldwide. Found in moist woodland and beside streams.

SITE
Partial shade.

SOIL
Moisture-retaining, fertile soil.

PROPAGATION
Sow seeds in the fall. Divide in fall or spring.

FLOWERING
Early summer.

USES
Herbal medicine, chocolate-flavored drinks.

Geum urbanum

Herb bennet

blessed herb, European avens, star-of-the-earth, yellow avens

This is a common wildflower in woodland and on wasteland. It was an extremely important medicinal herb in medieval times and was often grown by the Benedictine monks, hence its common name. It has small yellow flowers held aloft on stalks, and large dark green leaves, divided into three parts, with indented edges. It occurs as a weed on cultivated soil.

The aromatic roots, which smell of cloves, were thought to give protection against evil and poisons. It had many uses. It was used as a cure for chest complaints and pains in the sides. If taken every morning in the spring it "comforted the heart, opened obstructions in the liver and was a good preservative against the plague." It was also supposed to clear the complexion and remove spots and skin blemishes from the face.

Today it is used in herbal medicine to reduce inflammation and to treat diseases of the bowels, as well as hemorrhoids, vaginal discharge, and sore throats and gums. It has the same properties and uses as water avens, but is stronger and more widely used. You can eat the young leaves in salads and the root was formerly used as a pot herb.

Many medicinal properties were attributed to this ancient herb, including the ability to cure poor eyesight and deafness.

vital statistics

FAMILY
Rosaceae

OTHER VARIETIES AND SPECIES
G. coccineum, G. montanum, G. reptans, G. rivale. There are many garden varieties available.

PERENNIAL ZONE 4

HEIGHT
1–2ft (30–60cm)

SPREAD
18in (45cm)

FLOWERS
Yellow flowers followed by purple-tinged fruits.

FOLIAGE
Deeply divided, dark green rosettes with indented edges. Central portion is the largest.

NATURAL HABITAT
Native of temperate regions worldwide. Found in woodland and on wasteland.

SITE
Sun or partial shade.

SOIL
Moisture-retaining, fertile soil.

PROPAGATION
Sow seeds in the spring or fall. Self-seeds.

FLOWERING
Summer.

USES
Herbal medicine, culinary.

Gillenia trifoliata
Indian physic
American ipecacuanha

This attractive plant is native to North America, even though it was named after a German botanist called Gillenius. It is an emetic (causing vomiting) herb and can be prescribed by herbalists in very small doses to treat fevers, constipation, and chronic diarrhea. The herb also acts as a tonic and expectorant. It was formerly used in the treatment of muscular pains and rheumatism.

As the Latin name suggests, the leaves are its most distinctive feature. They are bronze-green with deep veins and coarsely toothed edges, and are divided into three, with each part shaped like a narrow oval with a pointed end. The flowers appear in early summer and are white to pink and star shaped, with red-tinted calyces (outer petals). They are held in clusters on red stalks and, although not large, can look striking in a display. Grow the herb in light shade and well-drained soil that does not dry out.

The most striking feature of the plant is the flower, which is white, tinged with pink, with exceptionally narrow, pointed petals.

vital statistics

FAMILY
Rosaceae

OTHER VARIETIES AND SPECIES
G. stipulata

PERENNIAL ZONE 3

HEIGHT
2–3ft (60–90cm)

SPREAD
2ft (60cm)

FLOWERS
White to pale pink, star-shaped, with open petals.

FOLIAGE
Deeply divided into three. Bronze-green, long, oval-shaped. Deeply veined with coarse toothed edges.

NATURAL HABITAT
Native of North America. Grows in open woodland.

SITE
Shade or partial shade.

SOIL
Well-drained, fertile soil.

PROPAGATION
Sow seeds in the spring or fall. Divide in spring or fall.

FLOWERING
Early summer.

USES
Herbal medicine.

Glycyrrhiza glabra
Licorice
sweet wood

Licorice is a fairly large plant with a long yellow, fibrous taproot, and stems that may reach 5ft (1.5m) in length. Various species of licorice are important in herbal and Chinese medicine today. Its name comes from the Greek, *glyks*, meaning "sweet," and *rhiza*, meaning "root." The oval, pale green leaves appear in opposite pairs (pinnate) down the whole length of the stem. It carries pea-like, blue, violet, or white flowers, held in sprays on upright stalks that appear in late summer. These are followed by long, brown seedpods in the fall. The plant has been an important source of food flavoring since the 15th century.

Licorice has been an effective treatment for coughs, wheezing, and shortness of breath for centuries and it is often used in cough medicine and lozenges. It is used as a laxative for children, since it calms the stomach. At one time it was believed to be a cure for infertility in women. Today it is used in the treatment of respiratory disease and commercially as a flavoring.

Caution: Excess use can raise the blood pressure and have other serious side effects. Use only in consultation with a qualified practitioner.

Licorice is used in the manufacture of candies. In Chinese medicine *G. uralensis*, Chinese licorice, is thought to be able to prolong life.

FAMILY Leguminosae/Papilionaceae	**PERENNIAL** **ZONE 4**	**FOLIAGE** Sticky, green, narrow, oval leaves appear in pairs on stalks.	**SOIL** Well-drained, fertile moist soil.	**FLOWERING** Late summer.
OTHER VARIETIES AND SPECIES *G. echinata, G. lepidota, G. uralensis*	**HEIGHT** 5ft (1.5m)	**NATURAL HABITAT** Native of southwestern Asia and the Mediterranean. Found in wasteland but various species have different habitats.	**PROPAGATION** Sow seeds in the spring or fall. Divide in roots in the spring.	**USES** Herbal medicine, culinary.
	SPREAD 3ft (90cm)			
	FLOWERS Pea-like blue, pale violet, and white flowers on long spikes.	**SITE** Sun.		

Hamamelis virginiana
American witch hazel
snapping hazel, spotted alder, tobacco wood, winterbloom

Witch hazels are a popular small tree grown in many gardens. It was a sacred medicinal herb of the Native Americans, who used it to heal bruised eyes. The leaves turn brilliant yellow and red in fall, and the flowers emerge in the early part of the year on the bare branches, like twisted yellow stars, with many long, thin, intermingled petals, which are incredibly fragrant. Plant them in soil that is moderately fertile, moist, acid to neutral. They will not flourish in alkaline soil. The two most popular garden species are *H. japonica* and *H.* x *intermedia*, both of which have a number of named varieties. These generally have larger, sweeter smelling flowers.

Witch hazel extract can be bought in any drugstore and is a traditional lotion for bruises, sprains, varicose veins, and wounds, while an ointment made from the herb is used to treat piles. Commercial preparations are made from the young flowering twigs. It is also prescribed for stomach ailments, and to treat dysentery, hemorrhages, and prolapses. It is an ingredient in a number of cosmetics.

Witch hazel is a well-known country remedy for a number of ailments, especially bruising. The leaves turn yellow and red in fall and the fragrant flowers emerge in late winter.

vital statistics

FAMILY Hamamelidaceae	**DECIDUOUS SHRUB OR SMALL TREE ZONE 4**	**FOLIAGE** Oval and long with coarsely toothed edges. They turn brilliant yellow and orange in the fall.	**SOIL** Moist, fertile soil that must be acid to neutral.	**FLOWERING** Winter.
OTHER VARIETIES AND SPECIES *H.* x *intermedia, H. japonica, H. mollis* (Chinese witch hazel) *H. vernalis* (Ozark witch hazel). There are many garden varieties available.	**HEIGHT** 12ft (4m) **SPREAD** 12ft (4m) **FLOWERS** Yellow twisted clusters. Red or brown centers in winter.	**NATURAL HABITAT** Native of North America. Grows in moist woodland. **SITE** Sun or partial shade.	**PROPAGATION** Sow in the fall. Take softwood cuttings in the summer.	**USES** Herbal medicine, cosmetic.

Helianthus annuus ⊕ ✻ ⊗ ⬦ ○
Sunflower

The annual sunflower is a multipurpose plant. It is grown commercially for the oil contained in the seeds. When the oil has been processed, the waste product is then used for cattle feed. The plant has herbal qualities, the seeds are used in the kitchen, and the fibers of the tough stems are used to make paper.

The sunflower is also the great family plant that children love to grow competitively to see which is the largest. The flowerhead is the image of the sun, with the giant yellow petals and a large brown, central disk that contains hundreds of small flowers that turn into seeds. The Latin name comes from the Greek *helios*, meaning "sun," and *anthos*, which means "flower." Keep sunflowers well watered, and cut and dry the heads when they start to droop. The plant is high in potash and any waste should be added to the compost heap.

Apart from its uses in the kitchen as a cooking oil and flavoring, sunflower is used in the manufacture of margarine. It is taken internally in herbal medicine for malaria and bronchial infections. The oil is used for some massage oils.

Caution: Contact with the leaves and stalks may cause skin allergies.

Sunflowers are an important commercial crop. In Russia the heads were steeped in vodka and used to treat malaria.

vital statistics

FAMILY Compositae	**ANNUAL**	**FOLIAGE** Large, green, hairy leaves.	**SOIL** Any, but the plant must be kept well watered.	**FLOWERING** Mid- to late summer.
OTHER VARIETIES AND SPECIES *H. a.* 'Autumn Beauty' (smaller with dark flowerheads), *H. a.* 'Russian Giant' (tall yellow flowerheads)	**HEIGHT** 10–15ft (3–6m) **SPREAD** 18in (45cm)	**NATURAL HABITAT** Native of Mexico and Peru. Found on dry prairies or in damp swamps depending on the species.	**PROPAGATION** Sow seed in spring at 61°F (16°C).	**USES** Culinary, commercial, herbal medicine.
	FLOWERS Large flowers with yellow rays and a brown-gold center made up of many small flowers.	**SITE** Full sun.		

Flavored oils & vinegars

Rather than purchase flavored oils and vinegars you can always flavor your own at home, using herbs you have grown. Basil can be used to flavor olive oil, and tarragon or marjoram can be used to flavor vinegar.

Basil-flavored olive oil

YOU WILL NEED:

2½ cups (20 fl oz/575 ml) olive oil

6 tbsp chopped basil

Add the basil leaves to the oil and let it stand for two weeks, shaking the bottle every 2–3 days. At the end of the period, check the flavor and then strain off the leaves and rebottle.

Sambucus nigra Black elder

Ocimum basilicum Sweet basil

Tarragon vinegar

YOU WILL NEED:

2½ cups (20 fl oz/575 ml) white wine vinegar

6 tbsp (or equivalent) tarragon

Warm the vinegar, do not boil, and then add the tarragon. This can be added in sprigs. Leave for 2 weeks and then check the flavor. Strain and rebottle if you wish.

Elderflower vinegar

Follow the recipe above substituting 6 heads of elderflowers for the tarragon. This vinegar should be strained after 2 weeks.

Rosemarinus officinali Rosemary

Essential oils

These are prepared by adding 2 tablespoons finely crushed fresh herbs to ¾ cup (6 fl oz/175 ml) pure vegetable oil. Add one tablespoon plain (not malt) vinegar and leave in warm sunlight to mature for 3 weeks. To make an extra strong oil strain the mixture at the end of each week and replace the herbs with fresh ones.

Excellent essential oils are made from lavender flowers, rosemary, marjoram, lemon grass, and cloves but the possible range is infinite. All essential oils must be used with care, in excess they are poisonous and need careful measuring even when used externally.

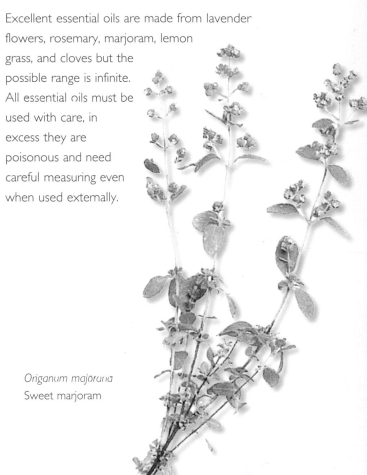

Origanum majorana
Sweet marjoram

Cymbopogon citratus Lemon grass

Lavendula Lavender

Helichrysum italicum ssp. *serotinum*
Curry plant

This evergreen subshrub, with thin, silver-gray leaves and small, yellow flowers, is sometimes used in the kitchen to add flavor to soups, stews, and vegetables. The leaves have an intensely aromatic scent, and they give off an uncanny smell of curry when brushed against.

Grow it as an edging plant or at the front of a sunny border. The plant will flourish in poor soil but it will not tolerate cold, damp conditions over winter. Make sure it is grown in a well-drained spot. You can cut and dry the flowers for flower arranging. The essential oil from *H. orientale* is used in the perfume industry. A number of helichrysums once had minor uses in herbal medicine. They were used as an herbal tea and to aid breathing problems, but their use has become obsolete, as doubt has been thrown on their safety for consumption.

Caution: Prolonged use is not recommended. If consumed, the leaves of the plant may cause an adverse reaction.

This is not a plant that should be used regularly in the kitchen; doubts have been cast on its safety.

vital statistics

FAMILY Compositae	**EVERGREEN SUBSHRUB ZONE 6**	**FOLIAGE** Silver-gray, narrow leaves.	**SOIL** Any well-drained soil.	**FLOWERING** Summer.
OTHER VARIETIES AND SPECIES *H. milfordiae, H. milliganii, H. orientale, H. petiolare, H. splendidum, H. stoechas*	**HEIGHT** 2ft (60cm)	**NATURAL HABITAT** Native of the Mediterranean. Found on dry, rocky hillsides.	**PROPAGATION** Take softwood or semiripe cuttings in summer.	**USES** Dried flowers, culinary, formerly medicinal.
	SPREAD 2ft (60cm)	**SITE** Full sun.		
	FLOWERS Small, deep yellow flowers on long stalks.			

Heliotropium arborescens
Heliotrope

The heliotrope, or cherry pie, is a native of Peru and was formerly an ingredient in herbal medicine, but is no longer used today. In temperate climates heliotropes are most often grown as half-hardy annuals and planted out in summer bedding schemes. A number of annual varieties have been developed. They have an intense scent and are often used in potpourris for their fragrance. Their name comes from the Greek *helios*, "sun," and *trope*, which means "turning," and refers to the flowers, which follow the course of the sun as it travels from east to west during the day. The flowers are a beautiful deep violet-blue and the leaves are narrow, oval to lance-shaped, dark green, deeply veined and sometimes tinged with bronze.

H. arborescens makes a bushy shrub in frost-free climates but it needs a minimum winter temperature of 45°F (7°C) to survive. In temperate climates grow the plant in a container and bring it inside to a cool greenhouse, or indoors in a cool room, during the winter months. Heliotropes are good butterfly plants.

Caution: Contact with leaves may cause skin and eye irritations.

The heliotrope is very strongly scented and makes a good container plant in temperate climates where it can be given shelter from cold weather in the winter months.

---

vital statistics

FAMILY
Boraginaceae

OTHER VARIETIES AND SPECIES
H. arborescens 'Chatsworth', *H. a.* 'Marine', *H. a.* 'Mini Marine', *H. a.* 'Princess Marina'

FROST-TENDER EVERGREEN SUBSHRUB

HEIGHT
2ft (60cm)

SPREAD
2ft (60cm)

FLOWERS
Intense violet-blue to lavender-blue flowers in large clusters.

FOLIAGE
Dark green, sometimes bronze tinged, oval, and deeply veined.

NATURAL HABITAT
Native of Peru. Found on dry, sandy pasture.

SITE
Full sun.

SOIL
Fertile, well-drained soil.

PROPAGATION
Sow seeds in spring at 61–64°F (16–18°C). Take stem-tip cuttings or semiripe cuttings in the summer.

FLOWERING
Summer.

USES
Dried flowers, potpourri, butterfly plant, formerly medicinal.

Helleborus niger
Christmas rose
black hellebore

This is a poisonous plant and the Latin name comes from the Greek *helein*, "to cause death," and *bora*, which means "food," a direct reference to its deadly qualities. *Niger* describes the roots of the plant, which are black. This plant has been used in homeopathic medicine for several centuries but it is rarely used today.

The Christmas rose is unlikely to flower on Christmas day in temperate zones in the northern hemisphere, but it flowers soon after and is one of the loveliest plants in the garden in the early part of the year. The flowers are usually white, tinged with pink and green, and many varieties are attractively spotted inside. They last for several weeks if they are not ruined by rain, and the single heads, carried on stalks, hang down in rather shy clumps.

The plant was used in herbal medicine to treat leprosy, fevers, madness, convulsions, and jaundice, and in powder form to heal ulcers. Goat's milk was the prescribed antidote if too much of the deadly herb was taken at a time.

Caution: All parts of the plant are poisonous. Avoid contact with the skin or eyes.

Hellebores are a much-loved flower of late winter. *H. niger*, the Christmas rose, has attractive white, pink, and purple spotted flowers. *H. viridis*, illustrated here, has green flowers.

vital statistics

FAMILY
Ranunculaceae

OTHER VARIETIES AND SPECIES
H. niger ssp. *macranthus*, *H. orientalis*, *H. foetidus*, *H. lividus*, *H. viridis*. There are many species and garden varieties available.

PERENNIAL ZONE 4

HEIGHT
12in (30cm)

SPREAD
18in (45cm)

FLOWERS
White with yellow centers, some varieties green or pink.

FOLIAGE
Dark green, deeply divided, rough leaves with seven or more oblong, toothed leaflets.

NATURAL HABITAT
Native of central Europe. Found in the mountains and open woodlands.

SITE
Shade or partial shade.

SOIL
Fertile, well-drained, moisture-retaining alkaline.

PROPAGATION
Sow ripe seeds in spring, but it is better to divide named varieties after flowering is over.

FLOWERING
Winter.

USES
Formerly herbal medicine.

Hesperis matronalis
Dame's rocket

This old-fashioned, short-lived perennial can be grown as a biennial. It has attractive terminal spikes of four-petaled white, purple, or violet flowers. You can pick the narrow leaves and use them in salads, to which they add a bitter taste. Pick the leaves before the plant comes into flower. Plant dame's rocket in fertile, well-drained soil, with sun or partial shade. There are a number of special varieties that have been developed for the garden, including *H. m.* var. *albiflora* 'Alba Plena', with double white flowers, and *H. m.* 'Lilacina Flore Pleno', with double lilac flowers. The Latin name comes from the Greek *hesperos*, "the evening," referring to the flowers that emit scent in the evening.

It was formerly used as a wound herb, and as an ingredient in enemas. It was taken in the form of a syrup in the treatment of asthma, to relieve congestion of the lungs, and to cure persistent coughs. It is high in vitamin C and was used in the treatment of scurvy.

Dame's rocket was important in the 16th and 17th centuries as a medicinal herb, and was used to treat cattle as well as humans.

vital statistics

FAMILY
Cruciferae

OTHER VARIETIES AND SPECIES
H. m. var. *albiflora* 'Alba Plena',
H. m. 'Lilacina Flore Pleno',
H. steveniana

SHORT-LIVED PERENNIAL OR BIENNIAL
ZONE 5

HEIGHT
3ft (90cm)

SPREAD
18in (45cm)

FLOWERS
White, purple, or violet.

FOLIAGE
Dark green, oval, pointed leaves.

NATURAL HABITAT
Native of central and southern Europe and western Asia. Found on wasteland and in woodland.

SITE
Sun or partial shade.

SOIL
Prefers rich, moisture-retaining soil, but tolerates most soils.

PROPAGATION
Sow seeds in spring. Take basal cuttings in spring.

FLOWERING
Summer.

USES
Culinary, evening scent, formerly medicinal.

Humulus lupulus
Hop

H ops are one of the most vigorous climbers and are best known as a flavoring and preservative used in beer. Today modern breeding has reduced the growth rate of most plants. They are still an important ingredient in the brewing industry. They make spectacular annual climbers: Grow them over a trellis or pergola. The leaves are very attractive; the variety 'Aureus', with its golden foliage, is the one most commonly grown. They will quickly engulf any unsightly garden objects you wish to cover up, such as an old shed. Buy female plants rather than attempt to grow hops from seed, as technically they are dioecious, which means that the male and female plants are separate.

Hop plants have been important medically for hundreds of years. They were used to clean the blood and as a cure for venereal disease, sores, ringworm, and intestinal worms. Today the cones of the female plant are used in herbal medicine to treat nervous tension, irritability, and insomnia. In fact, many people still use a hop pillow to sleep on.

Cut and dry the flowerheads for winter flower arrangements. You can also cut the young shoots that appear in the spring and cook them in the same way as asparagus. These are said to "purify the blood, and keep the body gently open." The fibrous stems of the plant are sometimes used in the textile industry.

Hops are best known as a flavoring for beer. Gerard stated that "hops make it [beer] a physicall drinke to keepe the body in health, than an ordinary drinke for the quenching of our thirst."

vital statistics

FAMILY
Cannabaciae

OTHER VARIETIES AND SPECIES
H. l. 'Aureus', *H. japonicus*

PERENNIAL CLIMBER ZONE 3

HEIGHT
10–15ft (3–4.5m)

SPREAD
4ft (1.2m)

FLOWERS
Greenish-yellow, hanging cones on the female plants.

FOLIAGE
Dark green, heart-shaped leaves with three to five lobes and toothed margins.

NATURAL HABITAT
Europe, western Asia, and North America. Grows wild in woodland in temperate zones.

SITE
Sun or partial shade.

SOIL
Rich, moisture retentive, and well-drained.

PROPAGATION
Sow seeds at 59–64°F (15–18°C) in spring or take softwood cuttings in spring.

FLOWERING
Late summer.

USES
Culinary, herbal medicine, dried flowers, textiles.

h

Hyoscyamus niger

Henbane

black henbane, devil's eye, hogbean, poison tobacco, stinking nightshade

This is a poisonous herb that is closely related to deadly nightshade, *Atropa belladonna*. Nevertheless, it is used today in herbal and homeopathic medicine as a relaxant and sedative. It is notorious for its use by sorcerers in the Dark Ages to cause hallucinations and death, and it is the herb that was used by Claudius to kill Hamlet's father in Shakespeare's *Hamlet*.

> *Upon my secure hour thy uncle stole,*
> *With juice of cursed hebenon in a vial*
> *And in the porches of my ears did pour*
> *The leperous distilment...*

The plant grows wild on dry, sandy soils and wasteland. It is distinguished by its large, felted, pale green, hairy, sticky leaves with lance-shaped points and large, purple-veined, creamy flowers with a deep purple center, which appear throughout the summer, either singly or in pairs. The name comes from the Greek *hys*, meaning "pig," and *kyanos*, "bean," which refers to the strange fact that pigs can eat the seeds of the plant without being poisoned. It is also sometimes called hogbean. The plant's distinctive, obnoxious smell gives it another common name, stinking nightshade.

Henbane is one of the ingredients in some travel-sickness remedies. It was formerly used to cure various inflammations and to alleviate pain caused by gout, headaches, and swellings. The juice was frequently mixed with vinegar and applied to the forehead. If swallowed by mistake, goat's milk, honey water, and mustard seed were considered the best antidotes.

Caution: All parts of the plant are poisonous and should not be taken in any form. Contact with the skin may cause irritation.

Henbane has rather sinister-looking, light purple, flowers, warning the would-be user of its poisonous properties.

FAMILY Solanaceae	**ANNUAL OR BIENNIAL ZONE 5**	**FOLIAGE** Large, felted, pale green, hairy, sticky leaves.	**SOIL** Well-drained, alkaline.	**FLOWERING** Summer.
OTHER VARIETIES AND SPECIES *H. albus* (Russian henbane), *H. aureus, H. muticus* (Egyptian henbane)	**HEIGHT** 2–4ft (60–1.2m) **SPREAD** 3ft (90cm)	**NATURAL HABITAT** Europe and western Asia. Usually found on wasteland, banks, and cliffs.	**PROPAGATION** Henbanes are sometimes grown by herbalists, although this is not recommended for private gardens. Henbanes self-seed freely.	**USES** Herbal medicine.
	FLOWERS Large, creamy, purple-veined, bell-shaped. Single or in pairs.	**SITE** Sun.		

Hypericum perforatum
St. John's-wort
amber, goatweed, Klamath weed, Tipton weed

Hypericums form a large genus. *H. perforatum* was, and remains, an extremely important herb medically. It was thought to have magical properties, as the flowers produce a red liquid when crushed, which can be used as a dye. In the Dark and Middle Ages it was placed above religious icons to ward off evil. It is a tufted perennial and carries the star-shaped yellow flowers common to so many of the genus. It looks attractive in a wildflower garden.

For centuries the herb was used to treat fevers, bruises, wounds, and snake bites. It was a diuretic and a cure for sciatica, palsy, and agues. A tincture of the flowers taken in wine was recommended for melancholy and madness.

Today it is used in herbal medicine for bruises, wounds, especially burns, and to ease painful joints. It is an antidepressant and is taken in dried form internally for depression, nervous tension, premenstrual syndrome, and complications during the menopause. Lately it has been used in trials to test drugs to combat AIDS.

The related species *H. androsaemum* used to be commonly used in herbal medicine and was regarded as an excellent remedy for wounds.

A controlled drug trial in Germany recently confirmed that St. John's-wort was the most effective and least harmful antidepressant.

vital statistics

FAMILY
Hypericaceae

OTHER VARIETIES AND SPECIES
H. androsaemum (tutsan, park leaves), *H. calycinum* (Rose of Sharon, Aaron's beard), *H. × inodorum*, *H. olympicum*, *H. reptans*

PERENNIAL ZONE 3

HEIGHT
3ft (90cm)

SPREAD
1ft (30cm)

FLOWERS
Bright yellow, small, five-petaled with gold stamens.

FOLIAGE
Pale green, veined, with large dots, held in opposite pairs.

NATURAL HABITAT
Native to Europe and western Asia. Found on dry, limestone areas, wasteland and in woods.

SITE
Sun or partial shade.

SOIL
Most, well-drained, preferably alkaline soils.

PROPAGATION
Sow seeds in spring or fall. Divide in spring. Take softwood cuttings in spring.

FLOWERING
Summer.

USES
Herbal medicine.

Hyssopus officinalis
Hyssop

Hyssop is one of the oldest herbs in cultivation. You can use the leaves to make hyssop tea, which is considered a cure for bronchitis and chest complaints in herbal medicine. Also use the leaves in soups, salads, and stews to add a bittermint flavor. However, the flavor is strong and not universally popular. The herb was used in biblical times and, according to St. John's Gospel, it was mixed with vinegar and given to Jesus on the cross. It was also used by monks and is one of the ingredients of both Chartreuse and Benedictine liqueurs. The oil extracted from hyssop is used in perfumes. It is an attractive plant with brilliant blue flowers held on a spike and grows well with other scented herbs, such as lavender and sage. Trim them well and the flowers will made a good, dense display. The plant is also a great bee and butterfly attractor.

It is a bitter, astringent, herb that is used in herbal medicine to reduce inflammation, and it has a tonic effect on the nervous system. It is also used to treat bronchial disorders, coughs, and colic, and externally for cuts and bruises. It was formerly considered a cure for dropsy and spleen, tinnitus, and head lice.

Hyssop was one of the cure-all herbs of the Middle Ages. It is still an effective treatment for bronchial complaints. It is also used as a flavoring in the liqueur Chartreuse.

vital statistics

FAMILY
Labiatae

OTHER VARIETIES AND SPECIES
H. o. f. albus, H. o. ssp. *aristatus, H. o. roseus.*

PERENNIAL EVERGREEN SHRUB
ZONES 4–5

HEIGHT
2ft (60cm)

SPREAD
18in (45cm)

FLOWERS
Rich blue two-lipped flowers.

FOLIAGE
Dark green, narrow, pointed aromatic leaves.

NATURAL HABITAT
Native of central and southern Europe and western Asia. Found on dry, limestone soils.

SITE
Full sun.

SOIL
Well-drained, light.

PROPAGATION
Sow seeds in fall. Take softwood cuttings in summer.

FLOWERING
Summer.

USES
Herbal medicine, culinary, bee and butterfly plant.

Inula helenium

Elecampane

elfdock, elfwort, horse-elder, horseheal, scabwort

Many properties were attributed to this plant. It was held to be a "cure for kidney and bladder stones, a resistance to poison of serpents and pestilential and putrid fevers, and even the plague itself."

The roots, flowers, and oil of elecampane are all used in herbal medicine. The plant is considered particularly effective in the treatment of bacterial and fungal infections. Grow this tall, stately herb on its own to form a focal point in a border. It can reach as high as 8ft (2.4m), and has large, spidery, yellow flowers, like a smaller version of a sunflower. Elecampane belongs to the daisy family and the flowers are similar to most of its members. They stand out against the dark green foliage.

Once popular as a flavoring for desserts and fish dishes, the roots are still used to flavor some liqueurs and may be candied. It has been used to cure bronchitis and hay fever for hundreds of years, and in the words of Culpeper "has not its equal in the cure of whooping-cough in children, when all other medicines fail." An infusion of the leaves is prescribed to be inhaled for chest complaints and sinus conditions. A decoction of the leaves, if drunk regularly, is said to strengthen the gums and get rid of worms.

vital statistics

FAMILY
Compositae

OTHER VARIETIES AND SPECIES
I. magnific, I. hookeri, I. orientalis, I. royleana

PERENNIAL ZONE 3

HEIGHT
4–8ft (1.2–2.4m)

SPREAD
3ft (90cm)

FLOWERS
Large, bright yellow, like smaller sunflowers.

FOLIAGE
Green, long, very woolly beneath.

NATURAL HABITAT
Native of central and southern Europe and western Asia.

SITE
Full sun or partial shade.

SOIL
Fertile, moisture-retaining soil.

PROPAGATION
Sow seeds in spring or in the fall when ripe. Divide in the fall.

FLOWERING
Midsummer onwards.

USES
Herbal medicine, culinary, dye plant, flavoring.

Iris pseudacorus
Yellow flag iris
fleur-de-lys, flag lily, pale yellow iris

The yellow flag is a spectacular, invasive plant that flourishes in damp places beside ponds and streams. *I. pseudacorus* has been used in herbal medicine for several hundred years as a purgative, to cure colic, and as a guard against the plague. The plant carries large yellow flowers with distinctive drooping petals and gray-green, long, sword-like leaves that spring from the rhizome and grow taller than the flower spikes. The rhizome is the part used in medicine, while the flowers are attractive to bees.

A yellow dye is made from the flowers, and a black dye from the roots. The fragrant, dried roots of the iris have long been known as orris, or orris root. These have an intense violet smell and are used in the perfume industry, and you can use them at home in potpourris. Today the chief species used in herbal medicine is *I. versicolor*. It is used to stimulate the gall bladder, reduce inflammation, and to treat all manner of skin complaints, such as psoriasis and acne. The plant is not given to pregnant women.

Caution: All parts of the iris are poisonous if eaten. This applies particularly to the roots. Contact with the skin may cause skin allergies. Avoid during pregnancy.

The yellow flag is a vigorous plant that spreads freely in the right conditions and might need to be controlled.

vital statistics

FAMILY Iridaceae	**PERENNIAL** ZONE 3	**FOLIAGE** Green, long, sword-like, springing in a tight bunch from the rhizome.	**SOIL** Fertile, moisture-retaining soil.	**FLOWERING** Early summer.
OTHER VARIETIES AND SPECIES I. cristata, I. pallida, I. versicolor, I. virginica	**HEIGHT** 3ft (90cm–1.2m) **SPREAD** 2ft (60cm) **FLOWERS** Deep yellow with three drooping sepals.	**NATURAL HABITAT** Native of Europe, western Asia, and North Africa. Found beside streams and ponds. **SITE** Sun or partial shade.	**PROPAGATION** Divide in spring or fall.	**USES** Herbal medicine, dye plant, bee plant.

Isatis tinctoria
Woad
dyer's weed

Woad is the traditional dye of the ancient Britons, who painted their faces and bodies with it before battle. The plant has long been recognized in herbal medicine for its ability to staunch the flow of blood from a wound, and it is probably this property that encouraged warriors to use it, rather than its ability to terrorize their enemies. Woad is an attractive herb—upright, with bright yellow small flowers held in clumps on branches springing from a main stem. The leaves are blue-green, oblong or lance-shaped.

The dye, which is produced from the leaves by distilling them in ammonia, was used to color cloth. The resulting smell was so vile that Elizabeth I, queen of England in the 16th century, declared that it could not be manufactured within 5 miles (8km) of any of her palaces. It was replaced by indigo in the 17th century.

Formerly, woad was not taken internally but applied as a plaster or ointment, particularly to wounds or enlarged spleens. Today herbalists have found it to be strongly antiviral and effective in the treatment of skin rashes, abscesses, and sore throats, as well as fevers and serious conditions such as encephalitis and meningitis. It is also thought to have anticancer properties.

Woad is an increasingly important herb in medicine today and it is thought to contain anticancer properties.

vital statistics

FAMILY Cruciferae	**BIENNIAL** **ZONE 5**	**FOLIAGE** Blue-green, oblong or lance-shaped, rising up the stem.	**SOIL** Fertile, well-drained alkaline soil.	**FLOWERING** Summer.
OTHER VARIETIES AND SPECIES *I. glauca*	**HEIGHT** 4ft (1.2m)	**NATURAL HABITAT** Native of Europe and western Asia. Most often found growing on chalky wasteland.	**PROPAGATION** Sow seeds in the spring at 55–64°F (13–18°C) or fall in a cold frame.	**USES** Herbal medicine, dye plant.
	SPREAD 2ft (60cm)			
	FLOWERS Bright yellow, prolific flowers with four petals held in sprays.	**SITE** Full sun.		

Jasminum officinale
Jasmine
poet's jasmine

The common jasmine is a popular climber found on the walls of many gardens. It was one of the old official medicinal herbs. Unlike a number of other species, common jasmine is deciduous, although it may retain some leaves in mild winters. It is vigorous and beautifully scented, with white, star-shaped flowers. The English 19th-century poet, Shelley, wrote about its scent in his poem, *The Sensitive Plant*;
And the jessamine faint and the sweet tuberose.
The sweetest flower for scent that blows.

The essential oil distilled from the form *J. o. f. affine* is still used in the perfume industry. A number of other species are important today. These include *J. grandiflorum*, royal jasmine or Spanish jasmine, which is an important herb in branches of Indian medicine for treating fevers and various cancers, and *J. sambac*, Arabian jasmine, which is used in China to make jasmine tea from green tea and jasmine flowers.

Today the plant is used mainly in aromatherapy to treat depression, impotence, frigidity, nervous tension, and respiratory disorders, but it was formerly regarded as an herb that would help in difficult cases of childbirth, assist the milk flow, treat disorders of the uterus, and as an aphrodisiac and antiseptic.

The variety *J. o.* 'Aureovariegatum', shown here, has splashed yellow leaves. It is less effective as a climber than the species plant.

vital statistics

FAMILY Oleaceae	**DECIDUOUS CLIMBER** **ZONE 6**	**FOLIAGE** Dark green, oval leaves divided into 5–9 leaflets.	**SOIL** Fertile, well-drained soil.	**FLOWERING** Summer.
OTHER VARIETIES AND SPECIES *J. grandiflorum, J. nudiflorum* (winter jasmine), *J. o. f. affine*, *J. o.* 'Argenteovariegatum', *J. sambac*	**HEIGHT** 6–16ft (1.8–5m) **SPREAD** 10ft (3m) **FLOWERS** Very fragrant white, star-shaped flowers in clusters.	**NATURAL HABITAT** Native of northwestern Himalayas and the Middle East. **SITE** Sunny, sheltered.	**PROPAGATION** Semiripe cuttings in summer, layer in fall.	**USES** Perfume, tea, herbal medicine.

Juniperus communis
Common juniper

A number of junipers grow into large trees up to 20ft (6m) high, but there are slow-growing dwarf forms that are suitable even for the smallest gardens. The ripe berries give a pleasant flavor to potatoes and stews, and are also used as an ingredient in gin. Junipers have loosely arranged, needle-like leaves that are often very scented. Its green fruit ripens over two to three years, turning blue, then black.

Junipers contain a variety of properties, but many of them are highly toxic and they should not be used for medical purposes unless administered by a qualified practitioner. In previous centuries juniper was regarded as a cure-all for a variety of ailments, including dropsy, gas, coughs, shortness of breath, consumption, cramps, scurvy, and piles. Today it is used in herbal medicine to treat disorders of the urinary system, and an oil made from the unripe berries is used for gout and rheumatic pain.

Caution: Do not use the plant medicinally without suitable supervision. It can be an irritant when used externally.

Junipers are used both in the kitchen and in herbal medicine. Culpeper thought that oil drawn from the berries was a remedy for gas and colic.

vital statistics

FAMILY
Cupressaceae

OTHER VARIETIES AND SPECIES
J. c. 'Depressa Aurea' (yellow leaved), J. c. 'Compressa', J. c. 'Depressa Aurea', J. c. 'Hibernica', J. c. 'Prostrata'

EVERGREEN TREE OR SHRUB

HEIGHT
To 20ft (6m) or more

SPREAD
To 20ft (6m)

FLOWERS
Small, yellow-green flowers.

FOLIAGE
Thin needle-like leaves, blue green with white band on the inner leaves.

NATURAL HABITAT
Found in all temperate zones in the northern hemisphere.

SITE
Full sun or partial shade.

SOIL
Any.

PROPAGATION
Grow from seed but germination may take five years.

FLOWERING
Early summer.

USES
Culinary, herbal medicine.

Laurus nobilis
Sweet bay
bay laurel, bay tree

In the wild or grown in a sheltered garden the bay tree can reach 40ft (12m) or more. It has smooth, pointed leaves, which are dried and used to flavor stews and sauces. It is an excellent tree for any garden and is particularly useful grown in pots and containers in town or country gardens. You can trim bay into various topiary shapes: pyramids, balls, and semicircles. To maintain a bay topiary, prune the tree twice a year, using small pruning shears to avoid cutting the leaves in half. On the mature plants the yellow flowers are followed by black berries which, when pressed, produce an oil for perfume.

The leaves were traditionally used in ancient Rome to crown successful generals returning from the wars, as well as athletes victorious in competition. They were also once used in medicine, mostly as a purgative. They were given to women to speed up childbirth, to promote the flow of urine, and to expel gas. Externally, it was applied to sprains, bruises, ulcers, and skin complaints. Although it is used less frequently as a medicine today, bay is sometimes prescribed by herbalists to treat indigestion, colic, and gas, and is also used as an antiseptic.

Bay trees are trees of legend. The trees were considered magical, and were able to resist witchcraft, ward off evil, and avert lightning.

vital statistics

FAMILY Lauraceae	**EVERGREEN SHRUB OR ORNAMENTAL TREE ZONE 6**	**FOLIAGE** Dark green, smooth pointed leaves.	**SOIL** Any well-drained soil.	**FLOWERING** Early summer.
OTHER VARIETIES AND SPECIES *L. n.* f. *angustifolia*, *L. n.* 'Aureus' (golden-yellow leaves)	**HEIGHT** To 40ft (12m)	**NATURAL HABITAT** Around the shores of the Mediterranean and in the Canary Islands. Grows in scrub and open woodland.	**PROPAGATION** Sow seed in fall or take semiripe cuttings in summer.	**USES** Culinary, herbal medicine.
	SPREAD To 30ft (9m)			
	FLOWERS Small, creamy-yellow flowers.	**SITE** Sun or partial shade.		

Lavandula angustifolia (L. officinalis)
Lavender
English lavender

Lavender is probably the most popular low-growing hedging plant. The scented flowers are used in herbal sachets to sweeten bed linen and ward off moths.

Lavender is a wonderfully scented plant. It has been used as a medicinal herb for centuries. Grow it against a sunny wall close to the house, or as a lavender walk on either side of a path, where it will be especially effective. The flowers are very attractive to honey bees. The lavenders most commonly grown in gardens are varieties of *L. angustifolia* and *L.* x *intermedia*.

All lavenders are used in potpourris, scented pillows, and herbal sachets, and you can use the flowers in the kitchen to flavor jams or ice cream. Herbalists regarded the herb with a certain amount of suspicion, because the oil made from the flowers was "of a fierce and piercing quality," and a few drops only was recommended for the treatment for most conditions. It was used to treat stomach complaints, as well as fits, fainting, and dropsy.

Today it is used in herbal medicine to treat depression, coughs, and indigestion, as well as for burns, rheumatism, and a number of skin complaints. You can also burn it on fires to perfume a room. The oil from *L. angustifolia* is highly valued in aromatherapy and in the perfume industry. French lavender, *L. stoechas*, is used to treat nausea and as an insect repellent.

vital statistics

FAMILY
Labiatae

OTHER VARIETIES AND SPECIES
L. angustifolia 'Hidcote',
L. canariensis, L. stoechas.
Low-growing lavenders include *L. angustifolia* 'Little Lady', *L. a.* 'Little Lottie',
L. a. 'Imperial Gem',
L. a. 'Walberton's Silver Edge'

EVERGREEN SHRUB ZONES
5–8

HEIGHT
2ft (60cm)

SPREAD
To 3ft (90cm)

FLOWERS
Purple, blue, white, or pink, on long spikes in tight heads.

FOLIAGE
Gray or gray-green thin leaves growing from a stem.

NATURAL HABITAT
Native of the Mediterranean. Found growing on poor soil on dry rocky hillsides.

SITE
Open, sunny.

SOIL
Prefers poorish, well-drained, alkaline soils.

PROPAGATION
Sow seed in spring in a cold frame. Take semiripe cuttings in summer.

FLOWERING
Summer.

USES
Herbal medicine, scent, potpourri, insect repellent.

Leucanthemum vulgare
Oxeye daisy

Often called the marguerite or moon daisy, the oxeye daisy is a common wildflower. An old medicine herb, you can add the fresh young leaves to salads. The flowers are fairly small, with a ring of white petals and a yellow center. They grow on stalks 1–2ft (30–60cm) high. The plant self-seeds prolifically, so be ruthless and remove unwanted plants if they spread too widely. Plant oxeye daisy in well-drained soil in a sunny position. The flowers look very attractive in a wildflower garden; a bank of them in full bloom is a truly dramatic sight in the early summer.

Oxeye daisy was one of the traditional medicinal wound herbs, considered especially effective in treating chest wounds. It was also used externally to treat ulcers, bruises, and other sores, and it was particularly effective in treating infected wounds that were slow to heal. An ointment was made from the leaves, and a tincture was used for coughs and bronchial infections.

Marguerite was the name given by Gounod to the heroine in his opera *Faust*, which includes the famous love song, "He loves me, he loves me not," as Marguerite plucks off the petals of the daisy, one at a time.

FAMILY
Compositae

OTHER VARIETIES AND SPECIES
L. v. 'Maikönigin' ('May Queen')
L. maximum

PERENNIAL ZONE 3

HEIGHT
1–2ft (30-60cm)

SPREAD
1ft (30cm)

FLOWERS
Daisy flowers with pronounced yellow centers, held upright.

FOLIAGE
Small, toothed, green, with rounder leaves at the base.

NATURAL HABITAT
Native of Europe and temperate zones in Asia. Found on grassland and wasteland and in meadows.

SITE
Full sun.

SOIL
Fertile, well-drained.

PROPAGATION
Sow seeds in late summer or spring. Divide plants after flowering.

FLOWERING
Early summer.

USES
Culinary, herbal medicine.

Levisticum officinale
Lovage
sea parsley

Lovage is a large plant traditionally grown in kitchen gardens. The chopped leaves make a delicious flavoring for soups and casseroles. You can blanch and eat the stalks, but not the central flower stem. Use the seeds to flavor home-baked bread. The taste is like a peppery celery. It is a clump-forming perennial with dark green, celery-like, deeply divided foliage. In the summer it carries large, flat heads of small, yellow flowers.

As the common name implies, the plant was regarded as an aphrodisiac in medieval times and was frequently included in love potions. Lovage was also used to treat indigestion, and a distilled water made from the seeds was used as a cure for sore throats, quinsy, and as an eye bath. A tea made from the leaves is considered to promote digestion. It is still used for these purposes in herbal medicine, and is employed commercially to flavor alcoholic drinks and in the preparation of food.

Lovage tastes a bit like peppery celery and is used to flavor soups and casseroles. It also had many uses in herbal medicine.

vital statistics

FAMILY
Apiaceae/Umbelliferae

OTHER VARIETIES AND SPECIES
Ligusticum porteri (Porter's lovage, Colorado cough root), *L. scoticum* (Scots lovage)

PERENNIAL
ZONE 3

HEIGHT
4ft (1.2m) or more.

SPREAD
3ft (90cm)

FLOWERS
Star-shaped, small, yellow-green, carried in large, flat heads.

FOLIAGE
Dark green, shiny leaves shaped like celery. The leaves are very aromatic.

NATURAL HABITAT
Native of the eastern Mediterranean. Found in mountainous regions.

SITE
Full sun.

SOIL
Rich, well-drained, moisture retentive.

PROPAGATION
It is easiest to buy young plants from a nursery, but if you want to raise your own, sow seeds in fall or spring. Mature plants can be divided in spring.

FLOWERING
Midsummer.

USES
Culinary, herbal medicine.

Ligustrum vulgare
Privet
European privet

Privet is often grown in gardens since it is easy to keep under control and is semi-evergreen, generally retaining its leaves for much of the year in most temperate climates. The herb has a number of medicinal qualities. It has small, oval-shaped, green or gold leaves, depending on the variety grown, and sprays of white flowers in summer that smell somewhat unpleasant. These are followed by black berries. A yellow dye is made from the leaves.

Privet was not an important medicinal herb in previous centuries, but it was used in lotions to wash sores and cool inflammations. A sweet water distilled from the flowers was considered a cure for cases of dysentery. Today the most important member of the family medically is *L. lucidum*, Chinese privet, which is used in the treatment of cancer to prevent bone marrow loss during chemotherapy. Extracts from this shrub are also used to treat menopausal problems, cataracts, and insomnia. It is also used in Chinese medicine as a treatment for Parkinson's disease, hypertension, and hepatitis.

Caution: All parts of these plants are poisonous and should not be taken in any form.

Common privet is a popular hedging plant. Chinese privet has become an important herb in the treatment of cancer as well as liver and kidney complaints.

FAMILY Oleaceae	**DECIDUOUS OR SEMI-EVERGREEN SHRUB ZONE 4**	**FOLIAGE** Dark green, small, oval-shaped.	**SOIL** Any well-drained soil that is reasonable fertile.	**FLOWERING** Midsummer.
OTHER VARIETIES AND SPECIES *L. amurense, L. japonicum* (Japanese privet), *L. lucidum* (Chinese privet), *L. ovalifolium, L. sinense*	**HEIGHT** 6ft (1.8m) **SPREAD** 3ft (90cm) **FLOWERS** Small, white, held in clumps.	**NATURAL HABITAT** Native of the Europe, and southwestern Asia. Found growing in woods and scrubland. **SITE** Sun or partial shade.	**PROPAGATION** Sow seed in spring or fall in a cold frame. Take semiripe cuttings in summer or hardwood cuttings in winter.	**USES** Herbal medicine.

Linaria vulgaris

Butter and eggs

pennywort, toadflax, yellow toadflax, wild snapdragon

Butter and eggs was an important herb in medieval times. Today it is grown chiefly for its attractive flowers.

Butter and eggs is an herbaceous perennial that spreads by runners. Once used as an herbal medicine, it is now normally grown for its attractive flowers. The plant produces a swathe of upright spires with many blooms that remain throughout the summer. It self-seeds freely and you may need to control it. The flowers yield a variety of dyes—yellow, red, and brown. In the Middle Ages the flowers were boiled in milk and used as a fly killer. It is closely related to *Cymbalaria muralis*, Kenilworth ivy.

It was formerly used in herbal medicine to treat gallstones and many skin conditions, such as leprosy, dandruff, and pimples. Today it is rarely used, but is sometimes employed by herbalists and in homeopathic medicine as a treatment for diarrhea, cystitis, and jaundice, as well as a number of skin complaints.

Caution: Butter and eggs should not be used by pregnant women as it can cause miscarriage.

vital statistics

FAMILY
Scrophulariaceae

OTHER VARIETIES AND SPECIES
L. alpina (Alpine toadflax), *L. maroccana, L. purpurea, L. reticulata* (purple-net toadflax). There is a number of annual series available for summer bedding.

PERENNIAL ZONE 5

HEIGHT
2ft (60cm)

SPREAD
3ft (90cm) or more.

FLOWERS
Small, bright yellow flowers like those of a snapdragon.

FOLIAGE
Blue-green, narrow leaves growing from the main stalk.

NATURAL HABITAT
Native of Europe and Great Britain. Found on dry, sunny scrubland and wasteland.

SITE
Full sun.

SOIL
Grows in most soils but prefers well-drained, dry conditions, rich in sand or gravel.

PROPAGATION
Sow seeds in spring or fall. Divide established plants in spring.

FLOWERING
Throughout the summer.

USES
Dye plant, insecticide, herbal medicine.

Linum usitatissimum
Flax

flaxseed, linseed, lint bells, winterlien

The perennial flaxes, *L. perenne* and *L. narbonense*, are the most common flaxes. Grow them for their lovely, delicate blue flowers, which sometimes look as if they are floating in mid-air. The annual flax, *L. usitatissimum*, which has similar flowers, is more important both commercially and medically. It has been used as a medicinal herb for centuries and is one of the oldest plants in cultivation. It has two distinct types, one with longer stalks than the other. The tallest kind provides the raw material for linen; the stalks are rotted away in water, leaving the fibers that are used to manufacture the cloth.

Annual flax is a significant commercial crop grown and harvested for the seeds, which yield linseed oil—used in oil paints, varnishes, and putty, and to preserve baseball bats and gloves. The residue and the oil are sold as animal feed.

It was formerly used in herbal medicine to treat diseases of the breast and lungs, and heal sores and tumors. Today herbalists use it to treat indigestion, and to cure burns, boils, and ulcers. It is also an ingredient in cough medicines.

Caution: Large doses of the herb can be poisonous when taken internally.

Flax has been cultivated since Roman times. The seed stamped with the roots of wild cucumber were thought to draw forth splinters, thorns, and even broken bones.

vital statistics

FAMILY Linaceae	**ANNUAL**	**FOLIAGE** Narrow, gray-green strap-like leaves.	**SOIL** Well-drained, dry, sandy soil.	**FLOWERING** Summer.
	HEIGHT 3ft (90cm)			
OTHER VARIETIES AND SPECIES *L. flavum* (golden flax), *L. grandiflorum* (flowering flax), *L. narbonense, L. perenne* (perennial flax)	**SPREAD** 12in (30cm)	**NATURAL HABITAT** Temperate zones throughout the northern hemisphere. Found in dry grassland and scrub.	**PROPAGATION** Sow seeds in spring.	**USES** Herbal medicine, animal feed, linen manufacture.
	FLOWERS Clear, pale blue, delicate, open, five-petaled flowers shaped like shallow cups.	**SITE** Full sun.		

Lobelia siphilitica
Great blue lobelia

Lobelias are named for Matthias de l'Obel, a 17th-century botanist, who was physician to King James I of England. Many of the species are native to North America and a number have a variety of uses in herbal medicine. Great blue lobelia and the cardinal flower, *L. splendens*, are popular garden perennials, the former for its large, lavender blue flowers with white striped throats, and the latter for the brilliant scarlet flowers. Both flower at the end of the summer when many other plants are over.

As its Latin name implies, great blue lobelia was used by the Native Americans as a treatment for venereal disease. The cardinal flower was taken to treat cramps, rheumatism, nosebleeds, and as a love potion. *L. inflata*, an annual that has no real decorative merit, is also important medically and was smoked as a cure for asthma. It has the common names of wild tobacco and vomitweed. It is still used in herbal medicine to treat asthma and is also used externally for whiplash injuries.

Caution: All members of the genus are toxic and require medical supervision. They can cause vomiting and respiratory failure. Contact with the skin can cause rashes and irritation.

Lobelias were important in herbal medicine but they are now grown mainly as decorative plants, both perennials and annuals.

vital statistics

FAMILY
Lobeliaceae

OTHER VARIETIES AND SPECIES
L. cardinalis (cardinal flower), *L. chinensis*, *L. inflata*, *L. paludosa*, *L. splendens*, *L. tupa*

PERENNIAL ZONE 3

HEIGHT
3ft (90cm)

SPREAD
18in (45cm)

FLOWERS
Lavender-blue, tubular with a white stripe, held on a spire.

FOLIAGE
Light green, oblong, leaves that are slightly hairy.

NATURAL HABITAT
Native of eastern North America. Likes damp ground.

SITE
Sun or partial shade.

SOIL
Fertile, moist soil that does not dry out.

PROPAGATION
Sow seeds in spring.

FLOWERING
Late summer.

USES
Herbal medicine.

Lonicera periclymenum
European honeysuckle

The wild honeysuckle is a common plant in woodland, gardens, and farmland in Europe and western Asia. It was formerly used in herbal medicine as a gargle for sore throats. It grows in most soils and a large number of garden varieties have been developed. The flowers are creamy white to yellow, trumpet shaped, and quite small individually, but they appear in large rounded clumps at the end of the flowering stems. They are amazingly fragrant, a popular plant with bees and moths, and are used in the perfume industry. All honeysuckles are extremely rampant, so cut them back hard, otherwise they will turn into a tangled mass.

The leaves were used in medicine and an oil distilled from them was formerly used to treat cramp and convulsions. Bruised leaves were also used to treat skin disorders. However, the plants are poisonous, especially the berries, and the use of honeysuckles is now prescribed only for external applications. *L. japonica*, Japanese honeysuckle, has a number of uses in Chinese medicine and is used in the treatment of fevers, pneumonia, and rheumatoid arthritis. There are a number of good garden varieties.

Caution: No parts of the plant should be eaten. The berries are particularly poisonous.

Honeysuckles were a recommended treatment for sore throats but are no longer used in herbal medicine today. They remain popular garden plants with fragrant flowers.

vital statistics

FAMILY	PERENNIAL CLIMBER	FOLIAGE	SOIL	FLOWERING
Caprifoliaceae	ZONE 4	Gray-green, oval, and pointed, held in pairs.	Well-drained, fertile, sandy soil.	Summer.
OTHER VARIETIES AND SPECIES	**HEIGHT**		**PROPAGATION**	**USES**
L. × americana, *L. × brownii*, *L. caprifolium* (Italian honeysuckle), *L. fragrantissima*, *L. henryi*, *L. japonica*	To 30ft (9m)	**NATURAL HABITAT** Native of Europe and western Asia. Found in woodland and farmland.	Layer in the summer, take semiripe cuttings in the fall. Sow seed in the fall.	Formerly herbal medicine.
	SPREAD 5ft (1.5m)			
	FLOWERS White to yellow, tinged with red and pink, held in clumps.	**SITE** Sun or partial shade.		

Lythrum salicaria
Loosestrife
purple loosestrife

This is a plant of river banks and damp places and there are a number of garden varieties. It is still used in herbal medicine. *L. salicaria* is a rhizomatous perennial with spires of deep purple flowers that become invasive when grown in a favorable place. The name comes from *lythron*, meaning "black blood," and refers to the color of the flowers. Although they come from different families, this plant has a lot in common with the other loosestrifes, *Lysimachia nummularia*, creeping jenny, and *L. vulgaris*, yellow loosestrife. These are not now used in herbal medicine, but were formerly used as wound herbs, as was purple loosestrife.

L. salicaria is a highly astringent herb with marked antibacterial qualities. It was regarded as a treatment for severe fevers, such as cholera. It acts as a diuretic, staunches the flow of blood, and soothes skin irritations. Today it is sometimes used in herbal medicine to treat dysentery, cholera, and typhoid, and to control hemorrhages and excessive menstruation. It is applied to skin infections, particularly for cases of impetigo and eczema.

Loosestrife is a common wild plant that flourishes in damp places. *L. vulgaris*, common loosestrife, was used to calm oxen when they were plowing, hence the common name.

vital statistics

FAMILY
Lythraceae

OTHER VARIETIES AND SPECIES
L. salicaria 'Feuerkerze', *L. s.* 'Florarose', *L. s.* 'Morden Pink', *L. s.* 'Rose', *L. virgatum* 'Rose Queen'

PERENNIAL ZONE 3

HEIGHT
2–4ft (60cm–1.2 m)

SPREAD
2–4ft (60cm–1.2 m)

FLOWERS
Star-shaped, deep purple to pink and red, on long spikes.

FOLIAGE
Dark green, long, pointed, willow-like, downy leaves.

NATURAL HABITAT
Native of Europe and western Asia. Found in marshes, river banks, ditches, and damp areas.

SITE
Sun or partial shade.

SOIL
Fertile, moisture-retaining, wet.

PROPAGATION
Sow seeds or divide established plants in spring.

FLOWERING
Mid- to late summer.

USES
Herbal medicine.

Malva sylvestris
Mallow
high mallow

The mallow is a wildflower often found in coastal areas. It was used as a pot herb and the young leaves were eaten raw in salads or cooked like spinach. The young seedpods were also eaten raw, but the plant should not be eaten in large quantities. It is a bushy, woody stemmed perennial or biennial that you can grow as a flowering plant in the garden. The flowers, which have five petals and appear in clusters, are pink, white, or mauve, veined, and shallowly cupped. All mallows have pretty flowers.

Formerly, mallow was used to treat a urinary disease called the strangury—the inability to pass water. Drinking a decoction of the roots or leaves helped to promote the flow of urine. Today the herb is used in herbal medicine to relieve inflammation and stings, and in poultices to ease ulcers. A tea made from an infusion of the flowers is sometimes given for colds and bronchitis. Although all mallows have the same properties, *M. sylvestris* has the strongest effect.

Caution: Care should be taken if consuming the herb, which acts as a purgative. Large amounts may cause indigestion.

A number of mallow varieties have been developed with white, blue, and purple flowers. Its chief use in herbal medicine was as a diuretic and to ease urinary disorders.

vital statistics

FAMILY Malvaceae	**PERENNIAL/BIENNIAL ZONE 4**	**FOLIAGE** Dark green, heart-shaped to rounded, with shallow lobes.	**SOIL** Ordinary, reasonably fertile, well-drained soil.	**FLOWERING** Throughout the summer.
OTHER VARIETIES AND SPECIES *M. alcea* (hollyhock mallow), *M. moschata* (musk mallow), *M. neglecta* (dwarf mallow), *M. parviflora* (least mallow, little mallow)	**HEIGHT** 4ft (1.2m) **SPREAD** 2ft (60cm) **FLOWERS** White, pink or mauve held in clusters, veined.	**NATURAL HABITAT** Native of northern Europe and southwest Asia. Found on banks and wasteland, frequently in coastal areas. **SITE** Sun.	**PROPAGATION** Sow seeds in spring or fall.	**USES** Herbal medicine, culinary, tea plant.

Mandragora officinarum

Mandrake

duck's foot. European mandrake, ground apple, hog apple

More legends are attached to the mandrake plant than almost any other. The roots are thought to resemble the human body and they have hallucinogenic qualities.

The mandrake is a plant of magic and witchcraft. The root has a strange resemblance to the lower part of a human body and many are the legends associated with it, and the properties attributed to it. It could cure broken love affairs, it was an irresistible aphrodisiac, it was a cure for sterility, and it was a cure-all for grievous disorders when all else had failed. But the roots supposedly gave out such a ghastly shriek when they were dug up that men died of fright. Evil was supposed to fall on anyone who disturbed the mandrake root, and sometimes, when they were collected, a dog would be tied to the root to pull it from the ground, so that the bad luck would fall on the dog rather than on its master. The plant is related to deadly nightshade and henbane. It is a strong purgative and the leaves were used to treat wounds.

Mandrake is a strong narcotic with hallucinatory effects, and taken in sufficient quantities can induce oblivion. Shakespeare wrote about this in *Antony and Cleopatra*:

Give me to drink mandragora.
That I may sleep out this great gap of time.
My Antony is away.

Caution: The plant is poisonous and should not be taken in any form.

vital statistics

FAMILY
Solonaceae

OTHER VARIETIES AND SPECIES
M. autumnalis (Autumn mandrake)

PERENNIAL ZONE 8–10

HEIGHT
6in (15cm)

SPREAD
12in (30cm)

FLOWERS
Clusters of white to pale purple bell-shaped flowers.

FOLIAGE
Rosettes of roughly oval, upright, dark green leaves.

NATURAL HABITAT
Native of southeastern Mediterranean. Found in arid mountain regions.

SITE
Sun.

SOIL
Well-drained, dry, moderately fertile soil. Avoid disturbing the roots.

PROPAGATION
Sow seeds in a cold frame in the fall. Take root cuttings in winter.

FLOWERING
Spring.

USES
Formerly herbal medicine.

Marrubium vulgare
Horehound
hoarhound, white horehound

Horehound is a wildflower found on cliffs and chalky areas and is a useful medicinal herb. The plant's most distinctive feature is its white or silver color. Grow it as a foliage plant in an herb garden to make a charming backdrop to many flowering plants. It is quite a tall plant, reaching 3ft (90cm) in height. The leaves, which are green, hairy, and deeply creased above and pale silvery beneath, hang down from the stems. The flowers are small, white, with two lips, and circle the stems in dense rings. Horehound beer used to be a popular brew and the plant was used in the manufacture of candy that people sucked to relieve coughs.

The plant has been used to treat coughs, bronchitis, asthma, catarrh, and whooping coughs for hundreds of years. It is still often used as an expectorant today in herbal medicine. As its common name suggests, the leaves of the plant were once used to cure the bites of dogs. As an herb, it increases the perspiration rate and has a sedative effect on the heart. It is also used to treat minor cuts and bruises.

The strongly aromatic, deeply veined leaves of the common horehound are held on slender, downy, white stems.

vital statistics

FAMILY Labiatae	**PERENNIAL ZONE 3**	**FOLIAGE** Oval leaves, gray-green above, silvery white underneath.	**SOIL** Well-drained, dry, poor.	**FLOWERING** Summer.
OTHER VARIETIES AND SPECIES *M. incanum*	**HEIGHT** 2–3ft (60–90cm)	**NATURAL HABITAT** Native of southern and eastern Europe and the Mediterranean. Found on dry wasteland.	**PROPAGATION** Take cuttings in summer or divide established plants in the spring. Sow seed in the spring although germination is erratic.	**USES** Herbal medicine, cough sweets, formerly brew herb.
	SPREAD 18in (45cm)			
	FLOWERS Small, white, with two lips, carried around the stem.	**SITE** Sun.		

Matricaria recutita
Wild chamomile
German chamomile

Also known as mayweed, wild chamomile is closely related to Roman chamomile, *Chamaemelum nobile*, and has many of the same medicinal properties. It is found growing in its natural habitat on the sides of highways and in chalky soil in early summer. Its fragrant, small, white, daisy-like flowers with yellow centers make it an attractive plant for the garden. Wild chamomile is the species used to make chamomile tea, a calming drink that is supposed to aid digestion. It is less bitter than Roman chamomile and the tea has a sweeter taste. The essential oil is used in hair tonics—mostly as a shampoo or conditioner.

It is an important medicinal herb, as it has sedative and anti-inflammatory qualities. It is particularly used in herbal medicine for children's complaints, including upset stomachs, teething, nausea, and colic. It helps the digestion and improves the immune system. It is also used externally to treat sunburn, wounds, sores, piles and mastitis in nursing mothers.

Wild chamomile is easy to grow from seed and has white, daisy-like, flowers with yellow centers. It is similar to Roman chamomile, with many of the same medicinal properties.

vital statistics

FAMILY
Compositae

OTHER VARIETIES AND SPECIES
Chamaemelum nobile 'Flore Pleno', *C. n.* 'Treneague'

ANNUAL

HEIGHT
18in (45cm)

SPREAD
12in (30cm)

FLOWERS
Small daisy-like flowers with prominent yellow centers in terminal clusters.

FOLIAGE
Green, feathery leaves.

NATURAL HABITAT
Temperate zones in Europe, Asia and India. Found on wasteland and dry banks.

SITE
Open, sunny.

SOIL
Light, well-drained.

PROPAGATION
Sow seed in spring.

FLOWERING
Early summer.

USES
Tea, herbal medicine, cosmetics.

Melilotus officinale
Yellow sweet clover
hay flower, king's clover, yellow melilot

The yellow sweet clover is a common wild-flower found on pasture and wasteland in temperate zones. It has been a commonly used herb in medicine for several centuries. This substantial plant is also cultivated as animal feed, and cut and harvested as hay. The herb is a biennial that reaches 5ft (1.5m) in height, with slender branching stalks that carry spires of sweet-smelling, yellow flowers in the summer. The Latin name comes from the Greek *meli*, which means "honey."

Culpeper attributed a number of wonderful properties to yellow melilot, declaring: "The head often washed with the distilled water of the herb and flowers is good for those who swoon, also to strengthen the memory, to comfort the head and brain, and to preserve them from pain and apoplexy."

Today the plant is used in the manufacture of rat poison. It can be extremely dangerous when used to excess. A tea made from the plant is prescribed by herbalists in cases of indigestion, sleeplessness, nervous tension, and thrombosis. It is also used as a relaxant in herbal baths and as an anti-inflammatory compress to treat wounds and sores. The dried herb is used to flavor stews and in the manufacture of some cheeses.

Caution: Excessive consumption can cause dizziness and vomiting.

Yellow sweet clover is widely cultivated for hay and silage, and is a welcome addition to the wildflower garden.

vital statistics

FAMILY Leguminosae	**BIENNIAL** **ZONE 3**	**FOLIAGE** Three leaflets, toothed, springing from the stalk.	**SOIL** Light, well-drained, alkaline. Melilotus is drought tolerant.	**FLOWERING** Summer.
OTHER VARIETIES AND SPECIES *M. officinalis* ssp. *albus* (white flowered form, white sweet cover) widely grown as a fodder crop.	**HEIGHT** 2–5ft (60cm–1.5m) **SPREAD** 1–3ft (30–90cm) **FLOWERS** Small, yellow, honey-scented flowers that appear in spires.	**NATURAL HABITAT** Temperate zones in Europe and Asia. Found on wasteland and meadows. Cultivated for hay and silage. **SITE** Open, sunny.	**PROPAGATION** Sow seed in spring or fall.	**USES** Herbal medicine, culinary.

Melissa officinalis
Lemon balm
bee balm, common balm, cure-all, melissa, sweet balm

Lemon balm is a commonly grown herbaceous perennial, found in many gardens in temperate climates. It has been used in herbal medicine for thousands of years. It has hairy, deeply veined leaves that are light green or gold-splashed, according to the variety grown. The small, insignificant white or pale pink flowers emerge in late summer. The leaves are extremely fragrant, smelling strongly of lemons when they are crushed or brushed against.

Dioscorides, the ancient Greek physician, declared that the leaves steeped in wine were a remedy against the sting of the scorpion and the bites of mad dogs. It also had a reputation for driving away melancholy and lifting the spirits. It has long been a popular herb in the kitchen and was used to flavor sauces, stews, fish dishes, and custards. The herb has antiviral and antibacterial qualities and is used today in herbal medicine to treat depression, anxiety, nervous disorders, and digestive upsets, and to lower blood pressure. It is an excellent bee plant, hence one of its common names.

Lemon balm is grown for its leaves, which release a scent of lemons when bruised. Some garden varieties have variegated leaves. It is used to treat depression.

vital statistics

FAMILY Labiatae	**PERENNIAL ZONE 4**	**FOLIAGE** Light green, heart-shaped, hairy, toothed leaves. Varieties have gold-splashed leaves.	**SOIL** Fertile, well-drained soil.	**FLOWERING** Midsummer onwards.
OTHER VARIETIES AND SPECIES M. officinalis 'All Gold', M. o. 'Aurea'	**HEIGHT** 24in (60cm)		**PROPAGATION** Sow seed or divide established plants in spring. Take semi-ripe cuttings in early summer.	**USES** Culinary, tea, herbal medicine, bee plant, potpourris.
	SPREAD 18in (45cm)	**NATURAL HABITAT** Native of southern Europe. Found on wasteland and in mountainous areas.		
	FLOWERS Very small, white or pale pink flowers on loose spikes.	**SITE** Sun or partial shade.		

Mentha
Mint

Pennyroyal, *M. pulegium*, is one of the most attractive mints, with its pink flowers clustered along the stems. Today it is used in various cosmetic products.

Mints are a large family and a number of them have distinct uses, both in the kitchen and in herbal medicine. Botanically, they are somewhat difficult to classify, as they hybridize freely, and named varieties should always be raised by division, for they very rarely come true from seed.

Although there are many varieties of mint, all forms are perennials. They also all have invasive roots that spread vigorously by using underground runners, so you will need to contain them. The traditional way of doing this in the garden was to plant them in an old bucket sunk into the soil with the bottom removed. A large flowerpot treated in the same way works just as well. They do best in fertile, well-drained soil that retains moisture in a semishaded position.

Caution: Mints have hairy leaves that can cause skin irritations and rashes. Handle them with care. Similarly, mint tea should not be drunk continuously over a long period.

Watermint
Mentha aquatica. This is a marginal aquatic plant with attractive purple flowers that form a large elongated ball at the top of the flower spike in summer. It is used only in herbal medicine and you should not use it in the kitchen. It has been used for many centuries to treat indigestion, colic, and disorders of the stomach and bowels. Herbalists find it extremely effective in the treatment of flatulence.

Caution: This plant can cause vomiting.

Mint (continued)

Wild mint

M. arvensis. This is a wildflower that is found in cornfields and is rarely cultivated in gardens. However, it is an important medicinal plant that you can use in the kitchen. Traditionally, it was used to prevent milk curdling and to make mint tea. It is a pungent antibacterial herb and is used in herbal medicine to dry up the milk in nursing mothers and to treat colds, coughs, and sore throats. It also reduces inflammation.

Peppermint

M. x piperita. Peppermint is used as a flavoring for candies, ice cream, and liqueurs, and is also a popular ingredient in cosmetics and soaps. It is quite a large plant, reaching 3ft (90cm) in height. Plant it in a prominent position in an herb garden so that its pleasant red stems and crisp, red-tinted leaves are visible. Peppermint is a hybrid of *M. aquatica*, watermint, and *M. spicata*, spearmint. It is grown as a commercial crop.

The leaves of *M. spicata* are the least pungent of all mints, making it one of the most popular for cooking.

Medically, peppermint has been used to treat nausea and diarrhea for many centuries and today herbalists also prescribe it for colds, coughs, and catarrh. Mints contain the chemical menthol, which is both a mild anesthetic and decongestant. The form *M. x piperita citrata*, lemon mint or eau de Cologne mint, contains an essential oil used in oral hygiene and in the cosmetics industry.

Pennyroyal

M. pulegium. Pennyroyal is very free spreading and you can grow it as a useful ground-cover plant. It is low growing and the stems reach only 8in (20cm) in height. It is a deliciously pungent herb and was used in medieval times to conceal the taste of rotten meat. It can be dried and used in the kitchen to flavor sausages and pâtés. It has been used for many centuries to ward off fleas and to repel mice and rats. The oil is used in soaps, bath salts and shampoos.

Medically, pennyroyal was used for many ailments and conditions, including sore gums, the gout, cramps, convulsions, and earache. Today it is still used in herbal medicine, although the uses have changed. It is now used to treat indigestion, colds and influenza, bites and bruises.

Spearmint

M. spicata. Spearmint is the most commonly grown of all the garden mints, and is considered by many cooks as the best kind for making mint sauce and mint jelly or for flavoring drinks in summer. It is used commercially in the manufacture of chewing gum. In medieval times it was a very important medicinal herb and was used for a wide range of ailments: to alleviate diarrhea, cure indigestion, treat urinary diseases, prevent nausea, treat bad breath, prevent headaches, improve the appetite, and treat hiccups. It was also thought to "stir up venery and bodily lust."

It is not commonly used in herbal medicine today, but is still used to treat indigestion, colic, and various other childhood illnesses.

Other favored mints in the kitchen are *M. suaveolens,* (apple mint), or its variety *M. s.* 'Variegata', with its attractive white and green leaves, and *M.* x *villosa* f. *alopecuroides* 'Bowles' Mint', a popular mint particularly used for flavoring new potatoes.

The usually lilac flowers of *M.* x *piperita* are carried on erect spikes in dense whorls above rough, aromatic leaves.

vital statistics

FAMILY Labiatae	**PERENNIAL ZONE 3**	**FOLIAGE** Dark green, oval, extremely fragrant. Some varieties have variegated leaves.	**SOIL** Fertile, well-drained, moisture-retaining soil.	**FLOWERING** Summer.
OTHER VARIETIES AND SPECIES *M. requienii* (Corsican mint), *M.* x *gracilis* (ginger mint, redmint), *M. longifolia* syn. *M. sylvestris* (horsemint), *M. satureioides* (Australian pennyroyal)	**HEIGHT** 8in–3ft (20–90cm), depending on the variety. **SPREAD** 12–24in (30–60cm) or more. **FLOWERS** Mauve, purple, white or pink.	**NATURAL HABITAT** Native of southern Europe. Generally found in damp and shady sites. **SITE** Sun or partial shade.	**PROPAGATION** Divide runners in the fall. Take cuttings in spring and early summer. They can be rooted in water if required.	**USES** Culinary, herbal medicine.

Meum athamanticum
Spignel
baldmoney

A member of the parsnip or carrot family, spignel is the only species in the genus. You can use the leaves to give a slight curry flavor to salads and other dishes. It is an attractive plant and carries a mass of tiny, white, or pale pink flowers on large flat heads in summer. It grows in mountainous regions of northern Europe and is cultivated in wildflower gardens. It has never been used as a medicinal herb.

The name comes from the Greek *meion*, meaning "small." This is a reference to the small, feathery leaves, which are rather like those of the herb fennel. The roots, which are thick and white, were formerly eaten as a vegetable in Scotland. It is a popular herb in Scandinavian countries, where it is called *bjørnerot*, or bear root, and dedicated to the Norse god Balder, god of the summer sun.

Spignel is an attractive plant that resembles a small fennel with clusters of white flowers held aloft on long stalks. It is used in the Scandinavian countries to flavor egg dishes, salads, soups, and stews.

vital statistics

FAMILY
Umbelliferae

OTHER VARIETIES AND SPECIES
None

PERENNIAL ZONE 3

HEIGHT
12–24in (30–60cm)

SPREAD
8in (20cm)

FLOWERS
White or pink-tinged flowers in large, flat flowerheads.

FOLIAGE
Light to mid-green leaves with finely cut edges like fennel.

NATURAL HABITAT
Native of northern Europe. Found in mountain regions in open pasture.

SITE
Sun or partial shade.

SOIL
Sandy soil. This plant will not tolerate lime-rich soil.

PROPAGATION
Sow seeds in situ in spring and thin to 6in (15cm) apart. Divide mature plants in spring.

FLOWERING
Early summer.

USES
Culinary.

Monarda didyma
Oswego tea
bee balm, scarlet bee balm

A hardy native plant, it was formerly used to make tea by the Oswego Indians, which gives the plant one of its common names. The plant is attractive, with striking, deep red flowers that act as a focal point in an herbaceous border. It can be invasive, so it is best to confine it within a pot plunged in the soil, in the same way as mint. The leaves are oval, rough with serrated edges, and dark green, sometimes with red tints. The flowers are often used in potpourris for their strong, citrus fragrance, which resembles that of the bergamot orange. As the name bee balm implies, the flowers are very attractive to bees, as well as to butterflies.

The leaves are still infused as an herbal tea that has relaxing, antidepressant qualities, and the plant is prescribed by herbalists to treat minor digestive disorders. An infusion is inhaled for colds and it is used as an antiseptic for ulcers.

Oswego tea is a native plant. A number of garden varieties have been developed with more colorful flowers, but these are less fragrant than the species.

vital statistics

FAMILY
Labiatae

OTHER VARIETIES AND SPECIES
M. citriodora (lemon bergamot), M. punctata (horsemint), M. fistulosa (wild bergamot), M. menthifolia, M. 'Cambridge Scarlet'

PERENNIAL ZONE 4–6

HEIGHT
18–24in (45–60cm)

SPREAD
18–24in (45–60cm)

FLOWERS
Scarlet, ragged flowers with red-tinged bracts on stems.

FOLIAGE
Dark green, pointed, veined leaves. Some varieties have reddish veins.

NATURAL HABITAT
Native of North America. Found in pasture and woodland near Lake Ontario.

SITE
Sun or partial shade.

SOIL
Fertile, moisture retaining.

PROPAGATION
By division in spring or fall.

FLOWERING
Late summer.

USES
Culinary (tea), herbal medicine, potpourri.

Myrrhis odorata
Sweet cicely
anise

Sweet cicely is an attractive herb with soft, green, fern-like leaves, and pretty, small, white flowerheads, which are followed by shiny, brown seeds. It was one of the original "pot" herbs of medieval times and has a long history of use both in the kitchen and as a medicine. Try adding the leaves to salads or use them to add sweetness and the flavor of aniseed to stewed fruit. As its name implies, the plant contains a sweetener. You can also use it to flavor yogurt and ice cream. The roots are edible cooked and eaten as a vegetable, and the seeds can also be added raw to salads. They were traditionally ground and added to furniture polish as a scent.

The plant was used medically in the treatment of rheumatic complaints, to improve digestion, to prevent scurvy, and as a tonic and a gentle laxative. It was formerly regarded as an ideal remedy for all cases of stomach trouble. An ointment was prepared from the roots as a treatment for ulcers.

Sweet cicely is an ancient herb, much used in the kitchen and as a medicine. The leaves can be used as a sugar substitute.

vital statistics

FAMILY
Umbelliferae

OTHER VARIETIES AND SPECIES
None

PERENNIAL ZONE 3

HEIGHT
2–3ft (60–90cm)

SPREAD
2ft (60cm)

FLOWERS
Small, white and star-shaped, held in clusters in flat heads.

FOLIAGE
Bright green, fern-like leaves, held on hairy stems.

NATURAL HABITAT
Native of Europe. Found on mountain pastures.

SITE
Sun or partial shade.

SOIL
Rich, moist, well-drained.

PROPAGATION
Seed outside in fall or divide in spring.

FLOWERING
Early summer.

USES
Culinary, formerly herbal medicine, formerly furniture-polish ingredient.

Nepeta cataria
Catnip
catmint, catnep, catrup, catswort

Catnip is a popular garden plant. Cut them back after flowering to keep the plants tidy.

Catnip is best known for containing a volatile oil that is a feline aphrodisiac. It attracts cats, who make nests in the plant when it is grown in an herbaceous border, and the dried herb is used in the manufacture of cats' toys. The oil was formerly used in the perfume industry and you can use the leaves to make a mint-flavored tea. The flowers are attractive to bees. *N. cataria* is the traditional herbal catnip, but there are many garden varieties.

The plant has gray-blue, nettle-like leaves on long stalks. It has long tufts of flowers, which are usually mauve or lilac-blue on the tops of the branches. Its strong sweet smell and downy stems and foliage make it a very attractive edging to a flower border.

Catnip is a bitter, astringent herb that is used in herbal medicine today to treat fevers and to increase perspiration. It has a mildly sedative effect and is used generally in the treatment of stomach complaints. It was thought at one time that it could cure infertility in women, and it was a traditional treatment for headaches, piles, scabs on the head, and coughs.

---

vital statistics

FAMILY
Labiatae

OTHER VARIETIES AND SPECIES
*N. cataria 'Citriodora',
N. x faassenii, N. grandiflora,
N. nervosa, N. racemosa,
N. sibirica, N. 'Six Hills Giant'*

PERENNIAL ZONE 4

HEIGHT
2–3ft (45–90cm)

SPREAD
2ft (60cm)

FLOWERS
Lavender-blue or mauve flowers held in spikes.

FOLIAGE
Blue-gray aromatic leaves, downy and paler underneath.

NATURAL HABITAT
Native of the Caucasus, Caspian Sea, and Turkey. Found on dry and rocky ground and scrub.

SITE
Sun or light shade.

SOIL
Sandy, well-drained soil, tolerates dry conditions.

PROPAGATION
Divide established plants in the spring, or take cuttings in summer. Cut back the plants after flowering.

FLOWERING
Midsummer onwards.

USES
Cats' toys, culinary, herbal medicine, formerly perfume.

Nigella sativa
Black cumin

Black cumin, *N. sativa*, has white or pale blue flowers that appear in a green mist of delicate foliage. It is grown for the black, aromatic, nutmeg-flavored seeds used in curries, and as a substitute for pepper and in baking. It has been used as a spice for over two thousand years. Before the 5th century it was used instead of pepper, as black pepper arrived in Europe only in that century. It is no relation to fennel, although it has a similar scent. The plant should not be confused with the most commonly grown nigella, *N. damascena*, better known by the charming common name of love-in-a-mist. The two plants are similar in appearance but have different uses.

In medieval times the herb was rarely used in medicine—except occasionally to treat fevers—but it is now used in herbal medicine to stimulate the uterus during childbirth and to improve lactation. It is also sometimes used to treat bronchial complaints.

Nigellas are grown for their pretty, star-shaped flowers, fine foliage, and prominent seed heads. All varieties self-seed easily.

vital statistics

FAMILY
Ranunculeae

OTHER VARIETIES AND SPECIES
N. damascena, N. hispanica

HARDY ANNUAL ZONE 3

HEIGHT
18in (45cm)

SPREAD
6in (15cm)

FLOWERS
Pale blue, five-petaled flowers followed by seed heads.

FOLIAGE
Gray-green, slightly pointed leaves like long needles.

NATURAL HABITAT
Native of Syria. Found on rocky ground.

SITE
Open and sunny.

SOIL
Ordinary, well-drained.

PROPAGATION
Sow seeds in situ in spring or fall. Some protection should be given for varieties sown in fall.

FLOWERING
Summer

USES
Culinary, herbal medicine, dried flower arrangements.

Ocimum basilicum
Sweet basil

asil is a favorite herb in the kitchen and today is also often used in herbal medicine. In former times it was regarded with the gravest suspicion. One man supposedly grew a scorpion in his brain by sniffing the herb every day, and it was thought that if it was laid to rot in horse dung it would breed poisonous beasts.

Basil is a tropical herb from Asia. In temperate zones it should be grown in a hot, sunny place, in a window box or other container. In sheltered positions it can be grown in the vegetable garden, although it dislikes strong winds.

Many popular dishes feature basil as the main ingredient, including *Insalata tricolore*, *Soupe au pistou* and pesto, and it is frequently added to summer salads and sauces.

In herbal medicine it is a restorative herb that is used to treat colds, indigestion, gastroenteritis, depression, and exhaustion. It is used externally for stings, bites, and skin conditions.

Sweet basil likes sun and shelter. If grown in a container, it can be moved inside during cold weather. Its leaves can be picked at any time.

vital statistics

FAMILY
Labiatae

OTHER VARIETIES AND SPECIES
O. b. 'Dark Opal' (purple leaves), *O. b.* 'Green Ruffles' (green ruffled leaves), *O. b.* 'Purple Ruffles' (purple ruffled leaves), *O.b.* var. *minimum* (Greek bush basil), *O. gratissimum* (East Indian basil)

TENDER ANNUAL

HEIGHT
18in (45cm)

SPREAD
12in (30cm)

FLOWERS
Small, white, pink-purple tinged, two-lipped flower.

FOLIAGE
Intensely aromatic, bright, shiny green leaves, like small spinach leaves but held on a stalk.

NATURAL HABITAT
Native of southern Asia, Iran, and the Middle East. Found in hot, humid regions.

SITE
Sunny, sheltered.

SOIL
Rich, well-drained, moisture retentive.

PROPAGATION
Sow seed at 55°F (13°C) in spring or in situ in summer.

FLOWERING
Late summer.

USES
Culinary, herbal medicine.

Oenothera biennis
Evening primrose
evening star

This coarse biennial herb has a long taproot and a basal rosette of long, willow-like leaves, which are bright green with a red central stripe. It has a number of traditional and modern uses in herbal medicine. In summer it grows into a tall plant, reaching 4–5ft (1.2–1.5m) in height (it may need staking). It has lovely, bright yellow, shallowly cupped, fragrant flowers, which open in the evening or on dull days throughout the summer. The scent is most prominent as dusk falls. The flowers, held on a long spike with several blooms emerging at a time, are followed by long seed capsules.

The plant has recently been discovered to contain gamma linoleic acid. This is the main ingredient of Evening Primrose oil, which is taken as a supplement to treat multiple sclerosis, cirrhosis of the liver, coronary heart disease, premenstrual and menopausal syndromes, and other conditions. The oil is also added to skin preparations and cosmetics.

The evening primrose is a lovely plant and is grown in many herbaceous borders for its fragrant yellow flowers.

vital statistics

FAMILY
Onograceae

OTHER VARIETIES AND SPECIES
O. acaulis, O. caespitosa, O. deltoides, O. fruticosa, O. macrocarpa (Ozark sundrops)

BIENNIAL
ZONE 4

HEIGHT
4–5ft (1.2–1.5m)

SPREAD
18in (45cm)

FLOWERS
Yellow, four-petaled, fragrant flowers, held on long spikes.

FOLIAGE
Alternate, lance-shaped or oval green leaves, growing up a reddish stem.

NATURAL HABITAT
Native of North America. Found on dry, stony ground, and sandy soil beside highways.

SITE
Sunny.

SOIL
Sandy, well-drained, reasonably fertile.

PROPAGATION
Sow seed in late summer, self-seeds.

FLOWERING
Summer.

USES
Herbal medicine.

Ononis spinosa
Spiny restharrow
cammock, petty whin, stayplough

Restharrows are small shrubs that find a welcome place in rock and alpine gardens. They produce pea-like pink flowers and remain in flower for much of the summer.

The restharrow got its common name because the tough, spiny stems and roots resisted the harrow used by farmers to level the soil. It was regarded as an important medicinal herb for hundreds of years, although it is no longer used today. There are a considerable number of species, but the most commonly grown in gardens are *O. repens*, the common restharrow, and *O. fruticosa*, the shrubby restharrow. These are both small shrubs that are suitable for a rock or alpine garden. *O. spinosa*, spiny restharrow, is the only species with thorns and it has attractive, pink, pea-like flowers in the summer. It is a wild plant found in limestone areas and on grassland.

Spiny restharrow was prescribed as a powerful diuretic, a decoction mixed with vinegar was used to ease toothache, and the dried and powdered root was mixed with sugar and made into lozenges to use as a purgative. More recently, the root has been used to treat severe cases of gout and rheumatism.

vital statistics

FAMILY
Leguminosae

OTHER VARIETIES AND SPECIES
O. fruticosus, O. reclinata, O. repens, O. rotundifolia

PERENNIAL ZONE 4

HEIGHT
18in (45cm)

SPREAD
12in (30cm)

FLOWERS
Brilliant pink and pea-like, held in clusters.

FOLIAGE
Dark green, narrow, pointed three-part leaves, on hairy stems with long spines.

NATURAL HABITAT
Native of Europe. Found on grassland and limestone areas.

SITE
Sun.

SOIL
Heavy, fertile, moisture retaining.

PROPAGATION
Sow seed in spring.

FLOWERING
Summer.

USES
Culinary, formerly herbal medicine.

Onoropordum acanthium
Cotton thistle
Scotch cotton thistle

The cotton thistle is a striking looking plant with gray-silver leaves covered with white down, topped by the giant, purple, solitary flowers that emerge from large spiny buds. The seeds contain an oil that was used in the 16th and 17th centuries for lamps, and also for cooking, and the heads and young stalks were once peeled and eaten.

It has been the national symbol of Scotland since King James V of Scotland chose the plant for the country's emblem at the beginning of the 16th century. The Latin name comes from the Greek *onos*, meaning "ass," and *perdo*, "to explode"—a supposed reference to the effect of using the thistle as a whip. You can grow thistles as a feature plant in the garden, but give them plenty of room and also control them ruthlessly: They self-seed freely and can become rampant. They are extremely prickly, unpleasant plants to handle, and are probably best confined to a wildflower garden. They are commonly found growing on wasteland.

Thistles were not highly regarded as medicinal plants by herbalists, but a decoction made from the flower heads was at one time used to treat both baldness and ulcers.

The cotton thistle has been the national emblem of Scotland for nearly five hundred years. It is a striking plant for display, but the sharp spines make it unpleasant to handle.

vital statistics

FAMILY Compositae	**BIENNIAL** **ZONE 5**	**FOLIAGE** Thick, spiky, silver branches emerge in the second year with sparse, spiny leaves.	**SOIL** Light, dry, sandy.	**FLOWERING** Late summer.
OTHER VARIETIES AND SPECIES *O. bracteatum, O. nervosum*	**HEIGHT** 8–10ft (2.4–3m)		**PROPAGATION** Sow seed in spring and early summer.	**USES** Formerly culinary, formerly herbal medicine.
	SPREAD 4–5ft (1.2–1.5m)	**NATURAL HABITAT** Native of Europe and Asia. Found on wasteland and on dry banks.		
	FLOWERS Large, solitary, typical thistle-like, purple flowers.	**SITE** Sun.		

Origanum majorana
Sweet marjoram

Sweet marjoram is an all-purpose herb, used in the kitchen, as a medicine, and in aromatherapy. In temperate climates it is best grown as a container plant.

Two members of the genus *Origanum* are popular herbs in the kitchen: *O. marjoram*, marjoram, and *O. vulgare*, oregano. Although similar botanically, they come from different parts of the world and have distinct tastes. Marjoram originally comes from northern Africa and southwestern Asia, although it is often found in southwestern Europe on the Mediterranean coast. It has a sweet, rather floral scent. It is grown as a tender perennial and needs to be brought in during the winter. Grow the plant in a container so that it can be brought inside for protection when frost threatens. It is an attractive shrub, with evergreen gray-green leaves covered with soft hairs, and tubular white or pink flowers held upright in clumps.

It is used in the kitchen to flavor soups, stews and fish dishes, and the oil is a flavoring in sausages, mustards, liqueurs, perfume and soap. It has been a medicinal herb for hundreds of years and it is still used to treat bronchial complaints, insomnia, and painful menstruation. The oil is employed in massage and aromatherapy to ease muscular aches and arthritis.

vital statistics

FAMILY Labiatae	**TENDER EVERGREEN SHRUB** ZONE 5–7	**FOLIAGE** Soft, hairy, pointed, gray-green.	**SOIL** Rich, well-drained to dry.	**FLOWERING** Summer.
OTHER VARIETIES AND SPECIES *O. dictamnus* (Dittany of Crete), *O. microphyllum*, *O. × majoricum*, *O. onites*, *O. rotundifolium*, *O. vulgare*. A number of garden varieties have been developed.	**HEIGHT** 32in (80cm) **SPREAD** 18in (45cm) **FLOWERS** Tubular pink or white flowers.	**NATURAL HABITAT** Native of southwestern Europe, Turkey, and northern Africa. Usually found in open mountainous areas **SITE** Sun or light shade.	**PROPAGATION** Sow seeds in spring at 50–55°F (10–13°C). Divide established plants in spring or take basal cuttings in spring.	**USES** Culinary, herbal medicine, massage oil, bee plant.

Herbs in the home

Herbs are the main ingredients of a number of practical and attractive objects that can be used in the home or given as gifts. Take care to present each object as prettily and professionally as possible.

Lavender bags

Cut the lavender flowers on a dry, sunny day before they are fully open. Tie them in bunches and hang them upside down to dry in a cool, well-ventilated room. When they are dry, strip the flowers from the stalks and put them in small decorative cheesecloth or calico bags. Secure the tops. Use the bags to scent clothes, bed linen, pillows, and cushions.

Herbal moth bags

Many herbs have been used as insect repellents for several centuries. (In Europe another common name for elecampane, *Inula helenium*, was fleabane.) And a selection of scented herbs can be used to make moth balls to protect clothing.

A moth repellent can be made from dried tansy leaves, dried lavender flowers, and dried southernwood, *Artemisia abrotanum*. Use two cups of the last two herbs and one cup of tansy leaves. Add two crushed sticks of cinnamon and ½ teaspoon of orris root. Put the mixture in bags or sachets and store them with your clothes.

Herb and hop pillows

Hop pillows have long been regarded as an aid to sleep. Herb pillows are also used to help cure sleeplessness and they are more fragrant. The principle of drying herbs and flowers is the same for all. Pick the herbs and flowers before they are fully open on a dry, sunny day and hang them up to dry in a cool, airy room. When they are quite dry they can be stripped and used for pillows or sachets.

The exact proportions of herbs for an herbal pillow or cushion can be varied but a good mixture is 1 part mint, lavender, lemon beebrush, and rosemary leaves to 3 parts lemon-scented geranium leaves, all dried. Mix them together, put them into individual sachets, and then place the sachets inside the pillows or cushions.

Dried lavender nosegay

Nosegays and pomanders were common in the 17th and 18th centuries and were carried around to protect the gentlefolk from the appalling smells of the towns. Herbal pomanders were also carried into courtrooms and placed in front of the judges to ward off infection from jail fever.

Sprigs of dried lavender held in a pot or decorative jar are a simple halfway house between these and a potpourri mixture.

Cut a number of sprigs of lavender on a sunny day and dry them in an airy room. Collect them into bunches. Get some florist's foam and cut it to fit inside the pot or jar you plan to use. Push a bunch of lavender into the foam and then keep adding bunches of lavender until you have contrived a dense mass of purple lavender flowerheads.

Rosemary pomander

These look a bit like tiny green porcupines when they have rolled themselves into a ball.

YOU WILL NEED:
a ball of florist's foam
rosemary sprigs
a good pair of scissors

Cut the rosemary into fairly short sprigs and push them into the foam ball, dividing it in half. Then do the same the other way dividing the ball into quarters. Trim the stalks to about ½in (1.25cm) in height. Fill in each quarter, trimming the sprigs as you go; do this carefully. When the pomander is complete, look it over from all sides and tidy up any ragged edges. Pomanders can be made with other herbs, such as marjoram, lavender, and curry plant.

Herbal wreath

Herbs can be used to make decorative wreaths to welcome guests to the home on special occasions. You can vary the flowers and herbs used according to those available in your garden, but an attractive wreath can be made from a mixture of gray and green foliage plants: lavender cotton *Santolina chamaecyparissus*; lavender, *Lavandula angustifolia*; field holly, *Eryngium campestre*; and curry plant, *Helichrysum italicum*; bay leaves, *Laurus nobilis*; spearmint, *Mentha spicata*; and parsley, *Petroselinum crispum*; the white flowers of the feverfew, *Tanacetum parthenium*; safflowers, *Carthamus tinctorius*, orange; blazing star,

Liatris spicata, red; and a variety of roses. Ideally these should be the red *R. gallica var. officinalis* or the white and red *R. g.* 'Versicolor', but if you don't grow these, any scented rosebuds can be substituted.

Select a suitable wire ring and then secure damp sphagnum moss to it to make a base. Attach the green herbs in small bunches, spacing them out evenly. Then add small bunches of the gray-leaved plants. Finally, wire in the flowers, spacing them out evenly around the ring. The white daisy-like flowers of the feverfew hold the design together.

Other good combinations for herbal wreaths include hops and lavender. A special, fragrant Christmas wreath can be made from holly, dried sage, dried lavender, oregano, conifers (for blue and green evergreen foliage) and slices of oranges.

Herbal posy

These were originally known as nosegays or tussie mussies, and many different herbs and flowers can be combined attractively to make charming posies for brides or bridesmaids. Fine ladies carried them in the streets to ward off the smells of the cities.

The art of making a successful tussie mussie is to choose flowers and herbs that make a pleasing color contrast and to group them together in small bunches. Strip off the lower leaves from the stalks. Lay the bunches one over the other to build up the posy and then insert brightly colored flowers singly at the end to make color highlights. Secure the posy with a doubled rubber band and then tie it with string. Cover the string with a decorative ribbon.

An attractive posy could be made with marigolds, lavender, carnations, cornflowers, and lady's mantle. Choose the herbs and flowers that you have readily available in adequate quantities. The herbs will gradually dry, but they will retain their color and fragrance for a considerable period.

Eryngium campestre Field Holly

Pressed herb notebook

Dried and pressed flowers and herbs were much used in Victorian times for decoration. Special presses for herbs and flowers are readily available. Pick the flowers when they are at their brightest and keep them in the press until they are completely dry. They can then be arranged in patterns and pasted onto cards or used to decorate book covers.

To make a cover of pressed herbs and flowers for a personal notebook build up a design of pressed flowers on the front. When you are satisfied with the design, glue the flowers and leaves in position, using very small amounts of white latex adhesive applied with a fine spike or tapestry needle. Cover the design with a self-adhesive plastic film. As an additional touch, wipe the inside of the notebook with a tiny amount of scented essential oil (see page 176) or keep the book in a closed box with a strongly scented lavender bag.

Pressed herb cards

You can make your own Christmas and greetings cards using the same principle. This is time-consuming but the finished cards are very, very special, making them doubly welcome and attractive. They lift an ordinary message onto a different plane and will be treasured for many years.

Viola tricolor
Johnny-jump-up

Pappaver Poppy

Scented candles

Candlemaking at home is a popular pastime. To make your own candles at home:

YOU WILL NEED:

thin cardboard

paraffin wax	scissors
stearin	bowl
primed wick	pencil
wax dye	double boiler
candle mold	scented essential oil

Measure out the quantity of wax you need, plus the stearin, and then thread the wick through the mold. Secure it tightly at the base. Melt the wax in the double boiler and then add just a few drops of the essential oil. Be careful not to add too much. Pour the wax into the mold and place it upside down in a bowl of cold water to cool. Remove from the mold when ready and square off the base. More detailed instructions are available in any good book on candlemaking.

Good oils to use are lavender, rose, or citrus. You can experiment to see which ones you like best.

Potpourris

Potpourris, literally rotted pots, have been made for centuries and were used to scent rooms, fulfilling the function of the old-fashioned nosegay. They should include a variety of flowers and scented leaves. Good flowers for a potpourri include scented roses, carnations, lavender, orange, heliotrope, rosemary, violets, woodruff, and honeysuckle; scented leaves include marjoram, sweet balm, lemon beebrush, rosemary, and pennyroyal. Deep red roses and the blue flowers of borage are particularly welcome, and lemon and orange rind can also be added.

Pick the flowers and leaves in a dry period when there has been no rain for 24 hours and the morning dew has vanished. Dry them, preferably on a wire rack in an airy room. Make sure that all ingredients are thoroughly dry and no vestige of moisture remains, otherwise the potpourri will go moldy.

An old-fashioned potpourri

YOU WILL NEED:

1½ lbs (675g) kitchen salt

2 tsp orris root

grated nutmeg

½ tsp allspice

2 tbsp oil of bergamot

dried flowers and leaves as available

Mix the salt, orris root, nutmeg, and allspice together, then add the oil of bergamot. Mix again thoroughly. Put the salt mixture and flowers in a jar in layers, starting with the salt and finishing with the flowers. Close the jar tightly and turn it over frequently.

Rosa canina
Dog rose

A simple modern potpourri

If you wish this potpourri can be made with dried herbs only.

YOU WILL NEED:

4 good handfuls of dried leaves and flowers

10 slices dried orange

6 cinnamon sticks

4 nutmegs

1 tsp mint essential oil

1 tbsp sweet orange essential oil

1 tbsp orris root

china or glass bowl

Mix all the ingredients together except the orris root. When the oils have been absorbed, tip the mixture into a plastic bag, add the orris root, seal, and leave to mature for a week or two. Shake the bag from time to time. Tip the mixture into a china or glass bowl.

An herbal potpourri

A simple gray and red herbal potpourri can be made from dried eucalyptus leaves, dried lavender, dried marjoram, dried carnation petals and dried honesty (*Lunaria*) seed heads.

Strip the leaves from the eucalyptus into a bowl, rub off the heads of the lavender flowers on top of the eucalyptus, add the honesty seed heads, and then cut up some of the lavender stems to add to the mixture. Sprinkle the deep red carnation petals over the top. Add a few drops of essential oil, such as citrus oil, and let the mixture stand for a few days before putting it out in a decorative bowl.

Origanum vulgare
Oregano

Oregano is another favorite Mediterranean herb for flavoring stews and many pasta dishes. It is a bushy rhizomatous perennial that carries many flowers on upright stalks. These are most attractive to bees and insects, and emerge pinkish-white from deep red bracts, although there are a number of naturally occurring color variations. This is a popular herb for the herb garden and a number of varieties have been developed with variegated and colored leaves. These include *O. v.* 'Aureum', with gold leaves; *O. v.* 'Aureum Crispum', with curly gold leaves; and *O. v.* 'Compactum', smaller in habit. *O. v.* 'Heiderose' is more upright and has pink flowers. The flavor of oregano depends on the soil it grows in and the amount of sun it gets. Oregano from sunny areas is stronger than that found in colder regions.

In medieval times it was recommended as a cure for stomach complaints, flatulence, indigestion, and loss of appetite, and was prescribed for dropsy, scabs, scurvy, and jaundice. It is used today in herbal medicine to treat colds, indigestion, and other minor complaints. It is not given to pregnant women and the oil may cause skin irritation.

Oregano is closely related to marjoram, but the flavor is different and they come from different parts of the world. It is one of the most popular herbs in the kitchen.

vital statistics

FAMILY
Labiatae

OTHER VARIETIES AND SPECIES
O. dictamnus (Dittany of Crete), *O. microphyllum*, *O. × majoricum*, *O. onites* (French marjoram), *O. rotundifolium*, *O. hirtum* (Greek marjoram)

PERENNIAL ZONE 5

HEIGHT
12–24in (30–60cm)

SPREAD
8–12in (20–30cm)

FLOWERS
White to deep pink carried in dense terminal clusters.

FOLIAGE
Dark green to gold, round or pointed.

NATURAL HABITAT
Southwestern Asia, Greece and Turkey. Found in open mountainous areas or in bushy scrub.

SITE
Slight shade.

SOIL
Rich, well-drained to dry.

PROPAGATION
Sow seeds or divide in spring, self-seeds.

FLOWERING
Late summer.

USES
Culinary, herbal medicine.

Paeonia officinalis ✚✳⊗◯◯
Common peony

Peonies were popular medicinal plants in the early Middle Ages, but fell from fashion and are seldom used today. The name comes from Paeon, the physician to the Greek gods. The common peony has single, cupped, red to rose-pink flowers with prominent yellow stamens. It flowers in early summer. The two other peonies that are used in herbal and Chinese medicine are the Chinese peony, *P. lactiflora*, and the moutan or tree peony, *P. suffruticosa*. They have single white, pink, or red flowers. Many of the garden varieties now available have been developed from these species.

The common peony was formerly used as a treatment for epilepsy and was given to prevent nightmares. Today the roots of the plant are sometimes used in herbal medicine to treat convulsions and problems after childbirth. The Chinese peony is used for hypertension and skin complaints, and the tree peony is used in the treatment of menstrual and intestinal disorders, as well as whooping cough.

Caution: Parts of the plant are poisonous, especially the flowers. They must be used only by qualified herbal practitioners.

The common peony has single pink flowers, but a number of garden varieties have been developed with double flowers, such as 'Alba Plena', shown here.

vital statistics

FAMILY
Paeoniaceae

OTHER VARIETIES AND SPECIES
P. cambessedesii (Majorcan peony), *P. delavayi*, *P. emodi* (Himalayan peony), *P. humilis*, *P. tenuifolia*, *P. veitchii*. There are many garden varieties.

PERENNIAL ZONE 5

HEIGHT
2–3ft (60–90cm)

SPREAD
2ft (60cm)

FLOWERS
Large, cup-shaped, single flowers, red, pink, or white.

FOLIAGE
Dark green, large, deeply divided into nine segments growing from single stalks.

NATURAL HABITAT
Native to southern and western Europe. Found in scrub and open woodland.

SITE
Partial shade or full sun.

SOIL
Moisture-retaining, well-drained, fertile soil.

PROPAGATION
Sow seeds in fall, or divide roots in fall. The seeds may take three years to germinate.

FLOWERING
Early summer.

USES
Herbal medicine.

Papaver spp.
Poppy
corn poppy, field poppy, Flanders poppy, opium poppy

Corn poppies are also called Flanders poppy after an area that was the scene of heavy fighting in Belgium during World War I.

Poppies are probably the oldest of all the medicinal herbs. They were known in Sumerian times and their uses inscribed on Sumerian tablets at the dawn of the written word. Two members of the family are used in medicine. The first is the corn poppy, *P. rhoeas*.

This is the red poppy that has became a symbol of peace and remembrance, especially used to honor those who died in World War I. This is because it is a common plant of Belgium where much of the fighting took place. The second is the opium poppy, *P. somniferum*, the more important plant medicinally. The seeds of both species are non-toxic and you can use them in breads, cakes, and desserts.

The corn poppy contains an expectorant and is used in herbal preparations for coughs and chest troubles; it is also prescribed for indigestion. The opium poppy contains the alkaloid morphine, the source of opium and heroin. Morphine is an extremely effective painkiller but it is usually used only in cases of serious injury and terminal illness, since it is so addictive. It is used in homeopathy for shock and breathing difficulties, and in herbal medicine in preparations for coughs and diarrhea.

The properties of the opium poppy have long been known. Culpeper advocated the use of the corn poppy for medical purposes. But of the opium poppy he wrote "... an overdose causes immoderate mirth or scupidity, redness of the face, swelling of the lips, relaxation of the joints, giddiness of the head, deep sleep, accompanied by turbulent dreams and convulsive starting, cold sweats, and frequently death."

vital statistics

FAMILY
Papaveraceae

OTHER VARIETIES AND SPECIES
P. alpinum (Alpine poppy),
P. atlanticum, P. commutatum, P. croceum (Arctic poppy),
P. orientale, P. triniifolium. There are a large number of garden varieties available.

HARDY ANNUAL

HEIGHT
10–36in (25–90cm)

SPREAD
10in (25cm)

FLOWERS
Bowl-shaped, single flowers.
The opium poppy can be pink, purple, red, or white.

FOLIAGE
Oblong, deeply divided, light green leaves mainly at the base of the plant.

NATURAL HABITAT
Native of Europe, northern Africa, and western and central Asia. Grows in sparse soil.

SITE
Sun.

SOIL
Well-drained, dry, alkaline.

PROPAGATION
Sow seeds in fall or spring.
Self-seeds.

FLOWERING
Summer.

USES
Culinary, medicinal.

Parietaria judaica (P. officinalis)
Pellitory
spreading pellitory

This is a plant that grows on walls and old roofs, and the name comes from the Latin for "wall." It has long been used in herbal medicine. A number of other plants are also called pellitories, the grandly named pellitory of Spain, *Anacyclus pyrethrum*; masterwort, *Peucedanum ostruthium*; and sneezewort, *Alchemilla ptarmica*. Spreading pellitory is a creeping plant with soft, green, hairy leaves and reddish, spreading stems. It has insignificant pale purple flowers held in clusters in the summer, and these are followed by rough black seeds.

A tea was made from the leaves to alleviate coughs, chills, and sore throats. The tea leaves once brewed could then be applied to cuts, sores, and wounds to prevent infection. The juice of the plant was supposed to be a cure for tinnitus, and an ointment made from the juice was a cure for piles. However, the main use for the plant has always been as a cure for urinary infections, and it was used to expel bladder and kidney stones. It is still in use today, and is a respected herbal treatment for urinary infections such as cystitis.

This herb has been used to treat urinary infections since medieval times. It has insignificant flowers through summer, but the stems are red-green and colorful.

vital statistics

FAMILY
Urticaceae

OTHER VARIETIES AND SPECIES
P. judaica 'Corinne Tremaine'

PERENNIAL ZONE 5

HEIGHT
16in (40cm)

SPREAD
16in (40cm)

FLOWERS
Small, insignificant pale, purple flowers held in clusters.

FOLIAGE
Soft, green, hairy, lance-shaped leaves on reddish stems.

NATURAL HABITAT
Native of southern and western Europe and northern Africa. Found on wasteland and around walls.

SITE
Sun or partial shade.

SOIL
Well-drained, dry; alkaline.

PROPAGATION
Sow seeds in fall or spring. Self-seeds.

FLOWERING
Summer.

USES
Culinary, herbal medicinal.

Pelargonium
Scented pelargonium

A number of scented pelargonium species and varieties have specific scents.

Sweet-scented geraniums are welcome plants in the garden in summer for their leaves and flowers. Use the leaves in baking, to flavor cakes and desserts, or infuse them as an herbal tea. You can also garnish summer salads with both the flowers and leaves. Geraniums are grown commercially, and the oil distilled from the leaves is used as an insect repellent and as an ingredient in soaps and perfumes. The leaves release a sweet scent when touched and the flowers are attractive, usually white to pink and mauve.

The plants are not hardy. In areas that are liable to frosts, bring them indoors during winter and treat them as houseplants. Water them sparingly while they are indoors. Where the climate allows for them to be grown outdoors, they make good plants for a container garden. Propagate pelargoniums from softwood cuttings. You can cut them back hard in spring. Deadhead pelargoniums regularly throughout the growing season.

There are a considerable number of scented species and varieties, each with its own scent. Among the best known are: *P.* 'Attar of Roses', with purple flowers and rose scent; *P. crispum* 'Variegatum', with gold-variegated leaves, pale mauve flowers, and pine scent; *P.* 'Lady Plymouth', with lavender-pink flowers and eucalyptus scent; and *P.* 'Rober's Lemon Rose', with mauve flowers and rose-lemon scent.

vital statistics

FAMILY
Geraniaceae (geranium)

OTHER VARIETIES AND SPECIES
P. 'Attar of Roses', P. 'Prince of Orange', P. 'Clorinda', P. crispum var. minor, P. x fragrans, P. graveolens, P. grossularioides, P quercifolium, P. tomentosum.

PERENNIAL ZONE 8–10

HEIGHT
To 2ft (60cm)

SPREAD
To 16in (40cm)

FLOWERS
Mauve, pink and white, single or double flowers in clusters.

FOLIAGE
Vigorous, bushy, erect plant with mid-green leaves that are slightly rough to the touch and deeply lobed.

NATURAL HABITAT
Native of coastal southern Africa. Widely naturalized.

SITE
Full sun.

SOIL
Light, well-drained to sandy soil.

PROPAGATION
Take cuttings from non-flowering shoots in summer; sow seeds in spring.

FLOWERING
Summer.

USES
Culinary, perfumes, cosmetics.

Perilla frutescens
Beefsteak plant
perilla, shiso

Beefsteak plants are colorful annuals grown for their bronze leaves, smelling of cinnamon. They are used in salads in Japan, where the purple form is popular in pickling to add a deep red color.

This is a valuable culinary herb that is grown as an annual in gardens for its colorful foliage, which emerges in shades of bronze, dark green, or purple. It comes from the Far East, China and Japan, and it is also a valued herb in traditional Chinese medicine for the treatment of a number of diseases.

Beefsteak plants are erect and bushy and the oval, pointed leaves are held in pairs on the stalks. They are very aromatic and smell of cinnamon. The flowers are small, white, and insignificant, and appear on spikes in the middle of summer. In Japan the plant is known as shiso, and the green-leaved varieties are used in the preparation of sushi and tempura. The purple-leaved varieties are used in pickling, for they add color to the spices. The volatile oil is extremely sweet and is used to flavor candy, sauces, and dental products.

In Chinese medicine the beefsteak plant is given to treat colds, sickness, stomachaches, constipation, and for allergic reactions to seafood. The stems were also a traditional Chinese remedy for morning sickness in pregnancy.

vital statistics

FAMILY Labiatae	**ANNUAL**	**FOLIAGE** Fairly large green, purple or bronze, nettle-like oval aromatic leaves.	**SOIL** Rich, moisture-retaining soil.	**FLOWERING** Summer.
	HEIGHT 2–3ft (60–90cm).			
OTHER VARIETIES AND SPECIES *P. frutescens* var. *crispa, P. f.* var. *nankinensis, P. f. rubra*			**PROPAGATION** Sow seeds in spring at 55–64°F (13–18°C).	**USES** Culinary, Chinese medicine.
	SPREAD 12in (30cm).	**NATURAL HABITAT** Native of China and Japan. Found in moist, open woodland.		
	FLOWERS Small, insignificant, tubular white or lavender flowers held on short spikes.	**SITE** Partial shade		

Persicaria bistorta (Polygonum bistoroides)
American bistort
dragonwort, easter giant, red legs, snakeweed

A number of bistorts are used today in herbal medicine and they have recently been reclassified by the botanists under the genus *Persicaria*. They are more commonly known as polygonums. They are bitter, astringent herbs that are valued for their healing and tonic effect. They have been used in herbal and Chinese medicine for many centuries. *P. multiflorum* is famed as a restorer of color to gray hair in the elderly, while *P. odoratum*, popularly known as Vietnamese coriander, is used in Vietnamese cooking as a flavoring.

The roots of the herb are dried and powdered and made into a variety of decoctions, pills, and powders. They are used to treat all sorts of fevers, and in the Middle Ages had the reputation of being able to resist both the plague and smallpox. They were regarded as an antidote to all poisons, and were thought to be effective in cases of snakebite. The roots have a curious, snake-like appearance. Today the plants are used in herbal medicine to treat all manner of stomach ailments as well as being applied to sore and bleeding gums.

P. multiflorum is also employed in herbal medicine, mainly as a tonic to improve the liver and reproductive systems. It is prescribed to lower cholesterol levels and is used as an antibacterial drug. It is also taken to ease menstrual pains and for constipation in the elderly.

Bistorts are good plants for any moist, reasonably shady herbaceous border. They make excellent ground-cover plants.

vital statistics

FAMILY
Polygonaceae

OTHER VARIETIES AND SPECIES
P. affinis, P. amplexicaulis, P. campanulata, P. capitata, P. virginiana. There is a number of garden varieties available that have better flower forms than the species.

PERENNIAL ZONE 4

HEIGHT
1–2ft (30–60cm)

SPREAD
18in (45cm)

FLOWERS
Bell-shaped white or pink flowers, held upright.

FOLIAGE
Broad, green basal leaves with pointed ends that turn orange and red in the fall.

NATURAL HABITAT
Europe, Asia, and Japan. Found in many habitats, in shady woodland and beside streams.

SITE
Partial shade.

SOIL
Moist, fertile.

PROPAGATION
Sow seeds in spring or fall, or divide the rhizomes in spring or fall. The plants may become invasive in ordinary gardens.

FLOWERING
Summer.

USES
Herbal medicine.

Petroselinum
Parsley
curled parsley, flat-leaf parsley, Italian parsley

Parsley is one of the most popular herbs grown today and has many uses in the kitchen. These range from simple garnish for boiled potatoes and vegetables, to the essential ingredient of parsley sauce and the classic Burgundian galantine of ham, *jambon persillé*. Parsley is also one of the main ingredients of a *fines herbes* mixture. You can also fry it and sprinkle the crisp leaves on fish dishes.

The two commonest varieties grown are *P. crispum*, curly-leaf parsley, and *P. c.* var. *neapolitanum*, flat-leaf or Italian parsley. The first is the most decorative and is sometimes grown as edging along a path in the vegetable or herb garden or in a container. Italian parsley is a hardier plant and has a much stronger flavor.

Parsley was a popular medicinal herb in the late Middle Aes. It was used to cure urinary infections and gas, and to help with menstrual problems. The boiled roots were used more than the leaves. The leaves were applied to the eyelids in cases of conjunctivitis, and the juice, mixed with wine, was used as a cure for earache. Parsley is rich in vitamin C and has a reputation for curing bad breath, particularly where the cause is excessive garlic intake.

Petroselinum crispum, curled parsley, has an attractive, bushy appearance and slightly subtler flavor than its flat-leaf cousin. It is often used as a garnish.

---

vital statistics

FAMILY
Umelliferae (carrot family)

OTHER VARIETIES AND SPECIES
P. crispum 'Champion Moss Curled', *P. c.* 'Bravour', *P. c.* 'Darki', *P. c.* var. *neopolitanum*, 'French', *P. c.* var. *tuberosum*

BIENNIAL ZONE 6

HEIGHT
1–2ft (30–60cm)

SPREAD
12in (30cm)

FLOWERS
Greenish yellow, very small, in compound bunches.

FOLIAGE
Rich green, aromatic, much divided into featherlike leaflets, crisp and curled or flat.

NATURAL HABITAT
Native of Sardinia and the eastern Mediterranean, widely naturalized.

SITE
Full sun or partial shade.

SOIL
Fertile, moisture-retaining soil.

PROPAGATION
Sow seeds in early and late summer; self-seeds.

FLOWERING
Summer to fall.

USES
Culinary, herbal medicine, breath freshener.

Phacelia tanacetifolia
Phacelia
lacy phacelia

The flower color of the scorpion weed varies from blue through all shades of pink to white. They are hardy annuals, and their creeping roots help to break up heavy soil.

Phacelias are one of the most attractive hardy annuals, with flowers in varying shades of blue, lilac, deep blue, and white. They spread vigorously and can be grown as annual ground cover on any vacant ground in the garden. The plants make an effective green manure when dug into the soil. They are also extremely attractive to bees. The species *P. campanularia*, desertbells, is low-growing, reaching only 12in (30cm) in height, but *P. tanacetifolia* is much taller and will reach 3ft (90cm) with a spread of 12in (30cm). The leaves are long and the flowers are shaped like bells and are lavender-blue to purple in color.

Phacelia was formerly used in herbal medicine in the treatment of fevers. It should be handled with care, as the leaves may cause some skin irritation. Phacelias are extremely hardy and can be sown where they are to flower, either in the fall or early spring when the soil has started to warm up. Sow the seed thickly and the plant will grow dense rather than tall.

Plants raised from seed sown in the preceeding fall make better plants. They flourish in light soil in full sun. You can use them to break up heavy soil, as their creeping roots will break up surface particles. Plants used for this purpose will not usually flower.

Caution: May cause skin irritation if handled.

vital statistics

FAMILY
Hydrophyllaceae (waterleaf)

OTHER VARIETIES AND SPECIES
P. bipinnatifida, P. campanularia, P. fimbriata, P. linearis, P. purshii

ANNUAL

HEIGHT
To 3ft (90cm)

SPREAD
12in (30cm)

FLOWERS
Lavender-blue spikes, followed by curled, scorpionlike seed heads. Pale violet petals.

FOLIAGE
Deep green leaves, finely divided, feathery, alternating along the branches.

NATURAL HABITAT
Native of North America. Bushy and grassy areas.

SITE
Prefers full sun but will tolerate partial shade.

SOIL
Most soils, prefers some moisture.

PROPAGATION
Sow seeds in spring after frost; self-seeds.

FLOWERING
Summer.

USES
Bee plant, green manure, formerly medicinal.

Phytolacca americana
Pokeweed

American pokeweed, inkberry, pigeonberry, pokeroot, red weed

This dramatic plant, native to the eastern and southern parts of the country, is an extremely useful medicinal plant. Its branching, red stems have alternate, narrow, oval leaves growing up the stems, and grow to a massive size in suitable soil. The leaves put on a really spectacular fall show, turning a wonderful red and purple color. The flowers are white to pink and are held on long elongated spikes, sometimes pendant. They are followed by the black fruit. The whole of this plant is extremely poisonous. Do not grow it in any garden where there are, or are likely to be, children, for the berries look most attractive, rather like long clusters of blackberries. They are extremely harmful if eaten. The plant does have an unpleasant smell that helps to deter youngsters from sampling it.

Pokeweed is mainly used in herbal medicine in the treatment of autoimmune diseases, such as rheumatoid arthritis, and glandular infections, such as tonsilitis, mumps, and mononucleosis as it reduces inflammation and stimulates the immune system. It has a number of other uses and is used externally for many skin complaints. Juice from the plant is used as a dye, red ink, and food coloring.

Caution: All parts of the plant are poisonous, especially the berries and roots.

Pokeweed is a plant to beware of, for the berries look so luscious and succulent that any child might be forgiven for tasting them. They are extremely poisonous.

vital statistics

FAMILY
Phytolaccaceae

OTHER VARIETIES AND SPECIES
P. acinosa (Indian pokeberry), *P. polyandra*

PERENNIAL ZONE 3

HEIGHT
4–8ft (1.2–2.4m)

SPREAD
4ft (1.2m)

FLOWERS
White or pink, small, shallow and cup-shaped.

FOLIAGE
Medium-green, lance-shaped to oval leaves, carried alternately on reddish stems.

NATURAL HABITAT
Native of south and east U.S.A., found on wasteland, in fields, and beside highways.

SITE
Sun or partial shade.

SOIL
Rich, moisture-retaining, light, well-drained soil.

PROPAGATION
Sow seed at 55–64°F (13–18°C) in early spring.

FLOWERING
Summer to late summer.

USES
Herbal medicine, dye plant.

Pimpinella saxifraga
Burnet saxifrage
small pimpernel, solid stem saxifrage

This plant is closely related to *Pimpinella anisum*, aniseed, and they have both been important medicinal herbs for centuries. They are not usually grown for decorative purposes. Both plants have clusters of white, sometimes pink-tinged flowers in the summer; the burnet saxifrage has slightly larger flowers.

Burnet saxifrage was a favored herb of Culpeper, who considered it only a little inferior to betony. He advocated using the herb as a tonic because "the continual use of it preserves the body in health and the spirit in vigour ... Two or three of the stalks put into a cup of wine, especially claret, are known to quicken the spirits refresh and clear the heart and drive away melancholy." It is still used in herbal medicine to treat throat infections, indigestion, and urinary problems. The young leaves taste a bit like cucumber and can be added to salads.

Aniseed is a warming herb that improves the digestion and stimulates liver function. The young leaves can be eaten, and it is used worldwide as a flavoring. It is a common ingredient in cough medicines and is employed in herbal medicine to treat bronchial complaints.

The burnet saxifrage has many uses in herbal medicine, chiefly in cases of throat infections, breathing difficulties, sore gums, and external wounds. It is also an ingredient in liqueurs.

vital statistics

FAMILY
Umbelliferae/Apiaceae

OTHER VARIETIES AND SPECIES
P. major (greater burnet saxifrage, greater pimpernel), *P. major* 'Rosea', *P. saxifraga* var. *nigra* (black caraway)

PERENNIAL ZONE 3
(*P. anisum* is half-hardy.)

HEIGHT
2–3ft (60–90cm)

SPREAD
12–30in (30–75cm)

FLOWERS
Small, white flowers in clumps.

FOLIAGE
Green, narrowly oval leaves growing from the stalks.

NATURAL HABITAT
Europe, Asia, northern Africa, and South America. Found in rough grassland and open woodland.

SITE
Sun or partial shade.

SOIL
Tolerates most soils but does best in rich, moisture-retaining soil.

PROPAGATION
Sow seeds in a cold frame when ripe in the fall.

FLOWERING
Summer.

USES
Culinary, herbal medicine.

Plantago major ⊕ ○ ◑
Greater plantain

broadleaf plantain, rat's tail plantain, round-leaved plantain, waybread, white man's footprint

The greater and lesser plantains are best known as troublesome weeds of the lawn that most gardeners spend time and energy removing. However, they are also important in herbal medicine. They are common almost everywhere, and the common name of white man's footprint came because the seeds were carried, inadvertently, around the world by colonial administrators.

The use of *P. asiatica*, the Chinese plantain, as a medicinal plant was recorded at the time of the Han dynasty around 200 BC. Greater plantain was one of the nine sacred herbs of the Saxons and has been recovered from graves of the Iron Age. In the 16th century the seeds of the greater plantain were used to cure pains in the stomach and irritation of the bowels. They were also thought good wound herbs and were prescribed for sores and open wounds. The distilled juice of the plant was used for toothache.

Plantain contain mucilage, which swells in the gut when swallowed and acts as a bulk laxative. It is an astringent herb that acts as a diuretic and expectorant, and is used in herbal medicine for urinary problems as well as bronchial conditions, such as asthma and hay fever, and sinusitis.

The flower heads of this weed turn brown as the seeds ripen, which gives it its common name of rat's tail. It is used as a laxative, and to treat bronchial and urinary problems.

vital statistics

FAMILY
Plantaginaceae

OTHER VARIETIES AND SPECIES
P. asiatica (Asian plantain), *P. lanceolata, P. media, P. nivalis, P. sempervirens.* Some cultivated varieties have been developed suitable for herbaceous borders.

PERENNIAL ZONE 3

HEIGHT
18in (40cm)

SPREAD
18in (40cm)

FLOWERS
Yellow-green flowers are born on a long spike.

FOLIAGE
Long, oval leaves held in a round basal rosette.

NATURAL HABITAT
Europe, Asia, northern Africa, and South America. Found in many habitats, a common weed of lawns and grassland.

SITE
Sun or partial shade.

SOIL
Prefers sandy, well-drained soil but will grow in most soils.

PROPAGATION
Sow seeds or divide in spring.

FLOWERING
Summer.

USES
Herbal medicine.

Herbs in the kitchen

To the private gardener, herbs are of most interest because of their use in the kitchen. Cuisines around the world rely on the myriad of flavors that herbs can contribute to food. Growing and using herbs is both pleasurable and healthy.

SOUPS

For cold days when some seriously warming food is required, soups with fresh herbs and vegetables always go down well. Lovage and chervil are traditional herbs for the kitchen that are not used often today. Both make classic soup dishes, and it is worth growing the herb for these delicious rewards.

Jerusalem artichoke soup with lovage

YOU WILL NEED:

1 lb (450g) Jerusalem artichokes

2 tbsp butter

2 cups (16 fl oz/500 ml) each milk and chicken stock

2 tbsp light cream

salt and pepper

2 tbsp chopped fresh lovage

sprigs of lovage to garnish

Levisticum officinale Lovage

Scrub and peel the artichokes and chop them roughly. Put them in a heavy saucepan with the butter, cover the pot, and cook them very gently until they are soft. Sieve them or put them in the liquidizer. Return the pureed artichokes to the pot, stir in the milk and stock, season to taste, and simmer for 15 minutes. Stir in the cream and chopped lovage just before serving. Garnish with a few sprigs of lovage and serve with croutons.

Vegetable soup with chervil

Chervil is much used in France for flavoring egg dishes and soups; the flavor is rather like parsley but more elusive.

YOU WILL NEED:

¼ cup (2oz/60g) butter

8oz (225g) leeks

2 scallions

8oz (225g) potatoes

8oz (225g) cauliflower florets

8oz (225g) peas, you can use frozen

3¾ cups (30 fl oz/850 ml) chicken stock

⅔ cup (5 fl oz/150 ml) light cream

salt and pepper

3 tbsp chopped fresh chervil leaves

Chop the leeks and fry them gently in the butter in a large saucepan. Chop and add the scallions, potatoes and cauliflower. Fry them gently together for 3–4 minutes. Pour on the stock and then simmer the vegetables for 30 minutes until they are soft and tender. Add the peas at the last minute if they are frozen or 10 minutes earlier if they are fresh. Put all the vegetables in a blender and blend until they are quite smooth. Return the soup to the pot and reheat, seasoning with salt and pepper and add the cream at the last minute. Do not let the soup boil after the cream has been added. Finally, remove from the heat and stir in the chopped chervil leaves.

Anthriscus cerefolium Chervil

SALADS

A small bed of salad herbs can keep you supplied right through the summer months. Try some of these unusual dishes for variety.

Dandelion salad

In France dandelions (*pissenlits*) are grown to eat. To make a simple salad wash 6 cups of young dandelion leaves and shake them dry. Then fry 3–4 slices of bacon, chop them into small pieces, and put them on the dandelion leaves. Add 3 tablespoons of red wine vinegar to the bacon fat, let the vinegar bubble and mix with the remains in the skillet and then pour this over the leaves. Eat while warm.

Herb and flower salad

YOU WILL NEED:
1 Boston lettuce
8 sprigs of chervil
nasturtium flowers

Combine the lettuce leaves and chervil. Add half the nasturtium flowers. Dress with a light vinaigrette and scatter the remaining flowers over the salad as a garnish.

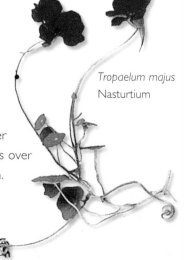

Tropaeolum majus Nasturtium

Insalata tricolore

One of the very best appetizers, which is simplicity itself to prepare and present.

YOU WILL NEED:
1 lb (450g) good quality beefsteak tomatoes: the better the tomatoes, the better the salad.
4 oz (110g) buffalo mozzarella cheese
20–30 fresh basil leaves
olive oil, salt, black pepper, wine vinegar

Peel the tomatoes if you want. Slice them thinly. Slice the mozzarella thinly. Alternate the slices of tomatoes and cheese around a dish. Scatter the basil leaves over them. Just before serving grind pepper over the dish, season generously with salt, and pour over about 2 tablespoons of olive oil, or a light vinaigrette.

OMELETS

Omelets are a true test of a cook. The secret of success is to use really fresh eggs, if you can get them. Beat them very lightly, have a good heavy non-stick omelet pan and heat it until the butter just starts to turn brown, then add the eggs. Add only a very little filling; you want to taste the eggs as well as the filling. The following omelets are delicious and light.

Omelette aux fines herbes

YOU WILL NEED:
4 fresh eggs
2 tsp butter
1 tbsp finely chopped herbs: parsley, tarragon, chives, and chervil
salt and freshly ground black pepper

Beat the eggs in a bowl, season with salt and pepper, and add half of the herb mixture. Heat the butter in an omelet pan and when it turns brown tip in the eggs. Add the remainder of the herbs on top of the eggs. Tilt the pan and allow the egg mixture to set. When there is just a little of the creamy mixture unset on the surface of the omelet, it is done. Fold it in three and slip it onto a plate. Eat immediately.

Sorrel omelet

Another good herbal omelet can be made with sorrel leaves.

Chop 3 or 4 leaves of sorrel and cook them in butter for 4–5 minutes before adding them to the omelet mixture when this is in the omelet pan. Cook as before.

MAIN DISHES

Herbs give can be used to enhance other flavors, or they can be the stars of a dish themselves.

Aioli

This typifies lunch on a hot summer's day in the south of France.

The dish is normally composed of a cold boiled chicken or fish surrounded by boiled and raw vegetables. A typical aioli might include chicken, shrimp, hard-boiled eggs, boiled potatoes, and a selection of cooked vegetables, such as carrots, beets and beans, and raw vegetables such as celery and tomatoes. In the center, a large bowl of yellow garlic sauce sits and each piece of food is dipped into it before being eaten.

YOU WILL NEED:

To make the sauce

4 garlic cloves (or more or fewer as liked)

2 egg yolks

1¼ cups (10 fl oz/300 ml) olive oil

1½ tbsp lemon juice or white wine vinegar

salt and pepper

Crush the garlic. Traditionally this is done with a mortar and pestle but you can also do it with a wooden spoon in a large bowl.

Add a little salt. Beat in the egg yolks and mix thoroughly before starting to add the olive oil, a little at a time. You can do this in a blender. If the sauce curdles, beat another egg yolk in a separate bowl and gradually add the curdled mixture to the fresh yolk, beating all the time. When the sauce is thick and shiny add the lemon juice or vinegar.

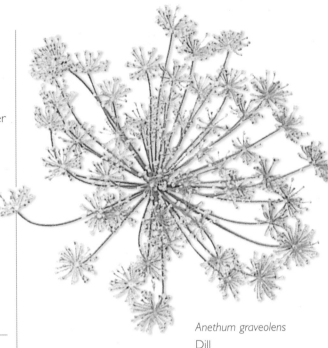

Anethum graveolens
Dill

Gravadlax

This is a popular method of serving salmon in Norway. The curing process can easily be carried out at home and the same treatment can be used for fish such as turbot or halibut.

YOU WILL NEED:

2 tbsp sea salt

1½ tbsp light brown sugar

1 tsp crushed black peppercorns

1 tbsp gin

3 tbsp fresh dill, finely chopped

1½ lbs (750g) fresh salmon in one piece, either the tail or a middle cut, boned and cut into two fillets

Put all the ingredients except the fish in a bowl and mix them together. Take a large plate or shallow bowl that will hold the fish and put a quarter of the marinade on the bottom. Lay one fillet on the marinade skinside down. Spread half of the remaining marinade on the top of the first fillet and then put the second fillet on top of the first, skinside up. Cover this with the rest of the marinade and rub it in. Cover the salmon with foil. Put a plate on top and weigh it down. Place the dish in a refrigerator for 3–4 days turning the fish over once a day. When the salmon is ready, slice the fillets thinly and serve with a sweet mustard and dill sauce (see page 267).

Roast sea bass with fennel

Fennel has an affinity with fish and this dish can also be made with trout, salmon, or any firm sea fish, such as turbot or cod. It is better if the fish is on the bone, but if you are cooking boneless fillets of fish in this way, then shorten the cooking time by 5 minutes.
I sea bass, approximately 1 lb (450g), per person.

YOU WILL NEED:

Quantity for each fish

½ tbsp fennel seeds

sea salt and black pepper

I red onion

I fennel bulb

2 tbsp olive oil

I lemon

parsley stalks (optional)

2 tbsp white wine

foil

Clean and scale the fish if this has not already been done. Cut off the head if you wish. Make three slanting incisions on each side of the fish, cutting down to, but not through, the backbone. Rub the

inside and outside of each fish with sea salt, grind over some black pepper, and put some fennel seeds in the inside. Slice the onion and fennel bulb thinly. Take a large enough piece of foil to wrap around each fish. Brush the foil with olive oil and then lay the fennel and onion on it. Put the fish on top, brush it with oil, squeeze the juice from the lemon over it and add the white wine and the parsley stalks, if using. Fold up the foil so that it forms a loose, airtight envelope around the fish.

Bake in a preheated oven at 375°F for 25 minutes. Serve the fish with some of the juices from the foil.

Easy Bolognaise sauce

The best Bolognaise sauce contains a number of herbs that give it a subtle flavor.

YOU WILL NEED:

2 small onions

I carrot (optional)

I stick celery (optional)

2 garlic cloves

2–3 tbsp olive oil

3 slices bacon

I lb (570g) ground beef

I tbsp tomato paste

I tbsp flour

I can Italian tomatoes

red wine, meat stock, or water

oregano, thyme, and basil

sugar

salt and pepper

Origanum vulgare Oregano

Chop the onions, carrot, celery, and garlic. Heat the olive oil in a deep skillet, add the bacon and vegetables and fry gently. Add the ground beef and brown it with the vegetables, breaking up any lumps. Stir in the tomato paste. Dust the flour over the fried meat and stir. Add the tomatoes, mixing them into the sauce and then add enough red wine to give the sauce, a good runny consistency. Substitute stock or water if necessary. Bring it to a boil, simmer, and let it thicken. Add all the herbs as well as a good pinch of salt, sugar, and ground black pepper. Check the seasoning

Foeniculum vulgare Fennel

and adjust. Cover the skillet and let the sauce simmer very slowly for 30–45 minutes. Remove the lid to reduce if the sauce is too thin or add a little water if it is too thick.

Roast pork with sage and rosemary

YOU WILL NEED:

4½ lb (2kg) boned loin or leg of pork

20 sage leaves

2 tsp rosemary leaves

½ cup (4oz/115g) unsalted butter

3 garlic cloves

1¼ cups (10 fl oz/300 ml) dry white wine

sea salt and pepper.

Cut off any fat and rind from the pork. Chop the sage and rosemary leaves finely and rub them into the meat with sea salt and black pepper. Melt half the butter in a heavy flameproof casserole and brown the meat thoroughly on all sides. Remove from the pot, pour off the fat, and then add 2 teaspoons butter, and the garlic. Shake over the heat for a short time.

Rosmarinus officinalis Rosemary

Add some of the wine and deglaze the pot. Return the pork to the pot, add the remainder of the wine, dot with the remaining butter, bring to a boil, and then cook, covered, in a preheated oven 300°F for 60–75 minutes. Slice and serve with the gravy from the pot. If you prefer your pork well done cook for 15 minutes longer.

Petroselinum crispum
Flat-leaf parsley

Roast lamb with parsley and rosemary

YOU WILL NEED:

1 leg of lamb about 4½ lb (2kg)

2 cups (6½oz/175g) or more fresh white breadcrumbs

3 tbsp chopped parsley

1 garlic clove

2 tbsp rosemary leaves

olive oil

sea salt

Rub the leg of lamb all over with olive oil and salt. Combine the breadcrumbs, parsley, garlic, and rosemary in a bowl and then spread this all over the lamb, making as thick a crust as you can. Roast in a preheated oven at 375°F for about 1¼–1½ hours, by which time it should be delicately pink in the middle. Run a skewer into the meat to test. If you like your lamb well done, cook it for slightly longer.

Mentha × piperita Peppermint

DESSERTS

Herbs bring fresh and delicate flavors to dishes that might otherwise be too heavy and sweet.

Rose cream tart

YOU WILL NEED:

I egg separated

10–12 petals of a red or pink rose

superfine sugar

8oz (225g) flaky pastry

1¼ cups (6oz/170g) whipping cream

⅔ cup (4oz/115g) plain yogurt

2 tbsp rosewater

Whip the white until it is stiff. Cover each rose petal with egg white, sprinkle them with sugar, and put them in the oven at 225°F to dry for about I hour. Roll out the pastry to about ¼ in (5mm) thick and cut a 10-in (25-cm) circle. Bake this at 400°F for 25 minutes until it has risen and is brown. Let it cool completely.

Whip the cream stiffly and then fold in the yogurt, egg yolk, and 2 tablespoons sugar. Whisk in the rosewater. Spoon the cream over the pastry base, decorate with the rose petals, and serve immediately.

Peppermint creams

These are easy to make and a popular way to amuse children on a wet weekend in winter.

YOU WILL NEED:

I lb (450g) confectioner's sugar

2 large egg whites

1–2 drops peppermint oil or 2 tsp peppermint essence

green food coloring if liked

Sift the sugar into a bowl. Whip the egg whites stiffly and add them to the sugar. Add the peppermint flavoring. Mix this to a stiff dough, add the food coloring, if using, and roll out the creams to about ⅛–¼ in (3–6mm) thick. Dredge with more sugar. Cut the creams into small circles with a small cookie or candy cutter and put them on a wire tray to dry for 24 hours.

If you want to cover the creams with chocolate, melt some chocolate in a bowl over hot water and dip the creams in it, holding them on a long, fine skewer. Let them dry on clean waxed paper.

Sugared fruit, flowers, and leaves

The flowers, fruit, and leaves of a number of edible herbs can be coated with sugar and used to make exotic decorations for desserts and drinks in the summer. Flowers of herbs such as borage and violets, and the scented leaves of some geraniums are all excellent for this purpose.

YOU WILL NEED:

To make the sugar mixture

I egg white

superfine sugar

Rinse the fruit, flowers, and leaves that you are going to cover and leave them to dry thoroughly. Whisk the egg white lightly in a bowl. Holding the dry leaves, flowers, or fruit in tongs or with a fork, coat them with the egg white. Shake off any excess and then coat them evenly with sugar. Allow coated objects to dry on a sugared surface for 30 minutes or until the sugar has formed a crisp, dry coating.

Sorbets

A number of herbs are used to make refreshing sorbets. All sorbets require two basic steps. Prepare the basic sugar syrup. The proportions are 1 lb (450g) of superfine sugar to 2 cups (16 fl oz/500 ml) water. Heat the sugar and water gently until the sugar has dissolved. Bring to a boil and simmer gently for 10 minutes. Store. Use this syrup for the following recipes unless otherwise indicated.

Freeze. Use an ice cream maker, or freeze the sorbet in a tray in the freezer until slushy. Remove from the freezer, beat vigorously to remove large ice crystals, and then return to the freezer until firm.

Elderflower sorbet

YOU WILL NEED:

3 large sprays of elderflowers

½ cup (4oz/115g) sugar

juice of 2 grapefruit and 1 lemon

1¼ cup (10 fl oz/300 ml) water

Dissolve the sugar in the water, bring to a boil, and boil for 5 minutes. Remove from the heat and push the heads of the elderflowers into the syrup. Leave to cool. When cool, add the grapefruit and lemon juice, mix thoroughly, then strain the syrup into an ice-cream maker. Freeze.

Sambucus nigra Black elder

Peppermint tea sorbet

YOU WILL NEED:

2 cups (16 fl oz/500 ml) water

1 cup (3¼oz/90g) peppermint leaves

½ cup (6oz/170g) sugar syrup

Boil the water in a saucepan and add the peppermint leaves. Set aside, covered, for about 3 hours. Strain. Mix the tea and sugar syrup together and freeze in an ice cream maker.

Ocimum basilicum
Sweet basil

Savory sorbets

Tomato and basil sorbet

YOU WILL NEED:

6 ripe tomatoes

juice of 1 lemon

¼ cup (3oz/85g) sugar syrup

3 chives

6–8 fresh basil leaves

¾ cup (6 fl oz/175 ml) tomato juice

salt and pepper

dash of Tabasco or hot pepper sauce if desired

Place the tomatoes in boiling water for a few seconds. Remove, then peel and scoop out and discard the seeds.

Put the tomato flesh, lemon juice, sugar syrup, chives, and basil leaves in a liquidizer and puree. Strain the mixture through a nylon sieve with a wooden spoon. Add the tomato juice, season to taste with salt, pepper, and Tabasco. Freeze.

Cucumber and mint sorbet

YOU WILL NEED:

1 tsp chicken stock granules

½ cup (4 fl oz/100 ml) hot water

½ cup (3½oz/100g) plain yogurt

1 tbsp fresh mint

freshly ground black pepper

2 large cucumbers, peeled, cored, and very finely grated

Dissolve the chicken stock in the hot water. Beat the yogurt and add the chopped mint and a grinding of pepper. Mix the yogurt, chicken stock, and grated cucumber together. Freeze.

This refreshing sorbet can be served with a small salad as a light lunch or appetizer.

Anethum graveolens Dill

CLASSIC HERBAL SAUCES

Herbs are the main ingredient of many of the classic sauces used in cookery.

Dill sauce

This is a traditional accompaniment for many Greek dishes, such as meatballs or lamb poached with vegetables in chicken stock. The dill sauce is then made using the stock and poured over the water.

YOU WILL NEED:

3 tbsp butter

2 tbsp all-purpose flour

2 egg yolks

¼ cup (2 fl oz/50 ml) lemon juice

3 tbsp chopped fresh dill

3¾ cups (30 fl oz/850 ml) stock

salt and pepper

Beat the egg yolks and lemon juice together with the dill in a bowl. Stir in 2 tablespoons of hot stock. Beat them together. Heat the butter and gradually stir in the flour. Add the stock and then pour the egg mixture back into the stock and stir constantly over a low heat for about 3 minutes. The stock must not even approach boiling point, if it does the eggs will scramble and this ruins the smoothness of the sauce. Pour the sauce over the meat and serve immediately.

Dill sauce for fish

This is made as above, substituting fish stock for the chicken broth and adding sugar to the seasoning.

Mustard and dill sweet and sour vinaigrette sauce

YOU WILL NEED:

⅔ cup olive oil

2 tbsp red wine vinegar

2 tsps French mustard

¼ cup (1½oz/45g)brown sugar

1 tbsp chopped dill

Put all the ingredients in a jar and shake vigorously.

Béarnaise sauce

A classic butter and egg sauce that is served with steaks and other broiled meat. There are a number of versions of the recipe.

YOU WILL NEED:

1 shallot

½ cup (3 fl oz/75 ml) white wine vinegar

1 sprig each tarragon and chervil

6 peppercorns

1 bay leaf

2 egg yolks

6 tbsp unsalted butter

1 small tsp each chopped tarragon and chervil

salt and pepper

Chop the shallot finely and put it, the vinegar, tarragon and chervil sprigs, peppercorns, and bay leaf in a saucepan. Reduce until only 1 tablespoon remains. Beat the egg yolks in a bowl over a gentle heat, strain the vinegar, add it to the egg yolks, and then beat in the butter piece by piece until it has all been absorbed and the sauce has thickened. Do not overheat or the sauce will curdle. Add the chopped chervil and tarragon. Taste and adjust the seasoning if necessary.

Sauce verte

YOU WILL NEED:

1¼ cups (6oz/170g) thick mayonnaise

1½ cups (6oz/170g) herbs—the leaves of young spinach, watercress, parsley, chives, tarragon, chervil. Allow 2 parts spinach and watercress to one each of the others.

Bring a saucepan of water to a boil and put in all the leaves for 3–4 minutes. Drain, dry the leaves, and then put them in a liquidizer. Traditionally, they were pounded and passed through a fine sieve. Add the puree to the mayonnaise just before serving.

Herb sauce

A simple herb sauce can be made by adding the finely chopped leaves of parsley, tarragon, chervil, and chives, making a thin, well-flavored béchamel sauce. Use 2 tablespoons of chopped herbs to every 2½ cups (20 fl oz/575 ml) of sauce.

Mint sauce

A traditional accompaniment to roast lamb. Use sparingly to avoid overpowering not just the delicate taste of the meat but also any wine that is being drunk with the meal.

YOU WILL NEED:

2 tbsp mint

¼ cup (2 fl oz/50 ml) boiling water

2 tbsp superfine sugar

2 tsp white wine vinegar

Pick some fresh mint. Chop it thoroughly. Put it in a bowl with the boiling water and sugar until the sugar has dissolved. Add the vinegar and let the sauce cool.

Nasturtium officinale Watercress (used in sauce verte above)

Mustard sauce

This is the traditional accompaniment for broiled herrings, which are now so seldom found. It is a delicious accompaniment to a very traditional dish.

YOU WILL NEED:

1 tsp dry English mustard or 1 tbsp yellow Dijon mustard

1 tsp tarragon vinegar

1 tsp white sugar

1¼ cups (10 fl oz/300 ml) white sauce made with milk, or half milk and half fish stock

2 tbsp butter

Mix the mustard and vinegar in a bowl. Add the sugar. Heat the white sauce to just below boiling and add the mustard mixture. Cut the butter in pieces and whisk each piece in, one at a time. The finished sauce will be creamy and quite thick.

Parsley sauce

The easiest parsley sauce is made by adding a good handful of finely chopped parsley to 1¼ cups (10 fl oz/300 ml) of béchamel sauce. Here is a richer version, usually served with hot ham.

YOU WILL NEED:

2 tbsp butter

2 tbsp all-purpose flour

1¼ cups (10 fl oz/300 ml) liquor in which the ham has been cooked

1 egg yolk

lemon juice

2 tbsp light cream

1 tbsp chopped parsley

Melt half the butter and all the flour in a saucepan. Add the ham liquor and stir until the sauce thickens. Combine the egg yolk, lemon juice, and cream in a bowl. Pour a little of the hot sauce into the bowl, stir and then return the mixture to the sauce. Stir very gently over a low heat for 2–3 minutes. Do not let the sauce boil. Remove from the stove, add the chopped parsley and the remaining butter cut in small pieces.

Petroselinum crispum Parsley

Rémoulade sauce

A traditional sauce often served with fish or broiled meat. It should have a good mustard flavor.

YOU WILL NEED:

yolks of 2 hard-boiled eggs

1 tbsp white wine vinegar

1 fresh egg yolk

1 tsp French mustard

⅔ cup (5 fl oz/150 ml) olive oil

1 tsp each chopped tarragon, chives, and capers

1–2 drops anchovy essence

salt and pepper

Pound the hard-boiled egg yolks in a bowl with the vinegar. Add the fresh egg yolk, the mustard and salt and pepper. Add the olive oil drop by drop, stirring all the time. When the sauce is thick, add the chopped herbs and anchovy essence.

Sauce ravigote

This sauce is served with salmon steaks or fried fish.

YOU WILL NEED:

2 shallots, finely chopped

3 tbsp white wine vinegar

1 tsp each, chopped chives, tarragon, and chervil

French mustard

1¼ cups (10 fl oz/300 ml) hot white sauce

Put the shallots and vinegar in a saucepan. Boil to reduce by half. Strain. Mix in the herbs and mustard.

Polemonium reptans
Greek valerian
Jacob's ladder

Both *Polemonium reptans*, the American species, and *P. caeruleum* are known as Greek valerian. Both were used for centuries in herbal medicine to cure fevers and treat cases of epilepsy, but they are very seldom used today. They are attractive plants, found in many gardens, with blue spires of flowers and narrow oval, green leaves. They received the name "Jacob's ladder" because the leaves and flower spikes resemble a floral ladder up which a weightless fairy could scramble.

P. reptans is a creeping, low-growing plant that makes good ground cover. The flowers are blue. 'Lambrook Mauve' is the most popular garden variety. All polemoniums prefer damp conditions and do best in moist soil and partial shade. They look good against a woodland background. *P. reptans* was often used by the Native Americans to treat bronchial ailments, such as coughs and pleurisy. It was also used to treat fevers. The roots were the part of the plant used and it was sometimes called "smells-like-pine," as the roots have a scent of pine needles.

Both *P. reptans* and *P. caeruleum* are attractive garden plants, found in many borders and in herb gardens. Neither is used to any extent in herbal medicine today.

vital statistics

FAMILY
Polemoniaceae

OTHER VARIETIES AND SPECIES
P. caeruleum var. *lacteum* (white flowers), *P. carneum*, *P. foliosissimum*, P. 'Lambrook Mauve', *P. pulcherrimum*. There are a number of garden varieties.

PERENNIAL ZONE 3

HEIGHT
2–3ft (60–90cm)

SPREAD
18in (45cm)

FLOWERS
Blue, five-petaled flowers with prominent orange stamens.

FOLIAGE
Bright green, pinnate leaves on branching stalks.

NATURAL HABITAT
Native of Europe, central Asia, and western North America. Found in damp soils by water and open woodland.

SITE
Sun or partial shade.

SOIL
Rich, moisture-retaining soil.

PROPAGATION
Sow seeds or divide in spring. Self-seeds.

FLOWERING
Summer.

USES
Formerly medicinal.

Portulaca oleracea
Purslane
little hogweed

It has recently been discovered that purslane contains omega-3 fatty acids, which are important in preventing heart disease.

Most portalucas are semisucculent trailing plants found in many warm countries. *P. oleracea*, purslane, is a native of southern Europe, where it is grown as a hardy annual. You can use the young, succulent shoots in salads, and the older shoots as a pot herb.

The plant has small, yellow flowers appearing in the summer. A number of varieties have been raised from the moss rose or sun plant, *P. grandiflora*, and these are grown as decorative annuals in borders. They include Sundance Hybrids and the Minilaca Series.

As well as their culinary qualities, purslane and the sun plant have both been used as medicinal herbs for many centuries. The juice of *P. grandiflora* was used for jaundice and as a cure for snake and insect bites, while *P. oleracea* is a diuretic and cooling herb sometimes used in herbal medicine to treat dysentery, mastitis, and piles. In the Middle Ages it was also used as a treatment for gonorrhea and to rid children of intestinal worms. Research has shown that it contains omega-3 fatty acids, which may strengthen the immune system.

vital statistics

FAMILY
Portulacaceae

OTHER VARIETIES AND SPECIES
P. oleracea var. *aurea* (gold leaves), *P. grandiflora*

TENDER ANNUAL

HEIGHT
6in (15cm)

SPREAD
9in (23cm)

FLOWERS
Small yellow flowers.

FOLIAGE
Fleshy, spatulate, thick, green, red-tinged leaves.

NATURAL HABITAT
The Mediterranean, India, and China. Found in dry wasteland and on hillsides.

SITE
Full sun, sheltered.

SOIL
Fertile, well-drained.

PROPAGATION
Sow seed at 55–64°F (13–18°C) in spring.

FLOWERING
Late summer.

USES
Culinary, herbal medicine.

Primula veris, P. vulgaris
Cowslip primrose

Cowslip primroses are charming wildflowers. They have a long history of use as medical herbs and have very similar chemical make-up, so they can be used interchangeably. In the Middle Ages cowslips were also called palsywort, and were used to treat palsy, cramp, convulsions, and pains in the nerves. They were also a treatment for sunburn and freckles. Cowslip primroses and primroses contain salicylates, the main ingredient of aspirin. Cowslips used to be more common than they are today; they have suffered from loss of habitat brought about by modern farming practices. In former times, when they were abundant, the flowers were picked to make cowslip wine, which was an excellent sedative.

Primroses are still very common plants and can be found growing on shady banks and in woodlands. Both primroses and cowslip primroses are used in herbal medicine today to treat bronchial complaints, whooping cough, and insomnia, or to cure minor wounds and sores. You can use both the leaves and the flowers of the two plants in salads. Also, try candying the flowers or use them in desserts.

Cowslip primroses are among the most beautiful of all wildflowers, with tall nodding flowers dotted with red-orange spots.

vital statistics

FAMILY
Primulaceae

OTHER VARIETIES AND SPECIES
P. alpicola, P. elatior, P. palinuri, P. sikkimensis. Many garden varieties have been developed.

PERENNIAL ZONE 3

HEIGHT
4–12in (10–30cm)

SPREAD
8in (20cm)

FLOWERS
Cowslips: deep yellow
Primroses: pale yellow.

FOLIAGE
Mid-green and veined. Downy on both sides.

NATURAL HABITAT
Native of northern Europe, found on banks and in damp woodland areas.

SITE
Sun or partial shade. Primroses do best in partial shade.

SOIL
Fertile, moisture-retaining soil.

PROPAGATION
Sow seed in spring.

FLOWERING
Late spring.

USES
Culinary, herbal medicine.

Pulmonaria officinalis
Lungwort
Jerusalem cowslip, Jerusalem sage, maple lungwort, spotted comfrey

Lungworts were thought to be able to cure lung disease because their curious spotted leaves look a bit like lungs. They are one of the most charming flowers of late spring, with blue, pink, and red flowers held in clumps on stalks. They make good ground-cover plants in a shady position in the garden. The young leaves used to be used to flavor soups, stews, and salads, and the plant is used in herbal medicine as a treatment for coughs and colds.

Lungworts are probably the best-known and most obvious example of the old belief, expounded in the Doctrine of Signatures by the 16th-century Swiss physician Paracelsus, that herbs resembled the diseases they could cure. This belief was very prevalent in medical circles in the 16th and 17th centuries.

In herbal medicine today lungworts are used to treat coughs, bronchitis, and catarrh, and they are also used for wounds and as an eye bath. However the plants are now thought to cause liver damage if ingested and so are seldom prescribed, although tea infused from the leaves is still drunk.

Caution: Handle the plants with care; the leaves may cause skin allergies. The plant may cause liver damage if ingested.

The chief glory of lungworts is the blue and pink flowers, very similar in shape and form to the cowslip primrose. They emerge in spring.

FAMILY
Boraginaceae

OTHER VARIETIES AND SPECIES
P. affinis, P. angustifolia, P. mollis, P. rubra, P. saccharata. There are many garden varieties.

PERENNIAL ZONE 4

HEIGHT
12in (30cm)

SPREAD
Indefinite.

FLOWERS
Pink, red, blue flowers similar to cowslips in terminal clusters.

FOLIAGE
Long, oval, pointed leaves with pronounced pale, white or silvery spots or blotches. The leaves are hairy.

NATURAL HABITAT
Native of Europe, found on banks and in woodland areas.

SITE
Shade or partial shade.

SOIL
Rich, well-drained, moist soil.

PROPAGATION
Divide after flowering or in the fall.

FLOWERING
Late spring.

USES
Culinary, herbal medicine.

Pycnanthemum virginiana
Virginia mountain mint
prairie hyssop, Virginia thyme

Mountain mints are probably used more often as herbs in the kitchen than for medicine. However, they were formerly used by the Native Americans as a medicine to treat a variety of complaints. They are not true mints, but the leaves and flowers are strongly aromatic and they impart a mint-like flavor to soups, stews, and desserts. You can also use them to make a peppermint-flavored tea. One of their main attractions is that they flower late in summer and into fall, when most other plants are over. They provide color and interest at a rather barren time of the year. They are also excellent butterfly plants. The leaves are thin and lance-shaped, and the white to lilac flowers are carried in dense clumps at the head of stalks.

The herb was once widely used by a number of Native American tribes as a general relaxing tonic that also soothed cases of indigestion. It is used in herbal medicine today to treat colic, chills, and fevers.

The prairie hyssop is an attractive plant with white flowers on gray-green hairy stalks. The herb relaxes muscle spasms, increases perspiration, and improves digestion.

vital statistics

FAMILY
Lamiaceae/Labiatae

OTHER VARIETIES AND SPECIES
P. muticum, P. pilosum, P. tenuifolium

PERENNIAL ZONE 4

HEIGHT
2–3ft (60–90cm)

SPREAD
2–3ft (60–90cm)

FLOWERS
Dense clusters of lilac-white flowers spotted with purple.

FOLIAGE
Light green, lance-shaped leaves held on radiating stalks.

NATURAL HABITAT
Native of North America. Found in dry thickets and woodland.

SITE
Sun, partial shade.

SOIL
Fertile, sandy soil.

PROPAGATION
Sow seeds in early spring, division in spring, take tip cuttings in summer.

FLOWERING
Late summer, fall.

USES
Culinary, bee and butterfly plant, herbal medicine.

Ranunculus ficaria ⊕ ✾ ⊗ ○ ◑
Lesser celandine
fig buttercup, pilewort

The lesser celandine is a small, quite attractive garden plant. An old medicinal herb, in modern gardens it usually appears where it is not wanted and is often condemned as a weed. It has dark, shiny, heart-shaped basal leaves, sometimes with silver or bronze markings and toothed edges. The flowers are small and yellow, like small buttercups, to which family they belong. They turn paler as they age. A number of garden varieties have been developed with double, white, yellow, or orange flowers.

One of the common names for this plant is pilewort. The roots of the plant were thought to look like hemorrhoids and therefore, according to the Doctrine of Signatures, a decoction made from the leaves and roots was the perfect cure for this ailment. It was also thought to be a cure for the king's evil (scrofula)—which was first thought to be cured by the touch of the king. Culpeper used the plant to cure his own daughter of the king's evil. Placing an ointment of the herb against her skin "...broke the sore, drew out a quarter of a pint of corruption, cured without any scar at all in one week's time."

According to herbal practitioners today, the lesser celandine does cure piles and is still used for this purpose.

Caution: The plant is poisonous. The sap of the plant can cause skin irritation

The lesser celandine is no relation of the greater celandine. It is one of those plants on the borderline between a weed and a garden plant. A number of good garden varieties have been developed.

vital statistics

FAMILY	PERENNIAL	FOLIAGE	SOIL	FLOWERING
Ranunculaceae	ZONE 3	Dark green, shiny, heart-shaped with bronze markings and toothed edges.	Rich, moisture-retaining soil.	Early spring.
OTHER VARIETIES AND SPECIES	**HEIGHT**		**PROPAGATION**	**USES**
R. aconitifolius (bachelor's buttons), *R. acris* (meadow buttercup), *R. aquatilis* (water crowfoot), *R. crenata, R. lyallii, R. parnassiifolius, R. repens*	2–10in (5–25cm)	**NATURAL HABITAT** Native of Europe, northern Africa, and Asia. Grows in moist places.	Divide the tubers in the fall or plant out bulbils in spring.	Herbal medicine.
	SPREAD Indefinite.			
	FLOWERS Small, yellow flowers that turn pale yellow or white with age.	**SITE** Shade or partial shade.		

Rosa
Rose

Roses make good informal ornamental hedges and are important plants in herbal medicine. Rose-hip syrup is a tried and tested tonic and a source of vitamin C.

Roses have long been used as medicinal plants, but when and where they were first used and by whom remains uncertain. They were mentioned in the works of ancient writers such as Homer, Sappho, Herodotus, Pliny, and Dioscorides, and there are recorded instances in Pliny's writings of the ailments that rose preparations could cure. Rose-scented oil, made by steeping rose petals in boiling sesame oil, was much used. According to legend, Aphrodite, the goddess of love, anointed the dead body of the Trojan hero Hector with rose water.

The main medicinal roses are the old species roses, *R. alba*, *R. canina* (the dog rose), *R. x damascena* (the damask rose), *R. eglanteria*, (eglantine, sweet briar), *R. gallica* var. *officinalis* and *R. g.* 'Versicolor', (the red rose of Lancaster), and *R. rugosa* (the hedgehog rose or Japanese rose). All these roses are used to produce attar of roses (rose oil), used in a large number of cosmetic preparations, perfumes, soaps, and rose water. Rose water was first produced in the first century AD and rose cream, made by mixing rose water and rose oil, in the same period. Today rose water is used in the manufacture of confectionery, especially Turkish delight, desserts, and gelatins.

Rose hips have been recognized as a good source of vitamin C for thousands of years. The hips of the dog rose are made into a syrup used in herbal medicine to treat coughs, colds, stomach troubles, diarrhea, and scurvy. Preparations from other species roses are used for stomach ailments, and to treat depression, lassitude, sore throats, skin complaints, urinary dysfunction, chronic diarrhea, and menstrual problems. The essential oil is used in aromatherapy and the dried flowers are almost always included in potpourri mixtures.

vital statistics

FAMILY
Rosaceae

OTHER VARIETIES AND SPECIES
R. rugosa 'Alba' (white),
R. r. rubra (purple-red),
R. gallica var. officinalis,
R. g. 'Versicolor'.

PERENNIAL SHRUB ZONE 5

HEIGHT
3ft (1m)

SPREAD
6ft (1.8m)

FLOWERS
Cupped single pink to red flowers with yellow stamens.

FOLIAGE
Dark green, wrinkled leaves.

NATURAL HABITAT
Native of western Asia. Found on hillsides and rocky places.

SITE
Sun or partial shade.

SOIL
Roses will grow in most soils but do best in fertile, moisture-retaining, heavy soil.

PROPAGATION
Take cuttings in the fall; rose nurseries propagate by budding.

FLOWERING
Summer.

USES
Culinary, potpourri, herbal medicine.

Rosmarinus officinalis
Rosemary

The flowers of most rosemarys are lilac or blue, although white varieties are available. They flower early in the spring.

Rosemary is an extremely important herb, both medically and in the kitchen. It is the herb of remembrance and friendship, and is supposed to stimulate the mind. Greek scholars wore a chaplet of rosemary when taking their exams, for it was supposed to aid the memory. In the kitchen it is the traditional accompaniment for roast lamb, but you can also use it to flavor a number of other dishes, particularly fish.

Old herbals tell of the many properties of the plant. The Myddfai manuscript, containing the writings of the 13th-century Welsh herbalists, claimed that "If the leaves be put beneath your pillow, you will be well protected from troublesome dreams and all mental anxiety. Used as a lotion, this herb or its oil will cure all pains in the head, and a spoonful of the herb, mixed with honey and melted butter cannot help but cure your coughing."

For many centuries rosemary was thought to be a cure for lethargy and dullness of the mind. In modern times the plant is recognized in herbal medicine as a treatment for depression, headaches, apathy, and migraine. It is applied externally to help rheumatism, muscular injuries, and dandruff.

Hungary water is made by distilling a pure spirit from rosemary. In the Middle Ages this was thought to cure poor sight and skin blemishes. A legend of the 14th century has it that Queen Isabella of Hungary used Hungary water, and at 72 she was still so beautiful that the King of Poland proposed to her.

vital statistics

FAMILY
Labiatae

OTHER VARIETIES AND SPECIES
R. officinalis var. *albiflorus*, *R. o.* 'Aureus', *R. o.* 'Benenden Blue', *R. o.* 'Jackman's Prostrate', *R. o.* 'Miss Jessopp's Upright', *R. o.* Prostratus Group, *R. o.* 'Sissinghurst Blue'

EVERGREEN SHRUB ZONES 6–10

HEIGHT
3–6ft (90cm–1.8m)

SPREAD
3ft (90cm) depending on the variety grown.

FLOWERS
Blue, white, or pink flowers.

FOLIAGE
Dark green, hard, needle-like leaves with gray underneath. The leaves are very aromatic

NATURAL HABITAT
Native of the Mediterranean. Mainly found on hillsides around coastal regions.

SITE
Sheltered and sunny.

SOIL
Well-drained, poor soil containing some lime.

PROPAGATION
Semiripe cutting or layering in summer.

FLOWERING
Winter to early spring.

USES
Culinary, medicinal, cosmetics.

Ruta graveolens
Rue
common rue, herb of grace

Rue is usually grown as a decorative plant for its attractive blue-gray foliage. It has a number of uses in herbal medicine and is an ingredient in the Italian drink, grappa.

Rue has tragic associations. It is given by Ophelia to her brother, Laertes, in Shakespeare's play *Hamlet*, just before she drowns herself. "There's rue for you; and here's some for me. We may call it herb of grace a Sundays." It is grown in many gardens. The variety 'Jackman's Blue' is evergreen with blue-green leaves that look attractive in the border throughout the year. It has long been used in herbal medicine and was traditionally thought to be an herb that provided protection from many ailments. It was also blessed by Mohammed after it had cured him of an illness. The seed taken in wine was an antidote for many poisons, and it was an ingredient of "thieves' vinegar," which protected robbers from infection when they robbed bodies of plague victims; possibly its reputation as a strong flea-repellent was well deserved. Posies of rue combined with southernwood were placed in courtrooms to ward off jail fever (typhus).

It was formerly used to treat stomachaches, bronchial infections, mental disorders, and sciatica, and today is employed in herbal medicine for epilepsy and rheumatic pain, as well as for sore eyes, earache, and skin diseases. The essential oil is used commercially as a flavoring.

Caution: Contact with bare skin causes severe blistering especially in sunlight. Wear gloves. Do not take internally in any form.

vital statistics

FAMILY
Rutaceae

OTHER VARIETIES AND SPECIES
R. chalepensis (fringed rue),
R. corsica (Corsican rue),
R. graveolens 'Jackman's Blue',
R. g. 'Variegata'

PERENNIAL EVERGREEN SUBSHRUB
ZONES 4–9

HEIGHT
3ft (90cm)

SPREAD
2ft (60cm)

FLOWERS
Small, yellow-green flowers.

FOLIAGE
Blue-green, waxy, small deeply divided leaves with many lobes. Very aromatic.

NATURAL HABITAT
Native of southern Europe. Found on poor, rocky limestone soils.

SITE
Sun.

SOIL
Well-drained, poor, alkaline soil.

PROPAGATION
Sow seeds in spring or take semiripe cuttings in early summer.

FLOWERING
Summer.

USES
Herbal medicine, insecticide, flavoring.

Salvia officinalis
Common sage
kitchen sage

Salvias are a large group of plants comprising annuals, biennials, perennials, and shrubs that are found throughout the world in many gardens. The common sage, *Salvia officinalis*, has been a culinary and medicinal herb for centuries. It is an upright plant with long spires of violet-blue flowers in summer and evergreen, pale, gray-green, hairy leaves, which are oval and rounded at the ends. The leaves are aromatic. A number of varieties have pleasant gold or purple leaves and *S. o.* Purpurascens Group is considered more effective medicinally than the species plant.

Sage has been used in herbal medicine since medieval times. It it an antiseptic, anti-inflammatory herb and has always been used in cases of fever to control profuse perspiration and excessive salivation. It is also thought to be good for the digestive system, liver, and bile, and to act as a general tonic. An infusion of the leaves and the young sprigs of the plant is used as a mouthwash in herbal medicine to ease and cure sore throats and gums, and a lotion is used to help cure sores, ulcers, and boils. Sage has long had a reputation for improving the memory and stimulating the brain, and in the 17th century was regarded as a cure for insanity.

There are a number of other salvias used in cooking and medicine. They include: *S. elegans* 'Scarlet Pineapple' (pineapple sage), used to flavor drinks, fruit salads, and sponge cakes; *S. fru-*

ticosa (Greek sage), used as a tea and medically to treat coughs, rheumatism, and fevers; *S. lavandulifolia* (narrow-leaved sage, Spanish sage), used for digestive and bronchial complaints and menstrual problems; *S. miltiorhiza* (red sage, Chinese sage), used for heart disease, to lower cholesterol levels, and lessen tension; *S. sclarea* (clary), used as an eye bath and to flavor some German wines. In the 17th century this herb was thought to be an aphrodisiac.

Salvias have a long history of use in herbal medicine. *S. officinalis* is used to treat Parkinson's disease and taken to relieve anxiety and depression.

vital statistics

FAMILY
Labiatae

OTHER VARIETIES AND SPECIES
S. officinalis 'Albiflora', *S. o.* 'Icterina', *S. o.* Purpurascens Group, *S. o.* 'Tricolor', *S. viridis* (bluebeard sage, painted sage), *S. horminoides* (wild sage), *S. pomifera* (apple sage), *S. pratensis* (meadow clary)

EVERGREEN PERENNIAL OR SUBSHRUB ZONES 4-8

HEIGHT
1–2ft (30–60cm)

SPREAD
2ft (60cm)

FLOWERS
Dark violet blue on long upright spikes.

FOLIAGE
Gray-green, oblong, rounded, woolly aromatic leaves.

NATURAL HABITAT
Native of the Mediterranean. Found in limestone areas.

SITE
Open, sunny.

SOIL
Well-drained, sandy soil.

PROPAGATION
Sow seeds under cover in spring, take semiripe cuttings in summer.

FLOWERING
Summer.

USES
Culinary, herbal medicine.

Sambucus nigra
Black elder
bortree, common elder, elderberry

Elderflowers have a delicious scent and flavor and are used to make elderflower wine.

The elder is a well-known tree found in hedges and woodland. Elders are trees of magic. They are worshipped by the Romany people, and the elder was supposed to be the tree from which Judas Iscariot hanged himself. The wood was used to ward off the attentions of demons, and was carried by undertakers to protect them from any unwelcome spirits to which their calling so frequently exposed them. Of all herbs, it was thought of as the best guardian against disease, with numerous virtues and healing properties. These virtues were so many that the tree was called the "poor man's medicine chest."

Both the white flowers and the berries are used in the kitchen. The flowers are the main ingredient in elderflower cordial, wine, and "champagne," and to flavor syrups and ice cream. They are also used to flavor the Italian liqueur Sambuca, which is named for the plant.

In herbal medicine, elders are used as the basis for treatments for coughs, colds, bronchial infections, and constipation, and a decoction is applied to heal burns, chilblains, and sore eyes. A balm of elder flowers is reputed to keep the skin smooth and banish wrinkles around the eyes. The juice of the fruit boiled with sugar to make a syrup is known as elderberry rob and was prescribed as a remedy to stave off an oncoming fever. Culpeper held that "fine levigated crab's eyes, half a spoonful of water, and six drams of the said rob would excite a gentle fermentation in the stomach, throw the person into a beneficial sweat, and produce a wonderful amendment."

vital statistics

FAMILY
Caprifoliaceae

OTHER VARIETIES AND SPECIES
S. canadensis, S. nigra f. laciniata, S. racemosa. There are a number of garden varieties with gold, purple and variegated leaves.

PERENNIAL TREE ZONE 4

HEIGHT
15ft (4.5m)

SPREAD
8ft (2.4m)

FLOWERS
Creamy-white, tiny flowers held on large, flat heads.

FOLIAGE
Dull green, subdivided into five leaflets.

NATURAL HABITAT
Native of Europe, northern Africa, and western Asia. Found in hedgerows and around open woodland.

SITE
Sun or partial shade.

SOIL
Rich, moisture-retaining soil.

PROPAGATION
Sow seeds in spring or take hardwood cuttings in winter.

FLOWERING
Early summer.

USES
Culinary, wine, herbal medicine.

Sanguinaria canadensis
Bloodroot

bangiunaria, Indian plant, pauson, red puccoon, tetterwort

The bloodroot is a member of the poppy family and contains many of the narcotic properties common to many poppies. It is a beautiful native plant with a lovely, white, eight- or nine-petaled flower that emerges in spring. The kidney-shaped, stalked, scalloped leaves follow the flowers and grow from a rhizome. The plant spreads slowly but in time establishes itself and forms a large clump of growth. The attractive variety 'Plena', which has many-petaled double flowers, is the most commonly grown.

It was a popular herb of the Native Americans and was used to induce vomiting. The sap from the plant is a deep red, hence its name, and this was used to dye clothing and weapons. The herb is both an expectorant and a diuretic, and slows the heart rate. It was used as a local anesthetic. Today it is sometimes used in herbal medicine to treat bronchitis, throat infections, and poor circulation.

Caution: Excess use can cause a slowing of the heart rate and even death. No part of the plant should be taken internally.

Bloodroot is an attractive wildflower. It is a member of the poppy family and has the same narcotic properties. It was formerly used as a local anesthetic.

vital statistics

FAMILY
Papaveraceae

OTHER VARIETIES AND SPECIES
S. c. f. *multiplex, S. c.* 'Plena'

PERENNIAL ZONE 3

HEIGHT
6–12in (15–30cm)

SPREAD
9in (23cm)

FLOWERS
Small, usually eight-petaled flowers with a yellow stamen.

FOLIAGE
Blue-green above, paler underneath, heart-shaped stalked with scalloped margins.

NATURAL HABITAT
Native of eastern North America. Grows in moist woodland and hillside areas.

SITE
Shade or partial shade

SOIL
Rich, moisture-retaining soil.

PROPAGATION
Divide the rhizomes in the fall.

FLOWERING
Spring.

USES
Herbal medicine, dye plant.

Herbal teas & drinks

The principle of making herbal teas is the same for all. Pick the flowers or leaves, whichever is to be used, in the early morning on a fine day. Bring them indoors and dry them in a cool, airy room. When the herb is quite dry, put it in an airtight jar until you wish to use it. As a general rule use between 1–3 teaspoons of the dried herb to 2½ cups (20 fl oz/575 ml) of boiling water. When making an infusion of fresh herbs, the average quantity used is between 1–3 handfuls to 5 cups (40 fl oz/1.1 liter) of water.

Chamomile tea

Allow 1 tsp of dried flowers for 2½ cups (20 fl oz/575 ml) of boiling water. Allow the flowerheads to infuse for 5 minutes. Add brown sugar or honey to sweeten if you wish.

Chamomile tea is mildly sedative and is a calming drink for cases of nervous disorder. It also helps to improve the appetite and cleanse the blood.

Dandelion tea

Pick 5–6 leaves from a young dandelion plant. Tear them in strips, put them in a mug, and then fill it with boiling water. Let it infuse for 5–10 minutes, then remove the leaves and add sugar to taste.

Dandelion tea is mildly sedative and also a mild laxative. It should not be drunk in large quantities.

Mint tea

Both peppermint, *Mentha x piperata*, and spearmint, *M. spicata*, are used. Use 2–3 teaspoons of dried leaves, according to taste.

Mint tea is excellent for indigestion, insomnia and cases of nervous disorders.

Caution: Mints can be an irritant and long term use of mint teas is not recommended.

Mentha spicata Spearmint

Blackcurrant & lemon verbena tisane

This is an excellent herbal tea.
Pour 2½ cups of boiling water over 1 tablespoon of fresh or frozen blackcurrants and 10 lemon verbena leaves torn into strips. Leave to infuse for about 5 minutes. Strain and sweeten with brown sugar if desired

Non-alcoholic strawberry punch

YOU WILL NEED:

1¼ cups (6oz/170g) clear honey

11 cups (88 fl oz/2.5 liter) water

1¼ cups (10 fl oz/300 ml) fresh lemon juice

2¼ lb (1kg) sliced strawberries

1¼ cups (10 fl oz/300 ml) fresh lime juice

5 cups (40 fl oz/1.1 liter) sparkling mineral water

ice cubes

3 scented geranium leaves

2 tbsp fresh rosemary leaves

2 sprigs rosemary

To prepare: Put the honey, 3 cups (25 fl oz/700 ml) water, ¼ cup (2½ fl oz/60 ml) lemon juice, and the rosemary leaves in a saucepan. Bring the mixture to a boil and stir until all the honey is dissolved. Remove the from the heat. Allow it to stand for a few minutes and then strain into a large bowl.

Press the strawberries through a fine nylon sieve into the bowl and then add all the other ingredients except the geranium leaves, rosemary sprigs, and ice cubes. Add the sparkling water last.

Just before serving add in the ice cubes and float the geranium leaves and rosemary on the top.

Mint cup

YOU WILL NEED:

2 sprigs fresh mint

½ tsp sugar

cracked ice

½ tsp lemon juice

2 tbsp grapefruit juice

soda or tonic water, as preferred

borage

Crush the mint and put it and the sugar in a tall glass. Fill the glass with cracked ice. Add the lemon and grapefruit juice, fill the glass with tonic or soda water as you prefer, and stir until the glass is frosted. Decorate the glass with flowered sprigs of borage.

TRADITIONAL DRINKS & COUNTRY WINES

Many traditional drinks are based on herbs, notably the great mint julep. Country wines were also made from a wide variety of ingredients, including fruit, the sap of trees, and herbs. Many of these have a considerable reputation for their taste and intoxicating properties.

A Victorian claret cup

YOU WILL NEED:

1 heaping tsp of white sugar dissolved in boiling water

1 cup (8 fl oz/250 ml) medium sherry

½ cup (3 fl oz/75 ml) brandy

½ cup (3 fl oz/75 ml) maraschino

1 strip lemon zest

1 strip cucumber

1 bottle claret.

Mix all the ingredients together and set aside for at least 1 hour in the refrigerator. Add a sprig of borage to the cup. Dilute to taste with soda water.

This cup was so popular in England in Victorian times that gardeners in large country houses grew borage under glass all year round for the express purpose of flavoring claret cup.

Borago officinalis Borage

Elderflower wine or champagne

Pick several flowerheads from an elder tree. Put them in a large jar. Pour 210 fl oz (4.5 liters) of cold water over the flowerheads, add 2½ cups (20oz/575g) of granulated sugar, 2 tablespoons white wine vinegar, and the juice and zest of 1 lemon. Stir until the sugar has dissolved. Leave for 24 hours. Strain the cordial and bottle it. It Improves in flavor if it is kept for up to six months.

Mint julep

Put 1 teaspoon of granulated sugar in a tall glass. Cover with just enough water to dissolve it and add a sprig of mint. Fill the glass with cracked ice. Add Bourbon to within ½in (1cm) of the top. Stir until the glass is thoroughly frosted.

HERBAL WINES

Traditional country wines are all made the same way. You can use fresh herbs or buy prepared dried herbs. Use an all-purpose wine yeast for fermentation, and wine jars with fermentation locks. Keep everything scrupulously clean. Expert advice can be obtained from one of the many books available on home winemaking.

Dandelion wine

YOU WILL NEED:

dandelion heads

210 fl oz (4.5 liters) of water

6 cups (3lb/1.35kg)sugar

1oz (25g) yeast

juice of 2 lemons

Pull the petals off the dandelion heads and put them in a fermenting vessel and pour over 100 fl oz (2.25 liters) of boiling water. Leave this to infuse, covered, for 6 days. Strain. Boil half the sugar in 5 cups (40 fl oz/1.1 liter) water, cool, then add this, plus the yeast and lemon juice to the mixture. Leave to ferment for 1 week. Strain again and then add the remaining sugar, dissolved in 5 cups boiling water as before. Leave until all the fermentation has ceased. Siphon the wine into bottles and cork.

Trifolium pratense Red clover

Clover wine

YOU WILL NEED:

red clover flowerheads

150 fl oz (3.45 liters) of water

6 cups (3lb/1.35kg)sugar

juice of 2 lemons

1oz (25g) yeast

Pull off the petals from the clover heads and put them in a container. Pour over 100 fl oz (2.25 liters) boiling water and then leave the mixture to infuse for 12 hours. This allows the flavor of the flowers to infuse into the liquid. Dissolve half the sugar in 5 cups (40 fl oz/1.1 liter) boiling water. Cool and then add to the flower mixture. Add the yeast and lemon juice. Allow to ferment for 7 days. Add the remaining sugar, dissolved in 5 cups water as before. Leave for 24 hours. Strain. Then allow to stand until fermentation has ceased (the liquid will have stopped producing gas). Siphon the wine into a bottle, and cork.

Broom wine

This wine is made with dried herbs and raisins. Broom is considered to be an excellent tonic for the the renal system.

YOU WILL NEED:

3oz (75g) dried broom flowers
100 fl oz (2.25 liters) water
4 cups (2lb/900g) sugar
1oz (25g) yeast and yeast nutrient
juice 1 orange and 1 lemon
1 cup (8oz/225g) raisins

Pour the boiling water over the dried herbs and set aside, covered, overnight. Dissolve half the sugar in 5 cups (40 fl oz/1.1 liter) boiling water. Add this to the herb mixture while it is hot. Stir the mixture thoroughly and re-cover. When it is cool, add the yeast and yeast nutrient, orange and lemon juice and the chopped raisins. Leave to ferment for 9 days, stirring daily. Keep covered. On day 10 strain the mixture, dissolve the remaining sugar in 5 cups water. Allow it to cool, then add it to the wine. Allow this to ferment undisturbed until all signs of fermentation have ceased. Siphon into a bottle.

Cytisus scoparius
Broom

Nettle beer

YOU WILL NEED:

nettle leaves
1½ lb (700g) malt
210 fl oz (4.5 liters) water
2 cups sugar
1oz (25g) hops
2oz (50g) sarsaparilla
1oz (25g) yeast

Boil the nettles and malt in the water for 30 minutes. Stir in the sugar, hops, and sarsaparilla. Set aside, and when cool add the yeast. Allow the beer to ferment, but bottle just before fermentation has ceased to give the beer more zest. Keep the bottles loosely corked in case the gases accumulate and cause the bottles to explode.

Humulus lupulus
Hop

Rose petal wine

YOU WILL NEED:

rose petals (dog rose, briar rose, or any perfumed garden variety)
150 fl oz (3.45 liters) water
6 cups (3lb/1.35kg) sugar
juice of 2 lemons
1oz (25g) yeast

Cover the petals with 100 fl oz (2.25 liters) of boiling water and set aside for 3 days in a covered container. Dissolve half the sugar in 5 cups (40 fl oz/1.1 liter) boiling water. Allow it to cool and then add it to the wine. Add the lemon juice and yeast, and allow to ferment for 6 days. Strain the wine and allow it to ferment for a further 3 days. Strain again, if necessary. The following day add the remaining sugar dissolved in water, as before. Set aside until all signs of fermentation have ceased. This wine is thought to drive away depression, and if only red roses are used to prepare it, it will also mend a broken heart.

Sanguisorba officinalis (Poterium officinalis)
Great burnet
Italian burnet, Italian pimpernel, official burnet

One of the charms of the burnets is the notched leaves, which look as if they had been cut out by a small tidy child.

With large bottle-brush flowers on terminal spikes, *S. officinalis*, greater burnet, is found in many herbaceous borders. It is one of the old medieval medicinal herbs and had a reputation for being able to staunch the flow of blood from wounds, as is implied by its name *sanguis*, which is the Latin for blood. Great burnet is a bitter astringent herb that is used in herbal medicine to reduce inflammation and to treat diarrhea, dysentery, ulcerative colitis, and abnormal uterine bleeding. The leaves are applied to cure sores, cankers, and burns.

The other principal species is salad burnet, *S. minor*, a pot herb that was much used in the kitchen to add flavor to soups, sauces, and cheese, and whose leaves were also eaten raw in salads. It has a delicate cucumber flavor and can be substituted for borage in fruit cups. It was also used medicinally. The leaves were dried and infused as a tea to cure digestive disorders and to treat diarrhea and hemorrhages. A decoction of the roots was a treatment for burns, and the roots were also used to make a black dye used in tanning.

vital statistics

FAMILY
Rosaceae

OTHER VARIETIES AND SPECIES
S. albiflora, *S. canadensis* (Canadian burnet), *S. obtusa*, *S. tenuifolia*

PERENNIAL ZONE 3

HEIGHT
6ft (1.2m)

SPREAD
2ft (60cm)

FLOWERS
Small red-brown petal-less flowers held in globular heads.

FOLIAGE
Gray-green pinnate, divided leaves with rounded leaflets.

NATURAL HABITAT
Native of Europe and northern and western Asia. Found in damp meadows and in other moist positions.

SITE
Sun or partial shade.

SOIL
Fertile, well-drained, moist soil.

PROPAGATION
Divide in spring or fall.

FLOWERING
Early summer.

USES
Herbal medicine, culinary.

Santolina chamaecyparissus
Lavender cotton

Lavender cotton looks nothing like lavender and is not related. It is a larger plant, with fine narrow, gray, aromatic leaves and small yellow flowers held out on stalks. They make excellent hedges if they are grown along the edge of a border, although they need a hot, dry position to give of their best. They can be clipped to shape in early spring.

The plant has a long reputation for being an effective moth repellent and in medieval times it was an important vermifuge, used to kill worms in adults as well as children. It is a good dye plant, producing yellow and gold colors. It was another plant that was used as an antidote for poisons, and to cure the bites and stings of insects. It was also used as a treatment for cases of diarrhea. Today it is sometimes prescribed in herbal medicine for digestive and menstrual problems, and the dried leaves are an ingredient of some herbal mixtures.

Santolinas are common garden plants but prefer a hot, dry position in the garden. They make good low-growing hedges and should be clipped in early spring.

---

vital statistics

FAMILY
Compositae

OTHER VARIETIES AND SPECIES
S. chamaecyparissus var. corsica, S. c. var. nana, S. incana, S. pinnata, S. rosmarinifolia. There are a number of garden varieties.

PERENNIAL EVERGREEN SHRUB
ZONES 5–7

HEIGHT
2ft (60cm)

SPREAD
2ft (60cm)

FLOWERS
Small, yellow and daisy-like.

FOLIAGE
Silver-gray narrow divided leaves forming long spikes. Very aromatic.

NATURAL HABITAT
Native of Mediterranean. Found on dry hillsides, frequently on coastal regions.

SITE
Sun.

SOIL
Well-drained, alkaline, dry soil.

PROPAGATION
Take tip cuttings in spring or summer.

FLOWERING
Summer.

USES
Formerly medicinal, insect repellent, dye plant.

Saponaria officinalis
Soapwort
bouncing Bet, bruisewort, dog cloves, old maid's pink, soap root

Soapwort is an attractive plant and is grown at the front of many borders. It is an old medicinal plant with pale pink to white, carnation-like flowers, which are held in dense terminal clusters. Its lance-shaped green leaves spring from an upright stalk. It is a close relative of *S. ocymoides*, rock soapwort, a popular spreading perennial that is grown in many rock gardens. The plant is rich in saponin and was much used for cleaning before the production of commercial soaps at the beginning of the 19th century. It is still used in museums and galleries to clean old furniture, tapestries, and pictures.

In medicine it was recommended as a treatment for bruises but in the 16th and 17th centuries it was really regarded as the principal remedy for the itch (scabies), as well as gonorrhea. It is seldom used in herbal medicine today, for it has an irritant effect on the digestive system. It also causes severe eye irritation.

Caution: This plant is poisonous, especially to grazing animals and fish.

Soapwort is an attractive spreading plant. It has a number of uses in herbal medicine and was regarded by Culpeper as a good cure for scabies as well as gonorrhea.

vital statistics

FAMILY Caryophyllaceae	**PERENNIAL** **ZONES 3–8**	**FOLIAGE** Mid-green, prominently veined, oval to lance-shaped.	**SOIL** Moisture-retaining soil.	**FLOWERING** Late summer.
OTHER VARIETIES AND SPECIES *S. caespitosa, S. ocymoides, S. x olivana, S. pumilio, S. o.* 'Alba Plena', *S. o.* 'Dazzler'	**HEIGHT** 2ft (60cm)	**NATURAL HABITAT** Native of Europe and western Asia. Found in wasteland and grassland.	**PROPAGATION** Sow seeds or divide in spring or fall.	**USES** Formerly medicinal.
	SPREAD Indefinite.			
	FLOWERS Pale, pink to white, carnation-like, held in dense clusters.	**SITE** Sun or partial shade.		

Satureja hortensis, S. montana
Savory
summer savory, winter savory

There are two sorts of savory, summer and winter. They have similar properties and are used in herbal medicine for the same purposes. They are also old culinary herbs, which have been found in kitchens for centuries.

Summer savory (*Satureja hortensis*) is an annual with a scent reminiscent of thyme. If grown for the kitchen, pull the plants up and allow them to dry naturally, and then pick off and store the leaves. Use them sparingly to enhance meat dishes and stuffings, and place the flowering shoots between clothes to repel moths.

Winter savory (*S. montana*) is a creeping, evergreen subshrub, and is traditionally thought to be the perfect flavoring for bean dishes; it is also sometimes used to flavor sausages.

Both summer and winter savory are used in herbal medicine to treat indigestion, nausea, bronchial infections, congestion and other gastric complaints. They were formerly used as a pick-me-up tonic and a cure for tinnitus. They were also thought to be a good remedy for the colic and iliac passion (the name for both a severe form of colic and for appendicitis).

Savory is an old-fashioned culinary herb seldom grown today. Both winter and summer varieties are similar to thyme and marjoram in flavor.

vital statistics

FAMILY Labiatae	**HARDY ANNUAL**	**FOLIAGE** Long, dark green, leathery pointed leaves.	**SOIL** Well-drained, sandy soil.	**FLOWERING** Late summer.
	HEIGHT 12in (30cm)			
OTHER VARIETIES AND SPECIES S. coerulea, S. montana (winter savory) S. m. prostrate white, S. spicigera	**SPREAD** 12in (30cm)	**NATURAL HABITAT** Found throughout the northern hemisphere on dry hillsides or cliff tops.	**PROPAGATION** Sow seeds in situ in spring when the soil has warmed up.	**USES** Culinary, formerly medicinal.
	FLOWERS Summer savory: white to pink. Winter savory: lavender-pink, throughout the summer.	**SITE** Sunny.		

Scabiosa columbaria
Dove pincushions
corn scabious

Dove pincushions, *Scabiosa columbaria*, grows wild in grassland and was often found in fields of corn. Hence one of its common names. This was a popular medicinal herb in the 16th and 17th centuries, one of the apothecary's cure-all herbs, and was used to treat coughs, bronchial disorders, skin disease, ulcers, spots, scabies, pimples, and dandruff. It was also taken to treat pleurisy and fevers and had the power to draw splinters and broken bones from the flesh. It has now fallen from favor and is seldom used in herbal medicine today.

The other common scabious, field scabious (*Knautia arvensis*), is a common flower of the fields and meadows and is normally lilac-blue in color. The flowers emerge at the end of long stems. Scabious are most attractive flowers and a number of excellent garden varieties have been developed for herbaceous and flower borders. They attract bees and butterflies and other beneficial insects.

Field scabious can be grown in the garden but it flourishes best in wild areas where the soil is poor and is generally found growing along hedges and roadsides. It is unlikely to do well in rich garden soil for the competition from other plants will be overwhelming.

Dove pincushions is usually lilac-blue, but pink varieties like this are available.

vital statistics

FAMILY
Dipsacaceae

OTHER VARIETIES AND SPECIES
Knautia arvensis, K. macedonica, Scabiosa columbaria. 'Butterfly Blue', *S. c.* 'Pink Mist', *Succisa pratensis*

PERENNIAL ZONE 3

HEIGHT
2ft (60cm).

SPREAD
18ft (45cm).

FLOWERS
Conspicuous lilac-blue flowers held on long stalks.

FOLIAGE
Green hairy lance-shaped leaves held in pairs.

NATURAL HABITAT
Native of Europe. Found on waste land, beside roads, and in open woodland.

SITE
Sun or partial shade.

SOIL
Well-drained, poor soil.

PROPAGATION
Sow seed in the fall. Take basal cuttings in spring.

FLOWERING
Summer.

USES
Formerly medicinal, bee and butterfly plant.

Scrophularia nodosa
Figwort
carpenter's square, heat-all kernelwort, scrofula plant, woodland figwort

Figworts form a large genus of perennials, annuals, and subshrubs. This species, the woodland figwort, has been regarded as a treatment for diseases of the throat for several centuries. It is a strong, rather unpleasant smelling, perennial with tuberous rhizomes. The plant is known in France as *l'herbe du siege*, because the roots were eaten during Cardinal Richelieu's siege of the Huguenot city La Rochelle in the 17th century. It is quite a large plant, with a square upright stem and pointed, heart-shaped, deeply toothed leaves. It has spires of sparse greenish-mauve flowers in summer.

A decoction of the leaves is an old herbal remedy for sore throats and inflamed tonsils, and is also used as a treatment for circulatory disorders, especially varicose veins. The herb acts as a mild laxative, increases the flow of uric acid, and was thought to be a cure for the king's evil (scrofula—which lends itself to the plant's Latin name). It was also used as a treatment for hemorrhoids. Today, it is sometimes prescribed in herbal medicine for various skin conditions, such as psoriasis and eczema. Shoreline figwort, another species (*S. auriculata*), was thought to be good for scabies.

Figwort was considered a good cure for all diseases of the throat. Culpeper said that it could cure "…(the king's evil) and any other knobs, kernels, bunches, or wens."

vital statistics

FAMILY Scrophulariaceae	**PERENNIAL ZONE 4**	**FOLIAGE** Green pointed and toothed leaves spring from a square stalk.	**SOIL** Moisture-retaining or wet fertile soil.	**FLOWERING** Summer.
OTHER VARIETIES AND SPECIES *S. auriculata* (water betony, shoreline figwort), *S. sambucifolia, S. scorodonia, S. vernalis*	**HEIGHT** 16in–4ft (40cm–1.2m) **SPREAD** 12in (30cm) **FLOWERS** Greenish-mauve held erect in loose spires.	**NATURAL HABITAT** Found throughout the Northern Hemisphere in moist meadows, woodland and scrub **SITE** Sun or partial shade.	**PROPAGATION** Sow seeds in spring or fall. Divide in spring. Take semi-ripe cuttings in summer.	**USES** Herbal medicine.

Sedum acre
Goldmoss stonecrop

A mat-forming evergreen perennial with erect branches with overlapping succulent leaves, stonecrop had a range of uses. It was thought to have the power to ward off lightning and was often grown on the roofs of houses for this purpose. In the summer flat-topped heads of greenish-yellow flowers cover the plant and continue for a long period. The plant grows wild in walls and in dry, stony soils. A number of small stonecrops are useful plants in rock and alpine gardens. You can eat the raw leaves and stems of Jenny's stonecrop, *S. rupestre* syn. *S. reflexum*, in salads.

Medically, it was used as a binding agent. It apparently stopped bleeding, and was used to heal sores and ulcers. It also helped with the king's evil (scrofula), and was one of the many remedies for hemorrhoids. The juice of the leaves was prescribed to remove corns and warts. The bruised leaves are a soothing treatment for burns and sores.

The plant is poisonous—even in the 16th century caution was advised in the treatment of piles—and it causes vomiting if eaten.

Caution: Poisonous—not for home treatment.

Stonecrop was grown on roofs to ward off lightning. Although the leaves of Jenny's stonecrop can be eaten, other stonecrops are poisonous.

vital statistics

FAMILY
Crassulaceae

OTHER VARIETIES AND SPECIES
S. caeruleum, S. cauticola, S. frutescens, S. lydium, S. pilosum, S rupestre, S. spectabile, S. telephium

PERENNIAL ZONE 5

HEIGHT
2in (5cm)

SPREAD
24in (60cm)

FLOWERS
Star-shaped, yellow-green flowers all over the plant.

FOLIAGE
Overlapping, pale green succulent leaves growing down the stems.

NATURAL HABITAT
Native to Europe, Turkey and northern Africa. Found in dry hillsides and on walls and roofs.

SITE
Sun.

SOIL
Rocky, sandy well-drained soil.

PROPAGATION
Divide in spring or fall, sow seeds in fall. Self-seeds.

FLOWERING
Summer.

USES
Formerly medicinal.

Sempervivum tectorum

Common houseleek

hen-and-chickens

Traditionally, houseleeks were used to heal skin ailments, such as sunburn, bites, stings, scalds, and itchy skin complaints.

This is another plant that is supposed to ward off lightning and fire if it is grown on the roof of a house. The Latin name comes from *semper*, meaning "always," and *vivo*, "to live," a reference to the long-lived, drought-tolerant nature of the plants. The leaves of the plant were traditionally halved and applied directly to bites or sores. Houseleeks are mat-forming succulents that form dense mounds of tightly packed open rosettes. The tips of each leaf often end in a bristly point, and the leaves are blue-green to red-purple in color. The reddish flowers emerge on stalks in the summer.

The common houseleek is used in herbal preparations today for the treatment of shingles and various skin complaints, but its most common use is still as a poultice to heal bites, stings, and sunburn. It was also supposed to remove warts and corns.

Caution: The plant is a purgative and internal use may cause severe stomach upsets.

vital statistics

FAMILY
Crassulaceae

OTHER VARIETIES AND SPECIES
S. arachnoideum, S. atlanticum, S. calcareum, S. × barbulatum, S. guiseppii, S. grandiflorum, S. montanum, S. patens. There are a number of garden varieties available.

PERENNIAL ZONE 5

HEIGHT
12in (30cm)

SPREAD
12in (30cm)

FLOWERS
Reddish-pink ,held in clusters on reddish hairy stems.

FOLIAGE
Overlapping, pale green, red-tipped, spiny succulent leaves growing in a tight rosette.

NATURAL HABITAT
Native to southern Europe. Found in dry hillsides and mountainous regions.

SITE
Sun.

SOIL
Rocky, gritty, well-drained soil. Grows in crevices on walls and on roofs.

PROPAGATION
Sow seeds in spring. Take offsets from established clumps in spring.

FLOWERING
Summer.

USES
Herbal medicine.

Silybum marianum
Blessed milk thistle
holy thistle, St. Mary's thistle

There is an old legend that the milky veins running down the leaves of this plant were caused by the milk of the Virgin Mary falling on them when the infant Jesus was being fed. Milk thistle is a stately and beautiful plant, a biennial that does not flower until the second year of its life, when you can trim and cook the purple-pink flowers as a vegetable in the same way as artichokes. Also try the stems and the leaves in the same way. The roots can also be boiled or roasted like parsnips.

The plant has long had the reputation for treating liver disorders and does in fact contain substances that protect the liver from damage and poison. It is used as an antidote to the deadly death-cap toadstool, *Amanita phalloides*. It is used in herbal medicine to treat jaundice, cirrhosis, hepatitis, and poisoning caused by by alcohol or drugs. In the past it has been used as a general tonic to benefit the heart, brain, and kidneys, and it is said to restore memory impaired by old age or sickness.

The milk thistle is an important medicinal herb that can be used to regenerate damaged liver cells. The young leaves can be cooked or eaten raw in salads.

vital statistics

FAMILY Compositae	**BIENNIAL** ZONE 5	**FOLIAGE** Spiny, pale gray- green leaves with prominent white veins.	**SOIL** Most well-drained soils.	**FLOWERING** Summer.
OTHER VARIETIES AND SPECIES None	**HEIGHT** 5ft (1.5m)	**NATURAL HABITAT** Mediterranean, Asia Minor, and the Caucasus. Found in rocky and stony places on wasteland and beside highways.	**PROPAGATION** Sow seeds in situ in spring or early summer. Self-seeds.	**USES** Culinary, herbal medicine.
	SPREAD 90cm (3ft)			
	FLOWERS Purple-pink fragrant flowers surrounded by thistly spikes.	**SITE** Open, sunny.		

Smyrnium olusatrum
Alexanders
black lovage

Alexanders was formerly used as a medicinal plant but it is now grown only for its culinary properties. It was cultivated by the Greeks and Romans, and the Latin name comes from *olus*, meaning "pot herb," and *atrum*, meaning "black"—which refers to the color of the seeds. It was a popular vegetable in Europe before celery arrived, for it has a pronounced celery taste. You can use the leaves, stems, stalks, and flowers in salads, stews, and fish dishes, or cook them as a vegetable after blanching. They have a delicate scent. The seeds can be dried and ground to make a condiment or spice.

It is a bitter herb and was formerly used as a diuretic to cure the strangury (difficulty and pain in urinating). Both the seeds and the leaves were used. Some herbalists thought that it was a cure for asthma and menstrual problems, and that a poultice of the leaves would cure wounds. The species *S. perfoliatum* is more frequently grown for its flowers, which you can dry for winter flower arrangements.

Alexanders is no longer used as a medicinal herb. It is still found in some kitchens, where it serves as an alternative to celery.

vital statistics

FAMILY Umbelliferae	**BIENNIAL** **ZONE 5–7**	**FOLIAGE** Large, shiny, dark green leaves divided into several leaflets.	**SOIL** Moist, well-drained, alkaline soil.	**FLOWERING** Summer.
OTHER VARIETIES AND SPECIES *S. perfoliatum*	**HEIGHT** 3ft (90cm)	**NATURAL HABITAT** Mediterranean and western Europe. Found mainly in coastal regions.	**PROPAGATION** Sow seed in spring or fall.	**USES** Culinary, formerly medicinal.
	SPREAD 2ft (60cm)			
	FLOWERS Small, yellow-green held in small clumps.	**SITE** Open, sunny.		

Solanum dulcamara
Climbing nightshade
bittersweet nightshade, felonwort nightshade, fever twig, staff vine, woody nightshade

Although not as dangerous as the deadly nightshade, all nightshades must be treated with caution. Herbal practitioners use this plant to treat skin diseases and rheumatism.

Solanums are a large genus of varied plants. These range from the potato, eaten throughout the world, to ornamental and dangerously poisonous climbers, such as *S. nigrum* (black nightshade).

Climbing nightshade is a common perennial found on wasteland and in gardens. It has trailing stems with pointed, veined, green leaves, rounded at the base, and pale, violet to blue, potato-like flowers carried in clusters in the summer. These are followed by red berries. Black nightshade has green berries that turn black as they ripen. Both plants contain poisonous alkaloids, and should be handled with care.

Climbing nightshade has long been used to treat skin ailments. It was a cure for sore throats, sore eyes, shingles, ringworm, and suppurating ulcers. The common name of felonwort came because it soothed inflammation of the finger joints, known as felons. It is still used by qualified herbal practitioners to treat skin diseases, and it is also used to ease bronchial ailments and for fevers, because it has a sedative effect. However, it must be treated with care. Excess use can cause paralysis of the central nervous system, a slowing of the heart rate, vertigo, delirium, convulsions, and death.

Caution: The plant is poisonous and must not be taken in any form.

vital statistics

FAMILY
Solonaceae

OTHER VARIETIES AND SPECIES
S. nigrum (black nightshade), S. capsicastrum (false Jerusalem cherry), S. crispum (Chilean potato vine), S. jasminoides

BIENNIAL ZONE 5–7

HEIGHT
13ft (4m)

SPREAD
Indefinite.

FLOWERS
Pale violet-blue, potato-like flowers held in small clusters.

FOLIAGE
Pointed, veined, green leaves, rounded at the base springing from the stalk.

NATURAL HABITAT
Throughout Europe and Asia. Found mainly in damp places and woodland.

SITE
Sun or partial shade.

SOIL
Moist, well-drained, neutral to alkaline soil.

PROPAGATION
Cultivation is not recommended.

FLOWERING
Summer.

USES
Herbal medicine.

Solidago virgaurea
Goldenrod

Goldenrod is a common wildflower growing in open spaces, heathland, and on hillsides, and in the wild areas of many gardens. It has a long history as an important wound herb.

There are a number of cultivated varieties of this plant. The species has sparse sprays of daisy-like yellow flowers in late summer and narrow, lance-shaped, toothed green leaves.

The leaves and stalks were pulped and applied externally to stop bleeding and prevent infection, and it was even thought that it could cure gangrene and tetanus. It was used in lotions to wash the affected parts in cases of venereal disease. The herb was also taken as an infusion made from the young leaves.

Goldenrod contains anti-inflammatory properties and is an ingredient today in herbal preparations to stimulate the kidneys and liver, and generally to reduce inflammation. It is specifically used for indigestion, stomachache, flatulence, nausea, morning sickness, hay fever, bronchial disorders, and whooping cough, and externally for bites and sore throats. A number of species have similar properties and are employed in the same way around the world.

Goldenrod is an extremely important medicinal herb with a number of uses ranging from a general anti-inflammatory to a specific treatment for kidney disease.

vital statistics

FAMILY Compositae/Asteraceae	**PERENNIAL** **ZONE 4**	**FOLIAGE** Small, narrow, pointed, green leaves.	**SOIL** Well-drained, moisture-retentive soil.	**FLOWERING** Summer.
OTHER VARIETIES AND SPECIES S. altissima, S. canadensis, S. carolinense, (horsenettle), S. flexicaulis	**HEIGHT** 4ft (1.2m) **SPREAD** 2ft (60cm)	**NATURAL HABITAT** Native to Europe. Found mainly in dry places and on wasteland.	**PROPAGATION** Sow seed in spring or divide in spring or fall.	**USES** Herbal medicine.
	FLOWERS Small, yellow, daisy-like flowers held in sparse clusters.	**SITE** Sun or partial shade.		

Stachys officinalis (Betonica officinalis)
Betony

hedgenettle, lousewort, purple betony, wood betony

Culpeper attributed numerous properties to betony. Gerard said "It maketh a man to have a good stomacke and appetite to his meate."

Betony is a common herb and can be found growing in woods and shady places. It has narrow triangular leaves with deeply notched edges arranged around a single upright, hairy stalk. The flowers are mainly purple, spotted with white, and look a bit like lavender, but the flower spikes are thicker and shorter.

The plant can be found under its original name (*Betonica offinalis*) in many books on wildflowers and old herbals. Wood betony was an ancient medicinal herb that was supposed to possess magical healing properties. It also had the power to ward off evil spirits, and was commonly found in herb gardens and churchyards in the Middle Ages. It is an attractive plant and the leaves are dried by herbalists to make a tea that has a mildly sedative action. It is taken for headaches and neuralgia.

It was a favorite herb in Roman times for the treatment of many ailments and conditions. These included the palsy, convulsions, shrinking sinews, gout, coughs, colds, wheezing, shortness of breath, the agues (malarial fever), consumption, griping pains in the bowels, and colic. It was also used as a treatment for rheumatic ailments. Today herbalists prepare a tea made from the leaves and flavored with half an orange or lemon as both a warming and strengthening beverage, bringing relief from the aches and pains of an illness. It is also used to cleanse the bladder and kidneys.

vital statistics

FAMILY
Labiatae

OTHER VARIETIES AND SPECIES
S. palustris (marsh woundwort),
S. sylvatica (wood woundwort),
S. alpina (Alpine woundwort)
S. byzantina, S. macrantha,
S. officinalis 'Alba',
S. o. 'Rosea Superba'

PERENNIAL ZONE 3

HEIGHT
12in (30cm)

SPREAD
4in (10cm)

FLOWERS
Purple flowers marked with white held on spikes.

FOLIAGE
Large, mid-green basal leaves, triangular with notched edges. Smaller narrower leaves spring from the stalk.

NATURAL HABITAT
Moist woodland in Europe.

SITE
Partial shade.

SOIL
Moist, well-drained.

PROPAGATION
Sow seeds in spring.

FLOWERING
Summer.

USES
Formerly medicinal.

Stellaria media

Common chickweed

Chickweed forms a mass of tumbled foliage and, despite its medicinal value, most gardeners find it an unwelcome visitor.

Chickweed has been an important herb in medicine for centuries. Culpeper declared that it was "a fine soft pleasing herb under the dominion of the Moon." It was used to heal ulcers and sores, particularly "of the privy parts of men and women," and as an eye tonic. The most unusual use was as an ointment made with the leaves of a red rose, muscadine, and sheep's trotters that was then rubbed on sinews when they had become stiff through cold or old age. Culpeper asserted that "with God's blessing it will help in three times dressing."

Today leaves of the plant can be used in the kitchen and added to salads, since they have a delicate and slightly salty flavor. They continue to be used in herbal medicine for most of the ailments that Culpeper advised especially for cases of rheumatism and skin complaints, including ulcers, boils, and abscesses.

Chickweed is a common weed found in many gardens. The name *Stellaria* comes from the Latin for "star," and refers to the small, white, star-shaped flowers. It can also be culti-vated by seed sown in spring.

vital statistics

FAMILY
Caryophyllaceae

OTHER VARIETIES AND SPECIES
S. nemorum (wood stitchwort), S. neglecta, (greater chickweed), S. pallida (lesser chickweed), S. alsine (bog stitchwort)

ANNUAL
Can be found in flower all year.

HEIGHT
2–5in (4–12cm)

SPREAD
8–16in (20–40cm)

FLOWERS
Very small, white, star-shaped flowers

FOLIAGE
Bright-green, oval leaves on brittle stems that have a line of hairs running down them.

NATURAL HABITAT
Native of northern hemisphere. Found on most cultivated land.

SITE
Sun or partial shade.

SOIL
Fertile, well-drained soil.

PROPAGATION
Sow seed in spring.

FLOWERING
Can be found in flower all year.

USES
Culinary, medicinal.

Symphytum officinale
Comfrey
blackwort, gum plant, knitback, slippery root, wallwort

Comfrey is another traditional medicinal herb, which for centuries had the reputation for being able to heal broken bones. It is a substantial plant, with large, hairy, green-veined leaves, pointed at the end and slightly rounded at the base. The flowers are small, bright blue, held in small clusters, but appear rather out of proportion with the leaves.

As well as its ability to heal broken bones, it was used to treat kidney complaints, hemorrhoids, gout, a variety of ulcers, sore breasts in nursing mothers, internal bruising, and also as an expectorant. It was also applied as a compress to eye injuries. However, research has shown that the alkaloids in the plant can cause liver damage and tumors. In view of this, the use of comfrey as a medicine has been banned in a number of countries and it should not be used internally at home under any circumstances. It is still used in synthesized form as a treatment for hemorrhoids and sore breasts.

Caution: Not to be taken internally; evidence shows the plant is carcinogenic. The leaves are irritant and may cause skin allergies.

Comfrey has recently been discovered to contain carcinogenic substances. The leaves may cause skin rashes. It is a good manure crop, for the leaves can be composted.

vital statistics

FAMILY
Boraginaceae

OTHER VARIETIES AND SPECIES
S. asperum, S. caucasicum, S. ibericum, S. × uplandicum (Russian comfrey), S. × u. 'Variegatum'

PERENNIAL ZONE 3

HEIGHT
4ft (1.2m)

SPREAD
3ft (90cm)

FLOWERS
Small bright blue, bell-like flowers held is clusters.

FOLIAGE
Large, mid-green leaves, hairy and rough, with pointed ends and rounded base.

NATURAL HABITAT
Native of Europe and Asia. Found in damp, shady places and wasteland.

SITE
Sun or partial shade.

SOIL
Moist, well-drained, fertile soil.

PROPAGATION
Sow seeds in spring or fall. Divide clumps in the spring.

FLOWERING
Late spring.

USES
Formerly medicinal.

Tagetes patula, T. lucida, T. minuta
French marigold
muster John Henry, sweet-scented marigold

French marigolds are often grown as companion plants in the kitchen garden for they deter a number of harmful insects, such as whitefly and carrot root fly.

Nowadays marigolds are divided into four main groups, African marigolds, French marigolds, Afro-French marigolds, and Signet marigolds, according to the habit and flower color. French marigolds are the group recognized for their herbal properties.

French marigolds are well worth planting in borders and in vegetable gardens as companion plants, for they deter whitefly, carrot-root fly, and cabbage white butterflies. They are pleasantly scented and the flowerheads can be used in potpourris. The leaves of *T. lucida*, sweet-scented marigold, taste of tarragon, for which it is a substitute. You can also use it to make a flavored tea or even to flavor chocolate drinks. *T. minuta*, sometimes called muster John Henry, contains sulfur compounds, thiophenes, which inhibit the spread of eelworms, and the plant is grown horticulturally for this purpose.

All three species are similar medicinally and are used in herbal medicine to treat constipation, colic, diarrhea, and stomach upsets. They are also used in eye lotions and to treat rheumatism. *T. lucida* may be hallucinogenic.

Caution: The leaves may cause skin allergies.

vital statistics

FAMILY
Compositae

OTHER VARIETIES AND SPECIES
T. lemmonii, *T. Aurora Series*, *T. Bonanza Series*, *T. Safari Series*

TENDER ANNUAL

HEIGHT
12in (30cm)

SPREAD
12in (30cm)

FLOWERS
Yellow, orange or bronze with five petals.

FOLIAGE
Dark green, deeply divided, aromatic leaves.

NATURAL HABITAT
Native of Mexico. Found in cultivated ground and on wasteland.

SITE
Open, sunny.

SOIL
Well-drained, poorish soil.

PROPAGATION
Sow seed in situ in late spring.

FLOWERING
Summer.

USES
Companion plant, potpourri, flavoring, herbal medicine.

Tanacetum spp. (Chrysanthemum spp.)
Tansy
alecost, costmary, feverfew, pyrethrum

Tanacetums have a number of uses in herbal medicine and in the home: Tansy was used to flavor cakes; feverfew to treat fevers; and pyrethrum was an insect repellent.

A number of the herbs that used to be known as chrysanthemums have now been reclassified under the genus *Tanacetum*. They are all members of the daisy family and make attractive garden plants, with, generally, white daisy-like heads surrounding a yellow center. They have a variety of uses in herbal medicine and some are cultivated commercially.

T. balsamita. This herb was originally called *Balsamita major* and has the common names of costmary and alecost. The plant has silver-gray foliage and myriads of tiny white and yellow flowers. It is a bitter herb with astringent qualities formerly used as a laxative and a hangover cure. It helped the digestion and the liver. The seeds were given to infants to treat worms.

T. cinerariifolium, pyrethrum. This is a decorative garden plant, with pure white, daisy-like flowers made up of many petals surrounding a yellow center. The flowers are held on stalks above gray-green foliage that looks attractive in any border. Pyrethrum is an aromatic herb that has been used since the 1920s in the manufacture of insecticidal sprays and powders.

T. parthenium, feverfew. As its common name implies, this herb has been used for centuries as a cure for fevers, indigestion, and as a sedative. It was formerly held to be of great benefit to women after childbirth. Culpeper was a devotee of the herb and declared that "the virtues of any sorts of Feverfew are beyond all praise and above all value." Chewing the fresh leaves can cause canker sores, and the herb should not be taken by pregnant women.

T. vulgare, tansy. This is an old cottage-garden herb with bright yellow flowers. The foliage is bright green and it makes a good foliage plant in a dry border because, like most other plants of the genus, it will not tolerate damp soil. The herb was used to treat sunburn and remove freckles. It was a cure both for stomachache and toothache, it helped to expel gas and was a cure for worms. It was used as a tonic to be taken in the spring; therefore tansy cakes were baked and eaten at Easter. Tansy can also be used as an insecticide, and the flowers and leaves produce green and yellow dyes.

vital statistics

FAMILY
Compositae

OTHER VARIETIES AND SPECIES
T. coccineum, T. vulgare var. *crispum, T. v.* 'Isla Gold', *T. v.* 'Silver Lace'

PERENNIAL ZONE 4

HEIGHT
2ft (60cm)

SPREAD
2ft (60cm)

FLOWERS
Button-shaped, bright yellow, daisy-like flowers in clusters.

FOLIAGE
Dark green fern-like with lance-shaped toothed leaflets.

NATURAL HABITAT
Native of Europe and Asia. Found on wasteland and woodland clearings.

SITE
Sun or partial shade.

SOIL
Well-drained, fertile.

PROPAGATION
Division in spring or fall. Sow seed in spring at 50–55°F (10–13°C)

FLOWERING
Late summer.

USES
Herbal medicine, culinary.

Taraxacum officinale
Dandelion
blowball, cankerwort, lion's tooth, priest's crown, puffball

The common dandelion is an old culinary and medicinal herb. It has a long taproot, long, narrow, and jagged leaves. The bright yellow, many-petaled flowers turn into a large puffball of gray down that blows away on the breeze and spreads the seeds far and wide. It was a traditional way of telling the time when children counted how many puffs it took to remove a whole seed head.

You can try the fresh leaves of the dandelion raw in salads, but not many people enjoy their bitter taste. More often they are blanched or cooked like spinach. You can pick the flowers and make them into dandelion wine. The roots are sometimes dried, roasted, and ground to make a type of coffee. They are also used to flavor herbal beers.

Medically, the herb is a strong diuretic; it "openeth the passages of the urine both in young and old." It is used in herbal medicine to treat gastric and internal disorders, especially gall bladder, liver and urinary complaints, and high blood pressure and heart disease. It is also used to treat arthritis and for a variety of different skin complaints.

Dandelions considered a weed here, but they are grown commercially in France as a salad vegetable. They are used to treat high blood pressure and heart disease.

vital statistics

FAMILY Compositae	**PERENNIAL** **ZONE 3**	**FOLIAGE** Green, long, toothed or jagged leaves held in a basal rosette.	**SOIL** Well-drained, fertile.	**FLOWERING** Spring onwards.
OTHER VARIETIES AND SPECIES *T. albidum, T. laevigatum* (lesser dandelion), *T. palustre* (little marsh dandelion), *T. pamiricum, T. spectabile* (bog dandelion)	**HEIGHT** 10in (25cm) **SPREAD** 12in (30cm) **FLOWERS** Button-shaped bright yellow, daisy-like, single flowers.	**NATURAL HABITAT** Northern hemisphere and temperate parts of South America. Found on wasteland and cultivated ground. **SITE** Sun or partial shade	**PROPAGATION** Sow seed in spring.	**USES** Herbal medicine, culinary.

Thymus vulgaris
Garden thyme

Thyme is an important culinary and medicinal herb. Creeping thymes flourish on stone paths, where they make an attractive flowering, scented carpet.

Thyme is a well-known and important herb, still used in the kitchen after many centuries to flavor meat, fish, and vegetable dishes, and in bouquets garni. It is also a charming, attractive plant for the garden. There are a number of thymes with varying flavors that can be used in the kitchen, including *T. herba-barona*, seed-cake thyme, with the scent of caraway, which was traditionally used to flavor a baron of beef and in baking; *T.* x *citriodora*, lemon thyme, and *T. serpyllum*, mother-of-thyme. All thymes are rich in volatile oil, mainly thymol, which is a powerful antiseptic. The essential oil is used in the perfume industry and as an insect repellent.

Garden thyme was formerly employed for bronchial complaints, to "strengthen the lungs," to cure coughs in children, and to treat gas and stomach pains. It was also given to children with worms, and an ointment made from the plant was a treatment for gout. An infusion of mother-of-thyme was a remedy for headaches and nightmares. Today thymes are used in herbal medicine to treat bronchial disorders including coughs, catarrh, bronchitis, and asthma, as well as indigestion, colic, and diarrhea.

vital statistics

FAMILY
Labiatae

OTHER VARIETIES AND SPECIES
T. caespititius (Azores thyme), *T. capitatus*, *T. pulegioides*, *T. herba-barona*, *T. serpyllum* (wild thyme), *T.* x *citriodora* 'Aureus', *T.* x c. 'Bertram Anderson', *T. v. aureus*, *T. v.* 'Silver Posie'

PERENNIAL SUBSHRUB ZONES 5–9

HEIGHT
12in (30cm)

SPREAD
12in (30cm)

FLOWERS
Small white to purple flowers in dense or loose clusters.

FOLIAGE
Gray-green with pale undersides on woody stems.

NATURAL HABITAT
Native of western Mediterranean and southern Italy. Found on rocky hillsides and dry sunny slopes.

SITE
Sun.

SOIL
Well-drained, sandy soil.

PROPAGATION
Sow seeds in spring under cover. Take semiripe cuttings in summer.

FLOWERING
Summer.

USES
Culinary, herbal medicine, perfume industry.

Trifolium pratense
Red clover
wild clover

Clover is a short-lived perennial that is sometimes grown as an annual forage crop. It has branching roots and long stems with pink-mauve flowers that last through summer and fall. The flowers are very sweet-tasting. Clover has been an important plant in agriculture since medieval times.

The dried flowers produce a volatile oil and a soothing tea. You can also use the flowers to make a pleasant herbal wine, and the plant also yields a yellow dye. A wide selection of garden varieties of clover has been developed. Many of these varieties have attractively colored leaves and are especially useful plants for rock gardens and the front of herbaceous borders.

Clover has been an herbal medicine for many centuries and was formerly employed in the treatment of gout, for hemorrhoids, to ease boils and swellings, and as a heart tonic and anti-depressant. It has a diuretic and expectorant effect. It is now used in herbal medicine to treat bronchial ailments and whooping cough, and is taken internally for skin complaints, especially eczema and psoriasis. It is also part of the treatment of a number of cancers, particularly breast cancer and cancer of the lymphatic glands.

Red clover is another herb that has become an important part of the treatment of cancers of the lymphatic system and breast cancer.

---

vital statistics

FAMILY
Papilionaceae/Leguminosae

OTHER VARIETIES AND SPECIES
T. alexandrinum, T. amabile (Aztec clover), *T. hybridum, T. repens* (white clover, Dutch clover)

PERENNIAL ZONE 4

HEIGHT
6in (15cm)

SPREAD
18in (45cm)

FLOWERS
Small white or pink-mauve flowers held in clumps.

FOLIAGE
Long-stemmed with the three-part clover leaf.

NATURAL HABITAT
Native of Europe. Found on scrub and grassland.

SITE
Sun.

SOIL
Well-drained, fertile, neutral soil.

PROPAGATION
Sow seeds in spring under cover.

FLOWERING
Summer.

USES
Herbal medicine, dye plant.

Trillium erectum

Birthroot

cough root, ground lily, red trillium, snakebite, wake robin

Most trilliums are native to North America, although there are some species that are native to the Himalayas and northeastern Asia. The herb is an attractive perennial for any garden that is moist with some shade. It has large, green, pointed leaves, three on each stalk, and blood-red, occasionally white, or yellow flowers also in three parts. The form *albiflorum* is white. The plants are slow to establish themselves and need both shade and acid soil together with a moist environment to show of their best. All trilliums make attractive plants in woodland or a shady rock garden.

Birthroot, as its name implies, was an old medicinal herb of the Native Americans and was taken as an aphrodisiac, applied to sore nipples, and taken to induce labor, and treat menstrual disorders. The plant has hormonal effects and is now used in gynecology and obstetrics, for it has a beneficial effect on the reproductive system. In herbal medicine it is also used for hemorrhages, menstrual problems, and for skin complaints.

Trilliums are unusual and attractive plants that need a shady environment and acid soil to flourish. They often take some time to become established.

vital statistics

FAMILY
Liliaceae

OTHER VARIETIES AND SPECIES
T. catesbyi, T. chloropetalum, T. grandiflorum, T. luteum, T. rivale, T. sessile

PERENNIAL ZONE 4

HEIGHT
18in (45cm)

SPREAD
18in (45cm)

FLOWERS
Red, or red-brown with three triangular petals.

FOLIAGE
Large, triangular, pointed, veined leaves just below the flower.

NATURAL HABITAT
Native of North America. Found in shady woodland.

SITE
Shade or partial shade.

SOIL
Moist or moisture-retentive, fertile, neutral to acid soil.

PROPAGATION
Sow fresh seeds in summer. Divide the roots after flowering in late summer and fall.

FLOWERING
Late spring.

USES
Herbal medicine.

Tropaeolum majus
Nasturtium
Indian cress

Nasturtiums are often grown for their young leaves, a popular salad ingredient. It is claimed that they have a tonic effect on the nervous system.

The common nasturtium is a good annual climber to grow in an herb garden. It has been a popular culinary and medicinal herb for centuries. It was called "Indian cress" because its pungent, bitter flavor is similar to watercress. Nasturtiums can be annuals or perennials, but most are grown as annuals, and a number of attractive series have been developed. You can eat both the leaves and the flowers, although the flowers are more often used as a garnish. Both have a hot, rather peppery flavor. The seeds are followed by spherical fruits that contain three seeds. You can pickle both these and the young flowers. The pickled seeds make an interesting alternative to capers in Mediterranean cooking.

Medically, the herb was used as a digestive and to cure urinary disorders. The seeds were used in poultices to heal boils and sores. The plant was also taken as an internal cleanser, of special benefit to the blood, with a tonic effect on the nervous system. Some herbalists have even claimed that it improves eyesight, and others that it postpones the onset of baldness. It is a diuretic and antibacterial herb and is now employed in herbal medicine to treat urinary diseases, and scurvy, and as a hair tonic.

vital statistics

FAMILY
Tropaeolaceae

OTHER VARIETIES AND SPECIES
T. majus 'Alaska',
T. m. 'Hermine Grashoff',
T. m. 'Red Wonder',
T. speciosum, T. tricolorum,
T. tuberosum

TENDER ANNUAL (PERENNIAL IN WARM CLIMATES) ZONES 8–10

HEIGHT
3–5ft (90cm–1.5m)

SPREAD
6–10 ft (1.8–3m) or more

FLOWERS
Red, orange, and yellow.

FOLIAGE
Green, wavy, round, kidney shaped leaves held on stalks.

NATURAL HABITAT
Native of South America. Found in scrub and wasteland and the margins of woods.

SITE
Sun, partial shade.

SOIL
Moist, well-drained. The plants flower best on poorer soils.

PROPAGATION
Sow seed in situ in late spring at 55–61°F (13–16°C).

FLOWERING
Late summer.

USES
Culinary, herbal medicine.

Tussilago farfara
Coltsfoot
bull's foot, coughwort, foal's-wort, horsehoof

Coltsfoot has long been used in herbal cough mixtures and it does sooth inflamed tissues. It can be found growing wild on scrub and along the margins of woods.

Usually regarded as an invasive weed, coltsfoot is a creeping perennial with large, rounded to heart-shaped green leaves and an erect, dandelion-like, yellow flower in spring. It has been regarded as a cough remedy since the dawn of medical knowledge and was smoked in Roman times to ease the symptoms of coughs and bronchitis. It has a licorice-like flavor and has long been used in herbal cough mixtures. The herb is a relaxant, soothes irritation, and stimulates the immune system. The name comes from the Latin *tussis*, meaning "cough."

The plant was also regarded as a suitable remedy for fevers, and the distilled water from the plant was applied to hot swellings and inflammations, and to assuage "the burning heat of the piles, or privy parts" (Culpeper). Today it is still used in herbal medicine to treat chest ailments such as asthma and bronchitis, and laryngitis, and is applied to sores, ulcers, eczema, and insect bites.

The name "coltsfoot" came from its ability to "madden young stallions" (Theocritus, the 3rd-century-BC Greek poet).

vital statistics

FAMILY
Compositae/Asteraceae

OTHER VARIETIES AND SPECIES
None

PERENNIAL ZONE 5

HEIGHT
12in (30cm)

SPREAD
Indefinite.

FLOWERS
Upright, yellow, dandelion-like flowers held on furry stalks.

FOLIAGE
Large, green, heart-shaped or rounded, toothed leaves.

NATURAL HABITAT
Native of Europe, Asia, and northern Africa. Found in scrub and wasteland and along the margins of woods.

SITE
Sun or partial shade.

SOIL
Moist, neutral to alkaline soil.

PROPAGATION
Sow seed in spring or divide in spring or fall.

FLOWERING
Spring.

USES
Culinary, herbal medicine.

Valeriana officinalis
Valerian

all-heal, garden heliotrope, garden valerian, setwall, vandal root

Valerian is an attractive, tall garden plant, and looks good in herbaceous borders. It has dark green, deeply divided leaves and small clusters of tiny pink, sometimes white, flowers held in clumps on the ends of stalks. It is also an important medicinal herb that has been used for thousands of years as a sedative and effective tranquilizer. It is not to be confused with the red valerian, *Centranthus ruber*, which has no medicinal properties.

Valerian is quite a strange plant and its exact properties, even now, are not definitely known. It has an almost magical attraction for cats; an oil prepared from the roots combined with aniseed can calm unfriendly dogs; horses are attracted to it, as are rats and mice, and it has been used to bait mousetraps. It has even been suggested that this is the herb that enabled the Pied Piper to charm away the rats of Hamelin Town. In World War I it was used to treat the victims of shell-shock. The name comes from the Latin *valere*, meaning "to be well," and refers to the many curative properties of the plant. It relieves pain, improves the digestion, and lowers blood pressure. It is also employed as a flavoring in a number of commercial edible products, such as ice cream and drinks.

It is still used today in herbal medicine to treat anxiety, hysteria, and insomnia. It is thought to be addictive if taken regularly and must be treated with caution.

Valerian is said to attract cats, calm unfriendly dogs, and is reputedly the herb that enabled the Pied Piper of Hamelin to rid the town of rats. It is used to treat insomnia and anxiety.

FAMILY
Valerianaceae

OTHER VARIETIES AND SPECIES
V. arizonica, V. montana, V. phu 'Aurea', *V. pyrenaica*

PERENNIAL ZONE 4

HEIGHT
3–5ft (90cm–1.5m)

SPREAD
3ft (90cm)

FLOWERS
Tiny pink, sometimes white, flowers in large clusters.

FOLIAGE
Dark green, opposite, deeply divided (pinnate) leaves.

NATURAL HABITAT
Native of Europe and western Asia. Found beside rivers, in moist meadows and woodland.

SITE
Sun, partial shade.

SOIL
Moist, fertile, moisture-retaining soil.

PROPAGATION
Sow seed in spring. Divide clumps in spring or fall. Self-seeds

FLOWERING
Summer.

USES
Herbal medicine, flavoring.

Verbascum thapsus
Great mullein

Aaron's rod, common mullein, flannel flower, shepherd's club, velvet plant

Great mullein is a stately plant, with long, felted, pale gray leaves and a giant spike on which a succession of small yellow flowers appear in the summer. It has a long history as an herb in medicine, and in the Middle Ages was regarded as a cure-all. Its chief use was to heal sore throats, but it was also a remedy for many stomach ailments, used to ease cramps, promote the flow of urine, and as a treatment for gout. The seeds and leaves boiled in wine drew out splinters and thorns when these became embedded in the flesh, and helped to mend broken bones.

The herb has soothing and antiseptic properties and today is used in herbal medicine for chest and bronchial infections. It is thought particularly beneficial in the treatment of asthma, pneumonia, pleurisy, and whooping cough. It is also employed as a general pain reliever and as a treatment for insomnia. Externally, it is applied to piles and chilblains, and olive oil, into which the flowers have been dipped, is a treatment for earache.

The great mullein is a tall imposing plant with felty gray leaves and long spires of yellow flowers. It can be grown in garden, but is more often found in the wild.

vital statistics

FAMILY Scrophulariaceae	**BIENNIAL** ZONE 4	**FOLIAGE** Gray, faintly green, felted, soft leaves. The basal leaves are very large, held in a rosette. The leaves are faintly scented.	**SOIL** Well-drained, light.	**FLOWERING** Summer.
OTHER VARIETIES AND SPECIES *V. bombyciferum*, *V. chaixii* (nettle-leaved mullein), *V. densiflorum*, *V. nigrum* (dark mullein), *V. phoenicum* (purple mullein)	**HEIGHT** 3–6ft (90cm–1.8m) **SPREAD** 2–3ft (60–90cm) **FLOWERS** Small, yellow, five-petaled, in clusters on a long tall spike.	**NATURAL HABITAT** Native of Europe and western Asia. Found on dry wasteland. **SITE** Sun.	**PROPAGATION** Sow seed in spring or in late summer when they are ripe.	**USES** Herbal medicine.

Verbena officinalis
Vervain
European vervain, enchanter's plant, herb of the cross, pigeonweed, simpler's joy

Vervain is not a spectacular plant to look at. It has sparse, greeny-gray leaves, and small, hooded mauve flowers. It is another herb that has long been used in herbal medicine as a calming agent for the nerves, to treat epilepsy and asthma, and to fortify the bladder, liver, and spleen. It was a sacred plant of the Druids, ancient pagan priests of northern Europe. It was employed in love rites in Roman times, and used in the Middle Ages to ward off the plague. Vervain's most popular use today is in vervaine, a soothing tea that relieves tension and reduces fevers. It was also used as a gargle and mouthwash for sore throats, and as an eye-bath.

Vervain is a diuretic herb that calms the nerves, reduces inflammation, controls bleeding, and increases perspiration. It is used externally to treat minor injuries, eczema, and sores. The native North American species, *V. hastata*, has the same properties and was used by the Native Americans. It is used in herbal medicine to treat liver complaints and respiratory disorders.

Caution: The herb should not be taken during pregnancy; if taken in excess, it may cause nausea and vomiting.

Vervain is often taken as vervaine, a soothing herbal tea. Blue vervain, *V. hastata*, the North American species, was commonly used by the Native Americans to treat liver complaints.

---

vital statistics

FAMILY
Verbenaceae

OTHER VARIETIES AND SPECIES
V. bonariensis, V. hastata, V. x hybrida. V. officinalis is cultivated commercially in France and other countries in Europe. Garden varieties are popular, striking plants, with showy flowers.

PERENNIAL ZONE 5

HEIGHT
3ft (90cm)

SPREAD
2ft (60cm)

FLOWERS
Small pale lilac-mauve, carried in slender terminal spikes.

FOLIAGE
Long, sparse, gray-green, three-lobed, toothed leaves.

NATURAL HABITAT
Native of Europe, western Asia and northern Africa. Found on dry wasteland.

SITE
Sun.

SOIL
Well-drained, moist.

PROPAGATION
Sow seed in spring or fall. Divide in spring.

FLOWERING
Summer.

USES
Herbal medicine, herbal tea.

Veronica officinalis
Speedwell
common gypsyweed, fluellen, groundhole, veronica

The common veronica is a prostrate, mat-forming, perennial with rough green leaves and pale blue flowers with a white eye, held in clusters all over the plant. It is regarded as an excellent cure for eye troubles. It was a popular herb throughout the Middle Ages, with a variety of medicinal purposes. It was used for catarrh, bronchitis, asthma and other chest complaints, and to treat minor sores and skin complaints, especially eczema. The herb is supposed to be named for St. Veronica, while the common name refers to the speed with which the flowers fall after the plant is picked. It is much grown as a ground-cover plant in gardens, and a number of garden varieties have been developed. Speedwell is still used as an herbal tea, sometimes called Swiss tea, which is drunk as a tonic and to aid digestion.

It is seldom used in herbal medicine today, although it is occasionally used for skin complaints or stomach upsets.

Veronica was a popular medicinal herb in medieval times, but it is seldom used today. It is sometimes taken as an herbal tea. Veronica is a good ground-cover plant

vital statistics

FAMILY
Scrophulariaceae

OTHER VARIETIES AND SPECIES
V. austriaca, V. beccabunga (brooklime), V. cinerea, V. gentianoides, V. prostrata, V. spicata. A number of garden varieties have been developed.

BIENNIAL ZONE 6

HEIGHT
18in (45cm)

SPREAD
Indefinite.

FLOWERS
Small, lilac-blue flowers on spikes with a tiny white eye.

FOLIAGE
Green, oval, finely toothed leaves, held in opposite pairs.

NATURAL HABITAT
Native of Europe and western Asia. Found on grassland, in woods and dry open ground.

SITE
Sun or partial shade.

SOIL
Well-drained, moisture retentive, acid.

PROPAGATION
Sow seed in fall. Divide in the spring or fall.

FLOWERING
Summer.

USES
Formerly medicinal, tea plant.

V

Vinca major, V. minor
Periwinkle
greater periwinkle, lesser periwinkle

Both periwinkles are good evergreen ground-cover plants with pretty blue flowers. There are garden varieties with different flower shapes and colors.

Both the greater and lesser periwinkle are similar in habit although, as might be expected, the lesser is smaller than the greater. They have similar herbal properties although the greater periwinkle contains reserpine, a substance that lowers cholesterol levels in the blood. Old herbalists, who believed in the theory that herbs were under the dominion of the planets, placed periwinkles under the governance of Venus; it was said that if two lovers ate a sprig of the herb together, they would stay in love for the rest of their lives. This rite is not recommended, for the plants are toxic and may cause stomach upsets. Both species have long creeping stems covered by opposite leaves and starry violet-blue flowers that emerge in spring. They are evergreen and make excellent ground cover in a shady part of the garden.

The herbs are a natural tonic and are used in homeopathy to cure stomach upsets, diphtheria, and diabetes as well as canker sores and sore throats. They are also used to treat menstrual problems and abnormal uterine bleeding. They are generally not prescribed to patients who are suffering from constipation, Culpeper referred to the herb as "a great binder."

vital statistics

FAMILY
Apocynaceae

OTHER VARIETIES AND SPECIES
*V. difformis, V. major var. alba,
V. m. 'Variegata', V. minor f. alba,
V. m. 'Argenteovariegata',
V. m. 'Atropurpurea',
M. m. 'Azurea Flore Pleno',
V. m. 'Gertrude Jekyll'*

PERENNIAL EVERGREEN ZONE 4

HEIGHT
1–3ft (30–90cm)

SPREAD
To 5ft (1.5m)

FLOWERS
Purple, violet to pale blue five-petaled solitary flowers.

FOLIAGE
Dark green, shiny, narrowly oval, opposite, growing down the long trailing stalks.

NATURAL HABITAT
Native of Europe. Generally found in moist ground or in mixed woodland.

SITE
Shade or partial shade.

SOIL
Well-drained, fertile soil.

PROPAGATION
Divide in early spring or take semi-ripe cuttings in summer.

FLOWERING
Late spring to summer.

USES
Herbal medicine.

Viola odorata

Sweet violet

garden violet

This is a charming flower of late spring, sweet-scented, as you can tell from its name. Posies of violets were picked to present to loved ones by romantic suitors. It was much prized by the Romans who used the herb as a flavoring in wine and who were much criticised by the Roman poet Horace for spending more time growing violets that the staple olive. The flowers can be deep violet, pale blue or white, and the flowers of the white violet were thought to be able to dissolve swellings and boils. It was considered a cooling herb and used to lower temperatures in fevers, especially quinsy, for epileptic fits in children and to treat bronchial conditions. The flowers were formerly used in the perfume industry. Try them raw in salads.

The violet is an extremely important herb medically. It is used in herbal medicine in the background treatment of cancer. It has been claimed that eating the flowers over a period has dissolved internal cancers. Violet is also used in the treatment of bronchial diseases, chest infections (it is a strong decongestant), and to treat heart disease.

Sweet violets are charming spring flowers and are now considered very important in the treatment of cancer. The Romans used to drink violet-flavored wine.

vital statistics

FAMILY
Violaceae

OTHER VARIETIES AND SPECIES
V. canadensis, V. cornuta, V. cucullata, V. elatior, V. gracilis, V. labradorica, V. odorata 'Alba', V. o. 'Alba Plena', V. 'Bowles Black', V. 'Johnny Jump Up', V. 'Prince Henry', V. palmata, V. rupestris

HARDY PERENNIAL ZONE 5

HEIGHT
6in (15cm)

SPREAD
12–18in (30–45cm)

FLOWERS
Violet-blue, white, pale blue, or pinkish, five-petaled, scented.

FOLIAGE
Dark green glossy, oval to kidney-shaped, bluntly toothed.

NATURAL HABITAT
Native of Europe, Asia, and northern Africa. Found in shady woodland.

SITE
Shade or partial shade.

SOIL
Moisture-retaining to moist, rich soil.

PROPAGATION
Sow seed in fall. Divide in late winter or early spring.

FLOWERING
Spring.

USES
Herbal medicine, culinary, perfume.

Viola tricolor
Johnny-jump-up
heartsease, stepmother, wild pansy

Johnny-jump-up has long been used in herbal medicine and has been attributed with magical properties. Today it is used for bronchial disorders.

This delightful flower has a long association with love and magic. Oberon, King of the Fairies, tells his mischievous servant Puck of its properties in Shakespeare's romantic comedy *A Midsummer Night's Dream*.

... maidens call it Love-in-idleness,
The juice of it on sleeping eyelids laid
Will make a man or woman madly dote
Upon the next live creature that it sees.

The flowers are edible and are sometimes sprinkled on salads to provide decoration. Culpeper believed the plant to be under the influence of Saturn, and described it as "cold, viscous and slimy." He thought it an excellent cure for venereal diseases, for convulsions in children, and for inflammation of the lungs and breasts. It is a cooling herb that is both laxative and diuretic. It is employed today in herbal medicine for chest and lung diseases, and as a blood purifier. It is also taken as a tonic for reducing blood pressure. It is used to treat ulcers, sores and various skin conditions.

The species *V. yezoensis*, the Chinese violet, is the basis for a treatment for eczema in children.

vital statistics

FAMILY
Violaceae

OTHER VARIETIES AND SPECIES
V. canadensis, V. cornuta, V. cucullata, V. elatior, V. gracilis, V. labradorica, V. odorata 'Alba', *V. o.* 'Alba Plena', *V.* 'Bowles Black', *V.* 'Johnny Jump Up', *V.* 'Prince Henry', *V. palmata, V. rupestris*

HARDY ANNUAL OR SHORT-LIVED PERENNIAL

HEIGHT
4–12in (10–30cm)

SPREAD
8in (20cm)

FLOWERS
Three-colored: violet, pale lilac, yellow tinged with white.

FOLIAGE
Dark green, toothed, lance-shaped with three leaflets.

NATURAL HABITAT
Native of Europe. Found in wasteland and cultivated fields

SITE
Open, sunny.

SOIL
Fertile sandy soil.

PROPAGATION
Sow seed in spring in containers under cover. Take tip cuttings in summer if wanted. The plant self-seeds.

FLOWERING
All summer.

USES
Herbal medicine, culinary.

Vitex agnus-castus
Chaste berry
chaste tree, lilac, monk's spice

The chaste berry was thought by ancient Greek warriors to guarantee the virtue of their wives. Today it is used in the treatment of menopausal complaints.

This is an aromatic tree or shrub with large, five- or seven-palmate leaves and long spires of fragrant violet flowers held in dense trusses. It has been an important herb for thousands of years. It was thought to guarantee chastity in wives left behind by warriors going to war in Grecian times. The flowers are a symbol of purity in southern Europe. It was a strewing herb (an early form of air freshener) in monasteries—which led to the name "monk's spice." The seeds are still used as a peppery condiment, and the branches to weave baskets.

Chaste berry is used in herbal medicine to regulate hormonal activity in both men and women, for menstrual problems, to promote lactation in nursing mothers, and to counter premature ejaculation in men. It should not be taken to excess, for it can cause formication (the feeling that insects are crawling under the skin).

V. negundo, Chinese chaste tree, is a sedative, cooling, antibacterial herb, which is used in the treatment of malaria and arthritis. Externally, it is applied to ringworm, toothache, and piles, and it is used to treat migraine and eye problems.

vital statistics

FAMILY
Verbenaceae

OTHER VARIETIES AND SPECIES
V. agnus-castus var. *latifolia*, *V. lucens*, *V. negundo*, *V. n. cannabinifolia*

DECIDUOUS SHRUB ZONE 6

HEIGHT
6–25ft (2–8m)

SPREAD
6–25ft (2–8m)

FLOWERS
Small tubular, lilac or violet, fragrant flowers held in spikes.

FOLIAGE
Dark green, large, palmate, opposite leaves.

NATURAL HABITAT
Mediterranean and western Asia. Found in woodland and open scrubland.

SITE
Sun or partial shade.

SOIL
Fertile, moist rich soil.

PROPAGATION
Sow seed in spring or fall. Layer or take softwood cuttings in spring.

FLOWERING
Fall.

USES
Herbal medicine, culinary.

Index

Index

Index

Credits & Acknowledgments

Photography
All photographs by
David Markson except:

Mary Evans Picture Library:
11, 15, 16l, 16r, 17, 18

The Garden Picture Library:
93, 234, 253, 258

Garden & Wildlife Matters:
49, 107, 121, 132, 148, 182, 184, 186, 191, 203, 241, 243, 251, 256, 271, 314, 316

Grateful thanks to the following nurseries and individuals for their help and assistance in locating plants:

Iden Croft Herbs
Staplehurst, Kent, England; special thanks to Rosemary for her patience and generous help

The School of Herbal Medicine and Phytotherapy
Bodle Street, Sussex, England; Mr and Mrs Zeylstra and staff

Wellingham Herb Nursery
Ringmer, Sussex, England

The Chelsea Physic Garden
London, England

The Loseley Gardens
nr Guildford, Surrey

Oakdene Alpine Nursery
Heathfield, Sussex, England

Michelham Priory
Sussex, England

Rudolph Steiner Community
Turners Hill, Sussex, England

Carolann Heming
for her plant identification prowess and general expert assistance

Also to **The Darkroom**
Tunbridge Wells, Kent, England

Pinpoint
Heathfield, East Sussex, England; for their reliable and professional film processing